Paul Ricoeur and Contemporary Moral Thought

Paul Ricoeur and Contemporary Moral Thought

Edited by John Wall, William Schweiker, and W. David Hall

Routledge
Taylor & Francis Group

NEW YORK AND LONDON

Published in 2002 by
Routledge
711 Third Avenue
New York, NY 10017, USA

Published in Great Britain by
Routledge
2 Park Square, Milton Park
Abingdon, Oxon OX14 4RN

Routledge is an imprint of the Taylor & Francis Group, an informa business

First issued in paperback 2016

Copyright © 2002 by Routledge

All rights reserved. No part of this book may be reprinted or reproduced or utilized in any form or by any electronic, mechanical, or other means, now known or hereafter invented, including photocopying and recording, or in any information storage or retrieval system, without permission in writing from the publishers.

Cataloging-in-Publication Data is available from the Library of Congress.

ISBN13: 978-0-415-86686-6 (pbk)
ISBN13: 978-0-415-93843-3 (hbk)

Contents

Preface   viii

Introduction: Human Capability and Contemporary Moral Thought
JOHN WALL, WILLIAM SCHWEIKER, AND W. DAVID HALL   1

Part I: Moral Selfhood, the Good, and the Right

CHAPTER 1
RICOEUR'S RECLAMATION OF AUTONOMY: UNITY, PLURALITY, AND TOTALITY

PAMELA SUE ANDERSON   15

CHAPTER 2
NARRATIVE ETHICS AND MORAL LAW IN RICOEUR

PETER KEMP   32

CHAPTER 3
MORAL MEANING: BEYOND THE GOOD AND THE RIGHT

JOHN WALL   47

CHAPTER 4
ANTIGONE, PSYCHE, AND THE ETHICS OF FEMALE SELFHOOD: A FEMINIST CONVERSATION WITH PAUL RICOEUR'S THEORIES OF SELF-MAKING IN *ONESELF AS ANOTHER*

HELEN M. BUSS   64

CHAPTER 5
THE SUMMONED SELF: ETHICS AND HERMENEUTICS IN PAUL RICOEUR IN DIALOGUE WITH EMMANUEL LEVINAS

MARK I. WALLACE   80

Part II: Moral Meanings, Human Fallibility, and Theological Ethics

CHAPTER 6
SEARCHING FOR A HEART OF GOLD: A RICOEURIAN MEDITATION ON MORAL STRIVING AND THE POWER OF RELIGIOUS DISCOURSE
DAVID E. KLEMM   97

CHAPTER 7
STARRY HEAVENS AND MORAL WORTH: HOPE AND RESPONSIBILITY IN THE STRUCTURE OF THEOLOGICAL ETHICS
WILLIAM SCHWEIKER   117

CHAPTER 8
THE SITE OF CHRISTIAN ETHICS: LOVE AND JUSTICE IN THE WORK OF PAUL RICOEUR
W. DAVID HALL   143

CHAPTER 9
VEILS AND KINGDOMS: A RICOEURIAN METAPHORICS OF LOVE AND JUSTICE
GLENN WHITEHOUSE   164

CHAPTER 10
JACQUES DERRIDA, PAUL RICOEUR, AND THE MARGINALIZATION OF CHRISTIANITY: CAN THE GOD OF PRESENCE BE SAVED?
LINDA M. MACCAMMON   187

Part III: Moral Practice, Responsible Citizenship, and Social Justice

CHAPTER 11
ETHICS AND PUBLIC LIFE: A CRITICAL TRIBUTE TO PAUL RICOEUR
FRED DALLMAYR   213

CHAPTER 12
RICOEUR AND THE TASKS OF CITIZENSHIP
BERNARD P. DAUENHAUER   233

Contents

CHAPTER 13
RICOEUR AND PRACTICAL THEOLOGY
DON BROWNING   251

CHAPTER 14
RICOEUR ON TRAGEDY: TELEOLOGY, DEONTOLOGY, AND *PHRONESIS*
MARTHA C. NUSSBAUM   264

Conclusion

ETHICS AND HUMAN CAPABILITY: A RESPONSE
PAUL RICOEUR   279

Contributors   291

Index of Names   292

Index of Subjects   294

Preface

This book is the result of several years of conversation among the editors on matters hermeneutical, theological, and ethical. Originally conceived by W. David Hall as a panel of scholarly papers for the American Academy of Religion, John Wall proposed the idea of a conference on Ricoeur's ethics when it became clear the panel would not materialize. With that idea in hand, my two coeditors, who at that time were finishing their own Ph.D. studies writing dissertations on facets of Ricoeur's thought, set about the many and varied tasks of planning and hosting a scholarly conference. The conference was finally held at the Divinity School of the University of Chicago in October, 1999. Before large audiences, the speakers whose work is represented in this book explored Ricoeur's work in the light of the most central issues in contemporary moral, political, and religious thought. The conference ended with a stunning address by Paul Ricoeur that appears as the conclusion to this book. With care and insight John Wall and David Hall ran an extremely important conference. We now see the project through to its publication. It has been my singular pleasure to work with my coeditors on the conference and this project.

We wish to express our gratitude to a number of people who helped make the conference and this book possible. Thankfully for us, Clark Gilpin, then dean of the Divinity School of the University of Chicago, was immediately supportive of the idea of a conference dedicated to Paul Ricoeur's work. Though Ricoeur was long a member of this University of Chicago faculty, the Divinity School had never hosted a conference in his honor. We are grateful to Dean Gilpin and the resources of the Divinity School for holding the event. As everyone knows, nothing is possible at the Divinity School without the wisdom and aid of Ms. Sandra Peppers, administrator in the Divinity School. We thank her for all her help and advice. In terms of the book, a special thanks is due to Nick Street of Routledge for helping us imagine the

Preface

volume and also seeing the book through to its completion. We are also thankful to Aimee Burant and Jon Rothchild for their diligence and care in the preparation of the manuscript. All of these individuals, and others as well, have worked to make this project successful. As editors we realize how great our debt is to those persons who help make our ideas and plans reality.

Finally, we want to thank Paul Ricoeur. His attendance and participation in the conference manifested once again a profound dedication to ponder the full range of human meanings. Through his personal presence and his many works, he continues to teach and to inspire. We hope that this book is a fitting tribute to his labor.

William Schweiker
University of Chicago
September 2001

Introduction
Human Capability and Contemporary Moral Thought

JOHN WALL, WILLIAM SCHWEIKER, AND W. DAVID HALL

The purpose of this book is to explore and propose new avenues for contemporary moral thought. The wide array of scholars who have contributed their voices to this work are bound together by common concerns and a sense of the moral possibilities and demands confronting us. At the center of this inquiry stands a figure. Uniting the essayists is the attempt to define and assess the significance of the writings of French philosopher Paul Ricoeur for ethics. While individual contributions often reach beyond Ricoeur's work and sometimes are at odds with his thought, the authors are one with him in a spirit of exploration about what matters most to persons and how best to sustain just communities. The purpose of the book can be most readily grasped by outlining debates within ethics, identifying several unifying themes to the book, and addressing briefly each essay.

Debates within Ethics

Paul Ricoeur is widely recognized as one of the most influential thinkers of the twentieth century. He has made original and daring contributions to phenomenology, hermeneutics, and narrative theory. Moreover, his work bridges the seemingly intractable divide between European styles of philosophy and Anglo-American analytic thought. Despite the obvious importance of Ricoeur's philosophy, his writings on ethics are surprisingly less well known. Yet as these essays aptly demonstrate, Ricoeur offers a unique and powerful option in moral thought.

Ricoeur's work belongs to the wide sweep of hermeneutical reflection concerned about the place of language and tradition in human understanding. The hermeneutical turn appears in his own work through ideas about the place of narrative, symbol, and image in the moral life and in human identity. And yet this hermeneutical claim is also precisely the point in which Ricoeur's unique contribution is most apparent. He centers interpretation theory not on the intentionality of pure consciousness (Edmund Husserl), being-towards-death (Martin Heidegger), or tradition and the event of understanding (Hans-Georg Gadamer). Ricoeur focuses on human capability, on "capable man." From his early work in the "philosophy of the will" through the long detours of investigation in Freudian thought, philosophy of action, and linguistic theory, Ricoeur has never lost sight of his focus on human capacities. And yet this focus, we should note, has taken different forms as Ricoeur has slowly, but consistently, moved reflection on the self into ever more subtle and complex formulations.

There is good reason for this movement in Ricoeur's corpus. Much twentieth-century thought tried to escape or revise the legacy of reflexive philosophy and the Cartesian ego. The transcendental subject, the thinking *I*, constituted by self-relation, has been exposed as empty. The critique of classical Cartesian accounts of the ego explains some of the criticisms of Ricoeur's early work insofar as he seemed to remain bound to that classical project. But as his project developed, the focus on the human subject has been rearticulated in ways that escape the critique of the Cartesian agenda. In his magisterial *Oneself as Another*, he explores our sense of self with respect to the capacities to act, speak, narrate, and impute responsibility. In his brilliant lecture that concludes this volume, Ricoeur clarifies the central importance of the notion of human capability to his entire philosophical corpus. This idea is so central to his ethical thought that we have taken it as the basic theme for the present volume.

Ricoeur's focus on human capability in ethics avoids two related dangers in the postmodern debate about the status of norms and values, namely moral particularism and the embrace of relativism. *Relativism*, as we use the term, is a moral outlook that denies the possibility of establishing the validity of norms and values. The values and norms people live by have no standing beyond individual preference or social convention. The world is, accordingly, the home of many, often incommensurable but equally "valid" moral outlooks. By moral *particularism* we mean the conviction that the values and norms by which people guide their lives have validity only within the specific community from which those norms and values arose and for which they mainly function. On this account, one can and must give nonpreferential and nonconventional warrants for the validity of norms and values (one might, say, appeal to a divinely revealed text), but the strategy of validating moral beliefs (interpretation of the revealed text) is always and irreducibly particular to a community or tradition (the interpretive method is coextensive with the community of interpretation). Ricoeur's ethical project holds up the possibility that diverse communities and traditions can enter into critical, yet genuinely constructive and mutual, dialogue. This possibility places Ricoeur in creative tension with many of the major positions on the contemporary philosophical and theological landscape, including communitarianism, narrative ethics, postliberal theology, discourse ethics, and proceduralism, to name but a few. More specifically, Ricoeur's critical hermeneutical ethics proposes a view of the moral life that is oriented in praxis, formed in tradition and community, responsive to plurality and otherness, and grounded upon core human capacities for interpretation, dialogue, and imaginative moral mediation. One way to isolate Ricoeur's ethics is with respect to debate in moral theory about the meaning and validity of moral norms and values in a pluralistic world.

One can thus locate Ricoeur's thought with respect to the legacy of hermeneutical reflection around the problem of subjectivity and self-consciousness, and also to debate in moral theory. Just how distinctive Ricoeur's ethics is can too easily be missed if one more arena of debate is not noted, however. A distinguishing characteristic of much ethics in the last few decades has been a concerted effort by a host of thinkers to overcome the excessive voluntarism associated with strands of existentialism. After all, existentialism was one of the first ethically charged modes of thought that rejected the primacy of the act of thinking in the constitution of the self. Yet it too centered on the self's relation to itself, merely shifting the constitutive relation of the "self" from the act of thinking to the concrete act of will, of choice, to be a self. Philosophers as diverse as Emmanuel Levinas, Iris Murdoch, Charles Taylor, Hans Jonas, and Alasdair MacIntyre have seen in the existentialist picture of the moral agent a grave danger. The same criticism of the "existentialist self" is found in the work of such theologians as James Gustafson, Stanley Hauerwas, and a host of feminist theologians ranging from Lisa Cahill to Beverly Wildung Harrison. The existentialist picture of the agent, paradigmatically seen in the work of Jean-Paul Sartre, imagines that the will can leap into action unencumbered by its past, basic needs and desires rooted in bodiliness, or the effects on consciousness of a community's traditions, moral beliefs, and values. It does not escape the emptiness or isolation of the Cartesian *I* so much as enact it in willing rather than thought.

In the context of the criticisms of both transcendental subjectivity and existential voluntarism, Ricoeur's focus on "capable man" is novel and fascinating. Ricoeur insists on focusing his ethics on human capability, further developing a "philosophy of the will." And yet, his account of the human capacity to act, to speak, to narrate, and to impute responsibility, far from removing the self from its embeddedness in relations, traditions, languages, and affectivities rooted in our bodiliness, in fact articulates precisely the way in which we are so situated humanly to what is other than self. To be sure, Ricoeur has not always developed in detail the importance of basic human needs necessary for a rich and encumbered sense of capability. Nevertheless, beyond the current critique of the will within a host of ethical positions, he does propose a new and enriched account of our moral possibilities, and also the fallibility and capacity for evil that tragically mark human existence in community. This specific focus on capability is the guiding thread of Ricoeur's work and, as noted, this volume as well.

Three orienting themes converge in an ethics that takes human capability as its focal point: self, meaning, and social-political practice. These three themes traverse all of the papers collected here, and they provide, with the benefit of hindsight, the editors' interpretation of the underlying unity of the volume. While none of the authors was asked to speak specifically to these themes, each emerges in one way or another in each essay. In the next section, we will expand upon the significance of these ideas for an understanding of capability and thus deepen our analysis of the situation in moral inquiry.

Themes and Human Capability

One level of reflection wherein Ricoeur charts new directions in ethics is distinctly anthropological; that is, his ideas about human beings as moral creatures. As noted, nothing characterized late-twentieth-century Western thought so much as the attempt to think with and yet beyond the legacy of modern reflexive philosophy. Begun by René Descartes, reflexive philosophy centers on the immediacy and certainty of self-relation. "Cogito, ergo sum," I think, therefore I am, Descartes put it. From the certainty of this reflexive self-relation it was believed one could build a complete and necessarily valid account of the world and human life. Later versions of reflexive philosophy sought the immediacy of self-relation in willing or feeling. Twentieth-century thinkers, rocked by radical advances in the sciences, sociopolitical critiques of false consciousness, the birth and growth of psychological inquiry, and the terrible forms of violence and suffering that scar the age, have jettisoned or radically revised the reflexive agenda. This is certainly true of the work of Ricoeur. Deeply influenced by Husserl, Heidegger, Gadamer, and others, Ricoeur has sought throughout his long career to show that the dream of self-immediacy is beyond our reach.

However, if there is reason to be suspicious of the imperious, self-posited *I*, in either its idealistic or its existential forms, how are we to make sense of the idea of a self at all? This suspicion has lead many thinkers to dislodge the question of the self from its place of prestige within philosophical speculation. Our initial twofold distinction of relativism and particularism becomes useful at this point as a heuristic device to address the various options by which this reflexive ego has come under attack. For instance, within the relativist camp we can place a number of antifoundationalist perspectives of various stripes. These positions tend to reduce the problematic of selfhood either to hegemonic, sociolinguistic forms of power (for example,

Michel Foucault, Richard Rorty), or, epistemologically, to untenable language games (say, Donald Davidson, Derek Parfit). These positions are frequently associatied with the continental, Nietzschean tradition or the Anglo-American, analytic tradition, respectively. Within the particularist camp, on the other hand, we can place positions that attempt to reduce the question of selfhood to proper enculturation into the particularities of a sociohistorical tradition of thought (for example, MacIntyre, Stanley Hauerwas). Such are often manifest in the positions of communitarianism and radical orthodoxy that stem from various neo-Barthian and neo-Thomist schools of thought.

While these positions are trenchant criticisms of the self-reflexive certainty of Descartes's ego, they are no less short-sighted from a Ricoeurian perspective. While the Cartesian position reduces the complex and manifold experience of the identity of the self to the rational faculty within the self, the critics of the transcendental ego too frequently reduce this same complex and manifold experience to one or another factor outside the self. In this case, analysis turns away from the *identity* of the self. For instance, Foucault focuses attention on locating and critiquing discrete practices of social power. MacIntyre directs his efforts toward the reclamation of the richness of cultural traditions from Enlightenment hegemony. But the attempt to avoid the problematic of selfhood as a fundamental concern raises particular problems for ethical reflection. If we cannot locate a capable self, or if we choose not to do so, then the relevance of concepts like the "human good" or "proper action" is open to question. That is to say, ethics entails some account of an agent; that is, a self who is capable of reflecting on possibilities and who is morally responsible for action.

One of Ricoeur's most profound philosophical contributions lies in this area of moral anthropology. In his account, the problematic of selfhood can be reduced neither to internal faculties nor to external social processes. Human identity is lived in terms of capabilities that are embodied in the flesh and embedded in the fabric of social existence. The chapters in this volume explore this account of the human self in moral thought. Among the positions taken are possibilities for a critical account of practical wisdom in response to moral tragedy, the dialogical character of human moral interaction, the manner in which cultural ideals serve as supports or hindrances to authentic selfhood, and the tasks of citizenship in relation to communal and global contexts.

This concern for the identity of the self opens directly onto the second organizing theme of the book, that of meaning. Conceiving the identity of the agent in terms of embodied capability embedded in a cultural world points to the fact that humans try to make sense of themselves and their world, that they look for meaning within shared existence. However, the elision of the question of the self to which we pointed above brings with it a reduction in the realm of meaning that is similarly problematic for ethical reflection. If our only possibility for meaningful existence lies in reclaiming pre-Enlightenment (medieval or ancient) cosmologies, as some thinkers seem to suggest, do we have any resources for meaningfully criticizing oppressive social regimes like those that ruled the roost in the Middle Ages? If consciousness is nothing but electrochemical brain activity, as Parfit tells us, is there even such a thing as meaning? To orient discussion around the idea of human capability is already to put up resistance to these kinds of reductive reasoning.

In a profound sense, moral particularists are correct to draw the connection between the context-bound nature of traditions of thought and the formation of our ideas of self. Capable agents are not simply transcendental egos, nor self-sufficient, autonomous wills. That is to say, human capability is defined as much by receptivity as it is by ability; this is especially the case in the realm of meaning. Humans do not create meaning ex nihilo. Meaning arises out of, and is continually influenced by, social histories and cultural and artistic traditions. However, these histories and traditions are not the monolithic apparatuses that communitarians and radical-orthodox thinkers are wont to claim. We can follow Foucault in claiming that societies do in fact exercise normative power, and that the exercise of power itself carves out places for resistance. However, we can and ought to question Foucault's attempts to articulate resistance as its own justification; we can and ought, likewise, to question Parfit's attempt to reduce human existence completely to biological processes, however true it may be that humans are, among other things, biological processes. If we characterize human capability in its profoundest dimensions as the striving for meaning and self-understanding, then this striving becomes the justification for acts of resistance to forms of power that unjustly limit our strivings. This remains the case even if we disagree about what kinds of resistance are justified and which forms of power are unjust. In this sense, meaning becomes the realm in which existence rises to moral norms and values that cannot be reduced to biology, or hegemonic power structures, or self-enclosed traditions of rationality.

Ricoeur's corpus is useful for moral reflection as a vast testament to the human capacity to strive for meaningful existence. This is the case from his early reflections on the phenomenology of the relation between the voluntary and involuntary, to his use of Freud to understand the self's archeology and teleology, to his insistence that symbol and metaphor not only reflect thought but also produce meaning, to his notion of tradition as a dialectic of sedimentation and innovation, and to his concept of narrative as the mode in which time becomes human. The writers who lend their insight and effort to this volume explore these human capacities for forming meaning in its various moral dimensions, from concepts of the human good and right, to responses to violence and moral tragedy, and to human being considered in terms of responsible citizenship and socially just action.

Introduction

For a number of contributors to this volume, the question of moral meanings raises decidedly theological questions. The book explores and assesses another underrepresented dimension of Ricoeur's thought; that is, his writings on religious matters. With regard to theological ethics, it is suggested that this volume contributes monumentally to an understanding of Ricoeur's contribution to the reemerging interest in the theology of culture. Ironically, the tendency to overlook or bypass Ricoeur's deep religious commitments and engagements with the Christian tradition is due, in part, to Ricoeur himself. Throughout his career, Ricoeur has consistently argued that while he was a philosopher who "listened" to the biblical witness, it was essential to distinguish theological and philosophical inquiry. No less astonishing than his insistence on the idea of capability as basic to his entire corpus, Ricoeur also argues in the lecture that concludes this book that a rapprochement between philosophy and theology is now needed. And, in fact, this is seen in other important contemporary thinkers: Levinas no less than Taylor; MacIntyre just as much as Jonas.

Ricoeur is a philosopher who is deeply influenced by a wide range of theological positions. To the frustration of many, his work moves between the two competing visions of kerygmatic theology and the theology of culture, à la Karl Barth and Paul Tillich, respectively. His hermeneutical approach is designed to handle at once "ordinary" moral reflection and moral reflection transgressed and reoriented by claims about the divine. Drawing some inspiration from his work, the new theology of culture displayed in various essays in this volume pursues a critical conversation between the human and the divine along the path of ethics. Engaged in a thick reading of texts and also cultures, mindful of the range and travail of human capability, resolute in addressing fallibility, evil, and violence, and with these the longing for transformation, this theological ethics of culture, as we call it, aims to show the meaning and truth of religious convictions for our time.

At this point, the last of our orienting themes emerges: the idea of social and political practice. An account of selfhood in terms of human capability must conceive of the self as embodied in the flesh and embedded in the fabric of social relations. Human capability rises to meaning within the public space of social histories, cultural realities, and traditions of thought. These claims point to the inescapable fact that human capability is a public phenomenon; capable, meaningful agency is lived in the social and political spheres where selves exercise power individually and in groups. This fact, in its turn, raises again the question of moral norms and values with which we began this introduction. What constitutes the human good? What is the proper action? What is the nature of justice? The realm of social and political practice is where human capability is concretely experienced as ethical concern and morally responsible selfhood.

To some extent we have encountered this experience at an inchoate level already. If there is reason to be suspicious of the hegemony of self-enclosed traditions of rationality it is because they have as much potential to stifle human initiative as they do to lend meaning to human existence. If there is reason to fear a morally neutral conception of power and a self-justifying resistance, it is because social and political action takes the form of violent gesture as often as, if not more frequently than, it takes the form of an impassioned plea for human liberation and social justice. The recognition that humans are capable beings becomes the impetus for ethical concern; the recognition that humans are beings capable of the most inhuman forms of violence gives us reason to ponder morally responsible limits.

People's capacity to form moral meaning moves debate onto new and more productive grounds. That is, the idea of human capability suggests a form of moral practice that mediates between the rights of a reflexive and interpretive moral agent and social goods embedded in larger historical, traditional, communal, and biological contexts. In this view, moral practice seeks to form meaningful aims and purposes within the parameters of respect for persons. That is to say, moral practice is not just adherence to fair procedures, but also striving to form moral goods by which diverse selves may live a meaningful life in common. At the same time, an understanding of moral practice is not aimed merely at historical and communal cohesion but, rather, at finite and provisional shared goods that are formed reflexively, critically, and creatively from out of conflicting teleological differences. Such a conception of moral practice is able to address the very real violence and tragedy by which human moral life is all too often characterized without losing sight of the human need to find meaning in relation to larger social and historical purposes. The kind of violence that the twentieth century has witnessed— world wars, ethnic cleansings, large-scale famines and poverty—demands a response from moral thought that holds up the dignity of the human person. At the same time, the twentieth century's growing appreciation for plurality and difference should not be allowed to descend into the moral particularism and the fear that has characterized much of the course of human history. Whatever the common goods that are embraced to overcome violence and relativism, these should not obscure the fundamental practical task of forging human differences into ever new and creative mediations.

The Essays

While it is fair to say that the three orienting themes of self, meaning, and practice discussed above are at play in all of the essays at one point or another, each places a particular focus upon and develops particular aspects within one of them. Therefore, the three sections that compose this volume attempt to gather together those essays that focus on the same theme. The essays in the first section deal in various ways with Ricoeur's moral anthropology. The essays in the second section, all of which are devoted to matters theological, focus attention on Ricoeur's understanding of the social and linguistic processes through which capable humans create and engage meaning. The essays in the third section attempt to shed light on the various contributions that Ricoeur has made toward an understanding of how humans practically live out their moral convictions within social and political structures. Once again, none of the contributors was asked to address specifically the idea of human capability; it is the editors' suggestion, following Ricoeur's lead, that this idea represents a potent organizing principle running throughout these essays.

Part I: Moral Selfhood, the Good, and the Right

The five essays in part I explore various dimensions of the manifold experience of actually *being* capable selves. Each argues in its own way that it is this capable self that sets apart a Ricoeurian critical hermeneutical ethics from other forms of ethics. The idea of capable selfhood helps us steer clear of the unproductive debates between relativism and particularism by virtue of the idea that capable humans have the ability to conceive of human goods critically and creatively with each other. The capable self is obliged to realize its moral capacities by recognizing and entering into a mediating relationship with other such capable selves. Each essay, however, offers a different angle of approach to the anthropological dimensions of Ricoeur's moral thought.

Pamela Sue Anderson turns her attention to the Kantian aspects of Ricoeur's ethical project, arguing that his tripartite *petite ethique* is thoroughly structured by the Kantian architectonic of unity, plurality, and totality. In tracing the implications of this architectonic, Anderson claims, first, that Ricoeur ought to be more explicit about this structure, and, second, that Ricoeur's revisioning of the Kantian project offers a path beyond debates surrounding the transcendental ego. Peter Kemp, in contrast, addresses the Aristotelian aspects of Ricoeur's ethical project. Kemp argues that the attempt to formulate an understanding of the moral law demands that one's obligations reside in a fundamental and robust sense of the inherited social narratives of one's community. John Wall focuses on the point of mediation of these two traditions. Wall suggests that the underlying value of Ricoeur's ethics lies in mediating human capacities for the good and the right in a more fundamental moral capacity for constructive and transformative dialogue with otherness. In a more critical vein, Helen M. Buss explores Ricoeur's conception of moral tragedy; in particular, his cautious agreement with Hegel's interpretation of *Antigone*. Buss argues that Ricoeur's approach necessitates a decidely male-gendered subject, and she offers for consideration another distinctly female-gendered model characterized by the idea of "placental consciousness." Mark I. Wallace turns to the more explicitly religious dimensions of Ricoeur's moral anthropology. Expanding upon Ricoeur's own engagements with Levinas, Wallace explores the points of convergence and divergence between the two with regard to the notion of a *called* subject or a "mandated self."

Part II: Moral Meanings, Human Fallibility, and Theological Ethics

Part II of this volume addresses the question of human capability from the perspective of the self's capacity to engage and to create meaning. As stated, the contributions to this section of the volume are all devoted to the theological dimensions of Ricoeur's thought. This should not be surprising. Ricoeur's engagements with the religious have always been oriented by questions and concerns of meaning. How do primary symbols and root metaphors within the myths and biblical texts give rise to critical reflection on human experience? How do the manifold genres that compose the biblical texts converge to "name" God? What are the possibilities that religious meanings can come to fill lacunae within philosophical speculation? The editors suggest that Ricoeur's most profound contribution in the realm of meaning in general and religious meanings in particular concerns possibilities for a new theological ethics of culture. While not all of the essays explicitly address this, all nonetheless contribute to a fuller understanding of where such a project might aim.

David E. Klemm explores the interplay of dialectical philosophy, ethics, religion, and theology in Ricoeur's corpus. Klemm argues that the theological perspective to be gleaned from Ricoeur's writings does not reside in an easy appeal to revealed texts or kerygma, but rather emphasizes the human capacity for affirming the "limits" of one's own moral perspective and embracing God's critical transformative power. William Schweiker addresses the question of moral responsibility in Ricoeur's theological writings by placing these writings at the intersection of the conflicting moral outlooks of a theology of hope and an ethics of responsibility. Schweiker questions whether Ricoeur's position adequately accounts for moral value and offers suggestions for how this value might be more deeply explored from a distinctive theological and hermeneutical perspective. W. David Hall attempts to draw out systematically Ricoeur's proposal that Christian ethics resides in the creative tension between unilateral love and bilateral justice. Hall explores the resources that Ricoeur offers for conceiving a systematic and meaningful Christian ethics and the possibilities for a critical rapprochement between religious and philosophical ethical claims. Glenn Whitehouse explores two important metaphors that undergird Ricoeur's ethical thinking in both its philosophical and its theological aspects: the veil and the kingdom. Whitehouse seeks a deepened understanding of Ricoeur's ethics through the complex interplay between these two metaphors at both the philosophical and the theological levels of discourse. Linda M. MacCammon concludes this part by arguing that Ricoeur offers an important remedy to the current "postmodern" ethical situation. Criticizing what she takes to be the marginalization of Christian voices, MacCammon addresses the relationship of faith and ethics in Ricoeur's thought in order to reintroduce Christian themes and concerns into public ethical discussion.

Part III: Moral Practice, Responsible Citizenship, and Social Justice

The four essays in part III direct our gaze to the level of social and political practice by addressing the significance of Ricoeur's ethical and religious writings for select concrete moral problems. However much ethics has to do with selfhood and moral meaning, it remains above all an expression of the human capability, despite finitude, ambiguity, and conflict. A return to practical conduct is no mere application of moral theory. Rather, it is an attempt to grasp what it means for the self's moral capacities to be realized or completed in actuality. The essays in this part are each an exploration into the possibilities of the human capability in a particular moral situation.

Fred Dallmayr offers a "critical tribute" to the political dimensions of Ricoeur's ethical thought. Dallmayr, while appreciative of Ricoeur's substantial contributions to post-Hegelian theories of the state, expresses reservations about a number of aspects of Ricoeur's thought, from his treatments of Hegel and Heidegger to his penchant for "detour" as a philosophical strategy. Bernard P. Dauenhauer uses Ricoeur to argue for a "communitarian liberalism" in which political life is grounded in the human capacity for citizenship. Of particular interest to Dauenhauer is Ricoeur's understanding of public memory and forgiveness in the international realm. Don Browning argues that Ricoeur stands behind a worldwide reconstruction of practical theology, which, as the essays on theology of culture above also suggest, depends on the human moral capacity to interpret religious traditions in relation to human concerns. Browning also insightfully critiques Ricoeur for failing to link the capacity for practical wisdom to a sufficiently realist account of "fundamental goods." Martha C. Nussbaum concludes this part by addressing Ricoeur's presentation of the progression from tragedy to *phronesis* and its implications for justice. Arguing that Ricoeur's understanding of *phronesis* deals far more adequately with tragic conflicts that affect the moral life than either Kantian deontology or utilitarian cost-benefit analysis, Nussbaum concludes by questioning how far *phronesis* might be pushed.

The essays found in the various parts of this book all revolve around the theme of moral capability. As we have shown, from this admittedly complex and even debated center the authors extend their reflection into the whole round of current thought as well as some of the most troubling, pressing, and exciting topics confronting us: the place of tragedy in our lives, the reality or illusion of goodness, the travail of meaning in the moral life, the connection and contest between love and justice, the demands of life together as political beings, the connection between moral conviction and our deepest longings for the sacred. In this way, the book not only provides a novel and important interpretation of the wealth of Ricoeur's thought, but it also, and perhaps more important, presents original thinking on some of the most engaging questions of our time.

The Labor of Humanity

This volume concludes with Paul Ricoeur's contribution. Ricoeur takes up the theme of capability as a lens through which to understand the central problematic of his entire philosophical career, including especially his ethics, and indeed it is this essay that initially suggested the thematic unity and title of this volume. We leave the concluding word about human capability to Ricoeur. Yet we hope that this is not the final word on the subject, but rather the basis for the continuation of the fruitful interchange that this volume founds. Each of the contributors to this volume is in his or her own way indebted to Ricoeur for the provocative and fecund way in which he has developed—and continues to develop—the concept of human capability in his many writings in ethics and theology.

As Ricoeur's concluding essay exemplifies, his work in ethics is distinguished by a stunning breadth of inquiry, attention to the multiplicity of alternative moral approaches, boldness in tackling the big issues, and most of all a creative capacity to open up moral reflection to previously uncharted possibilities. Ricoeur's remarkable body of work provides the basis for a rich and creative new approach to ethics and the theology of culture that has heretofore not been recognized clearly as a distinct position on the contemporary landscape. It is hoped that this volume of essays demonstrates the power and depth of Ricoeur's significance for moral thought, but also, and more important, energizes moral philosophy, theology, and public reflection beyond the confines of their current entrenched alternatives.

The path beyond these long-standing debates, this volume suggests, is a move into reflection on the peculiarly human capacity for forming meaning with one another. The call to undertake reflection in this way is to realize that after a century of untold terror and bewildering innovation, the twenty-first century confronts us anew with the great labor of our humanity.

PART I:

Moral Selfhood, the Good, and the Right

1
Ricoeur's Reclamation of Autonomy
Unity, Plurality, and Totality

PAMELA SUE ANDERSON

Ricoeur's Kantian Architectonic

Paul Ricoeur renders Immanuel Kant's moral and political principle of autonomy with these words: "Dare to learn, taste, savour for yourself!"[1] Interpreted loosely for my purposes this *threefold* imperative encapsulates Ricoeur's view of the ethics and meaning of autonomy in public life. His view is more engaging than the prosaic description often given of Kantian autonomy. As one feminist philosopher suggests, the description is in fact a caricature of "a moral superstar [standing] alone on a rock of rational will power,"[2] forcibly detached by his (*sic*) own sense of duty from other individuals and from the taint of emotions, or "care," which might connect him to the concrete vulnerabilities of life. This caricature will clearly not be compatible with Ricoeur's portrayal of autonomy and arguably not with Kant's own.

With the benefit of hindsight, Ricoeur reconfigures Kantian autonomy as the *capacity* of human subjects to make moral law for themselves and so bind themselves to an ethical life in community with other rational beings. Yet in reclaiming autonomy from contemporary disclaimers, his conception is potentially just as demanding as Kant's. Whatever else might be said of Ricoeur's relationship to Kant, I will contend that he takes up a thoroughly Kantian architectonic and that he persuasively reclaims autonomy from neo-Aristotelian, postmodern, and feminist disclaimers. The subtitle of my chapter, "Unity, Plurality, and Totality," contains Kant's categories of quantity. These three categories have informed Kantian discussions of autonomy in the spheres of both theoretical and practical reason. For some philosophers, especially moral philosophers, these terms will bring to mind Kant's elaboration of the three moments of a kingdom of ends; implicit are the moments in the progression from the categorical imperative formula of an end-in-itself (unity) to that of ends-in-themselves (plurality) and, ultimately, to that of the complete system of ends (totality).³ This threefold vision of the kingdom of ends should be kept in mind when assessing Ricoeur's reclamation of autonomy.

Ricoeur's Kantian architectonic denies neither the value of the formal functions of judgment (that is, universal, particular, and singular) as critical tools, nor the need to work with the material content of real life. Whereas the Kantian vision has tended to be presented as flawless, Ricoeur's vision of a community of persons as ends-in-themselves does not deny the inevitable gaps and possible inconsistencies in an account of autonomy that aims at completeness rather than simplicity.⁴ In particular, he recognizes that aporia plague the Kantian autonomy that begins reflection at a formal level of unity; and he attempts to confront three aporia at the "places" of (the self's) receptiveness, passivity, and powerlessness.⁵ I maintain that in confronting the aporia of (1) receptiveness of freedom to the law, (2) passivity of reason to the feeling of respect, and (3) powerlessness of the will to the propensity for evil, Ricoeur remains within a Kantian architectonic.

Ricoeur's Ninth Study, "The Self and Practical Wisdom," in *Oneself as Another* represents these aporia as three figures: (1) the other of freedom in the figure of the law (which freedom gives itself);⁶ (2) the other of feeling in the figure of respect—that is, passive-reason;⁷ and (3) the other of the good in the figure of the penchant toward evil.⁸ Bear in mind that Ricoeur progresses level by level to represent these figures of otherness, aiming to reverse—subsequently—the order of their appearance, and thus to reclaim the autonomy of the self as *ipse*, not *idem*; that is, selfhood, not sameness.⁹ Ultimately, he seeks to reconfigure the aporia—at the third moment—in the complete determination of the system of ends in trying cases of moral judgment as singular.¹⁰

A Kantian explanation can be given for the aporia as well as their reconfiguration. These impasses are inevitable insofar as the formal function of judgment, in its universal form, necessarily unifies by excluding the diverse sensible or material content and the complex of relations of real life circumstances. The aporia appear as a result of the exclusion of material parts and social relations. Yet Ricoeur's systematization of issues holds in view the three forms of judgment and the three categories of unity, plurality, and totality, while developing new arguments that both retain and reverse the distinctions of the conceptual, the sensible, and the full concreteness of action in concert with other persons.¹¹ His reconfiguration preserves the full meaning of autonomy, at each level, form, moment, category, and distinction of a Kantian architectonic, without losing either the flexibility necessary for the plurality of the embodiments of ethical life or the ultimate vision of a harmonious kingdom of ends.

Ricoeur's reclamation of autonomy develops at the heart of his account of the good and the right in the Seventh, Eighth, and Ninth studies of *Oneself as Another*.¹² It forms the core of his "little ethics," which is his retrospective name for these three studies. Against various schools of potential opponents, his account suggests that there is a deep connection between the good and the right.[13] The good, on the one hand, is understood, roughly, as living well. In Aristotelian terms, it is the aim of the ethical life, that is, living and faring well. The right, on the other hand, is understood, roughly, as doing what every finite rational being ought to do. In Kantian terms, it is acting autonomously, yet Ricoeur adds the proviso "for and with others in just institutions." In supplementing Kant, Ricoeur's complete account of the right becomes increasingly complex. It is, first, upstaged in the Seventh Study by what are Ricoeur's mediating analyses of the good in Aristotle, but also by what will become his elucidation of the good in the texts of Kant. Next, his account elaborates the right in terms of the norm of autonomy on three levels. These terms are represented by the Eighth Study, "The Self and the Moral Norm," in its three subsections: "The Aim of the 'Good' Life and Obligation," "Solicitude and the Norm," and "From the Sense of Justice to the 'Principles of Justice.'" The movement implicit in these terms means that the right covers both moral and political philosophy. Ultimately, his account reclaims the full meaning of autonomy in the reversal of the levels of judgment in the Ninth Study. This last study proposes that instead of beginning with the formal and universal, we should start with the complete action determined for and with others, and then reflect back upon the autonomy of selfhood (*ipseity*).[14] So from this, autonomy is not found to be the starting point, but the critical pivot for his little ethics; as Ricoeur will later argue, autonomy as a moral capacity is bound up with interdependence, or the "interpersonal," rather than independence.[15]

It is instructive to restate Ricoeur's own descriptions of the threefold levels of reflection in his analysis of autonomy before their reversal.[16] First, on the formal level of principles, or Kantian maxims, autonomy is achieved when the faculty of choice (*Willkür*) sets aside sensible inclinations (or natural desires), in order to follow the rational principle of the will (*Wille*); this renders universality.[17] Second, on the material level, autonomy is realized when instrumental reasoning is decentered by the respect owed to persons; that is, to others as much as oneself; this renders plurality.[18] Third, on the level of complete determination of all maxims, autonomy is accomplished when a will turned in on itself is recasted by the mediation of those institutional structures created for living well together. This renders justice, or the complete determination of ends-in-themselves, and hence autonomous willing in concert with others.[19]

Ricoeur suggests a connection between Aristotle and Kant—as representatives of the good and the right, respectively—in his reversal of formal conceptions of autonomy. Yet notice that he always progresses according to a Kantian architectonic—that is, according to three forms of judgment: of the universal, the particular, and the singular, to three spheres of acting: of unity, plurality, and totality, and to three levels of the formal, material, and the complete determination of autonomy in the harmony of persons who think and act attentive to the good. Moreover, the connection between Aristotle and Kant is played out upon the stage of Ricoeur's exploration of the self's intimate relations to otherness, in his words, of "oneself inasmuch as other."[20] Unlike many contemporary portrayals of the Kantian, or Aristotelian, *I*, Ricoeur represents *le soi* and not *le moi*.[21] The displaced *I* implicit here is the first-person subject, but it could also be thought to decenter the culturally specific *I* of Western philosophy that has been gendered as the man of reason. Ricoeur does not equate selfhood with the factual or empirical account of identity (*idem*) sought by Anglo-American or European philosophers. He does not claim to *attest to* the self on a first-person basis of an *I* alone. Instead Ricoeur's distinctive attestation of selfhood (*ipseity*) is made on the ontological basis of, initially, a *belief in* being self-identical (*ipse*), both active and receptive, but, ultimately and more strongly, a *conviction* of being oneself inasmuch as other (*soi-même comme un autre*) in acting and suffering.[22]

Ricoeur illustrates the role of attestation in a distinctive act of willing: that is, promising. Selfhood is being self-same at once bound in promise-keeping, despite change, and unbound in forgiveness, despite the past of shattered promises.[23] I intend to take a critical look at the originality of Ricoeur's account of promise-keeping in which he claims to disagree with Kant's assessment of the morality of false promises.[24] He also claims to advance beyond Kant with his conception of selfhood as *ipseity*. Yet a Kantian architectonic still shapes Ricoeur's conception of autonomy or, in his later terms, it builds *ipse*-autonomy upon a subject with a moral capacity. His essentially post-Kantian conception of a rational subject with certain capacities also creates the possibility and necessity of reconceiving related moral terms such as imputation, responsibility, and conviction.[25] I discuss this further later in this chapter.

Ricoeur also admits that the fragility of this picture of autonomy is personally embedded and reflexive. It is quite easily broken down by violence insofar as selfhood is discordant: always both agent and patient. Ironically, violence that disrupts the harmony of persons reveals retrospectively what had been possessed positively as power in common.[26] Ricoeur's distinctive manner of Kantian reasoning is both informed by and informs the larger picture of the hermeneutics of selfhood. Yet, admittedly, his notion of selfhood as *ipseity* has no exact parallel in Kant.[27] Unlike Kant, the autonomous self is neither his starting point (as a datum) nor an a priori concept. Nevertheless, he uses a Kantian framework to locate his ontological claims concerning the self. In this sense, he can be said to supplement Kant.

Ricoeur anticipates the distinctive reclamation of autonomy at the outset of his hermeneutics of selfhood. In his introduction to *Oneself as Another*, he fixes the autonomy of the self in its relations to otherness:

> Never, at any stage, will the self have been separated from its other. It remains, however, that this dialectic, the richest of all, as the title of the work [read as "oneself inasmuch as other"[28]] recalls, will take on its fullest development only in the studies in the areas of ethics and morality. The *autonomy* of the self will appear then to be tightly bound up with *solicitude* for one's neighbor and with *justice* for each individual.[29]

As stipulated by Ricoeur himself, "ethics" (in the above) refers to Aristotle's teleological account of the good life, while "morality" (above) refers to Kant's deontological account of acting on rational principles, that is, his account of autonomy. Solicitude should be understood, according to Ricoeur, as more fundamental than obedience to duty.[30] To explain solicitude, he refers to the "benevolent spontaneity" that is necessary for self-esteem and unfolds the dialogic dimension of beings who act and suffer.[31] Ricoeur claims that, although more fundamental than duty, solicitude is formalized in Kant's second formulation of the categorical imperative: "So act that you use humanity, whether in your own person or in the person of any other, always at the same time as an end, never merely as a means."[32] He also claims that "*justice* for each individual" (as quoted above) takes *equality* as "its ethical mainspring."[33] But he turns to the principles of justice, as in the fiction of a social contract,[34] in order to compensate for the "initial dissymmetry" between agents and patients. So both the rule of justice and solicitude's rule of reciprocity *respond to the dissymmetry of selfhood* that forms the basis of inequalities, suffering, and evil.[35] Thus, in reclaiming autonomy on the basis of a fundamental dissymmetry of selfhood, Ricoeur revises popular conceptions of Kantian morality; he demonstrates autonomy's deep connection with the good, Aristotelian teleology, and political theories of justice.

Autonomy and Ricoeur's Reversal of Kantian Formalism

At this stage allow me to contextualize—all too briefly—Ricoeur's Kantian conception of autonomy. Generally in his writings, Ricoeur has had an uncanny sense in anticipating those concepts in contemporary debates that will become and remain essentially contested. In particular, in choosing to focus on autonomy Ricoeur takes a highly contested concept in Kantian philosophy back to Aristotle.[36] In his fully revised Gifford Lectures, autonomy becomes pivotal in an argument that confirms, on the one hand, his debt to Kant and, on the other hand, his awareness of the dangers in Kantian formalism.[37] Ricoeur is readily aware of, and dissociates himself from, Kantian formalism and, in his words, the canonical Kant.[38] However, as I've begun to establish, Ricoeur's own exegesis and critique of Kant do *not* detract from his implicit Kantian framework. To establish this further, several things must be kept distinct: Ricoeur's own readings of Kant, the Kantian moral philosophy that has especially in this century formalized Kant, the more recent Kantian moral philosophers who are discovering the possibilities in yet untapped resources of Kant's practical philosophy, and finally, Ricoeur's Kantianism. These distinct views should not be confused.

The formalized Kant of twentieth-century philosophy restricts the reading and application of moral philosophy to tests of the universalizability of principles of action.[39] In this context, practical reasoning is formalized to such an extent that the fundamental role and several dimensions of the categorical imperative are lost sight of.[40] Ricoeur presupposes the formalized figure in rejecting this Kant, or at least this "path."[41] The obvious question would be, Is this fair to Kant? Some recent defenders of his practical philosophy might say it is not.

To assess critically Ricoeur's reversal of Kant's formalism, I have studied his reading of Kant's account of promising.[42] To summarize my findings, Ricoeur distinguishes two different paths to address the question of the morality of a false promise. He proposes that one path leads to the exclusion, and the other path to the inclusion, of the otherness of the other person (*l'altérité de l'autrui*); he often stresses that this includes the plural, that is, other persons.[43] According to Ricoeur, the first path is the formal one that Kant takes; but he will aim to take the second path involving a concrete situation in which the otherness of persons is recognized. It is Ricoeur's reduction of Kant to the first path that concerns me most here. Kant's formal path proceeds by verifying the moral character of a maxim, or subjective underlying principle, of an action by a two-step test: (1) The maxim is stated in such a way that it could be tested for its universalizability: Could the maxim—for example, "Refrain from making a false promise"—become a universal law? (2) The maxim is actually tested for its internal consistency: Does the maxim itself—"Refrain from making a false promise"—contain an internal contradiction?[44] Ricoeur largely equates Kant's two-step test to the question of his thought experiment: "Can the maxim of my action really become a universal law of nature?"[45] But this question adds to the test the prepositional phrase "of nature," confusing the matter of the contradiction. Perhaps it would have been less confusing had Kant himself added the phrase "a universal law of reason or freedom" in his thought experiment suggesting a causality on analogy with the laws of nature.[46] Ricoeur does not address this matter. Instead he rests with Kant's conclusion that in the case of "When I believe myself to be in need of money I shall borrow money and promise to repay it, even though I know that this will never happen,"[47] this maxim could never subsist as a system of nature; it would contradict itself.[48]

To consider some problems with this reading of Kant's account, I offer a rather complex discussion. First, I will indicate three of Ricoeur's criticisms of Kant on promising, explaining how each seems unfair. At the same time, I will suggest reasons why Ricoeur might have made these criticisms. In addition, I will contend that on each of these points he would have been better off if he had been more openly Kantian. Finally, in looking at Ricoeur's own approach I conclude that he would be better off with Kant as his support in that his conception of oneself inasmuch as other remains profoundly Kantian, especially in his singling out of promise-keeping to conceive *ipse*-identity.[49] More strongly stated, Ricoeur's original conception of *ipseity* is in fact more Kantian than he seems to think it is.

The First Criticism of Kant

Let me turn to the first of Ricoeur's three criticisms of Kant. Ricoeur claims that Kant's account of the contradiction in the maxim of the false promise is question-begging. In Ricoeur's words,

> [Kant] considers only a single route to be possible in the test of the maxim: the ascending route, subsuming the maxim under a rule;[50] . . . in what way does the maxim enter into contradiction with itself? In truth, the contradiction is apparent only if the agent has made the hypothesis that his maxim were to become a universal law;[51] [and] . . . a rule that admits of exceptions is no longer a rule.[52]

From the above assertions alone, this criticism of Kant's account of the first formulation of the categorical imperative, or as also said, the Formula of the Universal Law, seems unfair. Kant does *not* simply assume that the maxim is a rule before carrying out the test of universalizability. Instead he uses the test only on a maxim that appears to be a likely candidate for being a rule. So Kant does not beg the question. But why does Ricoeur think he does? It is not absolutely clear whether Ricoeur thinks that the question-begging is that Kant has already accepted the maxim as a rule (to be universalized), or that Kant assumes acceptance of the rule of noncontradiction as the test for the morality of a maxim. But either way, Ricoeur's criticism misses something: on the one hand, Kant considers the maxim only as a *possible candidate* for being a rule (that is, asking whether it should be willed as a universal law); and on the other hand, the rule of noncontradiction is neither sufficient on its own nor applied without prior practical judgment on a relevant maxim. This latter—that is, practical judgment—is not a simple matter.[53] For Kant, judgment cannot be taught, and algorithms, or a logical test, for applying rules in particular situations would end in an infinite regress: "to apply an infinity of rules for applying rules for applying rules . . ."[54] So the applicability of the rule in the test for the morality of an action cannot be carried out prior to the practical judgment concerning the maxim of the action; and judgment is an art, not a simple test.[55]

For instance, we might have to judge what the maxim is in making a cup of tea for a visitor; the making of tea involves many actions and intentions from taking out the teapot to pouring the tea into a cup in which one has already put a small amount of milk. But none of these intentions is clearly a candidate for being a rule, or for being a moral maxim. So what is the subjective underlying principle that might be a candidate for a rule and could be tested for universalizability? It could be that in some cases there is no moral maxim for the action of, say, making a cup of tea for a visitor. Yet we might decide that a possible candidate for the maxim is "Be generous to others in need." Once we think we have a candidate for a rule, it is next necessary to consider whether it could become a universal law. If it is, then, shown to satisfy the test of the first of three specific formulations of the categorical imperative, the question remains whether passing the test of the general formulation (or any one of three specific and equivalent formulations) of the categorical imperative on its own is sufficient for it to be a universal moral law.[56]

Whatever Ricoeur means by insisting that Kant's thought experiment only works if the agent has already accepted the maxim as a rule admitting of no exception, he could have developed a better strategy in response to his reading of Kant on false promises. A really interesting possibility for him would be to supplement Kant's thought experiment by employing his own account of self-constancy (*ipseity*) in promising. He could have provided a criterion for distinguishing which subjective underlying principle might serve as a serious candidate for a maxim being a rule. Kant's lack of criterion remains a burden for Kantian moral philosophers, but Ricoeur's hermeneutics of selfhood could contribute something to fill that lack. I will say more about this alternative strategy under discussion of the third criticism.

The Second Criticism of Kant

This criticism emerges in asking, What about the exception made on behalf of others? Implicit is the thought that Kant is not sufficiently aware of the otherness of other persons (note the plural here) in promising. This leads Ricoeur to propose his second path for assessing the singular situation of a false promise. But is it fair to say categorically that this second path is one that Kant never takes? It *is* true that Kant makes no exception for any person to an established duty. This would go against the categorical imperative. And yet for Kant the constraint of universalizability is supposed to preserve, not sever, moral interaction in the sense of relations between self and other; it is not to render them immoral. But doesn't Ricoeur seek these moral relations between oneself and another in Kant?

Some contemporary moral philosophers have found in Kant an irrevocable connection between the universalization of the maxim of action and the relation of self and other. In Onora O'Neill's words, "The Kantian picture of practical reasoning . . . requires the *capacity* to universalize, which is needed if the fundamental intentions of our lives are *not* to be ones that others can*not* share."[57] Furthermore, we have already seen Ricoeur holding together the categories of unity, plurality, and totality, which constitute the three formulations of the categorical imperative; this threefold vision makes certain that other persons are taken into account just as much as oneself. So it is not really clear that Ricoeur does himself any favor in apparently rejecting Kant's account of respect for the universal law of morality. He suggests that this rejection will render exceptions made on behalf of other persons possible. But, if so, he fails to accept that in disallowing any exception for one's own self, or another, Kant himself aims to preserve the morality of all persons as law-giving beings.[58] In brief, Ricoeur rejects Kant's point that persons are treated morally precisely because of the universal law, and insists that respect for the law devalues respect for persons.

Let me suggest one reason why Ricoeur makes his second criticism. And yet why he might still be better off if he had not. He wants to stress a distinction between the plurality of persons as ends-in-themselves and the unity of humanity as an end-in-itself, in order to raise a non-Kantian sort of exception. That is, the countenance, or face, of the other comes to signify "the genuine otherness of persons which makes each one an exception."[59] Perhaps he does something new insofar as a universalized maxim could not be rejected (by Kant) to make an exception for another person in a singular situation. Here he plays with an idea from the philosophy of Emmanuel Levinas concerning the face of the other. This new idea of otherness is, in his words, "potentially discordant in relation to" Kant's idea of humanity as a universal in the sense of a formal unity.[60] This assumes that universality can be extended to the detriment of others, that universality in plurality is an impossible category. Yet even with this assumption, is Ricoeur's own idea of the self's intimate relation to the other "discordant" in relation to Kant?

Kant's first formulation of the categorical imperative does not have to extend universality to the detriment of other agents. Again in O'Neill's words, "the notion of a plurality of interacting agents is already implicit in the Formula of Universal Law."[61] Nevertheless, what is the result of Ricoeur's playing with this apparently non-Kantian "factor of otherness"? In Ricoeur's words, "The promise then ceases to be connected to the sole concern for personal integrity and enters the space of application of the rule of reciprocity . . . tak[ing] into account the initial dissymmetry of agent and patient, with all the effects of violence that result from this dissymmetry."[62] Yet, to be fair, it has not been established (even if Ricoeur claims it has) that Kant connects promising solely with, in the above terms, "personal integrity" and not reciprocity. Instead Kant, or at least according to certain recent Kantian moral philosophers, agrees that the promise is kept because of the relation to another, that is, the duty to the self inasmuch as another. Alternatively, we could ask, in insisting on a "new" factor of otherness, does Ricoeur move away from Kant and closer to Levinas? This is also doubtful. He is clearly at odds with Levinas's ethics.[63] Ultimately he rejects Levinas's account of the injunction of the other because it renders impossible any reciprocal relation between self and other.[64] Levinas puts the self in a state of separation (as *le moi*, not *le soi*) from the other.[65] In contrast, Ricoeur attests to the relation of self (*le soi*) to the other in *ipseity*. But my point is that this places Ricoeur closer to Kant than he might recognize himself. This point becomes stronger in my response to the final criticism.

The Third Criticism of Kant

This has to do with the *moral* problem in the act of promise-keeping, which Ricoeur suggests is missing from Kant's account of promising.[66] Allow me to backtrack briefly. Before his little ethics in *Oneself as Another*, Ricoeur introduced the distinction between promising as defined by a "constitutive rule" of placing oneself under the obligation to do tomorrow what today I say I shall do and keeping one's promise as defined by a "moral rule" of fidelity.[67] This distinction from speech-act theory is introduced in the context of his preethical study "The Self and Narrative Identity" in order to solve the problem of *idem*-identity. That is, *idem*-identity as in the sameness that is constitutive of an agent dissipates in time but the moral rule of fidelity can create *ipse*-identity—that is, self-constancy—which endures despite temporal change. Later in the Ninth Study, "Self and Practical Wisdom," Ricoeur brings in the same distinction to claim that promising as an act can satisfy the conditions of "the promise" without our knowing anything about the success of promise-keeping. He asserts, "Promising is one thing. Being obligated to keep one's promise is something else again."[68] However, in this context a danger arises when he separates promising and promise-keeping: Ricoeur destroys a key support of his own account of *ipseity* as diachronically related to *idem*.[69]

I would contend Kant himself establishes that promising—when a moral action—is diachronic; that is, temporally shaped. For promising to be a moral action in Kantian terms it must be carried out freely and rationally. Kant's demonstration of the immorality of false promises is not intended to defend promising as either a virtually timeless act or a radically discrete act, but to represent the point at which an agent has the possibility of initiating rational action; hence, promise-keeping. In this way, Kant himself conceives what Ricoeur identifies as self-constancy in promise-keeping.[70] Without the moral rule of keeping one's word (or remaining faithful) to another, Ricoeur's account of *ipse*-identity would break down, but so would Kant's account of practical reason and autonomy. Without it, both accounts would, then, face the problems that plague the empiricist tradition of Locke and Hume, returning to identity as *idem*.

The further question is, Can Ricoeur achieve a socially embedded account of promise-keeping without building upon Kant? For his account to succeed he needs to maintain that (1) in the speech act, "I promise," promising and obligating are the same thing so that obligation is the force of an illocutionary act; (2) if moral, this act must also necessarily imply the self-constancy in keeping the promise in time and in relation to another; and (3) without the latter it is impossible to maintain an evaluative concept of selfhood as temporally embodied and socially embedded. Yet Kant is also committed to at least the first two contentions. Ricoeur rightly states that, in the example of promising, obligation raises the *moral* question, Will the promiser be faithful and stay committed to her promise? But this *is* a *Kantian* question. Kant must think that if the act of promising is to be rational and free, it cannot be separated from the moral rule of promise-keeping. Moreover, this might give us the criterion (sought above) for distinguishing which subjective underlying principle might serve as a serious candidate for a maxim being a rule: this criterion is that for a maxim (that is, a subjective underlying principle) to be a rule, it should render the action diachronic. Perhaps Ricoeur supplements Kant in the third contention above, but this would miss promising's relation to promise-keeping in Kant. For Ricoeur, *ipse*-identity in promise-keeping is an example of "the highest expression of selfhood" insofar as promising already reflects a desire to respond to an expectation, or request coming from another, with a commitment of self-constancy. But, then, Kant can provide a key support for *ipse*-identity in conceiving practical reason in promising as diachronic in giving shape to the lives of rational beings in a kingdom of ends.[71]

I have tried to demonstrate that Ricoeur's three criticisms of question-begging, of exceptions on behalf of another, and of promising are unfair to Kant's overall account of rules, judgment, and autonomy. How far can Kant support Ricoeur on the reflexive, personally embedded nature of freedom, whereby autonomy is closer to inter- or intradependence than to independence?[72] Despite his three criticisms, Ricoeur himself returns to employ "the requirement of universalization," which derives from Kant's formal level of judgment. Moreover, his account of autonomy, which includes the rules of reciprocity and justice, makes most sense in reclaiming, while supplementing, Kant's account of the self and the other. Precisely with a Kantian architectonic he *is equipped* to explain how to treat persons (stressing the plural) as ends-in-themselves and to recognize the initial dissymmetry in the reciprocity between self and other, agent and patient.[73] Further, his Kantian equipment can be seen as highly valuable in the light of contemporary debates in moral and political philosophy.[74]

Conclusion: Back to Kant

In conclusion, I return to Ricoeur's rendering of the Kantian imperative "Dare to learn, taste, savour for yourself." This reflects a position that challenges the popular (empiricist) accounts of a formalist autonomy as both disembodied and disembedded. The prosaic description of the Kantian autonomous man with which I began should have been decisively undermined by what

Ricoeur's Kantian architectonic has been found to offer. Perhaps unwittingly, Ricoeur has offered us the tools to challenge the account of Kant's autonomy assumed by philosophers such as Seyla Benhabib: "Kant's error was to assume that I, as a pure rational agent reasoning for myself, could reach a conclusion that would be acceptable for all at all times and places. In Kantian moral theory, moral agents are like geometricians in different rooms who, reasoning alone for themselves, all arrive at the same solution to a problem."[75]

Ricoeur's exegesis of the calculative test of the canonical Kant might agree with Benhabib's account of what she identifies as "the generalized other" who needs to recognize "the concrete other." Yet I have proposed that Ricoeur's reclamation of autonomy exhibits a deeper debt to, and insight into, Kantian philosophy than his explicit rejection of a formalized Kant would suggest. Far from leaving Kant behind in his hermeneutics of selfhood, Ricoeur offers a highly significant rereading of Kant's Enlightenment philosophy for the twenty-first century. With his daring words concerning the autonomous use of reason as inextricably bound to solicitude for one's neighbor and to justice for each individual embodiment of reason (that is, every person, self and other), I remain convinced that Ricoeur has made a significant contribution to new understanding of both Kantian philosophy and autonomy.

In 1993 I quoted Ricoeur's assertion that "Kant . . . is without a doubt the philosopher who has never ceased to inspire me . . . the philosopher who joins a precise architectonic of the power of thought to an intransigent sense of the limits."[76] I can confidently repeat this, while adding that Ricoeur's foresight on the debates concerning autonomy in moral and political (including feminist) philosophies and his ability to develop mediated positions at the points of contestation are remarkable. His style of doing philosophy is also something to which I will return as an attractive alternative for those feminist and nonfeminist philosophers who berate philosophy for its adversarial style of argumentation.

Many contemporary despisers of autonomy claim to be objecting to Kantian ancestry but fail to show knowledge of Kant's own arguments. Frequently these despisers reject autonomy on the grounds of broadly empiricist accounts of the self, action, and freedom. Perhaps they have followed Carol Gilligan's empirical studies of a different voice and her critique of autonomy, recognizing the missing dimensions of the concrete other in contemporary moral philosophy.[77] However, I would caution against the thought that any empiricist critique of autonomy uncovers a woman's way of thinking. Instead I hope to have shown that a reclamation of autonomy from its distortions by certain empiricist readings of the self and willing in Kant have implications for a much larger critique of our cultural thinking. This would be a critique of cultural thinking that is plagued by oppositions (which are not the same as a proper use of distinctions) between the good and the right, Aristotle and

Kant, women and men. Not only is treating these distinctions as stark oppositions inaccurate, but it can be harmful. Those who side with only the first term of this opposition include the misguided detractors of Kantian autonomy to whom Ricoeur's studies can speak. Ironically, sometimes this means speaking to himself insofar as, I think, he must be careful in how he criticizes a particular figure of a formalist Kant.

Implicit is my conviction that Ricoeur's writings offer an indirect demonstration of the importance of the larger systematic issues of selfhood and practical reasoning. He demonstrates these issues in constructing a careful and intricate, Kantian architectonic, which shapes his impressive studies on ethics, morality, and practical wisdom where conviction confronts choices rendered difficult by contexts of conflict. As discussed, his use of Kant's categories of quantity—that is, unity, plurality, and totality—give a framework to his account of autonomy. His reclamation of autonomy basically reverses Kant's ordering of the categories and so confirms what other philosophers who seek to understand Kant have found to be the necessity of a nonlinear reading and reconstruction of his philosophical writings. I see Ricoeur as part of moral philosophy's revival of new readings of Kantian autonomy. Thus Ricoeur and Kant remain partners in method and in critical dialogue.

More than partners, Ricoeur and Kant are two philosophers who have accompanied us into the twenty-first century. Despite strenuous efforts by their opponents and cultural despisers, neither of them has been silenced by the debates of twentieth-century poststructuralism, postmodernism, postfeminism, and the like. In the light of what some might take to be decisive disclaimers of Kantian autonomy—for example, its idealized caricature of the moral man (sic), its algorithmic reasoning, its disembedded and disembodied self—I have countered that Ricoeur offers us the means to reclaim autonomy for contemporary ethics, and moral and political debates. Crucially, this reclamation conceives autonomy as inseparable from the embodiment, the concrete otherness, and the vulnerabilities constituting the many dimensions of everyday life that, nevertheless, can together aim at a harmonious vision of the good. However unachievable, this vision is given expression by the symbol, or regulative ideal, of the kingdom of ends. As regulative and not constitutive, this symbol unites Kant's two questions, "What ought I to do?" and "What may I hope?" in longed-for possibilities.

Notes

1. Paul Ricoeur, *Oneself as Another*, trans. Kathleen Blamey (Chicago: University of Chicago Press, 1992), p. 276.
2. Jane Kneller, "The Aesthetic Dimension of Kantian Autonomy," in *Feminist Interpretations of Immanuel Kant*, ed. Robin May Schott (University Park, PA: Pennsylvania State University Press, 1997), p. 174.

3. Immanuel Kant, *Groundwork of the Metaphysics of Morals*, trans. and ed. Mary Gregor (Cambridge: Cambridge University Press, 1998), pp. 41–47 (4:433–40). Cf. Paul Ricoeur, "Freedom in the Light of Hope," trans. Robert Sweeney, in *The Conflict of Interpretations: Essays in Hermeneutics*, ed. Don Ihde (Evanston, IL: Northwestern University Press, 1974), pp. 411–24.
4. Ricoeur reads the simplified vision represented by the king, Creon, in the tragedy of Antigone as the cause of this character's moral downfall (Ricoeur, *Oneself as Another*, pp. 244, 249). Martha Nussbaum identifies this "strategy of simplification" in *The Fragility of Goodness: Luck and Ethics in Greek Tragedy and Philosophy* (Cambridge: Cambridge University Press, 1986), pp. 60–67. For a critical discussion of this strategy, see Pamela Sue Anderson, "Re-reading Myth in Philosophy: Hegel, Ricoeur, Irigaray Reading *Antigone*," in *Paul Ricoeur and Narrative: Context and Contestation*, ed. Morny Joy (Calgary: University of Calgary Press, 1997), pp. 52–59. Ricoeur also refers to Aristotle to support his understanding of the danger in "oversimplicity" (*Oneself as Another*, p. 262).
5. Ricoeur, *Oneself as Another*, pp. 212–17, 275.
6. Ibid., pp. 273 f.; also 212.
7. Ibid., pp. 262 f.; also 213–14, 218.
8. Ibid., p. 275; also 211–18, 223–24n35.
9. Ibid., pp. 2–3, 16, 18, 116–19, 274–75.
10. Ibid., pp. 263–83.
11. The idea of action in concert—or power in common—comes from Hannah Arendt, *The Human Condition*, 2nd ed. (Chicago: University of Chicago Press, 1998), pp. 200–3, 244–45. Cf. Ricoeur, *Oneself as Another*, pp. 194–97.
12. Ricoeur, *Oneself as Another*, esp. pp. 204, 207–18, 225–26, 228–29, 233, 238–39, 250, 273–83, 285, 330.
13. For a defence of both the connection and the distinction of the good and the right, see Christine Korsgaard, *The Sources of Normativity* (Cambridge: Cambridge University Press, 1996), pp. 114n26–15, 122–23.
14. Ricoeur, *Oneself as Another*, pp. 2–3, 18, 116–24, 207, 211, 267, 275–76, 285.
15. Paul Ricoeur, "Who Is the Subject of Rights?" in *The Just*, trans. David Pellauer (Chicago: University of Chicago Press, 2000), pp. 1, 5–6, 10.
16. On Ricoeur's use of reflection and analysis as characteristic of his hermeneutics of selfhood, see Ricoeur, *Oneself as Another*, pp. 16–21, 297.
17. Ibid., pp. 207–11. Ricoeur turns to Kant's "Analytic of Pure Practical Reason," in *Critique of Practical Reason*, to account for this split between reason and desire, bringing in the Kantian distinction between *Wille*, the fundamental rational structure of the will, and *Willkür*, the finite faculty of choice. See Immanuel Kant, *Critique of Practical Reason*, trans. and ed. Mary Gregor (Cambridge: Cambridge University Press, 1997), p. 19 (5:21).
18. Ricoeur, *Oneself as Another*, pp. 218, 222–26.
19. Ibid., pp. 229, 238–39. This can be usefully compared to his account of the moral capacity, "Who Is the Subject of Rights?" pp. 1–10.
20. Ricoeur, *Oneself as Another*, p. 3.

21. Ibid., p. 18.
22. Ibid., pp. 20–23, 299–302, 309n11. Consider Kant's various conceptions of the self, including the empirical self, the noumenal self, the transcendental self, and the practical self. Would *ipse* be closest to the latter? Or is selfhood deduced transcendentally as the condition of the possibility of the experience of a self who acts and suffers?
23. Ibid., pp. 264, 267; also 116, 118–19. On forgiveness as a model for the mediation of self-identity and alterity, see Ricoeur, "Reflection on a New Ethos for Europe," in *Paul Ricoeur: The Hermeneutics of Action*, ed. Richard Kearney (London: Sage Publications, 1996), pp. 9–12.
24. Ricoeur, *Oneself as Another*, pp. 265–69.
25. Ibid., pp. 288–89, 292–96, 302, 352. *Ipse* would modify autonomy as a moral capacity by stressing the reflexive and personally embedded, or interpersonal, nature of the reclaimed freedom as the self's own autonomy.
26. Ibid., pp. 194–97, 220, 256–57; cf. Arendt, *The Human Condition*, pp. 244–45.
27. Previously, I argued that the structure of *Oneself as Another* rested upon a transcendental argument whereby *ipseity* (like the transcendental subject) is shown to be the a priori condition for our experiences as speaking, acting, promising, choosing/willing, and suffering beings; see "Having It Both Ways: Self-Same and Other," *Oxford Literary Review* 15 (1993): 227–52. Now I recognize that Ricoeur's method of truth—i.e., attestation—affirms selfhood (*ipseity*) as an ontological condition; such truth is attested to as a state of being, and not deduced as an a priori condition or assumed as a basic datum.
28. Ricoeur, *Oneself as Another*, p. 3.
29. Ibid., p. 18.
30. Ibid., pp. 180, 190, 193.
31. On benevolent spontaneity, ibid., p. 190; on solicitude, pp. 180–94. Note that "self"-esteem is not to imply "myself"; the self is worthy of esteem because of its capacities, and not its accomplishments.
32. Kant, *Groundwork*, p. 38 (4:429); cf. Ricoeur, *Oneself as Another*, p. 222n33.
33. Ricoeur, *Oneself as Another*, p. 228; also 194.
34. Ibid., pp. 228–37, 260–61, 284, 288–89; cf. John Rawls, "Kantian Constructivism in Moral Theory," in *John Rawls: Collected Papers*, ed. Samuel Freeman (Cambridge, MA: Harvard University Press, 1999), pp. 303–58.
35. Ricoeur, *Oneself as Another*, pp. 219–23, 227–29. On the idea of "assymmetrial reciprocity," which recognizes differences of social and material positioning, an idea that might supplement Ricoeur's account of autonomy in its relation to the other, see Iris Marion Young, "Asymmetrical Reciprocity: On Moral Respect, Wonder, and Enlarged Thought," in *Intersecting Voices: Dilemmas of Gender, Political Philosophy, and Policy* (Princeton: Princeton University Press, 1997), pp. 38–59. Young contends that "Moral respect between people [Kantian persons] entails reciprocity between them, in the sense that each acknowledges and takes account of the other. But their relation is asymmetrical in terms of the history each has and the social position they occupy" (p. 41). On the assymmetry that has shaped the history of Western thought, see Luce Irigaray, "The Blind Spot of an Old Dream of Symmetry," in

Speculum of the Other Woman, trans. Gillian C. Gill (Ithaca, NY: Cornell University Press, 1985), pp. 13–129.
36. Ricoeur, *Oneself as Another*, pp. 172, 179–80.
37. Ibid., pp. 250, 274–83; also 228, 240.
38. Ibid., pp. 276–77.
39. See Kant, *Groundwork*, p. 31 (4:421); also 40–42 (4:433–34).
40. Ricoeur, *Oneself as Another*, pp. 209–11, 219, 222–27, 265n43, 286–87.
41. On "Kant's path," see ibid., p. 263 f.
42. Ibid., pp. 155, 207 f., 263–69.
43. Ibid., pp. 222–27. For a fuller discussion of "the otherness of other people," see ibid., pp. 329–41.
44. Ibid., p. 263; for more on Ricoeur's use of the universal, see ibid., pp. 274, 276n57, 277, 279.
45. Ibid., p. 264; cf. Kant, *Groundwork*, pp. 31–32 (4:421–22).
46. On the idea of freedom under the laws of reason, Kant, *Groundwork*, pp. 53–54, 57 (4:448, 452).
47. Ibid., p. 32 (4:422).
48. Ricoeur, *Oneself as Another*, p. 264.
49. Ibid., pp. 118–25. On the evaluative nature of this concept of personal identity, or selfhood, see A. W. Moore, *Points of View* (Oxford: Clarendon Press, 1997), pp. 220, 222–23, 231–32.
50. Ricoeur, *Oneself as Another*, p. 263.
51. Ibid., p. 264n40.
52. Ibid., p. 264.
53. On judgment, see Immanuel Kant, *Critique of Pure Reason*, trans. and ed. Paul Guyer and Allen W. Wood (Cambridge: Cambridge University Press, 1997), p. 268 (A 132–133/B 171).
54. Cf. Onora O'Neill, "Kant after Virtue," in *Constructions of Reason: Explorations of Kant's Practical Philosophy* (Cambridge: Cambridge University Press, 1989), p. 160.
55. On the difficulty in judging what is a maxim, see O'Neill, "Consistency in Action," in *Constructions of Reason*, pp. 81–85 f.
56. For background to Ricoeur's reading of Kant, see Rawls, "Themes in Kant's Moral Philosophy," in *John Rawls*, ed. Freeman pp. 498–506.
57. O'Neill, "Kant after Virtue," p. 160 (emphasis added).
58. Kant, *Groundwork*, p. 34 (4:425).
59. Ricoeur, *Oneself as Another*, p. 265. For a defense of the plurality and otherness of persons as ends-in-themselves, see Korsgaard, *The Sources of Normativity*, pp. 92, 126–28, 130–36, 166.
60. Ricoeur, *Oneself as Another*, p. 264.
61. O'Neill, "Consistency in Action," p. 94.
62. Ricoeur, *Oneself as Another*, p. 265.
63. Ibid., pp. 331, 335–41.
64. Ibid., p. 336. For Levinas the self (i.e., the *I* as *idem*) is in a state of rupture radically separated off from the other. The injunction from the other comes not as a call to relationship, but to responsibility without relation.
65. Ibid., pp. 336–37, 339.

66. Ibid., pp. 118–25, 266–72 f. Again this criticism will, first, seem unfair; second, there may be reasons for this criticism, but, ultimately, Ricoeur's position would have had more consistency and support if he treated his original ideas on promise-keeping and *ipseity* as supplementing Kant's account of autonomy.
67. Ibid., pp. 154–55.
68. Ibid. p. 266; cf. 154–55.
69. Ibid., pp. 118–25 f. For an account of the diachronic nature—or "temporality"—of a responsible action such as promising read in terms of both *idem* and *ipse*, see ibid., pp. 294–96.
70. Ironically, it is the false promise that could break down the coherent shape of a rational life; a false promise as immoral act is both irrational and temporally discordant (so not diachronic). For a discussion of the diachronic nature of practical reasoning in Kant, see A. W. Moore, "A Kantian View of Moral Luck," *Philosophy* 65 (1990): 297–321. Cf. Kant, *Critique of Pure Reason*, pp. 541–45 (A 550–56/ B 578–84); *Critique of Practical Reason*, pp. 37–44 (5:42–50).
71. Ricoeur, *Oneself as Another*, p. 267. Also, see Ricoeur, "Self as Ipse," in *Freedom and Interpretation: Oxford Amnesty Lectures, 1992*, ed. Barbara Johnson (New York: Basic Books, 1993), pp. 118–19.
72. On the relation of agent and recipient in Kant, see O'Neill, *Constructions of Reason*, pp. 128, 133, 142–43.
73. Kant, *Groundwork*, pp. 53–54, 57 (4:448, 452). For discussion of conflict, the social nature of obligation, personal relations, and reciprocity in a Kantian ethics of autonomy, see Korsgaard, *The Sources of Normativity*, pp. 5, 126–28, 135–38. Cf. Ricoeur, *Oneself as Another*, pp. 222–25.
74. Relevant texts for these debates include Carol Gilligan, *In a Different Voice: Psychological Theory and Women's Dependence* (Cambridge, MA: Harvard University Press, 1982); Benhabib, "The Generalized and the Concrete Other," in *Situating the Self: Gender, Community, and Postmodernism in Contemporary Ethics* (New York: Routledge, 1992), pp. 148–77; Young, "Asymmetrical Reciprocity," pp. 38–59; Thomas McCarthy, "Enlightenment and the Idea of Public Reason," in *Questioning Ethics: Contemporary Debates in Philosophy*, ed. Richard Kearney and Mark Dooley (London: Routledge, 1999), pp. 164–80. Maeve Cooke, "Questioning Autonomy: The Feminist Challenge and the Challenge for Feminism," in *Questioning Ethics*, pp. 258–82; and Natalie Stoljar and Catriona MacKenzie, eds. *Relational Autonomy: Feminist Perspectives on Autonomy, Agency, and the Social Self* (Oxford: Oxford University Press, 2000).
75. Benhabib, "The Generalized and the Concrete Other," p. 163. Also, see Susan Mendus, "Time and Chance: Kantian Ethics and Feminist Philosophy," in *Feminism and Emotion* (London: Macmillan, 2001), pp. 55–68.
76. Quoted in Pamela Sue Anderson, *Ricoeur and Kant: Philosophy of the Will* (Atlanta: Scholars Press, 1993), p. 115.
77. Susan Bordo, "Afterword: The Feminist as Other," in *Philosophy in a Different Voice: Critiques and Reconstructions,* ed. Janet Kourany (Princeton: Princeton University Press, 1998), pp. 304–12; Benhabib, "The Generalized and the Concrete Other," pp. 148–77.

2
Narrative Ethics and Moral Law in Ricoeur
PETER KEMP

Introduction: The Place of Narrative Ethics in the Work of Paul Ricoeur

Two great trends in modem philosophy meet in the work of Paul Ricoeur and have been integrated into an original synthesis: the philosophy of action and the philosophy of language. Having discussed Karl Jaspers and Gabriel Marcel in his first books, he presented in his dissertation from 1950, *Freedom and Nature,* his own thinking as a Philosophy of the Will focusing on the relationship between the voluntary and the involuntary in human action. The reflection on action concentrated in this book on a pure eidetical analysis of the will and its limitations, whereas ten years later he focused on the ethical dimension of the will, which brought him not only to develop an anthropology of Fallible Man, but also to consider symbolic language and in particular the symbolism of evil by which the human being has confessed its own fault. This was his first step in combining reflection on action with reflection on language.

Then he became aware of the conflicts between different languages of interpretation of human action; his phenomenological reenactment of ethical symbols and myths (narrative symbols) was challenged by psychoanalytic and structuralist interpretations of the same signs and stories. In order to manage these conflicts he proposed two equally valid ways of interpretation: interpretation as suspicion—that is, practiced as unmasking or reduction of illusions—and interpretation as listening—that is, practiced as recollection and restoration of meaning.[1] After this wrestling with psychoanalysis, and in other works also with structuralism, he concentrated more and more on the function of language as restoration of meaning; that is, on its metaphorical and narrative function.

However, the focus on action was not forgotten. He turned his hermeneutics of text toward a hermeneutics of action mainly by confronting, in his outstanding three-volume work *Time and Narrative* (from 1983 to

1985), the phenomenology of time, as it was inaugurated by Husserl and Heidegger, who both were indebted to the analysis of time in Augustine, with the analysis of history and fiction in modern reflection on language, including the renewal in literary theory of the Aristotelian idea of mimesis.

It is in this book on time and narrative that he sketched the concept that has been crucial as the basis for his later idea of ethics. I mean the concept of *narrative identity*, which he introduced in the third volume of the book and which is central for the philosophical anthropology, including an ethics in his last big work, *Oneself as Another*, from 1990, translated into English in 1992. It follows that his ethics, as well as his ideas of law and justice included in his ethics, cannot be understood without an examination of the way the concept of narrative identity appears and develops in his later work.

My chapter is divided into two parts. In the first part I present how Ricoeur contributes to the development of the concept of narrative identity and highlights its role for establishing an ethics in personal and public life today. In the second part I continue a discussion we have had together since 1987 regarding the role of narratives in the foundation of ethics. This discussion started before the issuing of *Oneself as Another*, when my paper, "Ethics and Narrativity," read in Rome, appeared in French in 1986.[2] Ricoeur's replies to me at that time were published in translation in two Scandinavian reviews.[3] Later, in another reply to the amplified version of my article in English in a volume of the Library of Living Philosophers, he asks whether *Oneself as Another* better responds to my expectations than did *Time and Narrative*, on which my questions were based.[4] My answer today is yes, but I still do not know whether we totally agree.

The Narrative Identity in the Ethics of Paul Ricoeur

The philosophy of Paul Ricoeur helps us to understand the importance of narrative for human life in at least three fundamental ways: (1) as foundation of temporal identity and in particular of the more or less coherent lifestory of everyone by which he or she understands himself or herself as agent and person; (2) as foundation of the ethical identity of a person, by offering narrative models of life that express intentions of the good life and give rise to ideas about liberation from evil and creation of happiness; and (3) as foundation of the identity of a society by offering ideologies that are in permanent tension with a utopian guide for common social life and law.

However, although he recognizes that the vision or intention by which we elaborate or configure ethics as an imagination of the good life must be expressed in narrative, he considers that the universal validity of obligation or moral law in the Kantian sense is non-narrative insofar as the particular narrative is subject to the test of the universally valid obligation of the categorical imperative. He finds this obligation expressed in the idea of the

Golden Rule and sees its foundation in the demand of love originating in loving encounter and in the necessity of its protection against violence. Thus, according to Ricoeur the concept of narrative identity cannot be the most fundamental concept in ethics. In aiming at universal validity, ethics needs to be more than narrative.

Temporal Identity

The question that leads Ricoeur in *Time and Narrative* to the concept of narrative identity is the question of how one relates the experienced imagination of subjective time to the observed and controlled dating of the flow of day-to-day events; that is, objective time, the time of existence and the time of things. His answer is that our life and the physical cosmos in which we live are connected by historical time, and this "third time" is always, at least to some degree, a narrated time. There is no history without a minimum of narration that tells us *who* did this or that, *who* was the agent or author, and *who* is to tell something of his or her lifestory.

But if the identity of a historical agent can be understood only through a story, it cannot be a substantial or a formal identity. It lacks the substantiality of things and has the fragility of a "character," which means that this self-constancy "can include change, mutuability, within the cohesion of one lifetime."[5] It is not the same thing, *idem,* but oneself as the same, *ipse.* Therefore it is not simply given, and there can, as Ricoeur says, be "different, even opposed, plots about our lives."[6] Thus, the narrative identity needs to be claimed by someone who tells the story; without this claim there is no coherency of life in time, no historical identity for others and for ourselves.

Nevertheless, the narrative self-understanding of an individual as well as of a community is indispensable for our identity. Here Ricoeur declares that this connection between self-constancy and narrative identity confirms one of his oldest convictions:

> namely, that the self of self-knowledge is not the egotistical and narcissistic ego whose hypocrisy and naïvete the hermeneutics of suspicion have denounced, along with its aspects of an ideological superstructure and infantile and neurotic archaism. The self of self-knowledge is the fruit of an examined life, to recall Socrates' phrase in the *Apology.* And an examined life is, in large part, one purged, one clarified by the cathartic effects of the narratives, be they historical or fictional, conveyed by our culture. So self-constancy refers to a self instructed by the works of a culture that it has applied to itself.[7]

This remark involves, as I see it, at least two levels of stories in the temporal identity that can be claimed. There is on the one hand the level of my personal lifestory as well as of the particular history of my society. These accounts may be very narrow-minded, egoistic, or nationalistic propaganda, as some autobiographies and historiographies surely are. On the other hand, however, such untruthful narratives need to be purged by storytelling on another level, namely the stories that—whether they are historical, fictional, or both (a poetization of history)—serve as models of the good life and thereby instruct our self-understanding both by their criticism of the tales we tell about ourselves and by their imagination, directly or indirectly, of a life in goodness and justice.

Ethical Identity

As we analyze these two contradictory levels of storytelling and find that one criticizes the narrowness of the personal or collective egoism of the other, we are already confronted with ethics. This is a fact that Ricoeur recognizes clearly in the paragraph on narrative identity in the third volume of *Time and Narrative,* from 1985. But he underlines also that if narrative identity shall be equivalent to true self-constancy, the choice of that identity assumes "ethical responsibility" as the highest factor in "self-constancy." On the one hand, narrativity is never deprived of every normative, evaluative, or prescriptive dimension, and the vision of the world, proposed by the narrator to the reader, "is never ethically neutral."[8] On the other hand, "it belongs still to the reader, now an agent, an initiator of action, to choose among the multiple proposals of ethical justice brought forth by reading." He concludes that it is "at this point that the notion of narrative identity encounters its limit and has to link up with the non-narrative components in the formation of an acting subject."[9]

I shall discuss this conclusion later. The question is whether this claim of non-narrative components in ethics means the claim of an a priori given, non-narrative ethical insight that might judge all our narrative ethical visions, or if it is simply a claim of the fact that the appeal of the story cannot be separated from the responsibility of the reader and agent for critical listening to what is told. Before answering this question, we must see how Ricoeur clarifies his position in *Oneself as Another.*

The distinction between identity as *idem,* sameness, and identity as *ipse,* selfhood, is decisive for the whole structure of *Oneself as Another.* But it is not simply used to claim a difference between personal life and physical things. The aim is to analyze the meaning of self that cannot be reduced to a substance or thing, although it is also always a thing. And the concept of narrative identity is advanced as the bridge between the semantic and pragmatic descriptions of action and the self as agent on the one hand, and the ethical and moral prescriptions of its possible good and its possible right actions on the other; that is, between conceiving the self as sameness and conceiving it as selfhood. The triad *describe, narrate, prescribe* is imposed on the analysis, because the need we have for an understanding of an entire life, of the *connectedness* of life, can only be satisfied by the emplotment of narratives that not only identify the living reality of a plot, but imply estimations, evaluations, and judgments of approval and condemnation and thereby help us to recognize ourselves and to aim at a good life for a whole life span.

But narrative identity is now, in *Oneself as Another,* recognized as a coherency of life in a permanence of time that is not only chosen, but always also given. It is in a way both *ipse* and *idem,* both selfhood and sameness. It is sameness as character or set of lasting dispositions by which a person can be recognized. This character is established by an emplotment capable of integrating with permanence in time diversity, variability, discontinuity, and instability. As a character I am this particular story by which I am known as the same person. If I lose this character I become like the title character in *The Man without Qualities,* the novel by Robert Musil. But I have selfhood as self-maintenance; that is, maintaining my self by truthfulness, fidelity, and involvement. By keeping my word I maintain my self as selfhood and become more than the same character known by others.

I can maintain my self according to the aim of a good life. And, as Ricoeur says, I cannot imagine this good life if it "were not gathered together in some way"[10]—that is, if it were not gathered in the form of a narrative, so that I can imagine what Alasdair MacIntyre calls "the narrative unity of a life," which he places above the notions of particular practices and specific life plans in professional life, family life, leisure time. I become the coauthor of my lifestory.

However, in *After Virtue* MacIntyre is mainly considering stories enacted in daily life. The "unity of an individual life"[11] is one's own lifestory. He is not considering, as Ricoeur does, the "refiguring of life by fiction"[12] and what I would call the efficacy of model stories on the way I understand my own lifestory. In fact, in order to acquire a narrative identity, I cannot be satisfied with my own life (story) as it is remembered and expected, because I cannot remember the narrative beginning of my life, and my death will be told only by those who survive me. Add to that the fact that it is possible to tell different stories about the same life, and that every narrative is caught up in the histories of others: of parents, friends, companions, and so on. Nevertheless, according to Ricoeur, the "narrative" incompleteness of life and the entanglement of my life with others do not "abolish the very notion of the application of fiction to life."[13] On the contrary, he considers that "it is precisely because of the elusive character of real life that we need the help of fiction to organize life retrospectively, after the fact, prepared to take as provisional and open to revision any figure of emplotment borrowed from fiction or from history."[14] But such figures help us to grasp our life as a whole, to stabilize real beginnings. And by giving form and imagination to the unknown end of our story, creating the shape of this or that death, they play the role of an apprenticeship of dying.

Ricoeur recognizes relations between narration and ethics at different stages of the storytelling. Already on the level of prefiguration of the narrative, when oral stories occupy the daily life and serve the exchange of experiences, the popular practical wisdom develops thanks to these stories: "in the exchange of experiences which the narrative performs, actions are always subject to approval or disapproval and agents to praise or blame."[15] On this ground, literary narratives, both in fiction and in historiography, are created and offer a real narrative dimension for our self-understanding and practices. Thus, ethics exists at the level of the "refiguration of action by the narrative."[16]

Finally, narratives play a role in the configuration of the vision of the good life, because moral judgment needs the art of storytelling in order to schematize its aim: "In narrativizing the aim of the true life, narrative identity gives it the recognizable feature of characters loved or respected."[17] Since this narrativizing happens in a world of literature that according to Ricoeur is an "immense laboratory for thought experiments,"[18] the ethical identity shaped as narrative identity depends on the responsible selfhood, and not the contrary. By itself the narrative identity cannot maintain itself because of the problematic character of the lifestory. The self refigured by the narrative "is in reality confronted with the hypothesis of its own loss of identity."[19] However, Ricoeur follows Lévinas and claims that it is capable of one thing: to the question "Who am I?" the proud answer can be "Here I am."[20] This is the non-narrative foundation of every ethical identity.

Social Identity

The narrative identity of a human being is not purely individual. Not only is every lifestory caught up in the stories of others—of parents, friends, companions, and so on. But together we also have a common tradition of ideas about how to organize our life in the best way, or rather we have in common a whole culture of testimonies about human experiences of the good life. The most important of these testimonies are founding stories that tell about the origin of society and the crucial events that determine the social imagination of what counts as good and right in the common life of a historical community.

In a 1983 article "Ideology and Utopia," Ricoeur calls this social imagination a narrative identity, perhaps the first time he uses this concept.[21] This narrative identity constitutes an ideology as far as it has the positive function of integration of individuals in the community.

In his analysis of the concept of ideology he follows Karl Mannheim's definition of ideology as opposed to utopia.[22] According to Mannheim, ideology and utopia aim respectively at justification and subversion of society: by the ideology the group understands its common life and strengthens it; by utopia it opposes the established order, claiming a radical change for society. But Ricoeur stresses their complementarity in a fruitful tension by which the established society remains open to new possibilities.

If we adopt the notion, as Ricoeur does, that ethics implies both a vision and a norm, and if we can follow Aristotle when he understood this vision as an imagination of the excellent way of life among friends and in society, then the social imagination to which both ideology and utopia belong must be an important element of the ethical vision that configures the good life of society, including its morality and law. And since Ricoeur believes that ideology has the capacity to provide society with a narrative identity, he has recognized narrativity as a founding element of ethics.

So, according to Ricoeur, there is a narrative ethics that imagines wise forms of action and communication and thereby expresses the practical truth of human life. But does the obligation or norm—in its most universal formulation—add a non-narrative dimension to ethics? This is the question that we now have to discuss.

The Foundation of Ethics: A Discussion

In my essay "Ethics and Narrativity," I claimed that "ethics is not tantamount to moral rules and norms, but that it constitutes their foundation or, rather, provides both the foundation of their permanence and of their transformation. Consequently, if ethics is a vision and not a rule, it consists of intuitive models for action and not of purely abstract principles."[23]

I also claimed that such intuitive models could only be narrative,

> because without emplotment there would be no sense in unfolding some models for action. Thus ethics must necessarily be the narrative configuration of the good life. Had this not from the start been configured by stories, it would not have been capable of being integrated (as Ricoeur has shown in his *Time and Narrative*) either into the author's works or into those of the historian as that vision which would never affect the reader in an ethically neutral manner.[24]

I was well aware of the fact that, if ethics is primarily vision and only secondarily normative, my argument could look like a vicious circle, since if ethics is itself a narrative configuration of the good life, how could we judge of the truest story among the infinite number of stories in the world without using one particular story or a particular kind of story as a measure for evaluation of narrative imagination? Is not my ethical evaluation of narratives, then, based on other narratives?

My answer was yes, but I argued that there are different levels of narrativity in the world, and that the narrative configuration of ethics to which we refer in order to justify the choice or evaluation of stories is to be found on a different level than that of these stories themselves. At the highest level in the hierarchy of evaluation of narratives we find stories "whose guiding power remains throughout history, and which, in times of crisis, have demonstrated their ability to encourage people to stop thinking in terms of fixed ideas."[25]

Thus, my claim was that ethics has to be totally narrative, and I could not see how Ricoeur could avoid accepting that.

Vision and Norm

However, in his two replies to me Ricoeur has claimed that there is a deontological dimension of the ethical intention that cannot be reduced to its teleological dimension; that is, that vision cannot be reduced to norm, or that Kant cannot be seen as Aristotelian. This is not, as he himself claimed, because of a contradiction between desire and obligation, but because of the violence that obliges us to demand the good and prohibit evil.[26]

Ricoeur considers, therefore, that we need the austerity of the moral norm in order to decide the order of priority of stories in the narrative hierarchy. The choice of valid stories in ethics and of the whole hierarchy of ethical stories must be founded in a non-narrative idea of the universal validity of obligation or moral law. He added that the moral norm that is the most universally recognized by the wisest among people is the Golden Rule, being "the imperative directly turned against violence and towards the recognition" of the other by the demand to everyone "not to do to your neighbor what you would hate to have done to you."[27] Thus, according to Ricoeur, the "moral power of some stories is due to their affinity with the Golden Rule."[28]

However, he agreed that the narrative has a power of schematization with respect to moral norms. This schematization happens in the witnessing by which "the imperative is transformed into 'a vision told about the good life,' "[29] and, in general, it is needed in order to transform the aim of the good life, the ethical intention, into a guiding vision.

This does not mean, he argued in his second reply to me, "that exemplary narratives can by themselves found ethics. One cannot be content with an argument that is ultimately utilitarian or, if one prefers, consequentialist, in order to account for the hierarchy that ensures the exemplarity of certain stories."[30] In *Oneself as Another* Ricoeur continues to distinguish between Aristotelian teleological ethics and Kantian deontological morality. And he recognizes the narrative schematization of Aristotelian ethics that is possible because "telling a story is deploying an imaginary space for thought experiments in which moral judgement operates in a hypothetical mode."[31] But whereas the ethical aim, according to his two replies to me, seems to include the norm, he claims in *Oneself as Another* an original primacy of ethics over morality. The moral norm then plays the role of the sieve through which the ethical aim must pass in order to be subjected to the test of its universal validity. But the norm does not have the final word. He considers that it is necessary to have "recourse by the norm to the aim whenever the norm leads to impasses in practice."[32]

He therefore presents his ethics in three parts, concerning, respectively, (1) the ethical intention "aiming at the good life with and for others, in just institutions;[33] (2) the moral norm by which the maxims of action, according to Kant, are submitted to the rule of universalization; and (3) the practical wisdom, *phronesis,* by which we can prescribe the right action in conflict situations in which there is no universally valid solution, but only a responsible solution, one based on a conviction about the sense of the original ethical aim.

I find that the triad Ricoeur constructs here—aim, norm, and wisdom—in order to develop ethics for our time in its most important aspects is very successful. But, if the aim is prior to the norm, and if the aim not only can but must be schematized in narratives, the narration must also be prior to obligation, even if the moral norm, in its turn, can subject the original narrative ethics to the test of universal validity. Add to that the fact that if practical wisdom finally is considered as a kind of return to ethics in order to highlight the good life in situations in which the law of universal morality cannot apply, then it seems unavoidable to confirm the narrative foundation of the whole ethical enterprise.

Two questions are brought up here. The first is this: What can we mean by speaking of the narrative foundation of ethics? The second, which is closely linked to the first, is the following: Can we think of a moral norm by which we test the ethical aim without a narrative foundation for this norm?

The Meaning of Narrative Foundation

By foundation I mean *necessary condition.* Saying that there is no ethics without narrative foundation means that it is not possible to imagine ethics without narrative language rendering a good life that takes time for its realization. To understand and guide life that takes time we must tell a story about actions that takes time. Emplotment of life needs emplotment of guiding language. Therefore, is not storytelling the only way of imagining the good life? And, therefore, I claim that narrativity is a necessary condition of ethics.

This is not less true if ethics is understood according to Ricoeur; that is, as the ethical intention "aiming at the good life with and for others, in just institutions." How should we imagine this life without telling about it? But it must also be true with respect to the moral law.

In his book *The Symbolism of Evil,* Ricoeur, analyzing the symbol of guilt according to the Jew, declares: "the giving of the Law is not abstract and non-temporal; it is bound up, in the Hebrew consciousness, with the representation of an 'event,' the exodus from Egypt, the 'going up' out of the 'house of bondage.' Consequently, the ethics itself is historical through and through; it is the ethics of the chosen people." Thus, "as a result of this bond between 'ethics' and 'history' the Law, for the Jew, could never be wholly rationalized and universalized."[34]

At that time, Ricoeur explained this bond as an interpretation done by the "theology of history of the Biblical writers."[35] Being opposed to the dichotomy between myth and history, I later proposed that we consider this vision of history as a poeticization of time by which was created *history as myth,* or the myth of history; for example, of the biblical account of the history of the Jewish people.[36] Thus, the Law was included in a narrative understanding of life.

I do not think that this can be otherwise today. What Kant has done by conceiving the moral Law as not only valid for a particular people but for all mankind is not imaginable without a world story to which every rational being belongs. The fact that this story was told and could be told at any time was the necessary condition of his idea of the categorical imperative prescribing the following attitude: "Act only on that maxim through which you can at the same time will that it should be a universal law."[37] I will even say that Kantian morality needs not less but more narration than Aristotelian ethics. It not only needs what Kant calls "popular moral philosophy," meaning moral stories or cases from daily life, and which he takes as his point of departure in the second chapter of *Groundwork* in order to analyze the concept of moral law, but he also presupposes a world history in which the world citizen develops a republican culture.[38] Kant's claim is that this citizenry rooted in both Jewish-Christian and Greek-Stoic ideas of morality and history is understandable both in terms of theoretical and practical reason and therefore has universal validity.

We know that Hegel developed this vision of world history into the speculative idea of the supreme plot that justified all evil in the world as the "cunning of reason" in order to realize an ultimate goal of man's final reconciliation with reality. And should we not renounce Hegel, as Ricoeur said in *Time and Narrative,* because of his lack of care for the individual, his cynicism in relation to the poor and the suffering? Surely. But a Kantian worldview is not yet speculative, but only ethical. Ricoeur himself develops in *Time and Narrative* this humble idea of history by following Reinhardt Koselleck, who introduced the idea of historical time as a tension between the "space of experience" and the "horizon of expectation."[39] Thereby he is brought back "from Hegel to Kant," as he says, "in that post-Hegelian Kantian style I favor." This means that, like Kant, he "holds that every expectation must be a hope for humanity as a whole, that humanity is not one species except insofar as it has one history, and, reciprocally, that for there to be such a history, humanity as a whole must be its subject as a collective singular."[40] Thus, the narrative vision of one history is the foundation of ethics and law in Kant.

But it is really possible to think of world history without reducing the Other to the Same, and has Hegel not thought through the Kantian idea of history to its end? This question accentuates the temptation in the Hegelian speculation and the need to speak as Ricoeur does about renouncing Hegel. But there is an alternative: we can speak as Levinas does and oppose Infinity to Totality.[41] Then the true world history is not the story of a Totality that consumes all differences in the Same Super-Individual (that is, the speculative System), but it is the story of an Infinity of others who each are irreplaceable and vulnerable.

This history of Infinity is not only rooted in the Jewish myth of history including Creation, Exodus, the giving of the Torah at Mount Sinai, the return from Babylon, and so on, but also in smaller model stories such as that of the Good Samaritan. According to Luke, this parable not only says that every other who suffers is my neighbor I have to take care of, but it explains that every human being has the duty to take care, even a Samaritan: "Which now of these three, thinkest you, was the neighbour unto him that fell among the thieves? And he said, He that shewed mercy on him. . . . Go and do thou likewise" (Luke 11:36–37, KJV).

If, now, as Ricoeur claims, the Golden Rule has the same universal validity as the Kantian moral Law, it is not only because it is known by most people in the world despite their different religions and traditions (taken alone this is truly a utilitarian or consequentialist argument, which cannot be sufficient), but primarily it is because we live in a world that we can consider as one world since we have heard and are summoned by a story about the community of one world to which we all belong, and since we still continue to imagine and reconfigure this world community through the story we tell about it.[42]

In the essay "Hermeneutics and Critique of Ideology," from 1973, translated into English in 1981, Ricoeur replies, to Habermas and others who since the Enlightenment have opposed critical consciousness to the tradition interpreted by hermeneutical consciousness, that criticism does not speak from a nonplace. "Critique is also a tradition," he says, and continues, "I would even say that it plunges into the most impressive tradition, that of liberating act, of Exodus and the Resurrection. Perhaps there would be no more interest in emancipation, no more anticipation of freedom, if the Exodus and the Resurrection were effaced from the memory of mankind."[43]

Here Ricoeur links the foundation of the critique of ideology to the world myth rooted in the Jewish story of Exodus and the Christian story of the Resurrection. Likewise, I think that we, being rooted in European culture, can link the foundation of the universal moral Law to the story of Sinai and Exodus, and—why not?—link the foundation of practical wisdom to the Christian account of the Resurrection.

It follows that the correction of the ethical imagination demanding universal validity of narrative visions about the good life—that which Ricoeur calls testing the narrative ethics by the norm—has in itself a narrative foundation. But in these cases the founding stories have been more convincing over time than others, thanks to their successful application having been shown not only in different social and cultural settings but in an international perspective as well. Thus, the obligation and its universal validity cannot avoid founding stories.[44]

The Non-narrative Conditions of Ethics

However, I agree with Ricoeur that there are non-narrative conditions of ethics. Thus, the narrative foundation of ethics is only one of its necessary conditions. I want to conclude my paper by referring very briefly to some of the other (non-narrative) conditions that have been highlighted by Ricoeur in his work.

There is the anthropological condition of fallibility expressed by Kant when, in his *Religion within the Bounds of Reason Alone,* he claims that the human being has both an original predisposition (*Anlage*) to good and a propensity (*Hang*) to evil, and developed by Ricoeur in his book *Fallible Man.* If ethics is a vision of the good life, it also presupposes the experience of evil—not only the evil of misfortune, but also the evil of destruction and self-destruction, as analyzed in *The Symbolism of Evil.* Moreover, it concerns both what we have experienced of goodness and an ideal, a hope, about the goodness that is to come, but is not realized. And we know that this lack of goodness is partly our own fault, and thereby we presuppose our fallibility.

Everybody knows evil from the personal experience of human relationships. But how do we come to know goodness? We know it through a loving encounter with the other. In his essay "Love and Justice," Ricoeur refers to Franz Rosenzweig's *Star of Redemption,* in which Rosenzweig interprets the praise of love in the Song of Solomon and shows "how the commandment to love springs from the bond of love between God and the individual soul."[45] In fact, to Rosenzweig "the commandment that precedes every law is the word that the lover addresses to the beloved: Love me!" The commandment to love, preceding the Law, is love itself, commending itself.

It follows that there is no narrative about the Law, no story of Moses receiving the tablets on Mount Sinai, without experience of the loving encounter. And the encounter between God and the human self can make sense for us only because we know what love is from the encounter with the other person. So it is from the loving encounter that we first know about goodness.

The next non-narrative condition of the ethical configuration of our life is our capacity for being responsible, as Ricoeur has explained it on many occasions, in particular in *Oneself as Another*[46] and in *Le Juste.*[47] And responsibility means imputability toward someone for doing something: I assume face-to-face with the other the consequences of my action.

But would there be responsibility without narration about the life for which we are responsible? I don't think so. And would there be moral obligation without both narration and responsibility? I don't think so either. The responsible self is also what Ricoeur in the last paper of his Gifford Lectures calls the summoned subject. The responsible self is the self "constituted and defined by its position as respondent to propositions of meaning issuing from the symbolic network."[48] In other words, the summoned subject follows a call, and therefore Ricoeur considers the call of the prophets according to narratives in the Old Testament as the first and most important figure of a responding self. And I would add that, just as sin and guilt, according to Ricoeur's analysis in *The Symbolism of Evil*, includes both an external power and the responsibility of the self for yielding to evil, there is both a call from the symbolic narratives that summon the self and the responsibility of this self to listen to and obey the narrative voice.

Another figure of the summoned subject since Paul and Luther is the testimony of conscience, but Ricoeur does not follow Heidegger and Ebeling when they identify God and the conscience. If salvation is a word-event, a *Wortgeschehen* according to the theology of Ebeling, then "the communication of this word-event does not take place without an interpretation of the whole symbolic network that makes up the biblical inheritance, an interpretation in which the self is both interpreter and interpreted."[49] So the autonomy of the self should not exclude its dependence on the symbolic mediation and its interpretation.

Ricoeur also notices that "this interpretation is the outcome of a struggle for veracity and intellectual honesty."[50] But, since there is such a struggle, we should not forget the figure of communication that Ricoeur has so often mentioned. I refer to the loving struggle so marvelously described by Karl Jaspers in his *Philosophy*.[51] This loving struggle (*liebender Kampf*) about existence is the last non-narrative condition of an ethics that nevertheless must express itself in narrations that summon the self.

Notes

1. Paul Ricoeur, *Freud and Philosophy*, trans. Denis Savage (New Haven and London: Yale University Press; 1970), pp. 9, 27.
2. Peter Kemp, "Ethique et Narrative," in *Aquinas, Rivista Internationale di Filosofia*, 1986 pp. 211–32.
3. Published in French as an appendix to Alain Thomasset, *Paul Ricoeur, une poétique de la morale* (Louvain, Belgium: Leuven University Press, Peeters, Leuven, 1996), pp. 655–58.
4. Paul Ricoeur, "Reply to Peter Kemp," in *The Philosophy of Paul Ricoeur*, vol. 91 of the Library of Living Philosophers, ed. Lewis Edwin Hahn (Chicago: Open Court Press, 1995), p. 396.
5. Paul Ricoeur, *Time and Narrative*, vol. 3, trans. Kathleen Blamey (Chicago: University of Chicago Press, 1985) p. 246.
6. Ibid., p. 248.
7. Ibid., p. 247.
8. Ibid., p. 249.
9. Ibid.
10. Paul Ricoeur, *Oneself as Another*, trans. Kathleen Blamey (Chicago: University of Chicago Press, 1991), p. 158.

11. Alasdair MacIntyre, *After Virtue* (Notre Dame, IN: University of Notre Dame Press, 1981), p. 203.
12. Ricoeur, *Oneself as Another,* p. 159.
13. Ibid., p. 161
14. Ibid., p. 162.
15. Ibid., p. 164.
16. Ibid.
17. Ibid., p. 166.
18. Ibid., p. 159; cf. p. 164.
19. Ibid., p. 166.
20. Ibid., p. 167; cf. Emmanuel Levinas, *Autrement qu'être ou au-delà de l'essence* (1974; reprint The Hague: Nijhoff, 1978), p. 186. Trans. Alphonso Lingis as *Otherwise Than Being or beyond Essence* (The Hague: Nijhoff, 1981), p. 146.
21. Paul Ricoeur, "Ideologie et utopie," in *Du texte à l'action* (Paris: Editions du Seuil, 1986), p. 391, s.v. The chapter "Ideology, Utopia, and Politics" in the English version of the book, *From Text to Action* (Evanston, IL: Northwestern University Press, 1991), pp. 308–24, is an older text, from 1976, and does not speak about "narrative identity."
22. Karl Mannheim, *Ideologie und Utopie* (Bonn: F. Cohen, 1929). Published in English as *Ideology and Utopia* (New York: Harcourt, Brace, 1936).
23. Paul Ricoeur, "Ethics and Narrativity," in *The Philosophy of Paul Ricoeur,* vol. 22 of the Library of Living Philosophers, ed. Lewis Edwin Hahn (Chicago: Open Court Press, 1995), p. 388.
24. Ibid.
25. Ibid., p. 389.
26. Paul Ricoeur, "Une réponse de P. Ricoeur à P. Kemp," in *Paul Ricoeur, une poétique de la morale,* ed. Alain Thomasset (Leuven University Press: Peeters Leuven, 1996), p. 655.
27. Ibid., p. 658.
28. Ibid.
29. Ibid.
30. Ricoeur, "Reply to Peter Kemp," p. 397.
31. Ricoeur, *Oneself as Another,* p. 170.
32. Ibid.
33. Ibid. See p. 172: The translator put "good life" in inverted commas to indicate the fact that Ricoeur put "vie bonne" in inverted commas, but he does so because "vie bonne" is an awkward expression in French; however, it is quite natural to speak about the "good life" in English, so the inverted commas for this expression are not necessary in the translation.
34. Paul Ricoeur, *The Symbolism of Evil,* trans. Emerson Buchanan (Boston: Beacon Press, 1967), p. 119.
35. Ibid., p. 120.
36. Peter Kemp. *Théorie de l'engagement, t. II, Poétique de l'engagement* (Paris: Editions du Seuil, 1973), p. 71.
37. Immanuel Kant, *Grundlegung zur Metaphysik der Sitten, Akademische Ausgabe* (Hartknoch, Riga: Academy Ausgabe, 1792), p. 421. Trans. H. J. Paton as *Groundwork of the MetaPhysics of Morals* (Harper and Row, 1953), p. 88.

38. Immanuel Kant, *Idea for a Universal History from a Cosmopolitan Point of View* (1784). Eighth and Ninth Thesis, in Kant, *On History*, ed. Lewis White Beck (New York: Macmillan/Library of Liberal Arts, 1963), p. 21.
39. Ricoeur, *Time and Narrative*, vol. 3, p. 208.
40. Ibid., p. 215.
41. Emmanauel Levinas, *Totality and Infinity* (1961; reprint The Hague: Nijhoff, 1978). Trans. Alphonso Lingis as *Totality and Infinity* (The Hague: Nijhoff, 1979).
42. My argument is expressed in terms of European culture including Jewish-Christian and Greek-Stoic ideas of history and morality, whereas those who belong to other cultures may express the universal dimension of ethics in other narrative terms according to their own cultural legacy.
43. Paul Ricoeur, "Hermeneutics and Critique of Ideology," in *Hermeneutics and the Human Sciences*, ed., trans., and intro. John B. Thompson (Cambridge: Cambridge University Press, 1981), p. 99.
44. I am grateful to Alain Thomasset for having been so comprehensive, careful, and fair in his book *Paul Ricoeur, une poétique de la morale* in describing my discussion with Ricoeur concerning ethics and narrativity (see p. 170 ff. and 623 ff.). He makes it totally clear that Ricoeur's resistance to reducing the deontological dimension of the demand of universal moral validity into a hypothetical dimension, or, say, to reducing the imperative to optative (see esp. 214 ff.), is the decisive reason for his support of a non-narrative moral law by which the universal validity of every narrative ethics can be put to a test. Moreover, he follows Ricoeur in asking how we should be able to choose stories about the good life without a "higher instance" of non-narrative judgment (ibid., p. 184). Thomasset himself considers that the critical dimension of hermeneutics must imply a utopian point of view (p. 219) that is "an indispensable non-narrative critical moment of the validity of moral argumentation" (p. 223; c.f. p. 626). But he doesn't explain how it is possible to imagine utopia or utopian criticism in a non-narrative language or without presupposing utopian stories. Also, he emphasizes that the narrator of a moral story must choose which moral evaluations shall be implied by the emplotment (p. 184), but forgets to explain how he can speak (pp. 388 ff.) as Ricoeur does about "the summoned self" without adopting the idea of an implied appeal in the story that is received and not chosen by the listener's self, whom he has summoned.
45. Paul Ricoeur, "Love and Justice," in *Figuring the Sacred: Religion, Narrative, and Imagination*, ed. Mark I. Wallace and trans. David Pellauer (Minneapolis: Fortress Press, 1995), p. 319.
46. Ricoeur, *Oneself as Another*, pp. 291 ff.
47. Paul Ricoeur, *Le Juste* (Paris: Esprit, Seuil, 1995), pp. 41–70.
48. Paul Ricoeur, "The Summoned Subject in the School of the Narratives of the Prophetic Vocation," in *Figuring the Sacred* (Minneapolis: Fortress Press, 1995), p. 262.
49. Ibid., p. 274.
50. Ibid., p. 275.
51. Karl Jaspers, *Philosophie II, Existenzerhellung* (3:93:2) (Munich: Piper Verlag, 1994), p. 65.

3
Moral Meaning
Beyond the Good and the Right

JOHN WALL

Paul Ricoeur's writings on ethics are not generally well known or recognized as constituting a distinct moral position on the contemporary landscape. This may be in part because they are developed only in occasional essays and often in the context of quite diverse issues like the nature of the self, hermeneutics, narrative theory, and biblical interpretation. The question I wish to address here is how best to interpret Ricoeur's philosophical-ethical project so as to understand its potential contribution to contemporary moral thought. This question involves three kinds of inquiry: How do Ricoeur's ethical writings relate to his larger philosophical project; how may they be related critically to major contemporary ethical alternatives; and how can we interpret coherently their overall constructive possibilities?

My argument is that Ricoeur's ethics is best interpreted as one that productively mediates an Aristotelian theory of the good and a Kantian theory of the right under what I would like to call *moral meaning*. What is unique about Ricoeur's view is that it locates moral meaning neither in a disembodied ego nor in broad social and historical conditions beyond the ego, but in an *interpreting self* that mediates these two. Put more generally, Ricoeur's view joins the chorus of critiques of the moral projects of modernity that are based on the self-reflective or transcendental cogito, but it also refuses the rejection of moral selfhood per se made by a variety of postliberal and postmodernist ethicists. Moral meaning is formed by interpreting selves who are capable of creatively mediating the diversity of their traditionally and historically constituted goods into shared goods that account for and recognize each self's interpretive otherness.

Developing Ricoeur's ethics further, however, I will also suggest that moral life mediates the good and the right in a way analogous to Ricoeur's larger phenomenological and hermeneutical dialectics, so that they lead to what I will call moral meaning as a critical teleological good. This critical good consists of dialectically shared ends between selves who nevertheless remain different from one another, and can be captured in terms like *conviction, promising,* and *critical community.* I leave aside for the purposes of this essay reference to the *theological* dimensions of the dialectics of the good and the right, which, in my view, depend to a large extent on, even if they are not exhausted by, the philosophical normative core I will explore here.

The Interpreting Self

Before moving into ethical theory per se, it is necessary first to understand Ricoeur's unique concept of *the interpreting self*. It is on the basis of such a self that Ricoeur's entire ethics is constructed.

The concept of *the self* is problematic for any contemporary ethical theory that takes seriously our constitution by our given traditions and communal contexts. Ethicists like Alasdair MacIntyre, Stanley Hauerwas, and Charles Taylor rightly point out how profoundly our individual moral choices and aims are conditioned by the particular historical, traditional, narrative, and ontological contexts that we inherit. Likewise, even ethicists of a more Kantian bent, like Jürgen Habermas and Karl-Otto Apel, reject the "monological" view of the self found in Kant himself in favor of moral principles that relativize the self within the context of an intersubjective moral world. Still other thinkers, like Michel Foucault and Jacques Derrida, would point out how profoundly the self is constituted by larger conditions like power and language.

But Ricoeur has insisted, all the way from his early phenomenology of the will to his hermeneutics and recent theory of narrative, that the constitution of the self by historical and social conditions does not rule out the self's strong capacity, indeed its necessity, to constitute itself. This is because, for Ricoeur, the wider contexts of selfhood have *meaning* only for a self constituted, as he puts it, "in front of" those conditions.[1] Historical, traditional, communal, and even interpersonal forces do indeed *precede* selfhood; but they are also themselves *completed in* the interpreting self in whom alone they are appropriated into understanding and rendered into meaningful practice.

This view can be traced back to Ricoeur's early phenomenology of the will, in which the self is viewed as the dialectical product of both our *involuntary* or passive nature and our *voluntary* or active freedom. Building upon Edmund Husserl, Martin Heidegger, and Hans-Georg Gadamer, Ricoeur argues that there is no such thing as a self *prior to* its always already projected being-in-the-world, no pure subjectivity, transcendental ego, or "original naiveté" upon which anyone can reflect immediately. But there *is* such a thing as "the self" in the sense of a concrete *will* or *intentionality* constituted as a "second naiveté" through its endless *detour* of *mediations* in the world.[2] Thus, for example, while the self's body is first of all passively given to the self as biological necessity, it is also, as Ricoeur puts it, "*my body*," an object in the world that I can move and will to form my own concrete intentions.[3] The same is true for desires and habits: they are first involuntarily present in one's dispositions, upbringing, and social and historical circumstances; but they are also *my* desires and habits since I appropriate and shape them as my own particular identity. The self's thrownness in the world is also, as Ricoeur puts it, an *attestation* of its capacity to be in the world *for itself*.[4]

The self's voluntary and involuntary dimensions are in fact for Ricoeur related *dialectically*. Negatively understood, this dialectic is an expression of our "fallibility," the self's ontological "disproportion to itself" as a freedom always already in tension with the conditions that make up its finitude (an "infinite finitude").[5] But, positively speaking, the dialectic of the voluntary and the involuntary is also the condition for the possibility of human self-understanding and practice. It is necessary for the self's appropriation of its passively given biological, historical, social, and traditional conditions into coherent and reflexive intentions.

Hermeneutically speaking, this dialectical self is developed in Ricoeur into a theory of *interpretation*, which is conceived of as a dialectic between what is already given to the self in its traditional, cultural, historical, and communal *backgrounds*, and the wider possibilities for the self's voluntary freedom opened up by the world of *texts*.[6] Ricoeur's concept of interpretive background is close to Habermas's concept of our ontological "lifeworld."[7] Both are working out of Gadamer's hermeneutical theory of "historically effected consciousness," the view that our "horizons of understanding" are historically, culturally, and socially prefigured.[8] Ricoeur calls this background horizon our world of "pre-understanding." But Ricoeur and Habermas part company over what it means to subject this traditional background to interpretive critique. For Habermas, one enters into the mode of a "critique of ideology" in which the lifeworld is reductively tested for its "systematic distortions." For Ricoeur, however, interpretation contains a more primary mode of critique through the interpretation of the manifestations of these backgrounds in their "distanciated" forms in texts.[9] Taking his cue in part from French structuralism, and adapting a distinction made by Wilhelm Dilthey, Ricoeur argues that traditions not only constitute ontological "understanding," but also thematize themselves as distinct *linguistic structures* that are open to systematic critical "explanation."[10] Arguably, this notion of texts in Ricoeur has roots in Husserl's theory of intentional objects.

In Ricoeur's view, "texts" are in fact any linguistic structure that, in contrast to the interpreting self's given background, are "fixed" and hence "distanciated" from it.[11] A text is any written, sung, painted, or ritualized object—or "work"—that escapes the background context of its author and hence is available as a possible new structure of meaning for any "reader."

The primary function of reading texts is not, as, for example, in Friedrich Schleiermacher's Romantic hermeneutics, to recapture the "genius" of its author, but rather for the reader him- or herself to discover therein their *ownmost possibilities for being*. Without textuality, I am simply the passive and undialectical product of my background. But with textuality, I gain critically reflexive perspectives within the field of language itself by which I can actively choose, for example, how sympathetic to be with such and such character in a story, what a particular prayer means to me, or on a very abstract level whether I am more persuaded by the writings of Luther or Aquinas, Habermas or Ricoeur.

It is at this point in Ricoeur's hermeneutics that we come closest to MacIntyre, for MacIntyre generally associates the interpretation of tradition with the explanation of the internal structures of a particular history of texts. For MacIntyre, a tradition is "an historically extended, socially embodied argument," such as one finds, for example, in Aristotelianism, Catholicism, the writings of the Enlightenment, and so forth.[12] But in contrast to MacIntyre, Ricoeur views texts not as themselves embodying meaning, but only as necessary distanciating *detours* in the larger process of understanding. Interpretation for Ricoeur is "completed" only in the fully dialectical moment in which the structures of texts are actively *appropriated* in relation to the vast complex of background assumptions that exist in the world of their reader. Ricoeur himself points out that MacIntyre does not thematize what it means for textual structures to have *meaning* for their interpreter, to transform a reader's own being-in-the-world.[13]

Interpretation for Ricoeur in fact involves a complex dialectic that moves an interpreting self's background and assumed horizons of preunderstanding through the detour of the structures of texts, in a never-ending hermeneutical circle toward *the self's* own more highly structured understanding. Interpretation plays upon the *conflict* of background assumptions and textualized possibilities to form a perpetual spiral of *refiguration* of the linguistic identity of the self. Meaning, in this view, can be reduced neither to the involuntary assumptions already given in the self's background nor to the self's voluntary agreement with a particular history of texts. It is instead constituted in *the self as such* as it transforms itself through the dialectic of interpretation that these two poles make possible.

The Narrative Good

Ricoeur's concepts of *the good* (teleology) and *the right* (deontology) grow directly out of this dialectical notion of the self. Each concept is constituted by an *internal* dialectic of voluntariness and involuntariness, and at the same time, on a higher level of analysis, they stand in dialectical tension with one another. Ricoeur rejects any narrowing of moral life to either the good or the right alone, and thus seeks to move beyond the contemporary debate over the acceptance or rejection of the basic ideas of Kant. An ethics that accounts for the interpreting self must account for both the teleological and the deontological dimensions of moral life at once.

In his earlier writings, Ricoeur described the good as the self's "ethical intentionality," which he defined as the self's "desire to be," its "capacity" to attest to its own being in works in the world. "I will call 'teleological ethics' therefore this movement (*parcours*) of actualization, this odyssey of freedom across the world of works, this proof-testing of the being-able-to-do-something (*pouvoir-faire*) in effective actions which bear witness to it. Ethics is this movement between a naked and blind belief in a primordial 'I can,' and the real history where I attest to this 'I can.' "[14] This realization of an "I can" in works in the world reflects the influence of Husserl. It suggests a phenomenological projection of the self as a specifically *ethical* intentionality.

During his later work in narrative, Ricoeur gives this abstract good more substance under the concept—borrowed but redefined from MacIntyre—of "the narrative unity of a life." Such a narrative good cannot be understood as a mere taking on of roles and responsibilities from tradition and one's community. It is instead an active and creative interpretation of those roles into a meaningful realization of self. The narrative unity of a life is an extension of the self's desire to be, its freedom to actualize itself in meaningful projects in the world.

More specifically, the good of a narrative unity of life is the realization of the self's capacity to form, shape, and render ever more structurally coherent the multiple aims by which it is already constituted. These aims come from diverse sources such as biology, psychology, relationships, society, tradition, and history. One's sexual practices, for example, may be counted as "good" insofar as they suggest a coherent narrative meaning to their various biological, psychological, interpersonal, social, and traditional dimensions. Insofar as these elements lack a larger narrative unity, they are further from fulfilling the self's sexual good.

It seems to be for these reasons that Ricoeur describes the good with the puzzling term *self-esteem*. By this he does not mean simply feeling good about oneself (which, with Aristotle, would be to confuse the substance of the good with one of its effects, pleasure). Self-esteem means the self's "attestation [to its own meaning in the world through] the conviction of judging well and acting well in a momentary and provisional approximation of living well."[15] "Living well" here means "putting my immediate actions in the perspective of larger projects, practices, professions, and plans of life [so that] I see myself as a history of life which has value, which merits existence."[16] It means forming, shaping, and interpreting one's ends and aims in accordance with a sense of larger meaning.

The good, in this broad definition, therefore includes the self's relations to others and to social institutions. The contexts within which the self has meaning to itself include not only biology, psychology, and personal history, but also relationships, society, culture, and politics. The full dimensions of the good include what Ricoeur calls "aiming at the 'good life' with and for others, in just institutions."[17] Thus, prior to any consideration of the right, the good of the self's narrative unity of a life itself requires what he calls a certain "solicitude" toward others, as well as participation in the goods of one's broader society. To take again the example above, the sexual good is not just a biological and psychological urge but also a social phenomenon involving sexual partners and, indirectly, potential children, one's larger family, social goods, and politics. Without critically incorporating these considerations into one's own narrative good, one fails to realize oneself as part of larger dimensions of meaning.

Here one comes to what I consider at once the greatest strength and greatest weakness of Ricoeur's concept of the good. Its greatest strength is that it views the good dynamically, interpretively, dialectically. The good is not just *given* to the self by external forces (like history, power, tradition, social relations, biology, and so forth). It is also, by definition, actively and voluntarily *interpreted* by the self into its own sense of narrative identity. This avoids the tendency of certain communitarian and postmodern ethics to reduce the good to external relations of history, power, and culture. At the same time, it refuses to fall back into a modernist idea of the good as predominantly private and subjective. The good of a narrative unity of a life is not just my interests, aims, and desires as I happen to choose them arbitrarily for myself. It is my reflexive appropriation of the multiple teleological ends of which I am constituted into a coherent narrative structure, a structure that, like a text, can be read and critiqued by others in the public domain. In this connection, one possible meaning of the suggestive title of Ricoeur's major book dealing with ethics, *Oneself as Another*, is a teleological one: the self is constituted as a narrative unity of life through its interpretive detour into the otherness of its own social, traditional, and historical contexts.

The problem, however, with such a view of the good is that it may also be too broad. How, for example, should the biological and social goods of sexuality be prioritized? A sociobiologist may interpret the former as needing greater weight than, say, someone concerned about its relational and familial dimensions. Indeed, each of these dimensions itself has multiple possible meanings. Can such a good be protected adequately from subjectivism after all? At least Ricoeur can say that such a vision can be appropriated meaningfully only within the public sphere and in relation to the self's social and historical contexts. And at least it provides us a new way through the Scylla and Charybdis of utter teleological relativism and the objectifying historical teleology of what Jean-François Lyotard has called "grand narratives."

The Critique of Otherness

But the narrative good is only half of Ricoeur's story about moral theory, for it does not thematize its related and indeed implied counterpart: the deontological right. The move from the good to the right is not a move from concern for the self to concern for others. As we have seen, the narrative good itself involves concern for others as fundamental constituents of one's own narrative unity. The move from the good to the right is instead a transition from how selves as such are perceived. It is a move from "esteem" for the self as pursuing narrative coherency to "respect" for *each* self as possessing its own narrative otherness. For Ricoeur, the right means viewing both oneself and selves generally as not only *parts* of larger social aims and goods, but also independent agents capable of interpreting and forming teleological aims *for themselves*. The deontological moment is what one could term a *critique of otherness*.

This critique is necessary, according to Ricoeur, because of what he calls "violence." Violence is meant as a broad term referring to any practice in which persons are "instrumentalized" for an alien or fragmenting teleological purpose. Like Ricoeur's term *text, violence* is based upon its paradigmatic expression (that is, it is not a transcendental abstraction but an experienced phenomenon). We usually think of violence in terms of the misuse of a person's body, as in physical abuse, murder, forced displacement, and torture. The body is paradigmatic for Ricoeur because it presents the most immediate ways in which the self can be prevented from realizing itself in the world. But in its general sense, violence in Ricoeur means *any* instrumentalization of the self for alien ends, including deceit, objectification, cultural marginalization, ideological manipulation, economic disempowerment, and so on. It is, as Ricoeur puts it, any "diminishment of the power-to-do."[18] Because of this, violence can be done to the self not only by other selves, but also by the self to itself (as in self-deception and self-destruction), or to selves by whole communities (as in failing to provide sufficient health care for children).

In fact, Ricoeur suggests that violence is an intrinsic, even if morally wrong, part of human life. Selves are inherently prone to the instrumentalization of others by the sheer fact of pursuing a narrative unity of life. Violence marks the point at which the dialectic of my goods and yours is reduced to conflict and competition, to a situation in which only one set of interests can endure. Ricoeur describes this situation as one of "asymmetry" between one person's or group's agency and another's passivity.[19] Under the conditions of asymmetry, certain selves become victims, their passivity overturning their capacities for voluntary self-constitution.

Ricoeur argues that the notion of respect in Kant does not respond to violence as fully as does the deontological formulation given in the more classic concept of the Golden Rule: do to others as you would have them do to you. The problem with Kant's categorical imperative is that it captures persons only as *agents* and not also as *patients* or *victims* of action. Ricoeur admits that Kant's second formulation ("Act in such a way that you always treat humanity, whether in your own person or in the person of any other, never simply as a means, but always at the same time as an end"[20]) acknowledges a certain passivity in selves in their capacity to be treated as "a means." However, the larger thrust of Kant's ethics, as the first and third formulations of the categorical imperative make clear, is to ground ethics in the person as a free agent, able to make and follow the moral law autonomously. The suppressed passivity of deontological respect is better captured in the Golden Rule because the latter makes clearer the fact that selves should be *done to* as one would like to be *done to* by others.

The deeper purpose of deontological respect, according to Ricoeur, is to "establish reciprocity wherever there is a lack of reciprocity."[21] Reciprocity has to do not with the give and take of favors and advantages, but with the mutual recognition of the dignity of selves in their otherness to each other. As I read it, respect or reciprocity in Ricoeur is a predominantly *negative* concept, the negative side, if you will, of the positive aim of the narrative unity of a life. It demands that one *not* instrumentalize others, that one acknowledge in others a certain "genuine otherness"[22] to which one must not do violence. Like the response to "the face" in Emmanuel Levinas, respect obeys the other's "absolute exteriority" (although, contra Levinas, Ricoeur claims that the self is also an *agent* in this responsiveness).[23] Genuine reciprocity places the limit on the self of "the willing of the other's freedom, the willing that your freedom might exist."[24]

For these reasons, Ricoeur describes the deontological right, not as a law, nor even as a procedure, but principally as a test. In this regard, Ricoeur sets himself apart, in several lengthy discussions, from John Rawls. Ricoeur views Rawls as having provided "a contractualist version of Kantian autonomy," meaning that Rawls's theory of the "original position" articulates autonomy as a fictional ideal.[25] Ricoeur's problem with Rawls is essentially that Rawls does not account for persons in their genuine otherness. His procedures of justice arrive only at "considered convictions" imagined by the decision-maker him- or herself to be shared by all. They bypass the problem of whose convictions are in the end "considered." The "fictional" Rawlsian contract involves the false assumption that one self or group of selves can adequately imagine the genuinely other nature of the goods of others.

For Ricoeur, the deontological right is a *test* in the sense of demanding that one account for the other in all one's strivings for narrative unity. It is a rule of exception for persons as such, exception for what lies at the margins of one's own teleological consciousness. This is why Ricoeur is particularly drawn to the rather negative formulation of the Golden Rule found in Hillel (which he regards as essentially saying the same thing as the better-known formulation above): "do not do unto your neighbor what you would hate him to do to you."[26] As this formulation suggests most emphatically, deontological ethics is a negative test not to do violence to the other. It is the constant and interminable demand, never fully realized, that otherness always be taken into account.

Interestingly, this negative prohibition appears to be viewed by Ricoeur as an implied counterpart to the positive aim of the good of a narrative unity of life. Insofar as I affirm my own capacity for the good, I also commit myself, by analogy, not to violating this capacity in selves generally. Here one could say, perhaps, that the phrase "oneself as another" takes on a second and more highly critical moral meaning: the self as not just another to itself but also another to other selves as well. Each self is also, irreducibly, another.

Moral Meaning

Ricoeur believes that the good and the right, as examined above, stand in dialectical tension with one another. This tension is analogous, it seems, to the dialectical tensions that pervade his larger mediating philosophy: between the voluntary and the involuntary, traditional texts and traditional background, and, more recently, narrative selfhood and narrative sameness. One way to describe the specifically moral tension at play here is as one between selves' *identity* as pursuing teleological aims in common and their *otherness* as pursuing narrative aims whose meaning is specific to them. But the critical question I would like to pose to Ricoeur is this: If *phenomenologically* speaking the self mediates the voluntary and the involuntary in the concrete intentionality of its will, and *hermeneutically* speaking it mediates its background and its encounter with texts in meaning, then *morally* speaking, in what precisely does the self mediate and render productive the dialectic of the good and the right? In other words, without reducing the good and the right to one another, to what does their dialectical tension give rise?

In my view, while Ricoeur has resources to address this question, he does not develop them systematically. This has led to a common misperception of what Ricoeur's ethics is really all about, namely the view that he is finally a Kantian after all who mediates the good and the right, happiness and duty, in a *theology of hope*. By acting according to duty, Kant argued, I can hope, as a philosophical postulate, for the reward of happiness from God in the afterlife. My own view is that theological considerations play an important role in Ricoeur's ethics, but that their role is not a *mediating* but rather a *limiting* one. As I have argued elsewhere,[27] and as other essays in this volume suggest, Ricoeur's theological ethics functions as a *radicalization* of ordinary, philosophical ethics on all three levels of the good, the right, and their mediation with one another. Hope is not the only theological ethical category, but is part of what Ricoeur calls an "economy of the gift," paralleling his philosophical ethics, that includes terms like *faith* and *love*.[28]

In bracketing these theological considerations, I do not wish to suggest their unimportance. However, Ricoeur does envision the possibility for a proximate, concrete, and finite mediation of the good and the right in what one could call a non- or pretheological *critical good* or *critical teleology*. Each self's otherness from others is not just difference but also an occasion for the possibility of forming new areas of *critical* meaning in common, fresh teleological aims by which conflicts are imaginatively mediated. This critical good is neither a communitarian reduction of selves' aims to those that are *already given* in their community, nor a proceduralist relativization of selves' aims under *overarching* universal procedures of discourse. It is rather the creative, poetic mediation of genuinely other and conflicting goods into new areas of now *critically shared moral meaning*.

Ricoeur provides a begining point for understanding the possibility for such a dialectically formed critical good in his concept of "practical wisdom," which he calls "critical phronesis" to indicate its origins in Aristotle but accountability at the same time to Kant. Practical wisdom is a response to what Ricoeur calls moral "tragedy," the tragedy of selves' inherent teleological "one-sidedness" or otherness from each other as self-interpreting agents. Ricoeur illustrates this with Sophocles' play *Antigone*, in which the characters Antigone and Creon are each caught in conflicting, but what from each character's own narrative point of view are legitimate, goods: Antigone the proper burial of her dead brother, and Creon the king of Thebes the prevention of this burial for the preservation of the city against traitors. The tragic one-sidedness of each of these characters illustrates the profound tension that exists between the good and the right. Each character pursues what to her or him are coherent goods for her or his own narrative unity of a life, but these goods nevertheless do violence (in both directions, one could argue, in this case) to the other's right to pursue her or his own proper goods as well.

Although for Sophocles this conflict of goods leads only to the tragedies of suicide, death, and the loss of family, Ricoeur insists that tragedy is also the grounds for the possibility of productive moral mediation. Practical wisdom (critical *phronesis*) averts moral tragedy through what Ricoeur calls "judgment in situation."[29] What he seems to mean by this is that practical wisdom is charged with dealing with selves' apparently intractable conflicts over goods. It seeks out new moral *convictions* that may be able to coordinate and draw together different interests and aims under larger common goods.

Ricoeur uses the helpful illustration of the debate over abortion.[30] Practical wisdom in this case would seek more than either to defend one conception of the good over others or to pay respect to the differences of the parties involved. It would seek out ever more productive mediations of the conflicting goods and rights involved. Some goods and rights may be more or less universally shared already (perhaps the good of the life of the mother, or the right to take part in the formation of laws). But the debate contains an element of "tragedy" in that the areas of greatest conflict between pro-choicers and pro-lifers involve claims in which both sides may have some prima facie legitimacy. This is why the debate has continued. Ricoeur illustrates the possibility for a phronetic mediation of these differences with the notion of graduated fetal rights corresponding to stages of fetal development (for example, from a right to nonsuffering, to a right to protection, to eventual respect as fully human). In any case, the way forward in genuine situations of conflict is ultimately not for one side or the other to *win*, but for new understandings of goods and rights that creatively mediate the oppositions. This is indeed where parts of the abortion debate are moving today, and where previous debates over religious liberties, labor working conditions, and so forth have been able to take us in the past.

This notion of critical *phronesis* distinguishes Ricoeur from both communitarianism and proceduralism. On the one hand, practical wisdom does not, as, say, in MacIntyre, evaluate teleological aims from what to Ricoeur is the morally *undialectical* perspective of the coherency of a given tradition or community. Practical wisdom in Ricoeur's sense takes seriously the tragedy of selves' interpretive otherness, so as to demand *new* forms of community and tradition ever more in accordance with selves' different narrative identities. On the other hand, practical wisdom is not, as, say, in Habermas, the application to actual life of formal argumentative procedures. As Ricoeur himself says about Habermas, critical *phronesis* refuses to reduce the difference between goods to a difference of relative "conventions," resolvable through correct rules of discussion. It instead faces the tragedy of the fact that goods belong to selves as "convictions" on which they are taking a rational stand.[31] Goods should not be *relativized* under discursive procedures because in cases of tragic conflict they must themselves be critically mediated and transformed.

But Ricoeur's concept of practical wisdom may not, I suggest, be sufficient for the kind of mediating ethics Ricoeur is proposing. Specifically, it is difficult to see exactly what *end* such critical interpretive dialogue aims toward, what *criterion* one could use to determine that practical wisdom has indeed achieved a *good* mediation of othernesses. What may be required is a notion of not just the narrative good but also the *critical good*, a notion that raises the good of the narrative unity of a life to a phronetic and fully dialectical level.

I believe it is possible to articulate such a critical good by developing further Ricoeur's concept of "mutual recognition." The chief advantage of this term is that it thematizes an intersubjective good that is neither a retreat back into a grand narrative of tradition nor a relativization of selves' goods under argumentative procedures. It can be developed, in my view, in three ways that correspond to three levels of analysis that Ricoeur himself uses in his concepts of the good and the right, namely the perspectives of the first, second, and third persons.

On the level of the first person, we can take Ricoeur's term *convictions* and suggest that it indicates goods that the self can affirm are actively *recognized by* others. How much a good is a conviction would be a matter of degree. The more that others recognize the worth and value of my own teleological aims, the more they can be affirmed *critically* as remaining accountable to otherness. In this sense, convictions would represent what Ricoeur calls "inchoate universals,"[32] or goods of my own that are also generally recognizable as good by others who are affected. Examples of such convictions might be that automobiles should be developed with fewer toxic emissions. Although this task might prove burdensome to members of the auto industry, most of us can agree that the current level of fuel emissions will lead to long-term environmental degradations that should not be tolerated. A creative mediation of the good of powerful cars and the good of a livable environment can result in the teleological conviction that we should pursue new kinds of energy-efficient transportation.

But convictions alone do not take the critical good to a fully dialectical level. Convictions are goods that ask in a somewhat *passive* sense for recognition *by* others. What of the self's entering into the more fully *active* mediation of goods in a mutual recognition affected by the different goods of others? A more fully dialectical level of the critical good is suggested in Ricoeur's concept of the *promise*, which he makes use of in different ways in various of his ethical writings. Most important for our purposes, a "promise" can signify in Ricoeur the formation of imaginative new ways of living together with one another. One example of promising could be marriage, where two selves with distinct narrative histories and their own particular narrative aims and hopes embrace what for them is the *new* good of a life spent legally joined together. Marriage from this point of view is in part the formation of a set of common purposes to which two different persons commit mutually. It involves each self's both active recognition *of*, and passive recognition *by*, the other as other under the sign of a promise of commitment to a larger unifying narrative.

Promising understood in this moral sense is a *critical good* that implies more than a mere incorporation of the other into one's own narrative identity. In the formation of promises, the other also participates and is equally recognized in his or her capacity for moral interpretation. Like the good of narrative conviction, a promise is a matter of degree, but it is a matter of degree in a more dialectical and critical sense. It is more than just the self's deontological "respect" for the other's otherness, because it goes beyond just negatively avoiding the other's instrumentalization. Instead, it implies a mutual formation of new teleological goods held in common amid the chaos and conflict of difference.

Promising in this sense is analogous to the interpretation of a text. By recognizing the structural *distance* of the other's otherness, the self reconfigures or reinterprets its own narrative identity in a more highly expansive and thoughtful way. Promises made with the intent to manipulate the other for one's own ends not only do violence to the other, but also, and more important, impoverish the self as capable of forming its own narrative ends more richly and broadly. Here the phrase "oneself as another" could take on yet a third and still more highly critical meaning of the self as literally *constituted in* the other's otherness. Interpreting selves are the kind of beings for whom selfhood is insufficient without the mediation of otherness. Promising is emblematic of this dialectical formation of the self on the level of moral life.

It is possible, finally, to take this dialectical notion of the critical good to a third-person, institutional and societal level of analysis in a new concept of "community," a term that provides an occasion for the sharpest point of comparison between Ricoeur's ethics and those of communitarians and proceduralists. Ricoeur uses the term *community* in his ethical writings only occasionally and without systematic intent, although as I wish to use it here it has analogies to his early phenomenological concept of "power"[33] and his midcareer hermeneutical concept of "the social imagination."[34]

The tragedy of the conflict of othernesses on this institutional level is articulated by Ricoeur as *social domination*, the fact that in pursuing certain general goods societies and groups often (perhaps inevitably) fail to recognize other goods that lie at their margins. The critical good of community responds to this tragedy by holding up the aim of greater mutual recognition between each and every member of society. It extends the notion of promising to the institutional level, where the teleological criterion becomes how well the vast diversity of social ends are imaginatively and critically mediated. And it presses individuals to extend their notions of participating selves as such into ever wider circles of dialogue. What is particularly suggestive here is the notion of community as not just a collection of rights or goods, but a creative *dialectic* aimed at concrete mediations of goods.

Community in this sense includes the communitarian hypothesis—for example, in MacIntyre—that interpretations of the goods that guide social life are made in a particular historical and traditional context.[35] But it goes further, to affirm that social goods should also be formed in recognition of each self's interpretive narrative otherness. We might take the continuing conflicts between Israel and Palestine as an example. Can a communitarian approach move beyond the deadlock of two entrenched cultures and traditions? Can it suggest more than that each side present arguments from its own traditional past? Ricoeur's suggestion is that such conflicts should be met with the more highly critical demand for mutual recognition, which is realized through the creative imagination of *new* forms of life in common. Because communitarianism lacks an element of deontological respect for otherness as such, built upon a recognition of persons' fundamental selfhood, it short-circuits the possibility for mediating goods in a genuinely dialectical way.

Community in a Ricoeurian sense can in addition include something of the proceduralist idea in Habermas that the formation of social ends involve the participation of all who could be affected.[36] But it adds to this deontological view a material social good: the more highly critical formation of the narrative unity of selves. We could take as an example the problem of the scarcity of medical resources. The proceduralist perspective suggests that so long as proper deontological guidelines are followed for distributing medical care and finances we can arrive at a mutually acceptable solution. However, as critics of proceduralism have maintained, fair procedures presuppose substantive criteria for judging *the value of the goods themselves* that are at stake. Can a fair procedure alone decide, for example, how to regulate expenditures on children's immunizations versus care at the end of life? Deciding this seems to involve some kind of dialectical mediation between the good of children's immunization and the good of dying well. While the different interests in the issue need to be given their voice in the discussion, an effort also needs to be made to generate ever more inclusive understandings of the narrative unity of a life, so that the relative goods in conflict can be evaluated critically alongside each other. Developing shared understandings of the critical good is the task of building, amid the diversity of perspectives on goods, ever greater senses of community.

Conclusion

Ricoeur's "little ethics," as he puts it in *Oneself as Another*, has not been developed with the same sustained rigor and attention that Ricoeur has given to his phenomenology of the will, hermeneutics, and theory of narrative. One has to dig deeply into almost every stage of Ricoeur's long and varied career to pull out the systematic force behind his moral ideas. However, as I have tried to suggest, such a systematic force does exist, and it presents us with the unique challenge of moving beyond current oppositions between the good and the right, rethinking the notion of moral selfhood, and grasping the dialectical and creative dimensions of moral life in common.

A fuller account of ethics by Ricoeur would involve facing, however, several important challenges. First, it would have to provide a more concrete sense of what the good of a "narrative unity of life" in fact consists in. Much rides on this idea for understanding how the diversity of human goods may be creatively mediated. While Ricoeur is right to insist, I believe, that any such notion of the good is not merely given in the order of nature, society, tradition, or history, he does not fully explain how such a good might actually be realized in practice. Ricoeur is to be applauded for developing a complex and reflexive understanding of the good, and this is one of the more innovative moves in his ethics. However, if we are not speaking here of a communitarian narrative unity of life tied to the coherency of traditions and communities, then it becomes necessary to develop a more stringent definition of "unity."

Second, Ricoeur's notion of moral *otherness* seems to me to depend on hidden theological presuppositions that Ricoeur is constantly at pains to cover up in his more philosophical writings. His use of Levinas in this regard is telling. As those familiar with Ricoeur's essays on love and justice will know, a superabundant excess of love is claimed to be required for truly recognizing the other's "singularity" and "nonsubstitutability."[37] The dialectic of the self and the other seems to require a sense for the ultimate *mystery* of the other, a sense that constantly goads each of us toward ever broader forms of life in common. We are therefore invited, at the very heart of Ricoeur's philosophical moral project, to ask if the implicit religious dimensions of which he is himself well aware can be bracketed in the way he has sought to do ever since his early philosophy of the will.

Finally, as I have tried to show at length, Ricoeur's notion of practical wisdom seems to require further development along the lines of some concept of the critical good. It is difficult to see how practical wisdom as "judgment in situation" finally helps guide moral dialogue substantively. Without returning to a nondialectical, Aristotelian concept of *phronesis,* and without, on the other hand, developing a full-blown Hegelian dialectic of *Sittlichkeit,* there remains the possibility for a third way in which practical wisdom is guided by the aim of ever greater mutual recognition. I have tried to show what this critical aim might look like through concepts like promising and community, and how it provides fresh possibilities for moral life beyond the opposed visions of communitarianism and proceduralism.

In the end, however, Ricoeur's central accomplishment remains to have shown that moral life—in all its teleological, deontological, and phronetic dimensions—is the task of the interpreting self. He insists that if no such self exists, or if it is relativized under the claims of community and tradition, then moral life ceases to function dialectically and creatively. We can rethink the moral self after the critiques of postmodernism and postliberalism only by understanding the self as a task to be accomplished, a freedom to be realized in the world, an inherently dialectical, historical, and social projection of meaning. It is in linking ethics to this great task of humanity that Ricoeur opens up new grounds for contemporary moral thought.

Notes

1. Paul Ricoeur, "The Hermeneutical Function of Distanciation" [French original 1975], in *Hermeneutics and the Human Sciences,* ed. and trans. John B. Thompson (New York: Cambridge University Press, 1981), p. 143.
2. Paul Ricoeur, *The Symbolism of Evil,* trans. Emerson Buchanan (Boston: Beacon Press, 1967) [French original 1960], p. 351.

3. Paul Ricoeur, *Freedom and Nature: The Voluntary and the Involuntary*, trans. Erazim V. Kohák (Evanston, IL: Northwestern University Press, 1966) [French original 1950], p. 10.
4. Paul Ricoeur, *Oneself as Another*, trans. Kathleen Blamey (Chicago: University of Chicago Press, 1992) [French original 1990].
5. Paul Ricoeur, *Fallible Man*, rev. trans. Charles A. Kelbley (New York: Fordham University Press, 1986) [French original 1960], pp. 3–4.
6. At one point, Ricoeur refers to this distinction between background and texts as one between "traditionality" and "traditions" (plural), in an effort to make a more fine-grained distinction than often exists in both the moral and hermeneutical literature. See Paul Ricoeur, *Time and Narrative*, Vol. 3, trans. Kathleen Blamey and David Pellauer (Chicago: University of Chicago Press, 1988) [French original 1985], pp. 219–27.
7. Jürgen Habermas, *The Theory of Communicative Action, Vol. 1, Reason and the Rationalization of Society*, trans. Thomas McCarthy (Boston: Beacon Press, 1984) [German original 1981], p. 335; Jürgen Habermas, *The Theory of Communicative Action, vol. 2, Lifeworld and System: A Critique of Functionalist Reason*, trans. Thomas McCarthy (Boston: Beacon Press, 1987) [German original 1981], pp. 113–97; and Jürgen Habermas, *Moral Consciousness and Communicative Action*, trans. Christian Lenhardt and Shierry Weber Nicholsen (Cambridge, MA: MIT Press, 1990) [German original 1983], p. 135.
8. Hans Georg Gadamer, *Truth and Method*, 2nd rev. ed., trans. Joel Weinsheimer and Donald G. Marshall (New York: Crossroad, 1989) [German original 1960], pp. 300–6.
9. Paul Ricoeur, "The Hermeneutical Function of Distanciation," in *Hermeneutics and the Human Sciences*, pp. 131–44.
10. Paul Ricoeur, "What Is a Text: Explanation and Understanding" [French original 1970], in *Hermeneutics and the Human Sciences*, pp. 145–64.
11. Paul Ricoeur, "The Hermeneutical Function of Distanciation," pp. 135–38.
12. Alasdair MacIntyre, *After Virtue*, 2nd ed. (Notre Dame, IN: University of Notre Dame Press, 1984), p. 222.
13. Ricoeur, *Oneself as Another*, p. 159.
14. Paul Ricoeur, "The Problem of the Foundation of Moral Philosophy" [French original 1975], *Philosophy Today* 22, no. 3/4 (Fall 1978): 175–92; 177.
15. Ricoeur, *Oneself as Another*, p. 180.
16. Paul Ricoeur, "L'ethique, la morale, et la règle," *Autre Temps: Les cahiers du Christianisme social* 24 (February 1990): 52–59; 54 [my translation].
17. Ricoeur, *Oneself as Another*, p. 172.
18. Ricoeur, *Oneself as Another*, p. 220.
19. Paul Ricoeur, "The Teleological and Deontological Structures of Action: Aristotle and/or Kant?" in *Contemporary French Philosophy*, ed. A. Phillips Griffiths (New York: Cambridge University Press, 1987), p. 107; see also Ricoeur, *Oneself as Another*, p. 222.
20. Immanuel Kant, *Groundwork of the Metaphysics of Morals*, trans. J. J. Paton (New York: Harper and Row, 1964), p. 96.
21. Ricoeur, *Oneself as Another*, p. 225.

22. Ibid., pp. 223–25, 339.
23. Ricoeur, *Oneself as Another*, pp. 336–37. See Emmanual Levinas, *Totality and Infinity: An Essay on Exteriority*, trans. A. Lingis (Pittsburg: Duquesne University Press, 1969), p. 67; and Emmanuel Lévinas, *Time and the Other*, trans. Richard A. Cohen (Pittsburg: Duquesne University Press, 1987), p. 56.
24. Ricoeur, "The Problem of the Foundation of Moral Philosophy," p. 178.
25. Paul Ricoeur, "Is a Pure Procedural Theory of Justice Possible? John Rawls' *Theory of Justice*" [French original 1995], in *The Just* (Chicago: University of Chicago Press, 2000), p. 39.
26. Ricoeur, *Oneself as Another*, p. 219.
27. John Wall, "The Economy of the Gift: Paul Ricoeur's Significance for Theological Ethics," *Journal of Religious Ethics* 29, no. 3 (summer 2001): 235–60.
28. For Ricoeur's work on this theological ethics of an economy of the gift, see "The Logic of Jesus, the Logic of God," *Criterion* 18, no. 2 (summer 1979): 4–6; "Evil, a Challenge to Philosophy and Theology" [French original 1986], *Journal of the American Academy of Religion* 53, no. 4 (December 1985): 635–48; "The Golden Rule: Exegetical and Theological Perplexities" [French original 1989], *New Testament Studies* 36 (1990): 392–97; "Love and Justice" [French original 1990], in *Radical Pluralism and Truth: David Tracy and the Hermeneutics of Religion*, ed. Werner G. Jeanrond and Jennifer L. Rilke (New York: Crossroad, 1991), pp. 187–202; "Ethical and Theological Considerations on the Golden Rule" [French original 1987], in *Figuring the Sacred*, ed. Mark I. Wallace, trans. David Pellauer (Minneapolis, MN: Fortress Press, 1995), pp. 293–302; and, with André LaCocque, *Thinking Biblically* (Chicago: University of Chicago Press, 1998), pp. 111–38.
29. Ricoeur, *Oneself as Another*, pp. 243, 249.
30. Ibid., pp. 270–73.
31. Ibid., pp. 286–89.
32. Ibid., p. 289.
33. See Ricoeur, *Fallible Man*, pp. 116–20.
34. See Paul Ricoeur, "Ideology and Utopia" [French original 1986], in *From Text to Action* (Evanston, IL: Northwestern University Press, 1991), pp. 309, 323–24; and Paul Ricoeur, *Lectures on Ideology and Utopia*, ed. G. H. Taylor (New York: Columbia University Press, 1986).
35. MacIntyre, *After Virtue*; Alasdair MacIntyre, *Whose Justice? Which Rationality?* (Notre Dame, IN: University of Notre Dame Press, 1988).
36. Habermas, *Moral Consciousness and Communicative Action*, pp. 65–66.
37. See in particular Ricoeur, "Love and Justice"; "Ethical and Theological Considerations on the Golden Rule"; and Ricoeur with LaCocque, *Thinking Biblically*, p. 131.

4
Antigone, Psyche, and the Ethics of Female Selfhood
A Feminist Conversation with Paul Ricoeur's Theories of Self-Making in *Oneself as Another*

HELEN M. BUSS

> [T]here is no ethically neutral narrative.
> —PAUL RICOEUR, *ONESELF AS ANOTHER*

In the tenth study of *Oneself as Another* Ricoeur concludes:

> an ontology remains possible today inasmuch as the philosophies of the past remain open to reinterpretations and reappropriations, thanks to a meaning potential left unexploited, even repressed, by the ... process of systematization and of school formation.... In truth, if one cannot reawaken and liberate these resources that the great systems of the past tend to stifle and to conceal, no innovation would be possible, and present thought would only have the choice between repetition and aimless wandering.[1]

My feminist conversation with Paul Ricoeur's meditations on selfhood, personal identity, and the ethical contexts of these concepts comes from a desire to "reawaken and liberate" the "unexploited, even repressed" materials in the philosophical resources of the past and the present, including those offered to us by Ricoeur. In Ricoeur's "Response" to a number of interdisciplinary essays (one of which is mine),[2] published in *Paul Ricoeur and Narrative: Contexts and Contestation,* Ricoeur opens what I now represent as a "conversation" when he observes that "I did not emphasize enough our difficulty, even our incapacity to bring to language the emotional, often traumatic experience that psychoanalysis attempts to liberate."[3] He adds, "I left unclear the face of impotence that goes with this ability [to act purposefully], owing not only to those infirmities of every sort that may affect the human body as the organ of action, but also to the interference of outside powers capable of diminishing, hindering, or preventing our use of our abilities."[4]

With these acknowledgments by Ricoeur of internal psychological and external oppressive hindrances to freedom of action of individual agents attempting to narrate a self and act ethically in the world, I enter the conversation to speak of the ways in which feminists can offer an edification of Ricoeur's concerns in *Oneself as Another*. My specific point of entry into the conversation is the moment in his "Response" when Ricoeur speaks directly of the feminist contributions to the interdisciplinary collection. He does so by asking a question: "Does the rootedness of narrative in memory, combined with the dialectic of acting and suffering, allow me to do justice to the narratives composed by women?"[5] He answers his question in three ways. The first two—his admission that his "analysis of common humanity suffers the limits of the male way of thinking and writing" and his welcoming of the "complements and corrections that women writers bring to my analysis"[6]—are answers that, in an actual conversation, would have me nodding and smiling in agreement, and probably—knowing my own feminist enthusiasm—preparing myself to speak some new "corrections and complements." However, almost immediately, my expression would suddenly change—in this imagined conversation—because in the same breath, the same sentence, in which Ricoeur speaks of his readiness to admit limitations and correction, he also asserts that such input does "not seem to me to require a basic revision of my sexually neutral theses."[7] He goes on to use the classical example of Antigone to illustrate that even when we have female figures challenging power and male figures holding power, what the story of Antigone finally illustrates is a "humanity at stake that surpasses both sexual roles."[8]

It is at this moment in an actual conversation that Ricoeur would find my gestures of agreement change, perhaps to a slight frown, a tentative raising of the hand in protest, but more likely the change would manifest itself as a deep and heartfelt sigh, one that is compounded of disappointment, impatience, regret, déjà vu. The sigh comes as I reexperience the helpless feeling a feminist has when she wonders how to get out of a situation that feminists often find themselves in when attempting to converse with other sympathetic intellectuals with whom we share common ground on the subjects of selfhood and ethics. There comes an impasse in such conversations caused by the sympathetic fellow traveler's tendency to foreclose feminist exploration of difference by too quick an appeal to our common humanity. Ironically, it is an extraordinarily difficult appeal for feminists such as myself to resist, since it appeals to our profoundest founding belief, that it is a revision and fuller realization of our common humanity that feminists are attempting to move toward.

However, in this conversation, as in all conversations that involve ungendered theories of the self, I must resist the call for unity, and continue what are often seen as divisive, even negative interruptions in order to explore the various different feminist "complements and corrections" that in the long run will make our concept of our common humanity less male-gendered and therefore offer the possibility—after many conversations with many ideas from many human agents over much time—of becoming, not so much the "sexually neutral theses"[9] that Ricoeur proposes, but the gender-inclusive theses that we all need to realize our unity.

In an actual conversation I would interrupt Ricoeur at the moment of his Antigone example, by asking him to try out another classical narrative patterning, one that I find speaks more fully to the female selfhood predicament. This is not to say that the Antigone story is not open to feminist inquiry, as in Pamela Anderson's revision in which she addresses the importance of gendering mythic material.[10] As well, Jean Bethke Elshtain offers convincing arguments that bear upon Antigone's importance to the plight of present-day women.[11] However, Elshtain's caution that women should not give up the wisdom and power of the private world for an uncertain public world is exactly why the Antigone myth can serve only limited illustrative purposes for me. So much of Antigone's private life is unknown to us. To retrieve that private world and the ethical matter that it generates for our conversation, it is necessary for me to move to a legendary/mythic figure whose personal life is the chief material of her story. This gesture can act not only as a caution as to the complicated nature of gendered narrative identity, but can also lead our conversation to a more productive examination of the ethical dimensions of moral agency. In making this interruption I claim Ricoeur's permission, since he himself asserts that "between [d]escription and [p]rescription" narration is an essential intermediary."[12] I would assert that Antigone's story is an insufficient narrative intermediary to carry the complexity of a conversation between Ricoeurian theory and feminist theory.

Antigone's story has other features that hamper a consideration such as mine. According to Ricoeur's reading of George Steiner's book *Antigones*, the Antigone story can, in Ricoeur's words, "help us in articulating the many dialectics this plot sets in motion: human/divine, moral absolutes/historical power, youth/age, life/death, male/female."[13] For me, the binary nature of the dialectics that has been typical of our understanding of the Antigone material along with its ungendered use are the very features that indicate the insufficiency of this mythic reference (by itself) to stand as patterning for women's narratives of self. Steiner points out that although "Sophocles' Antigone . . . held pride of place in poetic and philosophic judgment for over a century,"[14] the Antigone of philosophic and poetic discourse is not truly gendered female, but rather "belongs, hauntingly but safely, to the idiom of the ideal."[15] I claim that our culture needs to be more diversely informed in terms of its mythic exemplum.

In this regard, Luce Irigaray argues that in traditional narrative patternings women become an exchange commodity between men's systems: "Woman exists only as an occasion for mediation, transaction, transition, transference, between man and his fellow man, indeed between man and himself."[16] Agreeing with Irigaray in her discussion of Hegel's use of the Antigone story, Allison Weir points out that "woman is forced to *be* mediation, to unify human and divine law, individual and community, the male self with himself and with the universal. But in becoming the mediation of differences into a unity, she disappears. The connection she embodies is used to produce unity between opposites, and is thereby destroyed."[17] I would suggest that if I take up Ricoeur's offer of the Antigone illustration in order to move to our "common humanity," I would take up a form of narrative self-making that asks me to "disappear" as a female person, just as Antigone does after a lifetime of service to her blind father and the patriarchal norms of her society.

While I agree with Anderson's proposal that "what is clear in Ricoeur and of interest remains . . . myth's variability,"[18] I wish to offer the additional tactic of shifting to classical materials more productive of female difference and a gendered narrative of self-making. These are to be found in a feminist revision of the ancient Psyche story, as illustrated in Barbara Huber's recent book *Transforming Psyche*. Unlike traditional interpretations of the material of Apuleius's Cupid and Psyche tale—most notably in Eric Neuman's *Amor and Psyche*[19]—which tend to background Psyche's female gender in order to make her into a metaphor of the male (or at best, neutral) psyche or soul, Huber works with the story to draw out its implications for female ways of knowing, female self-narration. Huber sees the setting of the tale as a description of our world in which men have turned away from the worship of the proper source of beauty, sexuality, and fecundity, Aphrodite, to the worship of a mere girl, Psyche, who suffers from the "construction of female agency into beauty, sacrifice, and abandonment."[20] Merely the vehicle of men's desire to possess the female principle, Psyche herself has no choices and becomes the scapegoat for Aphrodite's anger. Aphrodite sends her son to punish the girl by enthrallment, and as we know from the familiar climax of the traditional retelling Psyche disobeys her lover Eros's instruction to not see him in the light and is punished with the loss of his love.

What Huber does is concentrate on the detail of the ancient tale that is overlooked in other interpretations, but, more important, for my purposes, she highlights what happens to Psyche after the moment of disobedience. For example, she emphasizes the dimensions of the symbolism of the love goddess, who is not a mere sex goddess as in most retellings, but is actually—in the Apuleius version of the tale—"mother of the universe, mistress of all the elements . . . mightiest of all the deities, queen of the dead."[21] This raises the stakes as to what is being lost in a world that traps women into being impersonators of the goddess. Aphrodite becomes "a Great Mother figure and life goddess in Psyche's tale and paves the way for an interpretation of Aphrodite as a mentor of wholeness, of holiness and of transformation for Psyche."[22] It is this transformative stage that most interests feminists such as myself who are concerned with how female agency and the narratives that can make it happen are different from (as well as similar to) the routes to agency outlined in other classical patterns.

While the traditional interpretations of the moment when Psyche sees her love in the light of the lamp emphasize the symbolism of the human soul seeking to bring the light of knowledge (more specifically reason) to what Eros represents (human instinct, loving, longing, yearning, and so on), Huber reads the moment with the lamp as Psyche's assertion of "an independence of desire—through the knowledge and ownership of her body and its erotic empowerment."[23] For feminist narrative patterning in general, it is what happens after the assumption of erotic empowerment that is most germane. Unlike Antigone, who ends in suicide or patriarchal marriage (the two favorite endings for all females in patriarchy), Psyche (after an unsuccessful suicide attempt from which nature saves her) actively seeks to renew her connection with Eros through undertaking a series of tasks under the guidance of Aphrodite, whom Apuleius called "the primal mother of all that exists, the original source of the elements, the bountiful mother of the whole world."[24] The narrative potential for self-making in the performance of these tasks empowers Psyche as a human female. Essential to that empowerment is the fact that the tasks are all undertaken while Psyche is pregnant, which is normally interpreted by patriarchal culture not as an agency-making, culturally significant condition, but as a passive, nature-bound condition. Ricoeur seems to (inadvertently perhaps) reinforce this cultural formulation when he takes up fetal development to illustrate the "degrees of actualization" of development into a person, and to outline an ethics that differentiates between "potential persons" and "persons." Ricoeur does not gender his discussion by noting that it is females who bear children, nor does he discuss women's agential power over the reproductive potential of their bodies. He refers in passing to "the maternal uterus" in the same way as he refers to the "separated embryo, conceived in a test tube,"[25] and he refers once to "the fetus and its mother"[26] without speaking of mothers as persons. In such a discussion, by implication, pregnancy is a more or less passive condition.

In the Psyche legend, the active tasks Psyche accomplishes during pregnancy involve the essential elements of becoming a mature actor in one's own lifestory. Psyche learns to sort seeds and thus understand "concrete realities" and effect their use in the physical world, where one must survive and provide for one's dependents. This everyday ordering extends to keeping track, not only of material realities, but also of affective realities as well: feelings, emotions, moods, and so on. Psyche then seeks a golden fleece—that much revered symbol of the hero's quest, standing for "male solar spirit" and "masculine power and courage."[27] In contrast, in a female quest the fleece symbolizes the traditional female tasks of spinning and weaving, which maintain civilized life and culture and also symbolize the spinning of new life; that is, the pregnancy that Psyche is engaged in at the time of her tasks. Her third task, collecting water in a jar, with its womb connotations, further emphasizes the life-giving nature of female development. Psyche's final task, her visit to Persephone in the underworld, is filled with symbolic representation of the sufferings and triumphs that are the inevitable part of a narrative of self-making that produces a human being capable of agency in the private and public world. Throughout her tasks, Psyche is actively learning to be a woman who knows how to make decisions about her responsibilities in life.

Huber asserts that Psyche is developing "[A]n ethic of recognizing and valuing the independent self within the community, and of being responsible for one's own needs and desires within the social contract."[28] For example, in Psyche's journey to the underworld she is warned not to give in to the multiple pleas for female nurturing to be spent in the interests of others. She learns that her own journey is as important as others' needs, and learns to prioritize the needs of others: "Psyche learns the limits of her personal responsibility for others' lives. This is an essential lesson on the limits of responsibility for someone about to be a mother."[29]

I would assert that Psyche's progress is an essential cautionary tale for any woman whose conditioning in patriarchal culture leads her to make herself into the mediating figure of the Antigone tale, who accepts responsibility without power, who gives unconditional nurturing to others whose acts—and the morality of those acts—she can have no control over. One of the facts that facilitates this misuse of the caring function in patriarchal society is the lack of female mentorship and alliance to teach women the proper use of their nurturing functions. In every legend of women in patriarchy, narratives from Antigone's to Marilyn Monroe's, women lack maternal and sisterly aid. Huber puts a great deal of emphasis on the importance of Psyche's sisters as oppositional, but very real allies, and, more important, she points out the ways in which Psyche is guided and instructed, at every step of her self-making, by Aphrodite—the very being that initiated her suffering as the result of Psyche becoming the impostor sex goddess of the patriarchy.

The fact that the Psyche story, unlike the Antigone story, goes beyond the moment of marriage/death allows me to return to my conversation with Paul Ricoeur's theories of self-making and narrative identity with a revisionary feminist viewpoint. As I read Ricoeur's important fifth and sixth studies in *Oneself as Another*, my Psychean concerns can be framed in the question: Where do women begin their stories in what Ricoeur names the "complex relations between action and agent"?[30] Ricoeur, in these studies, is addressing what he calls the "major lacuna" in his earlier works, a gap that involves the "*temporal* dimension of the self as well as of action as such."[31] With his usual generosity in admitting limitation, he sees that he needs to take "into account the fact that the person of whom we are speaking and the agent on whom the action depends have a history, are their own history."[32] I hope I have demonstrated, through the detailing of the Psyche legend, that it does matter which story you tell, which history you choose to start with, and where the agent is located in terms of the narrative moment of the story. Whichever story I tell of female self-making, I am still left with serious reservations in moving with Ricoeur through his goals for the Fifth, Sixth, and Seventh Studies in *Oneself as Another*, as he takes on the "notion of narrative identity" to bring it "victorious" through the "puzzles and paradoxes of personal identity" so that he can establish his thesis, "that narrative theory finds one of its major justifications in the role it plays as a middle ground between the descriptive viewpoint on action . . . and the prescriptive viewpoint which will prevail in the studies that follow."[33] However, I do work through the argument in those studies in good faith, since as Ricoeur himself assures me, "Suspicion is also the path toward and the crossing within attestation."[34]

Although I read with "suspicion" I do find much that is fruitful for feminists in the Fifth, Sixth, and Seventh Studies. I am particularly drawn by Ricoeur's assertion that "solutions offered to the problem of personal identity which do not consider the narrative dimension fail."[35] And as Morny Joy has observed, for feminists the "reflexive and existential connotations" of Ricoeur's concept of "ipse" are imperative to female acts of "writing as repossession" of selfhood.[36] Yet, in the past, as I have worked through Ricoeur's exploration of character and constancy, his discussion of the connection between the questions of "Who am I" and "What am I," even as I nod in agreement to his succinct enunciation of what is of bedrock importance to my own intellectual practice—the fact that "what sedimentation [of character] has contracted, narration can redeploy"[37]—I have had, nevertheless, a certain conversational reluctance in going forward with the philosopher who offers me the best support I can find for my own theorization and critical practice.

The Psyche story helps me go forward with Ricoeur by suggesting an essential revision. The moment where I can make that revision is when Ricoeur asks the crucial question regarding the possibility of an ethical self at the end of the Fifth Study: "But is not a moment of self-dispossession essential to authentic selfhood? And must one not, in order to make oneself open, available, belong to oneself in a certain way?"[38] Self-dispossession is exactly what patriarchy has always required of women as a precondition of their narratives inside a man's world—witness Antigone, witness Psyche at her abandonment on the mountain by her father and at her blind marriage to Eros. Patriarchy demands self-dispossession, not at a mature point of self-development (as in Ricoeur's formulation), but at the beginning of heterosexual relationship, and since women in patriarchy have never really belonged to themselves, their self-dispossession is not an act of making oneself open, available, but rather an act of sacrificing the possibility of ever having mature possession of a self. It is therefore not an act of agency at all, but rather an act of self-negation. (Patriarchy is defined here as "the structures and social arrangements within which women's oppression is elaborated. . . . [A]n ideology which arose out of men's power to exchange women between kinship groups; [the] symbolic male principle . . . the power of the father . . . men's control over women's sexuality and fertility . . . the institutional structure of male domination.")[39]

Once again the Psyche story becomes important for our understanding of gendered narratives of self-making. Many women today are in the transitional stage in patriarchy that Psyche experiences when Eros awakes and finds that, all unknowing of the consequences, his bride has shed the light of knowledge on the darkness his love has required. Psyche sees that her love is beautiful in the light, but she has broken his patriarchal rule that she can have Eros only if she does not seek logos. She is bereft, she is empty of what she had before and has no idea how to proceed to what she might have in the light of knowledge. Indeed, in the tale, she experiences such nothingness that she attempts suicide.

My realization of the aptness to many modern women of Psyche's position at the moment of her abandonment by Eros encourages me to revise Ricoeur's central question regarding identity and one's responsibility to another. Ricoeur asks: "Who am I, so inconstant, that *notwithstanding* you can count on me?"[40] As a feminist, I assert that women in patriarchal conditions of self-making cannot yet ask that question. Like Psyche, pregnant and abandoned by her lover at the very moment of discovering the potential of knowledge, I cannot ask a "Who am I" question, only a "How can I become a person" question, as in "How can I become a person, that *notwithstanding* my disempowerment and disability, you can count on me to enable others?" The questions are qualitatively different. Ricoeur's question can be asked only by an individual who is capable of self-esteem. In his seventh study Ricoeur says that if one is to achieve self-esteem one must have the "esteem of the *other as a oneself* and the esteem of *oneself as an other*."[41] He also says that I cannot esteem myself "*as* myself" unless I am "capable of starting something in the world, of acting for a reason, of hierarchizing [my] priorities, of evaluating the ends of [my] actions, and, having done this of holding [another] in esteem as I hold myself in esteem."[42] No wonder the Greek philosopher that Ricoeur brings up in the Seventh Study, Aristotle, defined friendship between two men, friendship that does not exist for physical pleasuring or practical utility, as the ideal of equal and ethical relationship. As Ricoeur himself comments, such reciprocity is "related to the condition of the free citizen, from which are excluded slaves, metics, women and children," and this restriction, as Ricoeur points out, narrows the "living together to thinking together."[43] I think that Ricoeur, who writes of "travel[ing] along this road with Aristotle for a moment,"[44] also needs to travel along a feminist road, if he, like me, wants a way out of defining relationship as only "thinking together."

If Ricoeurian theorizing is to move to a broader-based possibility of ethical reciprocity with others, what Ricoeur calls the "search for equality in the midst of inequality,"[45] the "Who am I" question needs recasting. It asks us to make ourselves accountable to others while admitting our inconstancy through an implied acceptance that we are indeed each a "who," a who capable of carrying out an investigation of the "whatness" of being a who. Thus, we are, "notwithstanding" all the inequalities caused by history and individual situation, capable of being counted on by others. This dispenses with the inequalities of race, class, and especially gender too quickly, moving us to a universal position of equality that may not exist in the world of deeds. My question asks us to go back a step to ask, "How can I be?" That is, how can there exist a way of being that makes me an "I" who then becomes capable of self-esteem, and who can then esteem another? At the same time as my question asks us to start at a point before "Who am I," it also recognizes that de facto, a female person always already carries responsibilities for enabling others in their coming to being as selves, even, ironically, as conditions in patriarchy require her to forbid her own self-making. Ricoeur's powerful "notwithstanding" clause becomes even more demanding in terms of female life, as we carry on the enabling responsibilities assigned to us in patriarchy, even as we question their relevance to our own self-narration.

How can feminism help us in this predicament of "How can I become"? Weir proposes that the central question of feminist philosophy is this: "Is it possible to affirm some sort of self-identity which does not repress the differences within the self, or the connectedness of the self to others and to do so without making false claims to authority and authorship?"[46] She sees the question as springing from the central problem of Western thinking, the tendency to binary identification in which all things must be one thing or another (as in the series of binaries brought up in the Antigone discussion), and thus all theories of identity tend to fall into either definitions of self-making that require repression and/or separation from connection to establish the self (usually gendered as male) or definitions that forbid individual identity by establishing the demands of connection of the self to others as the primary good (usually gendered as female). In her discussion of a series of prominent feminist theorists, Weir points out how the problem of self and other has preoccupied them, especially men's ability to have a self and women's position as othered. Weir is not very optimistic about the ability of feminist theorization since Simone de Beauvoir to construct a middle path between the dichotomies, considering the binary language traps that Western philosophical discussion entails. She does see, however, that language is at the crux of the problem.

For me, changing Ricoeur's question from "who" to "how" involves the how of self-making in language, since language must be used for any inquiring into identity. Weir identifies Julia Kristeva as the feminist philosopher most concerned, in her own language-making, with the traps that the polarities of language-making involve: "[her] work is characterized by a series of ambivalences, rooted in a fundamental ambivalence between a sacrificial model of identity and a theory of identity as something that can include difference and heterogeneity, and openness to change."[47] As well as in her work's ability to straddle binaries, constructing a both/and language of inquiry, rather than an either/or inquiry, Kristeva's work is useful for me because she points to the need for a contemporary ethics to have a contribution from "women who desire to reproduce. . . . From mothers."[48] She also suggests that "pregnancy seems to be experienced as the radical ordeal of the splitting of the subject: redoubling up of the body, separation and coexistence of the self and of an other, of nature and consciousness, of physiology and speech."[49] The explanatory power of the maternal subject position thus must be attended to in any philosophy of the self and its connection with others. We cannot afford, in a contemporary ethics, to dismiss, as Aristotle does, relationships of "utility" or "pleasure" as unequally reciprocal and unsuited for the construction of what Ricoeur calls an "ethics of reciprocity, of sharing, of living together."[50]

I find that at least part of the way to establish reciprocity and answer the question "How can I be a person" is that I must attend more carefully to the "utility" and "pleasure" that Aristotle rejects. The word *pleasure* is, coincidentally, one of the English translations of Kristeva's concept of *jouissance*. I need to find the *jouissance* in women's self-making narratives, use it to replace the disempowerment, the disabling that Weir names the "sacrificial logic" of binarized language usage, if I want to be a "who," a responsible person enabling myself and others. I require a nonsacrificial logic of identity since I must be able to enable at the same time as I gain a self-making narrative from the enabling process.

Jouissance is a word that pervades Kristeva's work and French psychoanalytic theory in general, and never seems to translate well into its obvious English substitute, "pleasure." In its elemental form the condition of *jouissance* comes as a result of fulfilling basic physical desires for food, water, sex, and so on. In Kristevian theory, *jouissance* becomes "joy," which is "another form of the 'unnamable'—the other side of reality as such—which together with Being and death, drives thought beyond itself, beyond its own limits, putting it in touch with infinity, particularly in the sense that the part becomes equal to the whole."[51] Kristeva refers to *jouissance* as the "nonsemanticized instinctive drive that precedes and exceeds meaning,"[52] thus, ironically, linking it to language making in its very positioning as a procedure that "precedes and exceeds" language. For me, it also links it to narrative self-making, a process that is itself dependent on a preceding and exceeding *jouissance*. *Jouissance* is our experience of what is normally not taken into account by the symbolic system, but is implicit in it—that is, the semiotic. It is our experience of what is not directly felt in our conscious world—that is, the unconscious. It is our way of experiencing the larger "unnamable" reality in which our little realities exist. It is what we experience in any vital connection between ourselves and all the otherness from which we feel separated, but instinctively know we are a part of. It is the unnamed first experience of connection, in which a pregnant woman begins to bring into imaginative being the otherness that inhabits her, a connection that underlies, informs and makes possible, such values as Aristotle's concept of "friendship."

Although I will use pregnancy as a metaphor for self-making, I am not here concerned with actual pregnancies. However, I am aware that my argument could be appropriated to the purposes of a "right to life" argument. Such an argument would have to ignore what I understand as the active character of pregnancy that involves the choice that a female person makes to either bring into imaginative being—as a desired child—the fetus that her body carries, or to choose not to take up that pathway, by refusing the further occupation of her body by the fetus. I, like Ricoeur, propose the use of "prudential judgment" in "the intermediary zone between things and persons."[53] Ricoeur proposes that the fetus begins to have the right to the "respect" we offer persons "once something like an exchange, even asymmetrical, of preverbal signs is begun between the fetus and its mother."[54] It is not clear to me who Ricoeur sees as establishing when "exchange" occurs: however the "asymmetrical" condition would suggest that if the agency belongs to scientists and ethicists, they could establish that some sort of exchange occurs as early as the implanting of the embryo. As well, Ricoeur does not make it clear if he means by "exchange" a voluntary act of acknowledgment on the part of a female person. More concerned with active agency of women during pregnancy, I choose to emphasize the decision of the individual woman (who may responsibly use the work of science and ethics, rather than being used by them) as to what are "preverbal signs" and when they can be said to begin. It is, for me, the recognition by the pregnant woman of the personhood of the fetal material she carries that establishes the fetus's move from thing to person. This is not a simple matter, and it is not the purpose of this essay to explore the ethical decisions involved in actual pregnancies. However, even when merely using pregnancy as a metaphor for talking about self-other relational activity, one gets into a much richer and more complex moral universe than can be explored in Aristotle's concept of "friendship."

For feminists, who need to find what Weir calls "new models of identity, of individuation, of agency, and of autonomy," we must start with finding out what other models exist, besides the cool Aristotelian one that forbids utility and pleasure, that sacrifices the body for the mind, that sees the only possible *jouissance* as the sharing of ideas. We must find what Kristeva calls "the unnamable repressed by the social contract."⁵⁵ We must also revise the contemporary Freudian/Lacanian model that posits the *mother, child, father* triad, where inevitable separation and continuing lack of the mother is the sacrifice we make for identity with the father. In both Aristotelian and Freudian/Lacanian models we must give up something of our fullness as human beings to begin to have an identity, and then use the freedom gained through sacrifice to form ethical alliances with others, in a kind of second-best substitute for the Eden of symbiosis with the mother.

To gain a nonsacrificial model for human self-making I think we need Psyche, particularly Psyche beyond the moment of the lamp. We need the pregnant Psyche, learning through her pregnant journey, evolving and changing into the mother Psyche, the woman who gives birth to the child she calls "pleasure" or "joy." Huber proposes that the Psyche story gives us a pattern for narrative identity that contains a new and productive metaphor for our identity-making that takes into account the independence of the self and connections between the self and others, what she calls a "placental" consciousness:

> Metaphorically, the placenta is the site of continuity. That which is absent in dualistic thinking—the gap or third in dichotomy—thus becomes available as a metaphor in any enquiry, and any enquiry may be said to be faulty if it does not examine this essential third element.... The placenta metaphor enables a revised image of the mind as well. The placenta is the third that operates as mediator between self and experience, between self and other.⁵⁶

Huber's "placental" metaphor of consciousness is similar to what Irigaray has called, in her discussion with biologist Hélène Rouch, the "placental economy." In her concern for finding more sufficient models of human relations than offered by patriarchally centered models, Irigaray asserts: "The placental economy is therefore an organized economy, one not in a state of fusion, which respects the one and the other. Unfortunately, our cultures, split off from the natural order—and the scientific methods used to get back to it more often than not accentuate that distance—neglect or fail to recognize the almost ethical character of the fetal relation."⁵⁷

In order to understand the possibilities of a "placental economy," and to use the metaphor of a "placental" consciousness, we must understand how a literal placenta operates as physical conduit. Huber explains that the placental relationship of mother and fetus, rather than being understood as the most unequal of relationships, as in a life cord from a dominant being to a completely dependent other, should be understood as a complex interdependency. We need to know that the placenta is not a simple cord of unity of mother and fetus, but rather, as Huber puts it quoting Gordon Bourne, a very distinct triplicity because of the separation of fetus and mother that is implemented by the placenta. Thus, the placenta is barrier, connection and conduit allowing the passage of nutrients and waste between the maternal environment and the fetus through the umbilical cord. The cord itself is biologically and physiologically triple, for it "carries the fetal blood from the fetus to the placenta via the two umbilical arteries, and the returning blood via the single umbilical vein." Its blood vessels are coiled in a spiral fashion, and finally, both cord and placenta ensure the "maternal and fetal circulations are entirely independent."[58]

As well, since the cells of the placenta are a product of fetal development, not maternal development, "the sharing of the maternal body by fetus and mother, does not imply union. . . . [N]either does it suggest loss of self in the mother. At the same time that the pregnant woman's bones, blood, and tissue cradle and sustain fetal development, the fetus may be said to initiate a connection that maintains separation even as it sustains life."[59]

I would add that just as in the case of actual pregnancies the involuntary initiation of connection by the fetus does not imply automatic acceptance of the personhood of the fetus, so in relational life, the initiation of a metaphorical "placental" bond by one person does not imply the automatic acceptance of responsibility by another. For my purposes, what is important about understanding that the placenta is part of the material of the fetus is to understand that in relationships in which one party is measurably more needy, more vulnerable than another, the strong party cannot simply diagnose and administer relational activity. The process of the needy person developing his or her own placental connections, reaching out and helping to define his or her own neediness, must be allowed to happen. Understanding the process of pregnancy at the level of bodies can help us to develop a metaphor of the relational activity of self-making with the concepts of barrier, connection, and conduit combined, which can, in turn, be helpful to a feminist theorization that can converse with Ricoeurian theories of self-making.

In placing this placental consciousness back into the specifics of the Psyche story we can begin to understand that learning to be a relational being does not have to be sacrificial, but rather consists in participating in a *jouissance* of self-development and social development. The tasks of self-making, interactive with nature, with life and death, with the goddess, with the lover—the journey that Psyche takes while pregnant—are the establishment of her own placental consciousness to the otherness of her universe. And her reward for an arduous journey well completed is her daughter, Pleasure/Joy. The figure of Pleasure/Joy, understood metaphorically, opens up new possibilities of how I can be a self in relation to others, and can allow me to go on to answer the Ricoeurian question "Who am I?"

I have taken some time to illustrate how our narrative patterning of individual life and cultural history must be widened from the usual patriarchal sources to include others. In conclusion I would like to make some suggestions as to how placental consciousness can converse with Ricoeurian identity theory. A productive engagement could be made in reexamining the *ipse* and *idem* of identity through a placental consciousness. In his fifth study in *Oneself as Another*, Ricoeur is at pains to explain the "overlapping" nature of *ipse* and *idem*, while noting that we must also "distinguish between them."[60] The aim, I think, is to suggest a less linear and logical operation, a less binarized operation of self-making than has been the case in the past. I think that Huber's model of the spiraling of the placental cord as metaphor of living, learning, and knowledge is useful in this regard. The spiral assumes a fixed center, but this fixity, or core, is not a preexisting subject, but a process and a product of the spatial and temporal acts of spiraling. The spiral also implies the circularity, the repetitiousness, of experience, the *idem* of life, but because the circles of a spiral always move in space and time the model speaks to the *ipse* of constancy through change, through continued performance of our narrative identities. As Huber affirms, "The spiral links transformative change and centered being."[61]

I began with an epigraph that quoted Ricoeur, who says that "there is no ethically neutral narrative," and I end by asserting that neither are there any sexually neutral theses, nor indeed any gender-neutral narratives. In pursuing this edification of Ricoeurian thought I have used a tactic that was suggested to me by Ricoeur when he says that much of what is "repressed" in traditional philosophy is "liberated" by revisioning. I have maintained that what is suppressed is gender consciousness and that it can be liberated by feminist theorization of alternative mythic materials. I assert that we may avoid what Ricoeur calls "repetition and aimless wandering" by revisioning a Psychean journey to realize that it represents a pathway to an understanding of ourselves as relational beings that is, as feminist revision teaches us, a much more complex and gendered mediation than we have previously thought.

Notes

1. Paul Ricoeur, *Oneself as Another* (Chicago: University of Chicago Press, 1992), pp. 298–99.
2. Helen M. Buss, "Women's Memoirs and the Embodied Imagination: A Gendering of Genre That Makes History and Literature Nervous," in *Paul Ricoeur and Narrative: Contexts and Contestation*, ed. Morny Joy (Calgary: University of Calgary Press, 1997), pp. 87–96.
3. Paul Ricoeur, "Response," trans. D. Pellauer, in *Paul Ricoeur and Narrative*, ed. Joy, p. xxxix.
4. Ibid., p. xl.
5. Ibid., p. xli.
6. Ibid., pp. xli–xlii.
7. Ibid., p. xlii.

8. Ibid., p. xlii.
9. Ricoeur, *Oneself as Another*, p. 115.
10. Pamela Anderson, "Re-Reading Myth in Philosphy: Hegel, Ricoeur, and Irigaray Reading Antigone," in *Paul Ricoeur and Narrative*, ed. Joy, pp. 87–96.
11. Jean Bethke Elshtain, "The Mothers of the Disappeared: Passion and Protest in Maternal Action," in *Representations of Motherhood*, ed. D. Bassin, M. Honey, and M. M. Kaplan (New Haven and London: Yale University Press, 1994), pp. 75–91.
12. Ricoeur, *Oneself as Another*, p. 152.
13. Ricoeur, "Response," p. xlii.
14. George Steiner, *Antigones*, (Oxford: Oxford University Press, 1984), p. 6.
15. Ibid., p. 10.
16. Luce Irigaray, *This Sex Which Is Not One* (Ithaca, NY: Cornell University Press, 1977), p. 193.
17. Allison Weir, *Sacrificial Logics: Feminist Theory and the Critique of Identity* (London and New York: Routledge, 1996), p. 97.
18. Anderson, "Re-Reading Myth," p. 53. Anderson points out Ricoeur's concern for the Antigone material in the "Interlude" portion of *Oneself as Another*, pp. 241–49, 256.
19. Eric Neuman, *Amor and Psyche: The Psychic Development of the Feminine: A Commentary on the Tale of Apuleius* (New York: Pantheon Books, 1956).
20. Barbara Huber, *Transforming Psyche*, (Montreal and Kingston, London and Ithaca, NY: McGill-Queen's University Press, 1999), p. 49.
21. Ibid., p. 52.
22. Ibid., p. 52.
23. Ibid., pp. 64–65.
24. Ibid., p. 52.
25. Ricoeur, *Oneself as Another*, p. 270.
26. Ibid., p. 272.
27. Huber, *Transforming Psyche*, p. 99.
28. Ibid., p. 79.
29. Ibid., p. 79–80.
30. Ricoeur, *Oneself as Another*, p. 113.
31. Ibid.
32. Ibid.
33. Ibid., p. 114.
34. Ibid., p. 115.
35. Ibid., p. 116.
36. Morny Joy, "Writing as Repossession: The Narratives of Incest Victims," in *Paul Ricoeur and Narrative*, ed. Joy, pp. 37–38.
37. Ricoeur, *Oneself as Another*, p. 122.
38. Ibid., p. 138.
39. Cheris Kramarae and Paula Treichler, *Amazons, Blue Stockings, and Crones: A Feminist Dictionary* (London: Pandora Press, 1992), p. 323.
40. Ricoeur, *Oneself as Another*, p. 168.
41. Ibid., p. 195.
42. Ibid., p. 193.

43. Ibid., p. 188.
44. Ibid., p. 181.
45. Ibid., p. 192.
46. Allison Weir, *Sacrificial Logics*, p. 1.
47. Ibid., p. 145.
48. Julia Kristeva, "Stabat Mater," in *The Kristeva Reader*, ed. Toni Moi (New York: Columbia University Press, 1986), p. 185.
49. Julia Kristeva, "Women's Time," in *The Kristeva Reader*, ed. Moi p. 206.
50. Ricoeur, *Oneself as Another*, p. 187.
51. John Lechte, *Julia Kristeva* (London and New York: Routledge, 1990), p. 22.
52. Julia Kristeva, *Desire in Language* (New York: Columbia University Press, 1980), p. 142.
53. Ricoeur, *Oneself as Another*, p. 272.
54. Ibid., p. 272.
55. Kristeva, "Women's Time," p. 200.
56. Huber, *Transforming Psyche*, p. 130.
57. Luce Irigaray, *Je, tu, nous: Toward a Culture of Difference*, (New York and London: Routledge, 1993), p. 41.
58. Gordon Bourne, *Pregnancy* (London: Pan Books, 1972), pp. 90, 85, quoted in Huber, *Transforming Psyche*, p. 129.
59. Huber, *Transforming Psyche*, p. 128.
60. Ricoeur, *Oneself as Another*, p. 122.
61. Huber, *Transforming Psyche*, p. 119.

5
The Summoned Self
Ethics and Hermeneutics in Paul Ricoeur in Dialogue with Emmanuel Levinas

MARK I. WALLACE

Paul Ricoeur's and Emmanuel Levinas's writings are a rich source for scripturally nuanced philosophical reflection on the question of the mandated self in relation to others. Former colleagues at the University of Paris-Nanterre, Levinas and Ricoeur have engaged one another in their writings over the years, making a comparison of their related proposals a potentially fruitful enterprise. In this essay, I will suggest that Ricoeur, in his sustained contrapuntal dialogue with Levinas, successfully mediates the dialectic between self-esteem and solicitude for others in his ethical thought. In this vein, I hope to show how both Ricoeur and Levinas use the biblical texts to construe the project of selfhood in terms of being summoned—beyond one's choosing and willing—to take responsibility for the neighbor—even at great cost to oneself. For each thinker, the individual becomes a self by allowing the divine Other to awaken it to its responsibilities for the human other. Nevertheless, the nature of the self being summoned to its responsibilities, on the one hand, and the hermeneutical method for understanding this summons within the biblical texts, on the other, are questions answered differently by each theorist. It is the answers to these questions that finally divide Levinas and Ricoeur from one another while still providing support for the deep affinities that underlie their related projects. While privileging Ricoeur's model of the summoned self in my exposition, I conclude with some comments about the aporetics of conscience in Dietrich Bonhoeffer's life and thought as a challenge to Ricoeur's analysis of the inner voice in moral decision-making.

I

Before I begin this conversation between Ricoeur and Levinas, let me first make some preliminary comments about Ricoeur's identity as a philosopher who uses the biblical texts to provide imaginary variations on the theme of the good life. As a philosopher, Ricoeur is a hermeneutical phenomenologist, to use Don Ihde's felicitous description of Ricoeur; and as a biblical exegete, he is an interpreter of the meaning of the Word within the words of the scriptural intertexts. Hermeneutical philosophy and biblical interpretation—these two tasks constitute the distinctive, but always related, fulcrums about which Ricoeur's thought turns. This dual description of Ricoeur's intellectual identity entails three characteristics.

First, as a *hermeneut,* Ricoeur argues that selfhood begins not with the philosophical hubris that the subject is an autonomous self but with an awareness that the subject enters consciousness already formed by the symbolic systems within its culture. Consciousness is never independent or empty—a tabula rasa—but always already interpenetrated by the founding symbols and stories that constitute one's communal heritage. Thus the journey to selfhood commences with the exegesis of the imaginary symbols and stories constitutive of one's cultural inheritance in order to equip the subject to become an integrated self by means of appropriating these symbols and stories as her own. Second, as a *phenomenologist,* Ricoeur puts into abeyance any judgment about—in Husserlian terms, he performs an *epoché* regarding—the reality status of the imaginary claims made by one's orienting textual sources. This bracketing exercise is performed in order to accord to these claims the status of lived possibilities—even if they cannot be established as referring to proven realities in the world.[1] Third, and finally, as a *theological thinker* within the biblical traditions—but not as a theologian per se, a label Ricoeur consistently refuses—Ricoeur maintains that it is in allowing oneself to be appropriated by the figurative possibilities imagined by the biblical texts that the task of becoming a full self is most adequately performed. A person's willingness to become an apprentice to the summoning voice of the text begins the performance of a life well lived in relation to self and others.

As a philosopher and interpreter of the Bible, it might appear, then, at least at first glance, that Ricoeur is a philosophical theologian, or perhaps a philosopher who engages in cryptotheology to promote his philosophical aims. But these readings of Ricoeur's project are a mistake. Ricoeur is not a philosophical theologian, if by that phrase one means a religious thinker who grounds reflections on God and the self on a particular philosophical foundation. By the same token, he is not a Christian philosopher, if by that phrase one means a philosopher who utilizes philosophical discourse to prove the truth of Christian faith claims in opposition to other rival claims. Faith, for Ricoeur, is always a wager and a risk and can never be established as apodictically certain based on the false security of a philosophical substructure. As a wager, faith eschews any triumphalism that posits one set of life choices as inherently superior to another set of choices. The only verification of the truth of such choices is found, over the course of one's existence, in the rich quality of a life well lived in harmony with self and others. No thought system external to these choices can adjudicate which, if any, alternative forms of life are superior to another.

In this respect, Ricoeur is a thoroughgoing Kantian, as Pamela Sue Anderson has shown, because like Kant he seeks to resolve the "conflict" between the "faculties" of theology and philosophy by erecting a rigid partition between the two disciplines: even as philosophy should be conceived as an autonomous, agnostic field of study that puts in suspension the question of God, so also should theology be regarded as a self-contained enterprise that refuses the temptation to ground its inquiries on a cryptophilosophical foundation.[2] In a Kantian vein, Ricoeur argues that it is productive to cautiously *borrow* language and concepts from one domain to elucidate the other mode of inquiry as long as such borrowing does not degenerate into *grounding* or *determining* the one discipline on the basis of the other.[3] Like Kant, who bifurcates the interests of critical philosophy and religious inquiry, Ricoeur defends his rigid partition by arguing that philosophy operates in the registry of reflective analysis, while theology functions as living testimony to the possibilities of biblical faith without the pseudosecurity of any metaphysical foundations.

In another sense, however, the trajectory of Ricoeur's work is not Kantian but Anselmian. Or, to put it another way, Ricoeur, as a scripturally informed philosopher, takes his cues from the Kant of *Religion within the Bounds of Reason Alone*, where biblical imagery is thoughtfully utilized for the explication of the moral life, and not the Kant of the three *Critiques*. If, as I have suggested above in labeling Ricoeur a hermeneutical thinker, all thought takes flight within the fullness of one's symbolically rich and textually mediated presuppositions, then biblical faith, while neither the queen of philosophy nor its handmaiden, is the generative *impulse*—but never the determining *ground*—for Ricoeur's whole enterprise. Religion, then, is the rich matrix that motivates and informs Ricoeur's autonomous and agnostic philosophy of the moral life. Unlike Kant—if one reads Kant diachronically from the first *Critique* onward—Ricoeur does not move from a presuppositionless critical philosophy to a regional application of the critical philosophy to religious questions. On the contrary, he begins all of his various projects in the fullness of his beliefs, and then strives critically to understand better the implications of such beliefs through the discipline of philosophical inquiry. Ricoeur's question, therefore, is not Kant's question in the first *Critique*—namely: How can knowledge be denied in order to make room for faith? Rather, his question is: In the fullness of faith, how can critical inquiry explicate the meaning of the presumptions and concerns generated by this faith? Or, as Ricoeur puts it in an earlier context, How can philosophy be pressed into the service of saturating faith with intelligibility?[4] In the introduction to *Oneself as Another*, Ricoeur states that his abiding interests in various philo-

The Summoned Self 83

ious philosophical problems—including the overall problem of the self—is motivated by the "convictions that bind me to biblical faith."[5] Ricoeur rejects the quixotic illusion of philosophy—to begin thought without presuppositions—by fully owning his positioned belonging to a rich heritage of biblical language and imagery as the wellspring of his philosophical itinerary.

II

To this point, I have sought to situate Ricoeur's hermeneutic of selfhood within the history of Western philosophical and religious thought. Now I would like to more explicitly take up Ricoeur's hermeneutic vis-à-vis his dialogue with Levinas concerning the dialectic of the self and the other. To begin this dialogue, let me first turn to an analysis of a central problematic in Ricoeur's moral philosophy: the question of the "broken cogito" and the role of conscience in mediating the fundamental discontinuity of the self with itself. For Ricoeur, the self is permanently "other" to itself because, contrary to Descartes, the self is not a fixed subject, in full possession of itself, that perdures over time. But while the self is not an immutable substratum, according to Ricoeur, it does not follow that there is no self, as some of Descartes's critics maintain. Some anticogito thinkers (for example, Michel Foucault) contend that insofar as there is no entitative core self, the subject is nothing other than the sum total of the discourses practiced by its particular culture. Similarly, some analytic philosophers (for example, Derek Parfit), who also criticize Cartesian essentialism, argue that the subject is reducible (without remainder) to its brain states and bodily functions. Ricoeur rejects both of these options—historicist and physicalist—through a tripartite analysis of the phenomenon of passivity or alterity within selfhood.[6] My self—as neither a fixed entity, discursive construct, nor biochemical cipher—cobbles together its identity by experiencing the "otherness" of my own body, the dissymmetry between myself and the other person in front of me, and, finally, and most important for my analysis, the originary phenomenon of being called by the voice of *conscience*—a voice both proximate and exterior to me—that summons me to my obligations and responsibilities.

What does Ricoeur mean by the term *conscience*? Conscience, Ricoeur writes, is

> the voice ... addressed to me from the depths of myself ... the *forum* of the colloquy of the self with itself.... We need, I think, to preserve within the metaphor of the voice the idea of a unique passivity, both internal and superior to me.... In this sense, conscience is nothing other than the attestation by which a self affects itself.... The point is that human being has no mastery over the inner, intimate certitude of existing as a self; this is something that comes to us, that comes upon us, like a gift, a grace, that is

not at our disposal. This non-mastery of a voice that is more heard than spoken leaves intact the question of its origin. . . . The strangeness of the voice [of conscience] is no less than that of the flesh or that of other human beings.[7]

In the depths of one's interiority, the subject is enjoined to live well with oneself and for others. The colloquy of the self with itself—the phenomenon of being enjoined—occurs in the place where the self appropriates for itself the demand of the other upon it. Conscience, then, is the forum for the summoning of the self to its obligations.

As I noted above, while Ricoeur scrupulously avoids grounding the disciplines of religious studies and philosophy upon one another, he does not object to borrowing concepts from one domain in order to illuminate problems within the discourse of the other field of inquiry. The upshot of this careful give-and-take interchange is the recognition, by Ricoeur, of certain deep affinities or homologies that exist between key terms that intersect the two disciplines. His analysis of the phenomenon of conscience is emblematic of this homologous approach to understanding the human condition. In his philosophical writing, Ricoeur is self-consciously agnostic about the origins of conscience, the experience of being enjoined by the other: "Perhaps the philosopher as philosopher has to admit that one does not know and cannot say whether . . . the source of the injunction, is another person . . . or my ancestors . . . or God—living God, absent God—or an empty place. With this aporia . . . philosophical discourse comes to an end."[8]

But in one of the two theological papers that Ricoeur excised from the original set of Gifford Lectures that constitute *Oneself as Another*, Ricoeur *does* identify the origins of conscience in the voice of God—a voice that enjoins the hearer to care for oneself and attend to the needs of others. In his omitted lecture on the summoned self, Ricoeur identifies conscience as the inner chamber where the divine mandate is heard and understood. In the interior voice of obligation, each person is called by God to exercise responsibility for oneself and the other. Indeed, conscience is now valorized as the inalienable contact point between the Word of God and human beings; it is the forum where divine forgiveness, care for oneself, and solicitude for others intersect. "Conscience is thus the anthropological presupposition without which 'justification by faith' would remain an event marked by radical extrinsicness. In this sense, conscience becomes the organ of the reception of the Kerygma, in a perspective that remains profoundly Pauline."[9] Without conscience, the divine voice that summons the self to its responsibilities falls on deaf ears. In Ricoeur's earlier writings, the *productive imagination's* capacity to interpret symbolic language played the role of a sort of *praeparatio evangelica* for the reception of the divine word.[10] While not denying this previous emphasis, the focus is now on the subject's *moral* capacity for an internal dialogue with itself that makes possible the hearing and understanding of God's voice in the life of the listening subject.

Ricoeur's analysis of conscience reflects the lifelong impact of Levinas on his thought, both religious and philosophical. As does Levinas, Ricoeur, in his theological writings on conscience, argues that the biblical scriptures consistently press onto the reader the obligation to appropriate God's demand—a demand definitively represented by the biblical prophets—to take responsibility for the welfare of the other. Along with Levinas, Ricoeur maintains that the ideal of the morally commissioned self is central to the biblical texts. In particular, the establishment of the prophetic *I*, through heeding the call of obligation for the other, is an underlying theme throughout these texts. In exegeting the Abrahamic/Mosaic response "here I am," Ricoeur writes, "I see, for my part, in this figure of a 'summoned subject' a paradigm that the Christian community, following the Jewish community, could make use of to interpret itself."[11] Ricoeur's position regarding the prophetic subject is analogous to that of Levinas, who writes that "religious discourse that precedes all religious discourse is not dialogue. It is the 'here I am' said to a neighbor to whom I am given over, by which I announce peace, that is, my responsibility for the other."[12]

In spite of this rough agreement, an important point of contention separates Ricoeur and Levinas in reference to the questions of conscience and the summoned self: whether the self is constituted solely by its obedience to the cry of the other for justice, or whether the move to selfhood and the capacity to respond to the entreaty of the other are cooriginary. In other words, is the self a product of the other's summoning it to its responsibilities, or is it not the case that the presence of the self itself, in the depths of its own conscience, is the necessary condition for hearing and responding to the other's attempt to awaken it to its responsibilities? For Levinas, I become a subject through radical self-divestment, by becoming hostage to the other. "The more I return to myself, the more I divest myself . . . I am 'in myself' through the others."[13] I have no self—I am not an *I*—without the other awakening me to my responsibility for the welfare of the other: "The word *I* means *here I am*, answering for everything and for everyone. . . . I exist through the other and for the other."[14] Ricoeur contends, however, that Levinas's idea of the passive self, singularly formed in response to unfulfillable obligation, undermines the dialectic between self and other, realized through the agency of one's conscience, essential to moral action. Conscience, as we have seen, is the site of intersection between selfhood and otherness, the place where my ethical ownness "within" and the commanding voice of the other "without" indwell one another, according to Ricoeur.[15] Only a self—as the subject and object, in its conscience, of its own internal dialogue—can have an other-than-self rouse it to its responsibility. Only a self—insofar as it esteems itself *as* a self capable of reason, agency, and good will—can exercise solicitude for others. Ricoeur argues that self-identity is not merely a *result* of one's response to the call of the other; it is also what must be *presupposed* for the call to be heard and understood in the first place. Pace Levinas, Ricoeur asks, "Would the self be a result [of its assignment to take responsibility for the other] if it were not first a presupposition, that is, potentially capable of hearing this assignment? ... [I]s it forbidden to a reader, who is a friend of ... Levinas, to puzzle over a philosophy where the attestation of the self and the glory of the absolute [or: the care of the other] would be co-originary?"[16] Self-attestation—the capacity for self-esteem—has its origin in my self-reflexive openness to being enjoined to give myself to meet the other's needs even as my hearing and understanding the voice of the other have their origin in my regard for myself as a moral subject. Ricoeur stubbornly insists on preserving self-love and other-regard in a correlative tension that he argues is snapped by Levinas's one-sided emphasis on self-emptying obedience in the face of the summons of the other.[17]

III

This disagreement over the question of the mandated self reflects the different hermeneutical orientations of both thinkers. In the mid-1970s at a conference on the topic of "revelation," Levinas and Ricoeur engaged in a spirited debate about the nature of revelation in Judaism and Christianity vis-à-vis the question of biblical exegesis. In the proceedings from that meeting, Levinas maintains that the gravitational center of the biblical texts is halakhic discourse; the commandments and their explication is the centripetal focus of the scriptures. In his comments, after registering his appreciation for Ricoeur's use of discourse analysis to explicate taxonomically the various revelatory modalities within the Bible, Levinas raises an important caveat:

> But perhaps, for a Jewish reading of the Bible, [Ricoeur's] distinctions cannot be established quite as firmly as in the pellucid classification we have been offered. Prescriptive lessons—found especially in the Pentateuch, the part of the Torah known as the Torah of Moses—occupy a privileged position within Jewish consciousness, as far as the relationship with God is concerned. Every text is asked to produce such lessons; the psalms may allude to characters and event, but they also refer to prescriptions ... [and] the texts of the Wisdom literature are prophetic and prescriptive.[18]

Biblical revelation centers on prescriptive teachings—regarding matters of behavior, morality, ritual, and law—to the degree that even in seemingly unlegal genres, such as the Psalms and sapiential literature, Levinas argues that there are prescriptive upheavals where God's commanding voice to the reader breaks through the literary surface of these texts.

Ricoeur sees matters very differently. His focus falls on how revelation is generated—how God is "named"—through the polyphony of diverse biblical genres. To be sure, Ricoeur's biblical discourse analysis is acutely aware of the function of prescriptive discourse in summoning the self to its responsibilities. But Ricoeur makes this point against the backdrop of a wider semiotic concern for reading the whole Bible as a point-counterpoint intertext.[19] Because attention to biblical genre diversity, according to Ricoeur, is necessary for a multifaceted understanding of the divine life, it follows that assigning privileged status to this or that particular genre threatens to flatten out the Bible's overall diversity and its regional zones of indeterminacy and discontinuity. Singular attention to any one discourse—including legal discourse—runs the risk of homogenizing the Bible's semantic polyphony. "The naming of God, in the originary expressions of faith, is not simple but multiple. It is not a single tone, but polyphonic. The originary expressions of faith are complex forms of discourse . . . [that] name God. But they do so in various ways."[20] It is only as any one biblical genre is interanimated by its crossfertilizations with the medley of other modes of discourse that the biblical texts effectively make meaning.

For Ricoeur, textual revelation is moderated by the play of literary genres. In the case of the Bible, the Bible's different modes of signification—narratives, hymns, wisdom sayings, laws, poems, gospels, apocalyptic writings, and so forth—generate a surplus of meaning outside the control of any one genre or particular theme. These various forms of articulation are not simply taxonomic devices for categorizing discourse but rather the means by which theological meaning is produced. "The literary genres of the Bible do not constitute a rhetorical facade which it would be possible to pull down in order to reveal some thought content that is indifferent to its literary vehicle."[21] The Bible's different registers of discourse are more than just classificatory codes or decorative literary trappings because the *content* of religious discourse is generated and determined by the literary *forms* employed to mediate particular theological understandings.

Ricoeur's discourse analysis of the Bible seeks to show how the stories and sayings of the Bible are not one-dimensional exercises in coherence but rather multivalent points of intersection for a variety of discourses and their contrasting theological itineraries. From this perspective, the scriptural figuration of the divine life—the phenomenon of revelation—is radically problematized by attention to the mixed genres employed by the biblical writers. "Throughout these discourses, God appears differently each time: sometimes as the hero of the saving act, sometimes as wrathful and compassionate, sometimes as he to whom one can speak in a relation of an I-Thou type, or sometimes as he whom I meet only in a cosmic order that ignores me."[22] In this approach, the Bible emerges as a heterogeneous intertext of oppositional genres—genres that alternately complement and clash with one another—

rather than a stable book unified by a particular discourse, including prescriptive discourse (pace Levinas).

Nevertheless, in spite of these important differences that separate Ricoeur and Levinas from one another on the questions of selfhood, ethics, and hermeneutics, I believe that Ricoeur, on a level that reflects his profound admiration of Levinas's philosophy, would, in one sense, have a deep sympathy for Levinas's biblical hermeneutic. Levinas is clear that as a positioned Jewish reader of the Bible, his goal is faithfully to recover the dynamically open invitation to obedience at the heart of the Bible—an invitation that is central to Jewish unity, and has been essential to its preservation, throughout the generations. "From the outset Jewish revelation is one of commandment, and piety lies in obedience to it."[23] For Ricoeur, insofar as biblical meaning is never frozen "in" the text, but made in the encounter "between" text and reader, then a Christian hermeneutic, understandably, has the right to subsume legal discourse to a wider concern for the panoply of other, nonlegal discourses that generate the surplus of meanings within the biblical texts. The hermeneutical difference between both thinkers is significant and to some degree irreconcilable but, nevertheless, productively illustrative of the equally principled religious locations—Jewish and Christian, respectively—from which both philosophers assay the meaning of being summoned by the other to meet our obligations for his or her welfare.

IV

Let me conclude with some comments regarding Ricoeur's notion of the summoned self in the spirit of an immanent critique. I say "immanent critique" because I want these final comments to stand alongside the broad assumptions of Ricoeur's project while still questioning some aspects of his construal of the notion of conscience. In this essay, I have sought to show how Ricoeur—in contrast, and in faithfulness, to Levinas—persuasively deploys a notion of conscience as a power of inward deliberation that mediates self-esteem and solicitude for the other. In this respect, Ricoeur's discussion of conscience has a distinctly Aristotelian cast: analogous to Aristotle's analysis of virtue, Ricoeur's understands conscience as the self's capacity for inward adjudication between extremes. Conscience is an exercise in prudential, reflective equilibrium. It is the colloquy of the self with itself where one's interior capacity for practical wisdom—*phronesis*—thoughtfully guides action directed to the care of self and other.

But what I find missing in Ricoeur's magisterial analysis of conscience is an equally powerful account of the phenomenon of the *war of the self with itself* in the interior adjudication of opposing life choices and moral options. In the colloquy of the self with itself, the character of this interior conversation is oftentimes more like an aporetic and conflicted *contest* between diverging voices than it is a careful and deliberative weighing of adjudicable options. Caught in the vicegrip of seemingly irresolvable extremes for action, the self, as it struggles with the voice of conscience within, must often run the risk of dissolving into an irredeemable jumble of broken pieces in its agonistic struggle to decide which path to pursue in responsibility to itself and others. Conscience, in this model, is not a hearkening to *a* voice or *the* voice within, but a confrontation with a plurality of *many different* voices—some of which are self-generated, others of which have their origin outside of the self. Conscience, from this perspective, is not a hearkening to one voice—be it the voice of the other or the voice of God or the voice of the nowhere—but a cacophonous echo chamber of many voices—many disparate and irreconcilably contested voices—all of which lay claim to the attention of the moral agent.

Ricoeur's recent work does make a partial turn to analyzing the role of irresolvable ethical conflict within the conscience of the moral subject. Nodding to Greek theater, he writes in the final essay of *The Just* about the "tragic dimension of action," where "strong evaluations relating to heterogeneous and sometimes competing goods" come into opposition with one another.[24] Moral conflict stems from the irreducible diversity of substantial goods. All of these goods cannot be brought together to form a larger synthesis in this or that particular situation of ethical decision-making. The results of such decision-making are tragic because there is no universal maxim that can adjudicate which goods are to be preserved and which are to be deemphasized or sacrificed altogether. For certain decisions, there is no formal rule—such as Kant's categorical imperative—that can mediate between contesting notions of the good. Such decisions are tragic rather than heroic: they often result in murky mediatorial positions that preserve the lesser of two evils rather than the elevation of a higher good over and against a transparent evil. "Wisdom in judging consists in elaborating fragile compromises where it is a matter less of deciding between good and evil, between black and white, than between gray and gray, or, in the highly tragic case, between bad and worse."[25] When incompatible goods or norms enter into conflict, practical moral wisdom consists of muddy compromises played out in the darker registers of human action.

Ricoeur's analysis of intractable moral disagreements is subtle and incisive. Nevertheless, he eases the tensions inherent within tragic decision-making through an appeal to group process in moral judgments. Within one's individual conscience the antinomies created by weighing different moral options appear to be hopelessly at odds with each other. But now conscience—the inner forum of self speaking to self—has a larger set of conversation partners to appeal to about the right course of action to pursue.

[T]he decision taken at the end of a debate with oneself, at the heart of what we may call our innermost forum, our heart of hearts, will be all the more worthy of being called *wise* if it issues from a council, on the model of our

French national consultative council on ethics, or on the model of the small circle bringing together relatives, doctors, psychologists, and religious leaders at the bed of someone who is dying. Wisdom in judging and the pronouncement of wise judgment must always involve more than one person. Then conscience truly merits the name *conviction*.[26]

Practical wisdom consists of moving outside of oneself toward a larger body of decision-makers—a relevant governmental body, for example, or the inner circle of one's immediate family—that can provide a wider reflective context for moral judgment. Indeed, such judgment is not truly moral, Ricoeur avers, unless it "always involves more than one person." Without a plurality of voices to attend to, moral judgment runs the risk of devolving into solipsism. No important moral decision should be taken alone—rather, one's conscience must always seek counsel with a larger *sensus communis* as a check and balance against one's own individual discernment about the application of the good (or goods) in particular circumstances.

Ricoeur's theory of conscience makes clear the role a wider social dialogue can play in forming good judgment. But the problem with his social model of conscience is that it appears unable to account for those acts of inner moral conviction that question the integrity of the wider circle said to be essential to moral judgment. If practical decisions are not truly "wise" apart from social mediation, then what role, if any, can an individual's distinctive moral certainties play in calling that individual to perform actions that undermine the beliefs and values of his or her cultural milieu? The problem with Ricoeur's social model of moral judgment is a certain tone-deafness to the importance of *alterity* in the formation of sound judgment. If conscience is ultimately subsumable to the larger social group, is there any place for the sometimes unique and distinctively "other" voice of "the good within" to question, even tear apart the fabric of one's social relations in an effort to work out the meaning and truth of *one's ownmost, radically individualistic, and oftentimes antisocial sense of the good*? Is not conscience often the voice of a profound sense of social unrelatedness—of the *totaliter aliter*—that allows persons to press beyond the limited confines and orthodoxies of their communal groups in order to realize new expressions of truth and goodness? Ricoeur's consistent emphasis on the relational context for moral judgment seems unable to account for the visionary excesses of the distinctive individual whose ethical praxis appears independent from, and a comprehensive challenge to, her lived surroundings.

Dietrich Bonhoeffer's life and work gives evidence of the irresolvable dilemmas that plague conscience—dilemmas that are not easily resolvable by appealing to a wider *sensus communis*. It is well known that Bonhoeffer's active resistance to the Nazis—culminating in his participation in the conspiracy to assassinate Hitler in 1944—eventually led to his execution in the

Flossenbürg concentration camp in 1945. However, Bonhoeffer's book *Ethics*, written prior to and during the time he was vigorously working to subvert the Reich government in the early 1940s, paradoxically lifts high the ideal of loyalty to the state. The irony here is that precisely at the time in which Bonhoeffer is plotting to overthrow the rule of the National Socialists in Germany, he is also imploring the readers of his *Ethics* to remember that the claim of government is from God and binding on conscience; that proper deference to the governing authorities is the proper rule for citizens of the state; that even when the government makes war against the church, the Christian should avoid any "apocalyptic diabolization of government"; and that while concrete acts of disobedience to government are occasionally licit, no regular and systemic disobedience of government is permissible, no matter how anti-democratic and anti-God the ruling powers have become.[27]

The ironic conflict that punctuates the division between Bonhoeffer's theological apologetic for government and his seditious activities to overthrow government elucidates the internal battle of opposing viewpoints within conscience. Bonhoeffer was well aware of this interior contest. He writes that in order to listen to and heed one's conscience—under the tutelage of the Gospel message—it is sometimes necessary to "bear guilt for the sake of charity."[28] In fidelity to conscience, one may find oneself running the risk of incurring guilt in pursuit of the responsible action in service to the neighbor. At times, one must do the wrong thing in order to pursue a higher good. Given his theology of the divine right of government, Bonhoeffer himself—in living out the dictates of his conscience to join the conspiracy to kill Hitler—also, fundamentally, trampled upon his conscience by assuming the guilt of murder through disobeying the commandment of the decalogue, "Thou shalt not kill." Of course, that Bonhoeffer was a pacifist—or, perhaps, a conditional pacifist—is a fact that only further complicates this aporetic division between his life and his writing. In taking the risk to become a killer, Bonhoeffer violated both his inner conscience and stepped outside the wider circle of received Christian opinion about the sanctity of human life.

Using Bonhoeffer, my criticism of Ricoeur here focuses on his relative lack of attention to the unassimilable welter of voices that make claims on the inner authority of conscience. My suggestion is that conscience, in many instances, is not a royal road to reflective judgment, a still point in the turning world of moral action, but a contested site of deep turmoil where the antinomic character of ethical decision-making is most keenly felt. As well, appeals to a wider *sensus communis* oftentimes does not help to mediate the plurality of contesting goods, but further exacerbates this conflict. This criticism is not to deny that Ricoeur is acutely aware, especially in his earlier work, of the tensive disproportionality of the self with itself in its incapacity to mediate the consciousness of freedom and brokenness of unfulfilled desire. But it remains unclear to me why Ricoeur does not thematize the phenomenon of conscience with the same awareness of the ineliminable oppositions that afflict the inner life that defined his earlier poetics of the will.

Is the internal conversation of the self with itself a level-headed process by which opposing options are weighed in the balance and a rational decision is then made in a deliberative fashion? In the interior debate with oneself can one adjudicate conflicts through rational appeals to a wider circle of decision-makers? Or is this inner colloquy less a dialogue between friends and more a disputation between combatants where the type of agonistic ethical dilemmas faced by Bonhoeffer are ultimately unfathomable and unresolvable? At times, Ricoeur's moderating appeal to the voice of conscience—whatever the ultimate origins of this voice—appears too sanguine about the interior capacity of the human subject to arbitrate between moral extremes in a fair and even-handed manner. With regard to the ultimate questions of the moral life—the life and death issues faced by Abraham at Mount Moriah or Bonhoeffer in war-ravaged Germany—these questions appear less like candidates for an inner colloquy and more like disputants in an ongoing struggle over irreconcilable ideals and choices. Ricoeur's philosophy of the summoned self—a self enjoined through the medium of conscience—can be broadened by a deeper appreciation of the abyssal chaos that lies at the center of all matters of the heart.

This caveat notwithstanding, I have sought to show how Ricoeur's Levinasian recovery of the biblical ideal of self-giving can be a transformative paradigm for integrated subjectivity in and with the other person. In Ricoeur's thought one can better comprehend the power and mystery of Jesus' ironic claim that unless one loses oneself one cannot find oneself. *Unless one forfeits oneself one cannot discover genuine selfhood.* The task of becoming a full self is most adequately performed by allowing oneself to be appropriated by the ethical possibilities projected by the biblical texts. In this gesture, a person's spiritual practice becomes her destiny as a moral subject: by taking the risk of becoming assimilated into the strange universe of the biblical texts, one makes good on the wager that a scripturally refigured self is the crown of a life well lived.

Notes

1. Paul Ricoeur, *The Symbolism of Evil*, trans. Emerson Buchanan (Boston: Beacon Press 1967), pp. 347–57.
2. Paul Ricoeur, *Oneself as Another*, trans. Kathleen Blamey (Chicago: University of Chicago Press, 1992), pp. 23–25; cf. Pamela Sue Anderson, *Ricoeur and Kant: Philosophy of the Will* (Atlanta: Scholars Press, 1993), pp. 1–39.
3. Paul Ricoeur, "Philosophy and Religious Language," in *Figuring the Sacred: Religion, Narrative, and Imagination*, trans. David Pellauer and ed. Mark I. Wallace (Minneapolis: Fortress Press, 1995), pp. 35–47; cf. Immanuel Kant, *Religion within the Limits of Reason Alone*, trans. Theodore M. Greene and Hoyt H. Hudson (New York: Harper, 1960), pp. 3–10.

4. Ricoeur, *The Symbolism of Evil*, p. 355.
5. Ricoeur, *Oneself as Another*, p. 24.
6. Ricoeur, *Oneself as Another*, pp. 1–39, 125–39, 297–356; cf. Paul Ricoeur, "Narrative Identity," *Philosophy Today* 35 (1991): 73–81.
7. Paul Ricoeur, "From Metaphysics to Moral Philosophy," *Philosophy Today* 40 (1996): 453–55.
8. Ricoeur, *Oneself as Another*, p. 355.
9. Paul Ricoeur, "The Summoned Subject in the School of the Narratives of the Prophetic Vocation," in *Figuring the Sacred*, p. 272.
10. Ricoeur, *The Symbolism of Evil*; cf. Paul Ricoeur, *The Rule of Metaphor: Multi-Disciplinary Studies of the Creation of Meaning in Language*, trans. Robert Czerny with Kathleen McLaughlin and John Costello (Toronto: University of Toronto Press, 1977), pp. 315–22.
11. Ricoeur, "The Summoned Subject" p. 267.
12. Emmanuel Levinas, "God and Philosophy," trans. Richard A. Cohen and Alphonso Lingis, in *The Levinas Reader*, ed. Seán Hand (Oxford: Basil Blackwell, 1989), p. 184.
13. Emmanuel Levinas, *Otherwise Than Being or beyond Essence*, trans. Alphonso Lingis (Boston: Kluwer, 1991), p. 112.
14. Ibid., p. 114.
15. Ricoeur, *Oneself as Another*, p. 341.
16. Paul Ricoeur, "Emmanuel Levinas: Thinker of Testimony," in *Figuring the Sacred*, ed. Wallace, p. 126 (bracketed additions are mine).
17. Ricoeur, *Oneself as Another*, pp. 329–56.
18. Emmanuel Levinas, "Revelation in the Jewish Tradition," in *The Levinas Reader*, ed. Hand, p. 193.
19. Paul Ricoeur, "'Thou Shalt Not Kill': A Loving Obedience," in André LaCocque and Paul Ricoeur, *Thinking Biblically: Exegetical and Hermeneutical Studies*, trans. David Pellauer (Chicago: University of Chicago Press, 1998), pp. 111–19; cf. Mark I. Wallace, *The Second Naiveté: Barth, Ricoeur, and the New Yale Theology* (Macon, GA: Mercer University Press, 1990), pp. 27–45.
20. Paul Ricoeur, "Naming God," in *Figuring the Sacred*, p. 224.
21. Paul Ricoeur, "Toward a Hermeneutic of the Idea of Revelation," *Harvard Theological Review* 70 (1977): 25.
22. Paul Ricoeur, "Philosophy and Religious Language," in *Figuring the Sacred*, p. 41.
23. Levinas, "Revelation in the Jewish Tradition," p. 200.
24. Paul Ricoeur, *The Just*, trans. David Pellauer (Chicago: University of Chicago Press, 2000), p. 154.
25. Ricoeur, *The Just*, p. 155.
26. Ibid.
27. Dietrich Bonhoeffer, *Ethics*, trans. Neville Horton Smith and ed. Eberhard Bethge (New York: Macmillan, 1965), pp. 339–53.
28. Ibid., p. 245.

PART II:

Moral Meanings, Human Fallibility, and Theological Ethics

6
Searching for a Heart of Gold
A Ricoeurian Meditation on Moral Striving and the Power of Religious Discourse

DAVID E. KLEMM

In this essay I want to focus our attention on an important connection within Paul Ricoeur's thought between ethics and religion. In particular I am interested in the relationship between ethics, construed as reflection on moral striving, and the power within religious discourse to affect a change of heart in the moral agent. My own standpoint in this meditation is philosophical theology. And it is ultimately for the sake of advancing theological understanding that I present, interpret, and at some points transform Ricoeur's own thoughts on the matter. My task in this essay is to construct a fundamentally Ricoeurian account of moral regeneration from diverse sources in Ricoeur's writings. At times the task requires me to expand or to modify what Ricoeur has done to make stronger theological sense of the power of religious discourse than Paul Ricoeur, the philosopher and listener to the Christian Word, has chosen to do.

It is a privilege to have this opportunity, because Paul Ricoeur, with relentless energy and impeccable honesty, has constructed a unique and important systematic reflection on ethics and religion within the context of his many philosophical concerns. Yet it is also humbling to do so, because Ricoeur pushes his reflections into a nearly infinite assemblage of detailed analyses of particular texts and thinkers. Who alive today can really understand the scope of his breathtaking philosophical project? In this volume we hope to make a few steps in the direction of appropriating Ricoeur's thought, focusing on Ricoeur's contribution to ethics and questions of meaning in public life.

To accomplish my task, I propose to arrange various elements from Ricoeur's thought into a structure that will enable me to think theologically about the relationship between religious power and the human desire for a good life. In doing so, I run against the grain of Ricoeur's own practice of thinking. Ricoeur himself always thinks systematically, but he resists articulating the elements of his thinking in terms of a system. Moreover, in his books and articles Ricoeur typically engages other thinkers on occasional disputed questions of the day. Consequently Ricoeur's readers become acquainted with the parts of his systematic project, but not with the principle of the whole. To some extent, I want to reverse this tendency by approaching my particular topic—the relationship between ethics and religion—with an account of the nature of thinking according to Ricoeur. My intention is to give a systematic account of my topic.

In taking this approach, I begin with the heading of *dialectic*, understood as the discipline that determines the nature, limits, and identity of human thinking as the moral striving of a bound and alienated freedom within an eschatological framework. Next, I consider rather straightforwardly Ricoeur's *ethics*, the discipline that determines the need for a fundamental change at the heart of human incentives, and that provides the norms and principles for guiding the will within the limits of human thinking in its efforts for such moral regeneration. A reflection on *religion* follows. Religion is on a different level from either dialectic or ethics. Unlike them, religion is not a reflective discipline but a real power in the world—a power that is manifest in the forms of religious discourse and ritual action. Religion, I hold, is contact with the power that can and does produce the sought-for change of heart. In religious language and action, people testify to their real contact with this power, and those testimonies can themselves assume religious power for others. I conclude with some theological thoughts on Ricoeur's account of religious power.

Dialectic

Readers of Ricoeur already understand that he does not assign a privileged place to the category of dialectic within a philosophical system in the way that, for example, Schleiermacher does. For Schleiermacher, dialectic is the art of thinking about thinking, or reflecting on reflecting, with regard to both the structural features of thinking and the absolute ground or transcendent/transcendental principle of thinking.[1] In Schleiermacher's system, dialectic determines both the very essence of thinking as such, as well as its self-differentiation into particular forms of thinking with respect to their basic principles, concepts, and rules. Dialectic is therefore for Schleiermacher, as it was for Plato, the pinnacle of philosophy.[2]

Now, I maintain that there is a dimension of Ricoeur's philosophical discourse that properly invites the name *dialectic* even though Ricoeur neither identifies it as such nor brings together his dialectical thoughts into a single treatise. Ricoeur, I believe, quite intentionally distances himself from the discipline of dialectic. His thinking is systematic, to be sure, in that it proceeds from clear principles and is always consistent with itself. However, Ricoeur's thinking does not aspire to the form of a closed system, whether deductively constructed or more loosely so. Ricoeur's thought is ever reconstituting itself in response to the pressing questions of the day and in dialogue with other major thinkers on those questions. I conjecture that engaging the traditional discipline of dialectic would constrain the open, always unfinished nature of Ricoeur's thought. Therefore, when the term *dialectic* does appear in Ricoeur's writings, its meaning is contextually rather than systematically determined. In a discussion of Kant or Hegel, for example, the term *dialectic* refers to the senses employed by those authors. But for the sake of my analysis and interpretation of Ricoeur's thought, I want to use the term *dialectic* as it appears in Schleiermacher, where dialectic is thinking about thinking's relation to being as an object of experience. I select Schleiermacher as a point of reference on dialectic for many reasons. One of these reasons is that I wholeheartedly agree with the principle held in common by both Schleiermacher and Ricoeur that neither thinking nor experiencing is possible apart from language. Therefore dialectic enjoins hermeneutic as its natural counterpart. Thinking about thinking is therefore always closely related to thinking about discourse and its manifold operations.[3]

Dialectical discourse appears in Ricoeur in discrete moments that tend to be embedded within other kinds of discourse. Most of us would acknowledge a dialectical method in Ricoeur. But I especially want to include those passages in Ricoeur's writings in which he reflects on the primary forms of reflective discourse rather than engaging directly in them. I have in mind dialectical reflections on such forms pure reflection (which in some ways is indistinguishable from dialectic itself), philosophical hermeneutics, ethics, philosophy of religion, political theory, aesthetics, and the like. For my purposes, Ricoeur speaks dialectically whenever he relates himself to the reflective forms of his philosophical project rather than to significant questions arising within it. Here is what Ricoeur accomplishes with dialectic so construed.

First, dialectic establishes the *nature* of thinking. Ricoeur distinguishes among mythological thinking (thinking in the form of images), critical thinking (thinking that dislodges the self-evidence of what is given and inquires about the conditions of its possibility), and speculative thinking (thinking that constitutes necessary forms of thought as necessary forms of being).[4] This distinction is, of course, a dialectical distinction. But when Ricoeur himself actually thinks, he always thinks critically. By this statement I mean negatively that by intention Ricoeur never engages directly in either mythological thinking (as does Karl Barth, for example) or in speculative thinking (as does Hegel). True, Ricoeur thinks critically *about* both mythological thinking and speculative thinking, but his own dialectic does not permit him to indulge in either extreme form of thinking himself. Let me now consider the nature of thinking in some more detail by rehearsing briefly that most dialectical of Ricoeur's books, *Fallible Man*. I want to do so, because I will return to the structure of thinking it presents in meditating on some new possibilities for religious discourse.

In *Fallible Man* Ricoeur constructs an abstract model of human being as the being whose thinking must mediate between disproportionate elements at three levels—namely, the theoretical, practical, and affective levels.[5] At the level of theoretical synthesis, the *I* constitutes objects of knowing by connecting elements that are quite different in kind, but that are quite equal in status, and cooriginal. Here thinking mediates between *seeing* (involving singular representations arising from bodily receptivity) and *saying* (involving general representations arising from conceptual determination in language) by means of the transcendental imagination. At the level of practical synthesis, the *I* projects images of the person that I could become by synthesizing the fixed qualities of selfhood with a vision of how that self could achieve happiness. Here thinking mediates between the givenness of finite character and the intention of a goal in life, by means of the moral feeling of respect for the person. At the affective level, we find the inner conflict of the heart. Here the *I* mediates—or at least tries to mediate—between vital feelings of pleasure and intellectual feelings of beatitude by means of the spirit (Plato's *thumos*). With each step, the fragile mediations brought about by thinking become more tentative and fraught with risk. At its core, the self is conflict—a sensed noncoincidence of the self with itself that is reflected on objects of knowing, sensed as the task of becoming a person in doing, and experienced as the alternation between misery and love in feeling.

The point I want to make is that *Fallible Man* dialectically establishes the nature of thinking as critical thinking, because *human beings are mediating beings*. In their thinking activities, humans are constantly bringing about mediations among disproportionate elements both in the world and in their own existences.[6] I think that it would be entirely fair to Ricoeur to add that dialectical thinking about thinking therefore means to question the meaning and truth of these mediations—and to put into question one's own being as thinking.

Second, dialectic establishes the *limits* of critical thinking both vertically and horizontally, as it were. Vertically Ricoeur establishes both a lower limit and an upper limit to thinking. At the lower limit, thinking arises out of an original *arche;* and at the upper limit thinking proceeds toward a final end or *telos*.[7] He calls the modes of discourse referring to these limits "originary affirmation" and "eschatological hope" to indicate the nonconceptual nature of thinking at both the lower and upper limits. Both affirmation and hope are forms of "conviction" that signify the end of mediation and hence a negation of thinking. On reaching these limits, critical thinking ceases to be possible and collapses into conviction. Dialectically speaking, we are left with the question of how to think these unthinkable limit-concepts. Ricoeur does not offer dialectical formulas by which to denote the postulated content of the limit-concepts, fearing a lapse into speculative or mythological thinking. However, it seems to me dialectically appropriate to designate the lower limit as the ground of unity prior to any difference between opposites of saying and seeing and the like, and the upper limit as the fully determinate unity of opposites.

Ricoeur establishes horizontal limits of thinking in his analysis of theoretical, practical, and affective syntheses. If one takes either side of the mediating activity in abstraction from its reciprocal other, one reaches a limit to thinking. For example, viewed from the standpoint of the theoretical synthesis, *saying* with no admixture of *seeing,* or conversely, seeing with no admixture of saying, each constitutes a limit. Viewed practically, *character* without *happiness,* or happiness without character, also each constitutes a limit. Similarly, at the affective level, purely sensible feelings of *pleasure* without spiritual feelings of *beatitude*, or purely spiritual feelings without sensible ones, each constitutes a limit. The principle of active synthesis is that neither element in a pair of opposites can appear in separation from the other element.

The dialectical point is that for Ricoeur thinking is the critical mediating of opposites, and all thinking occurs within these limits—both vertical and horizontal. To think at the limit is no longer to think, because mediating ceases when one attempts to think the limit-concept in isolation from its reciprocal other on which mediating activity depends.

Third, and this is an important point clearly articulated by Ricoeur, dialectic establishes the *identity* of such bounded critical thinking as moral thinking in a fundamental sense. It does this in three steps. In the initial step Ricoeur's dialectic establishes philosophy to be *philosophical anthropology*—in his case, thinking about what it means that the activity of thinking brings about fragile mediations of being within the limits of thinking. The meaning of human being—the being who brings about mediations at all levels of his being—is the preeminent topic of philosophy. The next step is that for Ricoeur philosophical anthropology is a *philosophy of the will.* The reason is that for Ricoeur thinking is not in the first instance a transcendental critique of knowledge but rather the appropriation in finite freedom of our desire to be and effort to exist. In other words, to claim, or rather to reclaim, freedom from alienation is the preeminent task of philosophy. Let's be clear on this point.

Ricoeur acknowledges that the starting point and foundation for all reflection is the positing of the being of the *I* in thinking: when I think, I am. For Ricoeur, however, the self-evident truth that I am a thinking being cannot constitute a substantive ontology. On the contrary, the truth of the cogito is "as abstract and empty as it is invincible."[8] For self-awareness to have content and therefore genuine meaning, the self must appropriate the expressions of its desire to be and effort to exist in the symbols, narratives, actions, and institutions that objectify it. Because for Ricoeur the "I am" always precedes the "I think," we live deeper than we think. Thinking is always attempting to catch up to itself by recovering the meaning of the self in its act of existing, and the meaning of the self that posits its being in thinking is freedom. For Ricoeur, thinking freely appropriates itself as freedom by deciphering its own expressions in the linguistic world around it. For this reason, and this is the final step, thinking qua thinking for Ricoeur has the identity of a moral striving. Because thinking is always appropriating a prior depth, and because appropriation signifies that the initial situation from which reflection proceeds is "forgetfulness," the practice of reflection is a moral task leading from alienation to freedom.[9]

Fourth, dialectic in the nature of the case establishes the *relationships* among other modes of reflective thought, such as ethics, hermeneutics, philosophy of religion, and ontology. On these interconnections—especially those between ethics and religion—I want now to focus. Let me begin by pondering how ethics arises from Ricoeur's philosophy of the will within the structure of his own thought.

Ethics

Fallibility, we have learned from Ricoeur, is not merely the structural possibility for error inscribed at the heart of human being. Fallibility is a potency for evil, a power to fail, which becomes fault when it is actualized.[10] Pure reflection cannot follow the leap from fallibility to fallenness, however, because reflection cannot derive the actuality of evil from its possibility. Freedom, not necessity, accounts for the fall; and freedom binds and impairs itself thereby. As a result, acknowledgment of fault is a decisive moment in the history of consciousness, whether collectively or individually considered.

First, the avowal of evil is a crucial material cause or occasion of *hermeneutics*, which is evoked in order to decipher the symbolic languages of confession. With the fall, freedom is in no sense transparent to itself; fallen freedom is an enigma, and its expressions in language require decoding. After the fall into evil, hermeneutics is the necessary reflective discipline for understanding, interpreting, and reappropriating the desire to be and effort to exist. In *The Symbolism of Evil* Ricoeur begins his long hermeneutical detour in order to understand expressions of astonishment at evil experienced successively as the stain of an infecting agent, as awareness of a broken relationship, and as my personal responsibility. The cycle of symbols and myths of evil push out and objectify the multileveled "experience of being oneself but alienated from oneself,"[11] Ricoeur says, "consciousness of self seems to constitute itself at its lowest level by means of symbolism and to work out an abstract language only subsequently, by means of a spontaneous hermeneutics of its primary symbols."[12] Hermeneutics thus arises in response to confessions of evil: someone agonizes—appalled at what he has done. Someone else interprets the meaning of the avowal of evil. Yet another person interprets the meaning of the interpretation. Someone else again questions the principles, concepts, and rules under which interpretations can be justified. Philosophical hermeneutics arises out of incremental steps leading from the fall. Ricoeur's multiple studies in the hermeneutics of texts—studies such as *Interpretation Theory*, *The Rule of Metaphor*, and *Time and Narrative*—thus bear a trace of the primary language of confession. Hermeneutics reflects on expressions of human moral striving.

Second, the avowal of evil, along with the hermeneutical debate arising from it, is at the same time the birthplace of the *ethical vision of the world*, by which Ricoeur means "our continual effort to understand freedom and evil by each other."[13] In other words, on the one hand freedom is the finite ground of evil's appearance in the world, and on the other hand the avowal of evil is the condition of consciousness of finite freedom. This guiding theme of Ricoeur's thought is extremely powerful, and to it he constantly returns with the notion of the bound will that claims its freedom by admitting its personal responsibility for evil. It is important to understand that consciousness of fault as my own also sets in motion a temporal dynamism to the guilty conscience. In remorseful contemplation of the past, the guilty conscience recollects itself in repentance; yet in hopeful anticipation of the future, the penitent projects the possibility of regeneration, reconciliation, and redemption. In this twofold temporal ecstasis, the distressed soul becomes aware of the vertical limits of thinking. Repentance harks back in recollection to the lower limit of primordial goodness. Ricoeur writes, "It is always *'through'* the fallen that the primordial shines through."[14] Hope peers forward in imagination to the upper limit of eschatological fulfillment. Within these limits, humanity is "the Joy of Yes in the sadness of the finite."[15]

According to Ricoeur, the ethical vision of the world comes to its mature philosophical form in Kant's "Essay on Radical Evil," to which Ricoeur refers in many of his writings. For Ricoeur, the "Essay on Radical Evil" both gives philosophical analysis to the moral struggle that human beings wage in their hearts and it provides conceptual clarification to the lower and upper limits of moral thinking and striving. Recall that Kant rejects the one-sided views that human being is by nature either morally good or morally evil. Instead, Kant argues a middle view. On the one hand, human nature possesses an original predisposition to good, on the grounds that the free power of choice (*Willkür*) by nature incorporates the feeling of respect for the moral law into its maxim. But on the other hand, human nature also possesses a propensity to evil. The reason is that the weakness of the heart leads every human being, even the best, to incorporate into his or her maxim the occasional deviation from the moral law in favor of selfish interest.[16]

Because the propensity to evil is ubiquitous, radical evil stands guard at the lower limit of human moral striving. The original good will appears only through the reality of radical evil. The condition of radical evil means that anyone who says "I" has always already subverted the moral law by adopting maxims for action on the basis of self-love, even as she or he nonetheless feels and understands his or her duty to a moral law of pure practical reason. An evil maxim becomes the ground of all maxims—namely, the maxim to make the incentives of self-love and its inclinations the condition of compliance with the moral law, rather than to make compliance with the moral law the condition of incentives of self-love and its inclinations. Radical evil is the inversion of the proper order of incentives, and it is the origin point of subsequent moral striving.[17]

At the same time, Ricoeur's interpretation of Kant's "Essay on Radical Evil" clarifies the upper limit or goal as well—namely, the highest good as synthesis of happiness and duty, which constitutes the unconditioned totality of the object of pure practical reason. Because proper subordination of incentives of self-love to the incentive of the moral law so often leads to suffering rather than happiness, the concept of the highest good is the concept by which Kant conceives the completion of the moral struggle. This concept takes the place of the Hegelian absolute for Ricoeur, in that it is not given as a speculative totality for knowing but is rather posited as a task for freedom in the light of hope.[18] We hope that the reward for a good will is duty in unity with happiness; that is the upper limit of moral thinking.

Third, the ethical vision of the world poses the challenge of moral regeneration, for the passage from radical evil to the highest good requires a change in the subjective ground of maxims—a conversion of fundamental incentive. The ethical vision of the world therefore enjoins the quest for a good will, a heart of gold. This challenge leads to the special discourse of *ethics* broadly speaking. For Ricoeur ethics functions as the moral schoolmaster for the alienated self who has sinned, has lost its way, and yearns for genuine freedom. Ethics is the reflective discourse that can teach us what constitutes that change of heart or moral conversion.[19] Constructed on the basis of the philosophy of the will, and formulated in the context of a hermeneutics of the self, Ricoeur's ethics finds its most complete expression in the seventh, eighth, and ninth studies of *Oneself as Another*.[20] In this text, Ricoeur brings his extensive hermeneutical detour back to a concrete reflection on what it means to be human. The topic of the book is the question of selfhood: Who is a "self"? In successive chapters Ricoeur asks: Who speaks in speaking? Who acts in acting? Who narrates in telling his or her story? Who assumes responsibility for his or her actions? Ricoeur's aim is to interpret the being of the self within each of these domains. Resisting reductions either to the exalted subject of the Cartesian cogito or to the humiliated self of Nietzschean rhetorics of the self, Ricoeur instead attests to the being of the self in the mediations appearing between third-person descriptions and first- or second-person experiences of selfhood.

To this end Ricoeur introduces two different notions of personal identity. *Idem* identity refers to third-person descriptions of what is permanent in time (for example, one's body) and therefore reidentifiable as the same from an outsider's perspective. *Ipse* identity, by contrast, refers to a person's character as what is constant through time and therefore capable of making and keeping promises in the midst of change. The two approaches are mediated in the notion of narrative identity, which shows how the self is author, narrator, and main character in the narrative unity of its own life. In writing and rewriting one's lifestory in the mode of the possible, the self suspends moral judgment even as it prepares one's consciousness for moral education.

Moreover, the self is always already dialogically related to other selves from the beginning. Again, Ricoeur takes a middle position between extremes. He argues against the view that the self is entrapped within the potentially solipsistic circle of its own world-constituting consciousness and must therefore argue on the basis of analogy to the reality of an intersubjective sphere of consciousness, as in Husserl's *Cartesian Meditations*. And likewise he claims that the self is also not one-sidedly accused by the wholly exterior and transcendent face of the Other—as Emmanuel Levinas in *Totality and Infinity* would have it. Rather, for Ricoeur the self in its temporal attestation to itself is always already in response to a threefold otherness. First, we encounter our own bodies as an ever present otherness; I am my own body, yet in another sense I can always distinguish myself from my body. Second, we are always open to the otherness of other people who are like us in their humanity, but who have different life narratives and values. Third, we carry with us the voice of conscience, which includes the values and norms of our own cultural heritage, and those of humanity as a whole. Nonetheless, the voice of conscience comes from beyond us, beckoning us to assume our own individual humanity.

Through this conception of the self as always already in reciprocal relation to this threefold otherness, and in response to the question "Who is the responsible moral agent?" Ricoeur reflects on the values, norms, and principles that ought to guide human life in its condition of radical evil. The human desire to be and effort to exist are now funneled into the ethical aim that responds to the reality of evil and violence. Ricoeur defines the ethical intention as *"aiming at the 'good life' with and for others, in just institutions."*[21]

In keeping with the teleological structure of Ricoeur's thinking in general, the first moment is Aristotelian in conception. Human agents desire the good life, and the ethical aim begins with the moral agent appropriating *values* and *virtues* that are embedded in culturally transmitted ethical institutions. Freedom actualizes itself precisely in the activity of fulfilling these values within the ultimate horizon of the good life. Correlatively, ethical fault appears in the gap between particular goods that an agent pursues and the open horizon of the good life. In response to fault, ethical reflection prescribes virtues for successful formation of character. The desire for the good life posits the virtue of self-esteem, the quality of living with and for others posits the virtue of friendship, and the aim of living in just institutions calls for the virtue of justice.

The second moment of Ricoeur's ethics is Kantian, and his terminology shifts from the discourse of ethical aim to that of the moral norm. Ethics requires the deontological moment in order to apply systematic critique to the ethical aim of the good life, which itself can become systematically distorted under conditions of actual evil and violence. The demand to universalize our maxims under the categorical imperative provides the key test to the desire to live a good life. Ricoeur favors the formulation of the categorical imperative that responds to the problems of evil and violence: Always treat humanity, whether in your own person or in the person of another, as an end in itself and never simply as a means. Self-respect is the quality of the moral agent who understands the necessity to pass all ethical intentions through the critical sieve of the moral norm.

In its third moment, Ricoeur's ethics culminates in a critical *phronesis*, a form of practical wisdom that mediates the Aristotelian desire for the good life and the Kantian test of the moral norm. Practical wisdom is the ethical analogue to appropriation in hermeneutics: the *phronimos* relates the critically tested mean of virtue to the practical decision at hand. Schooled in the lessons of tragic wisdom, the *phronimos* understands that personal autonomy is always limited by and performed within community, that the demand to follow rules must always measure itself against the expectations of others, and that institutional justice is best served by public debate and democratic decision-making.

Ethics for Ricoeur responds to the malaise of the fallen will, by diagnosing its plight and prescribing a cure. Two fundamental questions remain unanswered, however. First, how is the prescribed change of heart *possible* under conditions of radical evil? Second, how can that change of heart become *actual*? In addition, we will want to know how an actual change of heart might affect the structure of moral striving. I turn now to Ricoeur's hermeneutics of religious discourse, where we will seek the answers.

Religion

So far I have said the following. Dialectic both sets the limits within which and presents the conditions under which humans think. Ethics diagnoses the fallen form of human thinking and prescribes a change of heart. Now we reach religion, a form of discourse, which testifies to contact with a real power transcending the limits of critical thinking that can potentially produce the desired change. The steps I will follow in this section are these: First, I advance an interpretation of Ricoeur's account of religion. Second, I want to show how Ricoeur demonstrates the possibility of a fundamental change of heart from the standpoint of a hermeneutics of poetic texts—a major accomplishment. Third, I want to build on his notion of how religious hermeneutics can intensify and overturn the ethical hope for a good and just life through testimonies of the inbreaking of divine grace.

I propose that Ricoeur's starting point for thinking about religion is precisely the same one that he ascribes to Kant in *Religion within the Boundaries of Mere Reason*.[22] According to Ricoeur, Kant reflects on religion as just *there* in the world—as the Other of philosophy. Religion is extraphilosophical due to its positivity and its historical nature; philosophy can only take religion into account as "lying at its margins, at its boundaries."[23] Thus Ricoeur, like the mature Kant, does not present a philosophy of religion or a philosophical theology, but rather a philosophical hermeneutics of religious discourse. For Ricoeur, philosophical engagement with religion is not a matter of reasoning about the being of God. It begins instead by acknowledging religion as what is outside the limits of critical thinking. Critical thinking, we remember, always combines opposites—such as singular representations of reference with universal representations of meaning. Religion unites and transcends these opposites, because religious power combines saying and seeing (or meaning and reference): the meaning of religious discourse is itself its real reference in the world. In other words, in religious discourse what is said is also seen. The image does not refer beyond itself to the perceived world, such that its truth is its correspondence between the image and perception. In religious discourse the image is more real than the perceived world. The meaning of the religious image instantiates its own being. Let me explain this point with reference to Kant's philosophy of religion.

In *Religion within the Boundaries of Mere Reason*, Kant writes that for critical thinking, "How it is possible for a naturally evil man to make himself a good man wholly surpasses our comprehension." Philosophy cannot achieve that comprehension, because it is inconceivable how a human will could reform itself once it has adopted an evil maxim as its basic principle. For an evil will to reform itself would be self-contradictory, hence unthinkable. Moral regeneration requires grace, but a critical philosophy cannot think grace, for it would have to ascribe agency to some reality other than the will—namely, a divine being that is unthinkable without violating the limits of critical thinking. Christian religion, by contrast to critical philosophy, does not seem to have such problems. Christian religious discourse has as its center a representation of what Kant calls the triumph of the good principle over the bad, the representation of Christ as humanity pleasing to God. Kant admits that we cannot ascribe this latter representation to our own thinking as its origin point. Indeed, we cannot even understand how human nature could be receptive to this idea. According to Kant, "It is better to say that that prototype has *come down* to us from heaven, than that it has taken up humanity." Christian religion is the depository and guardian of this representation. To this point, Ricoeur and Kant run together. But with the next step, Ricoeur altogether surpasses Kant.

Ricoeur rightly claims that Kant backs away from the real issue for a philosophical hermeneutics of religion. That issue is how Christ becomes *more* than a hero of duty, even while being less than an actual *kenosis* of the absolute in Hegelian style. In other words, the real issue is how it is possible that the Christ symbol (in Kant's phrase) "takes on power" to set people free for righteousness. Kant properly rejects the mythological answer of a vicarious sacrifice, of a substitute victim to repay the debt for radical evil, because such an answer removes the incentive for ethical striving and negates moral responsibility. Yet Kant cannot altogether dismiss the core of the religious answer, which is not merely a matter of *will* but in addition and supremely a matter of *grace,* although Kant has no clue how to think grace because Kant lacks an understanding of religious imagination. Nonetheless it remains inconceivable that a good disposition might proceed from a corrupted will without a divine gift; that is, without some unfathomable aid.[24] At this point Ricoeur carries us past Kant's impasse by means of his marvelous conception of religious imagination, grounded in the hermeneutics of poetic discourse. Let me try to explain the power of religion for Ricoeur, beginning with the poetic imagination.

From the standpoint of Ricoeur's hermeneutics, Christian faith is inseparable from the mode of discourse in which it is embodied. Religious texts are species of poetic texts for Ricoeur. That is, they display the characteristics of the metaphoric process at the level of text: the "is not" of the literal meaning evokes an "is like" of figurative meaning, which projects a network of meaningful connections—a "world of the text"—as horizon for a possible "mode of being." The poetic text is a model for the imagination that has the capacity to redescribe reality in the mode of possibility through semantic innovation. Philosophical hermeneutics makes possible the conceptual interpretation of the imaginatively proposed world of the text. All of this is quite well known as part of Ricoeur's hermeneutics. What is less well known is that Ricoeur's theory of metaphor also extends the mediating function of imagination below the threshold of the productive capacities of cognitive understanding to the level of attunement and feeling.[25] This extension bears directly on the religious possibility of a change of heart through hearing or reading the word. Let me explain.

Feeling is for Ricoeur integral to the act of schematizing the metaphoric meaning. When the imagination forms an image of the new predicative congruence, the emergent meaning is not fully objectified but is also *felt.* The hearer or reader is thereby assimilated to the meaning precisely as she or he performs the predicative assimilation. Ricoeur says, "We feel like what we see like" in metaphor, which in part means that the icon structures a mood.[26] What is more, feeling plays an important role in the imaginative projection of a new mode of being within the metaphorically formed world of the text. Just as the imagination suspends the first-order referential world when reading poetic texts, so imagination reverberates on feeling in order to affect an *epoché* of bodily emotions directed to literal objects. With the clearance of first-order feelings, a deeper attunement to being as such can come to the fore. The poetic experience thereby can "insert us within the world in a non-objectifying fashion."[27] In the act of appropriating the specifically metaphorical level of meaning—in which the *I* claims the emergent meaning as its own and the *I* is restructured affectively in accordance with that meaning—the real possibility for a positive change of heart appears. Let's see how this possibility plays out at the level of religious texts.

Religious texts are, for Ricoeur, biblical texts—namely, poetic texts with a difference. Ricoeur writes, "It is the naming of God by the biblical texts that specifies the religious at the interior of the poetic."[28] Ricoeur devotes considerable time analyzing the different subgenres of biblical language. Whereas poetic texts intend new modes of being, these religious texts intend the infinite source and goal of any possible mode of being, because they possess a reference to God within them. "The God-referent is at once the coordinator of these varied discourses and the index of their incompleteness, the point at which something escapes them."[29] The reference to God inverts the interpretive relationship: instead of interpreting the new mode of being in the world of the text, the reader finds his or her interpretive imagination thwarted and overturned. The God-referent interprets the reader's existence and is revelatory of it.[30] How does religious language modify poetic language in order to perform this inversion?

According to Ricoeur, poetic texts are models of redescription that are religiously modified by the presence of "limit-expressions." Limit-expressions function to transgress or overturn the normal course of metaphorical process and to intensify its effect so that forms of poetic language "converge upon an extreme point, which becomes their point of encounter with the infinite."[31] In his analyses of various New Testament texts, Ricoeur shows how the expression "Kingdom of God" functions as a limit-expression together with tropes of extravagance in the parables, techniques of overturning in the eschatological sayings, and instances of paradox and hyperbole in proverbial formulas. Through the use of limit-expressions, the interpretive intention *breaks out* of the closure of the narrative and the God-referent *breaks into* the act of interpretation. Let's focus more closely on the New Testament, which Ricoeur repeatedly cites as a paradigmatic religious text.

In the New Testament, Jesus as Christ is the teller of the parables, sayings, and formulas, which open up the God-referent in these texts. Jesus as Christ is also, however, the hero and hence subject of the inclusive New Testament passion narrative in which the parables, sayings, and formulas appear. Consequently, these texts individually and collectively refer the reader or hearer precisely to the new being of Jesus as Christ as revelatory of the being of God. The name *Christ* humanizes the infinitely self-negating Name of

God; the name *Christ* signifies the advent of a Wholly Other God from beyond the limits of human thinking. At the same time that the "Christ" of the gospels manifests what it means for God to be God, "Christ" reveals the transformed human being of the individual and collective readers or hearers. The name *Christ* discloses what it finally means to be human. Let's continue to reflect directly on Ricoeur's own use of limit-expressions in religious language, connecting them to the metaphoric process in poetic language in order to understand how this image may take on religious power.

We can quite properly view religious language as the body of a faith-community, wherein disclosures of divine being and new being can and do occur through biblical limit-expressions. Now, we know that limit-expressions both intensify and overturn the metaphorical process of imagining new possibilities to be—a process that occurs within the ethical aim of a human life defined through its moral striving. Religious limit-expressions add something to the capacity of metaphor to shape moral agency, to affect moral sentiments, and to provide a vision of the good life to the imagination. Within the corporate body of religious language, limit-expressions point to and actualize *limit-experiences*, which in the Christian context are encounters with the Christ figure of the Gospels.[32] What are these limit-experiences? Ricoeur himself does not say much to determine what he means by "limit-experience." In strict conceptual terms, limit-experiences are impossible experiences; they cannot be conceived because they arise outside the limits of thought. But religiously speaking, limit-experiences are necessary experiences; they give meaning and power to religious discourse precisely because they break into the structure of thinking from beyond it. The sought-for change of heart occurs on the basis of religious experience or not at all. At this point I propose to ask, Where and how does religious discourse take on power? I aim to give determinate content to the notion of limit-experiences by referring back to the limits of thinking and being articulated at the level of dialectic.

Recall the distinction between vertical and horizontal limits in Ricoeur. Vertically, Ricoeur establishes both a lower limit and an upper limit of thinking. The lower limit is the original ground or source of unity prior to difference; it signifies the goodness of creation prior to the separation of being and thinking. The upper limit is the final end of fully determinate unity; it signifies the highest good for moral striving—the restored unity between willing according to the moral law and justly deserved happiness. Limit-expressions testify to an experience that intensifies and overturns the ethical aim of human life. How can we conceive it?

We must start at the heart, with the affective conversion. For Ricoeur the New Testament narrative of the life, death, and resurrection of Jesus as Christ is a testimony of superabundant divine love. As a poetic text, it projects a possible mode of being that is not my own. For the sake of discussion, call this mode of being, with Ricoeur, "fallibility without fault," or the mode of timing all one's activities through the good will of moral regeneration or the mode of being of "openness to the good."

Now, at this point I want to carry my analysis somewhat beyond Ricoeur by means of Ricoeur. I propose that the limit-expressions within this narrative additionally function to make the signified mode of being into a sign with a metaphorical referent of its own—namely, the goodness of creation in undisrupted unity with the highest good of human moral striving. In other words, qualified by the limit-expression the mode of being depicted in the New Testament narrative can in turn point to the open horizon of being-itself within which any mode of being is possible. Further, the qualified mode of open being can summon that open horizon as the presence of an unthinkable God whose being is goodness. How does this happen? The metaphorical process of understanding the limit-expression coins an image in the mind of the hearer or reader, and this image in turn evokes a feeling of superabundant love as the *Selbstgefühl* of an inspired mood. The reader or hearer now identifies the mode of being called "fallibility without fault," a "good will," or simply "openness" as one's own. In appropriating this mood and stabilizing it in one's being through practice, a change of heart occurs and one's narrative identity is transformed. What we have traced so far is the inbreaking of religious power from beyond the limits into the human heart. I shall now extend this analysis to the horizontal limits of thinking.

If the vertical limits point to and manifest divine reality at the ground and height of finite reality, the horizontal limits reveal the right and the left hand of an image of a potentially transformed humanity. Recall the horizontal limits Ricoeur establishes in his analysis of theoretical, practical, and affective syntheses. Theoretically, the limits are saying and seeing (or thinking and being); practically, they are character and happiness (or who I am and who I could be); and affectively, they are spiritual feelings and sensible feelings (or intellectual beatitude and bodily pleasure). Critical thinking cannot in the nature of the case think these limits, yet the testimonies of religious imagination present us with an image that comes to it from beyond the limits of thinking. Can we think the content of a limit-experience on this horizontal axis?

The answer is again suggested by Ricoeur's dialectic, but it requires me to go further. I propose that rather than assuming that limit-expressions point to the polarized limit-concepts taken separately, we instead seek the reference of limit-expressions at the point of the fully differentiated unity of the limits on the right and left hands. If the New Testament narratives of Jesus the Christ poetically signify the mode of being of fallibility without fault, the qualifying limit-expressions, such as "Kingdom of God," point the religious imagination to this limit, where feeling can internalize the image formed. The image of humanity pleasing to God, for example, pushes us to imagine and to experience the consummate unity of thinking and being in one's cognitive capacity. It is to experience the unity of one's actual finite self and the open background of one's infinite happiness in one's practical capacity. It is to experience the unity of spiritual feelings and sensible feelings in one's affective capacity. This experience of the unity of finite opposites springs from the center of one's being, because each one of us already is that unity of opposites at the depth of our beings. That depth of being is the image of God within, the finite ground of the heart of gold. To appropriate this image, no matter how fleetingly and partially, and to claim it as one's own is to humanize divine grace. It is to be empowered by a living God.

The power of religion, I hold, is the power to intensify and to overturn the ethical aim of human life through encounter with the limits. What are some of the transformations of moral striving that can and do result from these experiences at the limit? An encounter with the power of religion can affect moral striving in these ways: First, experiencing and appropriating superabundant love can empower the original disposition to good, on the basis of receiving through the image of Christ a renewed experience of unbound freedom. Second, experience of religious power can produce or bring about the sense of happiness or flourishing as already here and no longer merely in the eschatological future. Love of life, not as a reward for accomplished duty, but as the basic attunement of a religious person transforms the will and its projects. Third, the virtues of self-esteem, friendship, and justice are similarly intensified and overturned through grace. No longer measured by a rule of reciprocity, these virtues can be transformed in the direction of agape. Fourth, the categorical imperative similarly is changed into the extravagant command to love one's enemies. Fifth, the call of conscience can now be heard not merely as the call to moral striving, but additionally as the call to bring God's abundant love into the world. The self-critical *phronimos* now brings a superabundant heart into the concrete situations that call for prudential decisions.

Let me conclude with some thoughts that go beyond biblical hermeneutics to philosophical theology.

Theology

First, I think that Ricoeur gives us some extremely powerful tools with which to think theologically the religious power that is ingredient in certain forms of discourse. However, I think that in appropriating Ricoeur for theology, it is important to remove the constriction Ricoeur places on religious discourse. Religious discourse in the nature of the case is not merely biblical discourse but any instance of language, which drives thinking and experiencing to the limits by means of limit-expressions. In addition, I think that it is important also to give a higher evaluation to meanings manifest in sacramental settings, where images and material symbols convey religious power. Ricoeur's magnificent essay "Manifestation and Proclamation" unfortunately subordinates the religious world in which the sacred is sacramentally present in symbolic things to the power of the proclaimed Word. I think, however, that dialectically speaking the sacramental word and the verbal sacrament are cooriginal and coequal. We have no dialectical warrant to diminish the powerful mysteries of sacraments and the materiality of bread and wine as symbols imparting religious power.

Second, I think that it is important for theological reasons to provide a deeper analysis of religious feeling in relation to dialectical thinking than Ricoeur does. The question here is whether religious feelings, which form the core of religious experiences and make possible any change of heart, should be thought as personal, private, and idiosyncratic or rather as somehow universal and necessary. In other words, can religious feelings be given dialectical justification? Let me attempt an answer.

Feeling has an intentional structure; feeling is not purely receptive, although the separation between the act of feeling and the object felt is minimal. In the case of religious discourse, what is felt is the meaning of some individual representation or mode of being; that is, its relation to the whole and manifestation of the absolute unity of opposites that is beyond the limits of thinking. Feelings of course include different contents. They can either be idiosyncratic for the person who has them (such as the feeling of conviction that might accompany private opinions or quirky maxims) or universal and necessary for all people (such as the feeling of conviction accompanying rules of logic and the moral law). What about the content of religious feeling—that is, the feeling accompanying religious power?

To justify the appeal to religious feeling as universal and necessary rather than personal and contingent, it is necessary to show precisely that the content of the feeling corresponds to a universal and necessary intentional object of the feeling. I propose that this task should be attempted at two levels. The first leads us to the most fundamental felt experience of being a self. Recall that for Ricoeur the human being is a mediating being—bringing about mediations between disproportionate opposites at theoretical, practical, and affective levels. Such mediations occur under the transcendental condition of what Schleiermacher calls feeling or immediate self-consciousness. The content of immediate self-consciousness is the same as in Fichte's notion of the intellectual intuition of the self-positing *I*. Immediate self-consciousness is the nonobjective, preconceptual, nonpropositional acquaintance of the subject with itself. Immediate self-consciousness is the essence of the finite subject as a self-positing that is a being-posited. Clearly, immediate self-consciousness is always already presupposed by any act of objective self-consciousness, but its meaning can also be hermeneutically mediated through the engagement of the imagination in deciphering texts, words, or images.

Immediate self-consciousness is not necessarily religious. It becomes so precisely with the felt insight that the self's positing itself as being posited is itself posited by the absolute ground and goal of all human thinking—that is, what Schleiermacher calls the Whence of the feeling of absolute dependence or "God." What does Schleiermacher mean by "religious feeling" so described? Ricoeur has the best answer. It is precisely the lived feeling—psychological and empirical—of the Joy of the Yes in the Sadness of the finite. The felt element of joy arises from the free activity of self-positing; the felt element of sadness arises from the sheer contingent givenness of being-posited. The felt element of Yes—the affirmation and love of life—grounds both joy and sadness. The Yes is the felt capacity to embrace both the joyful and the sorrowful. In its absence the self oscillates between joy and sadness—seeking joy, fleeing sadness. Together they constitute the feeling of the love of life, gratitude for the goodness of finite being. There is nothing arbitrary about this religious feeling; it expresses the dialectically conceived essence of the self. When it is aroused by religious discourse, we humans receive the religious power that can change the heart.

Finally, what about the God who is beyond the limits of thought? Should we abandon the living God, from whom religious power comes, as a regulative principle of thinking? Or should we keep an eye on God as an infinite vanishing point, perhaps calling God "X," or "Being" crossed-out, or simply the unknowable Whence of religious power? It is true that God appears to thinking at the limits of the structure of thinking, as the absolute ground or unity of all opposites—a necessary and universal ideal—albeit inconceivable. In metaphysical theology, this God was called Uncaused Cause, because it grounded the entire system of causation that determines finite human thinking, and critical reflection on causality removed the warrant for applying this or any other concept beyond the limits of thinking. But does it really make sense to think that the necessary idea of God as the absolute ground and goal of thinking within the limits bears no analogical similarity to the deep structure of being within which our thinking is embedded? I think not. If not, how could we conceive a possible analogy between the structure of religious feeling and the idea of God in order to give the idea content?

I understand that in a literal sense all we can think about God is the inability to think God as absolute unity of opposites. Thinking about God reveals a lack at the heart of thinking. But it is precisely this lack—this rigorous and necessary lack—that takes on power when brought into meaningful correspondence with the religious feeling of holy awe at the joy and sadness at the heart of the human creature. In our failure to think the being of God we have too little from which to make a theology. In our felt response to the living God of religious power, we have too much from which to make a theology. But in the relation of the too little and the too much, we might indeed have enough to reflect meaningfully on the theological meaning of religious experiences through words and sacramental things.

Notes

1. Friedrich Schleiermacher lectured on the topic of dialectic at the University of Berlin in the years 1811, 1814, 1818, 1822, 1828, and 1831. He always intended to prepare these lectures for publication, and he produced an introduction to his intended book in 1834, but he died before seeing the project through to completion. Editions of the lecture notes, supplemented by student notes, are as follows. *Dialektik* (1811), ed. Andreas Arndt (Hamburg: Felix Meiner Verlag, 1986); *Dialektik* (1814), ed. Andreas Arndt (Hamburg: Felix Meiner Verlag, 1988); *Dialektik* (1814): *Aus Schleiermachers handschriftlichem Nachlasse*, ed. L. Jonas (Berlin: Reimer, 1839) (in *Sämmtliche Werke, Part III*, vol. 4, pt. 2); *Dialektik* (1822), ed. R. Odebrecht (Leipzig: Hinrichs, 1942; reprint Darmstadt: Wissenschaftliche Buchgesellschaft, 1976); *Dialektik* (1831), ed. Halpern (Berlin, 1903), *Dialektik* (1814), ed. Andreas Arndt (Hamburg: Felix Meiner Verlag, 1988).
2. Other major philosophers may have used other terms—Fichte has his *Wissenschaftslehre*, Hegel has his *Logic*, Heidegger has his fundamental ontology—but in these and other cases we find dialectic renamed.
3. Friedrich Schleiermacher, *Hermeneutics and Criticism*, trans. and ed. Andrew Bowie (Cambridge: Cambridge University Press, 1998), p. 7.
4. Paul Ricoeur, *The Symbolism of Evil: Philosophy of the Will*, vol. 2, pt. 2, trans. Emerson Buchanan (Boston: Beacon Press, 1967), pp. 3–10, 347–57. See also Paul Ricoeur, *Critique and Conviction*, trans. Kathleen Blamey (New York: Columbia University Press, 1998), chap. 7: "Biblical Readings and Meditations," pp. 139–70.
5. *Fallible Man: Philosophy of the Will*, vol. 2, pt. 2, trans. Charles Kelbley (Chicago: Henry Regnery Company, 1965).
6. Ibid., p. 6.
7. See, for example, Paul Ricoeur, "A Philosophical Interpretation of Freud," in *The Conflict of Interpretations: Essays in Hermeneutics*, ed. Don Ihde (Evanston, IL: Northwestern University Press), pp. 173–76.
8. Paul Ricoeur, *Freud and Philosophy: An Essay on Interpretation*, trans. Denis Savage (New Haven and London: Yale University Press, 1970), p. 43.
9. See the important pages in Paul Ricoeur, "The Hermeneutics of Symbols: II," in *The Conflict of Interpretations*, pp. 326–30. The quoted term *forgetfulness* is on p. 328.
10. Ricoeur, *Fallible Man*, p. 223.
11. Ricoeur, *The Symbolism of Evil*, p. 8.
12. Ibid., p. 9
13. Ricoeur, *Fallible Man*, p. xxiii
14. Ibid., p. 221
15. Ibid., p. 215
16. Immanuel Kant, *Religion within the Boundaries of Mere Reason*, ed. Allen Wood and George di Giovanni (Cambridge: Cambridge University Press, 1998), pp. 50–55.
17. Ibid., pp. 44–59.
18. Paul Ricoeur, "Freedom in Light of Hope," in *The Conflict of Interpretations*, pp. 416–22.

19. See Paul Ricoeur, "The Problem of the Foundation of Moral Theory," *Philosophy Today* 22 (fall 1978): 175–92.
20. Paul Ricoeur, *Oneself as Another*, trans. Kathleen Blamey (Chicago and London: University of Chicago Press), 1990.
21. Ibid., p. 172.
22. See Paul Ricoeur, "A Philosophical Hermeneutics of Religion: Kant," in *Figuring the Sacred: Religion, Narrative, and Imagination*, trans. David Pellauer and ed. Mark I. Wallace (Minneapolis: Augsburg Fortress, 1995), pp. 75–92.
23. Ibid., p. 75.
24. Kant, *Religion within the Boundaries of Mere Reason*, p. 80.
25. Paul Ricoeur, "The Metaphorical Process as Cognition, Imagination, and Feeling," *Critical Theory* 5, no. 1 (1978).
26. Ibid., p. 156.
27. Ibid., p. 157.
28. Paul Ricoeur, "Naming God," *Union Seminary Quarterly Review* 34, no. 4 (1979): 219.
29. Paul Ricoeur, "Philosophy and Religious Language," *Journal of Religion* 54 (1974): 83.
30. Paul Ricoeur, "Philosophische und theologische Hermeneutik," *Evangelische Theologie* (Sonderheft 1974): 40.
31. Paul Ricoeur, *Essays on Biblical Hermeneutics*, ed. and intro. Lewis S. Mudge (Philadelphia: Fortress Press, 1980), p. 109.
32. Ricoeur, *Figuring the Sacred*, pp. 61–81, 95, 234.
33. Ibid., pp. 48–67.

7
Starry Heavens and Moral Worth
Hope and Responsibility in the Structure of Theological Ethics[1]

WILLIAM SCHWEIKER

Ethics and the Space of Reasons

The title of this essay recalls the famous words of Immanuel Kant. Two things, Kant said, filled him with unending wonder, the starry heavens above him and the moral law within him. Aside from expressing a profound grasp of the dignity of human existence and the grandeur of nature, these words inscribe a major issue for modern ethics. The space of reasons about human action, and thus the realm wherein the moral law reigns, is seemingly forever and necessarily distinct from causal laws that explain natural events. The human mind is strung between, on the one hand, theoretical and empirical knowledge, and, on the other hand, capacities for practical reasoning. Of course, it might have been the case that in more "religious ages" there was some coherence between the natural and moral orders, some synthesis obtained in myth and ritual between God, human, and cosmos. But the religious synthesis did not survive the modern world.[2] The breakdown of this synthesis between a natural and a moral order has led to unending debate about how, if at all, one can articulate the relation between moral values and norms and claims about the workings of the natural world, including basic features of human existence. The burden of human existence, if the breakdown of a religious synthesis is the defining fact of modernity, is to create value within the senseless expanse of reality rather than seeking to discern and enact the moral order of reality.

While nature and the moral life might inspire wonder, most of modern ethics is characterized by the insistence that nature and morals, scientific rationality and practical reason, or (abstractly stated) being and goodness, remain distinct. My concern in this essay is to enter the debate about the modern consensus in ethics in terms of its most recent expression. With the help of Paul Ricoeur, I want to show how hope and responsibility designate *in nuce* different, even competing accounts of the moral space of life that address, albeit in different ways, the modern consensus about the separation of being and goodness. In this way, discourse about hope and responsibility enables us to probe the task of ethics at the far end of the modern project.[3]

In order to begin the inquiry, I want in the next section to clarify in more detail the current debate within ethics. With that background in hand, I then turn in the third section to Ricoeur's ethics in order to unfold within his work ideas about hope and responsibility. This will enable me to isolate Ricoeur's contribution to moral reflection. This essay concludes by striking out in a new direction in the attempt to overcome a possible return to the modern lacuna between being and goodness seemingly still present in Ricoeur's work. In a word, I seek to press forward the enterprise of theological ethics. And while my argument moves beyond, and at points against, Ricoeur's ethics, my debt and gratitude to him remain obvious.[4]

Conflicting Moral Outlooks

The ideas of hope and responsibility dominated mid- to late-twentieth-century Western conceptions of human existence. The importance of hope was given its most resounding expression by Ernst Bloch and within theology by Jürgen Moltmann in the 1960s in his famous *Theology of Hope*. Moltmann argued that after ages in which love and faith dominated the religious life, our time, marred by massive violence and eschatological anticipation, can ponder the divine reality and human life in terms of hope. Hope is the driving force of human initiative. Temporally speaking, the future, not the past or present, is decisive. Moltmann joined others, notably Bloch, in the work of ideology critique. The hoped-for future functions, as a counterfactual state of affairs, to provide critical distance on present life in order to isolate political and ideological distortions. Theologically construed, the inbreaking of the reign of God exposes the oppression of the present and liberates one to act. God is in front of us, Johann Baptist Metz insisted.[5] Christian theology explores how the resurrection—the absolute future—founds a dialectic between hope and the dangerous memory of Christ disruptive of the present. The coming absolute future undercuts any closed system—social or conceptual—based on the past or the present. Thus, the theology of hope gives priority to promise, not presence, and to the resurrection as the God "who comes" rather than the God "who is." This means a virtual rejection of all claims about the priority of creation to hope within theology. The banishment of the good from present being was tied to an account of time.

Phenomenologically considered, hope discloses the inner meaning of freedom as the power to transgress the captivity of life by desire, social systems, ideologies, and even death. Hope is not so much about the explication of actions; it is much more about creating a new and novel space for the very possibility of human flourishing. Hope bears the mark of the future irrupting in the present with new possibilities for life. As a passion for the possible, freedom in this form is, for Ricoeur, the capacity of "denying death and asserting the excess of sense over non-sense in all desperate situations."[6] Voices arising from prison camps and the survivors of violent relations testify that the loss of hope sinks life into the necessity of a closed present. Without hope, life is servile and freedom formless. This is why Christians—as well as Jews and Muslims and others—place their hope in a reality that cannot be grasped under the structures of present reality but must present itself, disclose itself, in coming to us. Hope lays hold of an expected reality, something or someone coming—the *adventus bonum*. Hope is a genuine gift; it subverts the strict demands of reciprocity.[7] As Ricoeur says, hope follows a unique logic of superabundance that bursts the demands of retributive justice.

Philosophers and theologians of hope insisted that the principle of intelligibility is openness to a future that delimits the present. In other words, the phenomenon of hope discloses that "thinking" is not defined by or limited to an analysis of causal laws, what is empirically given, or the a priori structure of thought needed to grasp those laws and events. Arising within our lives as practical beings, hope transgresses the epistemic limits outlined by Kant, even within his wonder about the starry heavens above. Not surprisingly, thinking that is defined by the logic of hope manifests a distinctive relation between theory and practice. Praxis is basic to thinking insofar as the principle of intelligibility is an open future that must be enacted rather than given in structures to be theorized. The norm of praxis—itself not an actual state of affairs—is what enables one to grasp genuine possibilities. We can call this norm the utopic principle of thought. Further, thinking moved by hope, under a utopic principle, and grounded in praxis is radically critical. It seeks to unfold the future as the condition of the possibility of thought and life. In this way an ethics of hope provides an account of our existence in the world as willing agents; it discloses within the limits of the present the conditions of freedom. To be human is to harken the destruction of tyranny; it is to be a harbinger of the possible.

What then of responsibility? Like hope, the idea of responsibility has dominated much twentieth-century ethical and theological reflection. The language of responsibility designates, if nothing else, the fact that we exist in a space of questions and reasons for conduct in which, come what may, we must orient our lives. The acts of assigning or assuming responsibility entail explications of action and patterns of human relations; responsibility is a way of reason giving about the shape and tenure of our actual lives. Yet while virtually all theorists of responsibility would accept these basic points, there is considerable difference among thinkers about how best to specify the nature and scope of human responsibility.[8]

Some thinkers, like the Jewish philosopher Emmanuel Levinas, speak of an infinite responsibility for the other.[9] Under the pressure of planetary endangerment, the Roman Catholic theologian Hans Küng and other religious and secular thinkers call for global responsibility and responsibility for the future.[10] For others, as diverse as Karl Barth and H. Richard Niebuhr, "responsibility" focuses on responsiveness to the other in patterns of interaction, or, as Barth put it, the command of God.[11] At issue is what or who makes a rightful claim on our lives and how best to live in responsiveness. Anglo-American philosophers like Marion Smiley, Peter French, and John Martin Fisher hold that responsibility is about the freedom or power of an agent to be accountable for their actions.[12] From this perspective the nature of action, freedom, and determinacy, as well as patterns of ascribing accountability occupy attention. Responsibility for actions, rather than responsiveness to the other, is the center of ethics.

Despite differences among theorists of responsibility, the basic point is that this moral outlook entails a distinctive account of our being moral creatures. Whereas Kantian-style ethics conceives of human beings under duties and virtue theory focuses on patterns of self-formation and well-being, the ethics of responsibility pictures humans as creatures existing in patterns of interaction. Responsiveness to others and responsibility for acts of power bespeak a mode of moral being extended into the future and receptive to others. But this means that an ethics of responsibility awakens us from the existentialist bacchanalia of freedom in which, as Jean-Paul Sartre put it, the will is sovereign over existence. Whether one insists on otherness or the command of God, the point for responsibility ethics is that the human will cannot leap into action unencumbered by what it encounters. We have some capacity to choose how to act amid the limitations on our freedom by the reality of others. Attention is directed to concrete others and accountability for specific courses of action. Responsibility to particular others, rather than pure duty, is the heart of the moral life.[13]

The importance of hope and responsibility in current thought bespeaks a tension at the core of human existence. I have intimated this tension with reference to different ethical positions. Descriptively, human beings strive to enact a future as well as exist in matrices of interaction and accountability. An ethics of hope articulates how practical freedom triumphs over the immersion of life in the necessary. In this triumph is an opening to claims about the future and even the coming God. Hope configures an openness in the very structure of thinking beyond the modern empirical and transcendental limits on knowing. Yet we should also note that "hope" entails a denial of any substantive contribution to ethics of reflection on creation or natural constitutions including our bodies. An ethics of responsibility, conversely, contends that all human willing is within the sphere of interaction and demand. The demand uttered in God's command or the face of the other manifests the depth and scope of worth beyond our projects. In this way, the language of responsibility denotes a break with the modern, Kantian claim that the "moral law within" is definable in terms of the self-relation of practical reason in the act of legislating maxims for action. If hope discloses the structure of thinking to be openness to the future, then responsibility exposes the self as constituted in responsiveness to past, present, and future others.

These alternative discourses of hope and responsibility are often at odds. From the perspective of an ethics of responsibility, an ethics centered on hope risks a denial of the concrete, the given, in the race for the utopic. Hope seems to drain concrete life of worth and collapse all value into our projects. But in view of hope, an ethics of responsibility might well be trapped in the grinding logic of equivalence. These stances taken alone say something true about life and yet seem to falter in giving a complete picture of moral existence. How then are we to carry on moral inquiry? With this question we return, perhaps surprisingly, to the modern consensus in ethics inscribed in Kant's words about the moral law and starry heavens. We also move a step closer to Ricoeur's ethics. The central conviction of the modern consensus is that ethics, and so moral reason, can and must get along without making substantive ontological claims about the good.[14] And no less than the debate about hope and responsibility, contemporary thinkers are divided about the relation, if any, of goodness to being.

One extreme of the debate is found among thinkers deeply concerned about the "other" and troubled by the legacy of ontotheology in totalistic systems of thought. Levinas, Jean-Luc Marion, and perhaps Jacques Derrida argue for good beyond being. Ethics is first philosophy, Levinas insists. The moral life centers on an infinite demand of responsibility for the other. Yet, ironically, one cannot speak of the being of the other as good. The drive of reason to specify the being of the other is characterized by totalizing ontology that, ironically, always effaces the moral claims of responsibility. These thinkers banish from ethics the connection of being and goodness and thus continue some form of the modern consensus. At the other extreme of the debate are those who insist on some kind of ontological ethics. For these thinkers moral rationality reaches into the very nature of things. Philosophers like Hans Jonas, Erazim Kohák, Iris Murdoch, and others herald a moral sense of nature or attention to the real, especially other persons. The moral law "bids us to honor the intrinsic claim of Being," as Jonas puts it.[15] To exist is good, and this goodness, graspable by human reason, grounds moral responsibility. Importantly, the idea of responsibility is basic to each of these options in ethics. The path beyond the modern consensus in ethics takes different directions: some thinkers deepen the rupture between goodness and being, while others seek to overcome it.

This brings us to the specific task of the remainder of the present inquiry. With some sense of the importance of hope and responsibility in contemporary discourse, I intend to engage Ricoeur's work with respect to the debate within ethics about being and goodness.[16] I believe this complex of issues (hope/responsibility; being/goodness) exposes Ricoeur's contribution for moving beyond the modern consensus but also the deepest ambiguity in his ethics. According to Ricoeur, philosophical thinking under the claim of hope is always on the way to ontology. The same would seem to be true of responsibility. The one to whom we respond is an actual existing self, a bearer of intrinsic worth, that we can and must respect and enhance. Insofar as we are responsible, we endorse the reality of moral worth in the world. This double focus about being and goodness is most obvious in the tenth study of *Oneself as Another*, "What Ontology in View?," in which Ricoeur unfolds ideas of responsibility and conscience.[17]

Ricoeur seems to weave a path between other options in ethics: thought aims at understanding being; the moral life entails responsibility for the other. Our concern for hope and responsibility draws us into debates about axiology, theory of value, and ontology in ethics. Yet while Ricoeur's work appears to mediate the debate in current thought, his account of the structure of thinking risks a return to the modern consensus in ethics. The goodness of being, even the other to whom I am responsible, is beyond thought. In *Oneself as Another* he calls this the "aporia of the Other." But is it the case, finally, that moral reason is limited in this way?

One must appreciate Ricoeur's attempt to navigate the thorny question of the connection between being and goodness. But, sadly, I judge we must depart his company on precisely this point, or, at the very least, radically extend the ethics.[18] This departure entails a different account of the connection of morals and religion as well as insistence on ontological claims within ethics. That is, Ricoeur's account of thinking seems to disallow a robust, nonreductionistic naturalism in ethics, since, as disclosed by hope, the very structure of philosophical thinking must remain open and not reduce the future to claims about present reality. And yet it is equally true that his account of responsibility for self and for other seems, at least at the level of a theory of value, to require claims about the goodness of being and so some kind of naturalism in ethics. It is then the tension between thinking and valuing, hope and responsibility, that opens up within Ricoeur's thought the demand for new directions in ethics. Of course, the route to axiological claims is always interpretive. As philosophers and theologians have long insisted, people do not see the good like other perceptible objects. We must examine symbolic forms, texts, narratives in order to explicate something about worth in the world.[19] Nevertheless, the high-sounding rhetoric about the claim of the other remains ethically meaningless without some way of showing that the worth of finite being in all of its vulnerability can and may and must evoke a sense of responsibility.

Like most arguments surrounding basic principles in ethics, my argument rests on a basic intuition. A primary datum of our lives as acting, bodily beings seems to be an enduring love of life. While some people claim to hate life, John Lachs is surely right that a "universal hatred of life seems . . . to be beyond our power. . . . The enemies of existence, therefore, love themselves while they loathe many, most, or all others."[20] A robust ethics of responsibility requires, in the face of suffering and violence, a primary conviction about the goodness of incarnate being and hence the love of life grasped in symbolic presentation. A central purpose of this essay is then to articulate this conviction, realizing that debates about the range and kinds of basic human goods must be left aside for the moment.[21] Stated otherwise, it is my contention that at the root of the very structure of thinking is responsiveness to or intuition of the worth of life (what Ricoeur might call a primary attestation) within which moral actions and relations in a narrow sense are understood and our experience of hope rendered intelligible.

While I depart from Ricoeur on the connection between ontology and axiology, I will do so, importantly, along lines suggested by his own work. As will become clear, my intention is to exploit an undeveloped connection in Ricoeur's thought in order to articulate the goodness of being in spite of evil. He claims that hope is given philosophical expression as "regeneration" and even, borrowing from St. Paul, "new creation" (cf. 2 Corinthians 5:17; Galatians 6:15). Ricoeur further argues that creation, linked to the love of enemy, backs the supreme moral principle, the Golden Rule. However, he does not, as far as I can see, delineate the connection between creation and new creation in the direction of moral realism. Insofar as the structure of thinking is defined by hope, then a robust naturalism is hardly possible. My tactic, then, is to think with and yet beyond Ricoeur on this point. I want to articulate via the idea of responsibility an affirmation of creation and also the richness of "new creation" as an object of hope. In this way, we can situate hope within a realistic ethics of responsibility. And this saves ethics from a return to the modern consensus within which moral values are, in the Humean strand of modern ethics, reports of preferences and desires lacking in cognitive content, or, in Kantian-style ethics, somehow separable from the question of the validity of norms about reciprocity.

Ricoeur: Hope and Responsibility

With the dispute about hope and responsibility as well as being and goodness in hand, I turn now to Ricoeur's complex, dialectical moral philosophy. The tensions he seeks to mediate are well-known and oft discussed: deontology and teleology; love and justice; esteem and respect; self and other; Kant and Aristotle. Rather than focusing on those mediations, I intend to read Ricoeur from the center of his moral concern: the problem of evil and violence rooted in the fragile noncoincidence of the self with itself. That is to say, I intend to examine his ethics along the lines of his work on human fallibility—namely, evil, violence, and gift. This should allow us to isolate the point in Ricoeur's ethics that threatens us with a return to the modern consensus about the necessary separation between ontological and axiological claims.

Hope, Evil, and Philosophical Systems

Ricoeur explores hope with respect to the structure of philosophical systems.[22] Unlike Descartes or Husserl, Ricoeur is concerned with the closing point or horizon of philosophical discourse. Yet he does not seek, as Hegel did, a complete system, closed to itself. Ricoeur asks the question of system from the practical perspective of our lives as willing creatures who must appropriate possible ways of life. Philosophy articulates the fallible but also projective character of human life. At the core of human existence is imagination as the capacity both to interpret symbolic language and to appropriate possible modes of being projected by such texts.

According to Ricoeur, at issue most profoundly in the question of the structure of philosophical systems is an unfulfilled claim and an admission of human limits. The claim is the requirement of a totality of meaning, of sense, with respect to our lives as agents who are able to fulfill purposes.[23] We act intentionally and as such implicitly endorse in our acting a condition in which purpose and reality become one. People want to bring about the existence of projects; we want to accomplish goals. We strive to make our desires real, give them existence. As Ricoeur puts this in *Oneself as Another*, self-esteem is linked to our capacity to realize projects. And yet, there are genuine limits to any simple or ready isomorphism of purpose and existence. The limit is not due to our failure to achieve goals because of ignorance, misfortune, or folly. As Aristotle already noted, ignorance, fate, and the like can in some circumstances render human action "involuntary" and thus not open to full ethical assessment. But for Ricoeur, and Kant before him, at issue is more radical disjunction in human action. There is, Ricoeur writes, "something broken in the very heart of human action that prevents our partial experience of fulfilled achievements from being equated with the whole field of human action."[24] In order to explore that brokenness in its most extreme form, Ricoeur adopts a Kantian-like account of evil. "If evil resides somewhere," Ricoeur notes, "it is surely in the maxims of our actions, by means of which we hierarchize our preferences, placing duty above desire, or desire above duty. Evil, in fact, consists in a reversal of priority, an inversion or subversion on the plane of the maxims of action."[25] The mystery of evil bespeaks an unfilled claim upon us for meaning but also a limit, a surd, in the very heart of action that shatters all thought. Is the human demand of meaning to remain unfulfilled?

Ricoeur turns to the symbolism of hope in the face of the surd of unfilled meaning. This symbolism denotes an excess, a superabundance, of sense that meets the rational, human demand of a totality of meaning. "Hope means," Ricoeur writes, "the 'superabundance' of meaning as opposed to the abundance of senselessness, of failure, of destruction."[26] We could say that hope is the saturation of experience by a power not our own but manifest in our lives and witnessed to in religious discourse. At the core of practical existence, hope is a yes to reality, a love of life, in spite of its brokenness. Importantly, Ricoeur's account of hope approximates the eschatological event—the resurrection of Christ—at the center of the theology of hope. As he notes, the argument moves from the destruction of absolute knowledge approximating sin and redemption, through a claim about the connection between purity of heart and the fulfillment of desire in an idea of the highest good, and onward to the meeting of these reflections in the idea of regeneration. As the philosophical approximation of hope, regeneration is the transformation of the will in the face of evil. As Ricoeur notes, "hope makes of freedom the passion for the possible against the sad meditation on the irrevocable. This passion for the possible is the answer of hope to all Nietzschean love of destiny, to all worship of fate, to all *amor fati*."[27] Like all theologians of hope, Ricoeur explicitly rejects the "idols of a cosmological vision," any appeal to being, nature, or reality to fund moral projects.

Hope articulates the horizon of thinking vis-à-vis the problem of evil. That is to say, hope answers a failure in the ethical aim of leading a good life, a failure that arises out of human fallibility but centers on the problem of evil. In this respect, we are at the turning point between "ethics" and "morals," as Ricoeur uses these terms.[28] And yet this turning point is fraught with ambiguity insofar as "morality" is not simply a matter of our aims but our response to others. Yet insofar as Ricoeur insists that hope is an answer to any love of destiny, a suspicion arises from the perspective of an ethics of responsibility important for the domain of morals. Does the brokenness and radical finitude of actual life, even the presence of evil in the world, make creatures unfit objects of love? Can we redeem a love of being in the face of evil without a fall into a Nietzschean consent to destiny or a totalized system? The next step in our inquiry is to trace the shift from hope and the structure of thinking to Ricoeur's ethics. "There are morals," Ricoeur insists, "because there is violence, which is itself multiform."[29] The shift from evil to violence would seem to make responsibility, not hope, basic in ethics. It would seem to signal openness to claims about the goodness of the being of the other.

Violence, Responsibility, and the Principle of Morality

Ricoeur insists that the Golden Rule (do unto others as you would have done unto you) is the supreme moral principle. That is to say, the Golden Rule specifies the test through which all our intended actions must pass if they are to be deemed right and just. Morality is, we might say, a moment of critical distanciation within our ethical lives, a deontic moment in which we are bid to test maxims and intentions with respect to our primal relation to others. Granting differences between Matthew's positive statement and Luke's negative formulas (cf. Matthew 7:12; Luke 6:31), this rule is located in what each Gospel presents as the epitome of Jesus' teaching—namely, the Sermon on the Mount and the Sermon on the Plain. One must explore the Golden Rule set "in the perspective delimited by the symbolic order underlying the Jewish and Christian Scripture."[30] In doing so, Ricoeur rightly links the rule to the radical demand to love one's enemies expressing a logic of superabundance that parallels the dynamics of hope. However, we must note that what Ricoeur does not see is that already within Jewish thought the command is tied to creation and Torah (cf. Leviticus 19:18) as the background to Christ's teaching. As the New Testament scholar Hans Dieter Betz has put it, "how do you love your neighbor? Look at creation: this is the way God loves the neighbor. God provides the bounty of life even to the enemy, to the rebellious and ungrateful humans."[31] In this symbolic light, I will set forth later the connection between creation and new creation. On the way to that point, we must grasp Ricoeur's argument.

According to Ricoeur, the Golden Rule enjoys three advantages over the Kantian categorical imperative as the best articulation of the supreme principle of morality. First, the Golden Rule focuses on the intersubjective nature of human action rather than autonomy and maxims of action. Whereas the categorical imperative might make sense at the level of thinking, and so the problem of evil is rooted in the subversion of maxims for action, in terms of human conduct one must stress relations between persons. For the "Golden Rule" it is not "humanity" (that is, the idea of rational freedom) in persons that is the focus of moral concern; what matters morally is the different and unique character of individuals. This makes the problem of actual "violence," rather than wrongful maxims per se, the central moral challenge.

A second advantage of the Golden Rule is that it centers on fears and desires. Kant sought to exclude reference to desire in the formulation of the categorical imperative in order to escape heteronomy. The price of this move is twofold: (1) it renders the categorical imperative formal in that it must be the "form" of any possible maxim of action to be moral; (2) it asserts that, morally speaking, reason as such must be the spring of action. Practical reason is conceived as a law-giving faculty, and Kant formulates his idea of practical reason seemingly abstracted from other features of distinctly human life. In other words, Kant's account of moral motivation is such that, in genuinely moral action, there is but one valid source of action (reason) and what determines the morality of a maxim of action is the form of the categorical imperative. Given his account of human fallibility, Ricoeur cannot endorse an ethics in which there is a simple coincidence of thought and desire. For him there is a noncoincidence between thinking and desiring that requires recognition of fallibility. Unlike Kantian rationalism, Ricoeur further acknowledges (rightly, I judge) multiple sources of action, including a moral act. The Golden Rule, with its concern for what is desired or feared, locates morality within the scope of basic human goods. Goods implied in our action as rational agents must be protected and promoted. Even though Ricoeur does not develop the idea of basic goods, it is clear that unjustified violence against these goods is immoral.

A third advantage of the Golden Rule over the categorical imperative brings us to moral responsibility. By focusing on human interaction as well as presuming basic goods, the Golden Rule "emphasizes the fundamental asymmetry between what someone *does* and what *is done* to another." The other, Ricoeur insists, "is potentially the victim of my action as much as its adversary."[32] The Golden Rule, centered on interaction, presupposes not only intersubjectivity and basic goods, but the power to act and the potential exercise of power over others. Whereas Kant provided a imperative to thwart desire's heteronomy in the will, the Golden Rule aims to thwart the tyranny of power on and over others. At issue is what someone does and what is done to another, an agent and a patient. The other person is potentially beloved, victim, or adversary. The moral life is about taking responsibility for the welfare of others within just institutions. The self is summoned to responsibility, as Ricoeur puts it in *Oneself as Another*. And conscience is where the obligation to the other resonates within the self. It signifies, he notes, "being enjoined as the structure of selfhood."[33] What must be grasped, I submit, is that for Ricoeur conscience in the domain of human interactions is correlate to imagination in the structure of thinking. Conscience designates one's being enjoined; imagination opens thinking to the horizon of human possibilities.

It is on these various levels of the Golden Rule—intersubjectivity, motivation and goods, and the connection between conscience and responsibility—that I will later need to revise Ricoeur's proposal for ethics. However, at this juncture in our inquiry we must note a challenge to the Golden Rule as the most apt formulation of the principle of morality. As theorists note, the Golden Rule rests on a suppressed premise, namely the good will.[34] It should read: Do unto others as you *ought* to have done to you. The evil will can endorse ill to itself and thereby legitimate violence under the requirement of universalizability. The horror of this possibility is seen, for example, in Adolf Eichmann, the Nazi, adamant in the face of war crimes that he followed the categorical imperative. Kant was aware of this dilemma. The moral law presumes that for which it is the norm: the good will. This is why Kant explored radical evil and moral regeneration not as a matter for ethics but as a religious topic. Ricoeur also takes the problem of the will with utter seriousness. His response to this challenge is also religious.

The Hypermoral Economy of Gift

I have been exploring levels of Ricoeur's ethics consistent with his work on human fallibility. We have traveled from hope within the structure of thinking through the Golden Rule in terms of human action to arrive at motive and desire in affective life. Now we must grasp the incapacity of the will to act on the Golden Rule given the reality of human fault and evil. Like Kant, the problem of evil in Ricoeur's thought is the connecting point of morality and religion, responsibility and hope.

Recall that Kant tries to answer human fault solely at the level of practical reason. Specifically, Kant insisted that the *idea* of a redeemer, the symbol of Christ as "humanity agreeable to God," can guide the labor of moral self-transformation. In terms of moral theory, this is one reason why Kantianism exemplifies the modern banishment of ontology from ethics. Insofar as the answer to fallibility and evil is delivered within practical reason, morality is vindicated on rational grounds without appeal to reality, God, or human nature. Can the structure of thinking as Ricoeur outlines it through hope perform the work of regeneration and vindicate the moral law?

In his recent writings, Ricoeur addresses the condition necessary to surmount the evil will in what he calls "the economy of the gift." He does so, significantly for me, with respect to the symbolism of creation. The face-to-face interaction of agent and patient governed by the Golden Rule is set within an environment—creation—that evokes, at the affective level, respect, admiration, and solicitude.[35] "The sense of our radical dependence on a higher power," Ricoeur writes, "thus may be reflected in a love of the creature, for every creature, in every creature—and the love of neighbor can become an expression of this supramoral love for all creatures."[36] Ricoeur examines religious symbolism for a power to evoke the desire to abide by the moral law in the face of evil, violence, and unrelenting self-interest. But note: it is the *sense* of creation and not the reality of finite being's worth that is of central concern. What is crucial for Ricoeur, so it seems, is a transformation of disposition and not the recognition of objective goodness. "Creation" as a symbol is about sensibility and subjective change and not axiology; that is, it is not a claim about the ontological status of value in the world. Put more precisely, the symbol of creation seems to reduce value to sensibility and thereby qualify real or objective value. At the very least, the ontological import of sensibility needs to be clarified.[37] This designates one point where we must, I submit, move beyond the confines of Ricoeur's ethics. It returns us to the modern debate in ethics about being and goodness noted at the outset of our inquiry.

Ricoeur argues that the symbol of creation is moral because it joins the idea of power with goodness. God creates, is sovereign, and yet recognizes, if we follow the biblical Genesis account, the goodness of what is other (cf.

Genesis 1:31). A sense of dependence on this God can, but need not, engender a love of being. Yet Ricoeur also insists that creation is supramoral in that it, as well as Torah and redemption, is not inscribed within the logic of equivalence, the demand of justice. The creature makes no valid demand on the divine for its existence or its ultimate redemption. These are gifts. In terms of the moral life, the supramoral character of creation comes pointedly to expression in the superabundant logic of love of enemies that can regenerate the will. Recall Hans Dieter Betz: God loves the neighbor by providing the bounty of life even to the enemy and thereby seeks conversion. Ricoeur is clear, of course, that radical love cannot be severed from the Golden Rule lest it risk becoming nonmoral or even immoral (say, in extreme self-sacrifice or the nondefense of the innocent). One must hold in tension unilateral love and bilateral justice.

How does this account of creation help to answer the question we are pursuing—namely, the problem of motive to abide by the Golden Rule? How does it relate to the larger question about an ontology of good? Whereas for Kant the religious is operative in the imagination of practical reason, Ricoeur focuses on the "sense" of religious experience backing the claim of conscience. This sense, as he puts it, is "the conjunction between a reverential humility and a compassion without limits in the benevolence of the all-powerful."[38] The symbolism of creation discloses a power working for moral regeneration at the level of sensibility. The economy of gift saturates affective experience, and, in principle, empowers one to act upon the Golden Rule motivated by a love of others. If hope is the triumph of sense over non-sense under the demand for meaning, then love of creatures is, I suggest, the victory of good will over the reality of violence under the dictates of the moral law.

The object of this religious sensibility that converts the evil will is, if I understand Ricoeur rightly, the conjunction of God as creator, the origin of being and goodness, and the God of hope, the source of unknown possibilities. Originary affirmation and eschatological hope meet in the supreme configuration or symbol of faith, God. "The God of beginnings is the God of hope," he says. However, Ricoeur adds that "because God is the God of hope, the goodness of creation becomes the sense of a direction."[39] Hope preserves the sense of directionality to the goodness of creation in spite of evil. The symbolism of creation, wherein power and goodness are joined, and eschatology, a source of unknown possibilities, infuse affective experience transforming moral motivation. This can only be the case because the very structure of thinking and the structure of the self as enjoined are symbolically united in God and "felt" in hope, humility, reverence, and compassion. Ricoeur seems to redeem a love of being beyond Nietzschean consent to destiny and also to escape the modern banishment of ontology from ethics. That is, unlike Nietzschean Yes-saying to reality, the love of being is tied for

Ricoeur not to the will to power or *amor fati*, the love of fate. Ricoeur seems to infuse within ethics an ontologically rich account of the good.

If only this ontology of value truly represented Ricoeur's ethics! I judge that it does not. Oddly enough, for Ricoeur creation with its rich symbolics about the depth of worth and the love of creatures derives *moral direction* from hope. Because of this fact, I submit that in an unstated way the suspicion of a theology of hope about creation uncovered earlier in this essay remains firmly in place within Ricoeur's ethics. Insofar as the symbol of creation must in the face of violence be redeemed by hope, then the very structure of thought dictates limits on what can be said about the goodness of existence and the love of life. Thinking triumphs over the affectivities that sustain it. Ricoeur's longstanding critique of totalized systems and his opposition to Nietzschean *amor fati* leads, apparently, to silence about the depth and reach of worth in the name of a philosophy of limits. The name for the limit within moral philosophy is "the aporia of the Other." With this aporia about goodness we reach the roots of the ambiguity in Ricoeur's ethics.

The Aporia of the Other

Ricoeur concludes *Oneself as Another* with the admission that the philosopher "does not know and cannot say" whether the Other as the source of moral injunction is a person, ancestors, the self, the living God, or "an empty place." "With this aporia of the Other," he writes, "philosophical discourse comes to an end."[40] What is this "end"? Are we to suppose that the goodness of the Other that enjoins the self is beyond thought? Conversely, is goodness the *telos*, the end or goal, of thinking?

It is not enough, I think, to disavow the need for an answer to the question of the source of responsibility by evoking Ricoeur's idea of originary affirmation and his contention that human beings are always under way, an incompleteness seeking wholeness. It is also not adequate to insist that we can designate the coherence and yet incompleteness of human life through narrative. Incomplete and temporal beings we surely are, but if one speaks of a love of creatures and even responsibility for the other, then claims about the goodness of finite being are implicitly made. The ambiguity in Ricoeur's ethics, then, is that these claims about the other are symbolically presented but not conceptually expressed. At this level—namely, how to think the being of the other as good—the symbol (creation) apparently *does not* give rise to thought.[41] Because of this, it is unclear whether or not Ricoeur escapes the modern consensus in ethics, the banishment of the being of goodness from ethics.

I want now to suggest a way beyond the ambiguity over axiology in Ricoeur's moral thought. If the aporia of the other is not to reduce us to silence about the depth of value, then we must render it productive by a new examination of the ethical potential of religious symbols. Reflection on creation and new creation is required if we are to affirm a love of being as the root of morality in the face of violence without a fall into a Nietzschean consent to destiny, a totalized system, or naive utopianism masked as hope. By conceptualizing the dialectic of creation/new creation through responsibility, the theme of being and goodness within the love of life can better be addressed. And we will also be in a better position to grasp the depths of the Golden Rule. I turn to this argument and thus conclude with constructive work in theological ethics.

Creation and New Creation in Responsibility Ethics

Please note the flow of my argument. I began with the modern consensus in ethics about the necessary and unbridgeable separation between claims about value, or moral claims, and those about reality. I tried to show the way in which this consensus informs the most pervasive forms of contemporary thought, forms emblematically designated through the ideas of hope and responsibility. What is uniquely "modern" about the patterns of thought defined by responsibility and hope is not those ideas per se. Thinkers from a variety of traditions, religious, philosophical, and political, have long mused on the importance of hope and responsibility in human life. What is new, then, is that these ideas so basic in human life would be linked to the modern banishment of ontology from axiology. But while that is no doubt true, hope and responsibility add an important twist to the modern debate about being and goodness. These ideas configure different moral orientations and even claims about the structure of thinking and selfhood. In other words, how one thinks about value and being and their distinction is fundamentally different if one explores (say) hope rather than responsibility. Indeed, I tried to show at the outset of this inquiry that it is with ideas about responsibility that the modern consensus is most hotly debated.

Armed with this complex set of issues, I turned in the previous section to Ricoeur's work in ethics. I wanted to unfold his position progressively, beginning with the problem of evil at the level of maxims for action, through violence and responsibility in the domain of real actions and relations, to, finally, religious symbols and sensibility aimed at a conversion of the will. This line of inquiry—stated too simply as a move from thinking to willing and then to feeling—was meant to grasp the richness of Ricoeur's ethics. And by adopting this route of inquiry I was able to show that Ricoeur seems to trace a convergence between the structure of thinking and the structure of the self in being enjoined. This convergence is rich for further exploration. Further reflection is required, I submit, because we have also isolated the way in which Ricoeur's work risks a return to the modern consensus. The dynamics of thinking via imagination and hope finally cannot validly assert the goodness of being even if this goodness is "felt." In a word, the connection between being and goodness while "felt" can never rise, validly, to the level of thought without seeming to sunder the very structure of thinking built on ideas about hope.

Of course, it might be the case that I have merely uncovered an enduring and central feature of Ricoeur's work. Human beings are forever mortal, always limited projects. But it could also be the case, as I have intimated, that the root difficulty is not an admission of human limits; the root difficulty in Ricoeur's position is that the ethics remains determined by the structure of thinking specified through hope. And against this difficulty I have suggested a different route of inquiry that begins with responsibility. This route of inquiry is no less insistent on human limits than Ricoeur's, and one must also be mindful of the profoundly hermeneutical character of all human understanding. Nonetheless, a different direction of inquiry seems to be possible. And this will mean, I submit, reversing the direction of inquiry, showing, that is, how religious texts and discourse articulate the structure of lived reality and thereby disclose the dynamics of "thinking." It is now time to undertake this new direction of moral reflection. The central constellation of ideas is responsibility, creation, and new creation.

The idea of "responsibility" commends itself for linking the levels of reflection we have traversed. Rightly understood, it provides the structure for an ethics that connects a sense of humility and compassion undergirding the moral law, accountability for acts and responsiveness to others, and the regenerate conscience as "new creation." But in order to see this, we must initially insist on a distinction many thinkers are not always careful to draw. Making this distinction allows us to think with and yet beyond the modern consensus in ethics even as it enacts, hermeneutically, a unique deployment of religious symbols and narrative within the work of moral inquiry.

In the symbolic frame of scripture as well as in the Christian imagination, creation is more than nature. Ricoeur seems to grasp this crucial theological point. He speaks of ongoing creation and identifies this with "a sense of radical dependence on a power that precedes us, envelops us, and supports us." And, further, creation is a "cosmos" in which we are set where "nature is between us, around us—not just as something to exploit but as an object of solicitude, respect, and admiration."[42] Yet nestled within these insights is also a problem that already bespeaks a hermeneutical problem. Dependence, power, nature, cosmos—the old conceptual hallmarks of ontotheology—are used by Ricoeur, after their rejection by the theology of hope, to interpret the symbolics of creation. While Ricoeur sees that creation is a construal of reality essentially related to the divine and endowed with a worth that evokes humility, respect, and admiration, he interprets this "reality" in concepts borrowed from an analysis of nature.[43] In other words, within Ricoeur's subtle analysis there is the possible confusion of creation with nature through the use of ontotheological concepts to speak of "creation." Those concepts are derived not from the symbolic power of the biblical texts but from reflection on the structures of finite being and the condition of its possibility. Insofar as this is the case, the symbolism of creation specifies the ground but not the *telos* of morality because as "nature" it is deemed morally purposeless. Little wonder, then, that creation so defined requires for Ricoeur hope and eschatology to provide it with a fully moral trajectory in spite of evil, a sense of direction.

We need to draw upon a subtle idea of creation in thinking about being and goodness rather than reverting to the old conceptual framework of dependence and power. In fact, if we devolve reflection to that older framework theological ethics falls prey to the Kantian criticism of heteronomy, and we lapse into yet another version of the modern consensus. In good hermeneutical fashion we should let the symbol (creation) give rise to thought (hence an account of the structure of thinking) rather than reducing the symbol to some conceptual frame. In terms I prefer and noted above, the hermeneutical task is to articulate the structure of lived experience as a field of reasons, a moral space of life. The "world" disclosed is not only "in front of the text," an opening of human possibility and freedom. It is, in my account, the articulation of the density of lived experience, including the possibilities and limitations that saturate our freedom as mortal creatures. In other words, the "referent" of religious symbols, metaphors, and texts is not defined solely from within the drive and reach of the imagination. We can practice this explicative interpretative act in outline form within the biblical creation narrative by uncovering therein a connection between the Golden Rule and the love of enemies.

Biblically construed, creation is a highly differentiated realm of relations (heaven/earth), forms of creatures (fishes/creeping things), modalities (light/dark), temporalities (evening/day) in which humans as incarnate beings act as culture creators. As one commentator notes, human beings participate in the "construction and maintenance of associations of different, interdependent creaturely realms"—that is, in creation.[44] Further, God's perception of goodness transpires amid the divine activity of creating and ongoing faithfulness. Human beings, and, interestingly, the Sabbath, actively participate in distinctive ways in the fecundity and blessing of reality. The divine action is to be imitated by human beings in all their dealing with reality, even the enemy. Compassion, reverence, and stewardship are symbolically and morally bound together. The love of life and responsibility for creatures is displayed textually in the symbolism of the creation narrative. Creation so understood hardly lacks moral direction! It is also clear that the traditional categories of "ontotheology" (dependence, power, brute nature) are not adequate to grasp the complexity of "creation." Creation is much more a space of reasons, a moral space, not reducible to simple causal explanation of events. The creation narrative explicates the space of reasons and thereby provides orientation for how people can and ought to live in response to the decidedly natural features of existence.

In this light, the shape of the moral life is how to respect and enhance the complex integrity of highly differentiated realms of life and the basic goods these entail. Evil and violence do not instigate the moral life; purpose and worth are written into the dynamics of reality. Human fault, manifest in the actions of Adam and Eve, is a disruption within the moral space called creation; it does not create, but rather disorders, the moral order of life. In a similar way, new creation is not simply the restoration of "natural man," a sort of religious overhaul of natural human capacities. It is, rather, a renewal of human existence enabling one to participate creatively and rightly in life. New creation is the ongoing regeneration of self that enables one to recognize and respond to others rooted in an enduring love of life, a testimony of conscience to created goodness. This regeneration, moreover, arises from a power not one's own but that resonates within the self. The picture of human existence inscribed in the symbolics of "creation/new creation" is then of people as participants in a complex and differentiated reality infused with worth who also, in the core of their being, are enabled and required to assume responsibility for existence—that is, to respect and enhance the integrity of life.

The question, then, is whether or not the idea of responsibility adequately specifies the moral meaning of the complex symbolics of creation. Ricoeur apparently lacks such a conceptual vocabulary to make this point; it is why he ends with the aporia of the Other. That is the case since the very structure of thought through hope is marked by "openness" rather than responsiveness to the worth of the other. Again, despite his genuine advance in moral inquiry Ricoeur's position risks a return to the modern consensus in ethics where, technically speaking, the goodness of being must remain beyond the purview of ethics. Can we deploy the idea of responsibility to provide the structure of an ethics?

By uncovering the sensibilities of solicitude, respect, and admiration in the creation narrative, I have isolated a fundamental responsiveness basic in life. The symbolism of creation means that these sensibilities are evoked by the proper relation between power and goodness and not brute dependence. That is to say, what evokes moral wonder is not simply the causal grandeur of the natural order (the starry heavens) nor even the moral law prescribed by pure practical reason, but the perception in and through the symbolics of creation that human life is situated in a space defined by the conjunction of power (creative capacity) and worth. If for Kant what elicits respect is "rational freedom" in persons, we can say, after our journey, that what initiates the moral life are sensibilities (solicitude, respect, awe) evoked by power made good as manifest in creation and its creatures. As Ricoeur puts it, it is the conjunction of reverential humility and compassion without limits. But these attitudes disclose more than subjective states of affairs; they are responses to the reality of a good creation. Moral attitudes (like humility and compassion) are cognitively laden; the cognitive content of these attitudes are partly displayed in religious symbols and texts. Cosmic order, the starry heavens, and ethical order and worth are linked in complex, nonreductionistic ways within the symbolic world of religious texts and narratives. For Ricoeur, given the structure of thinking rooted in the dynamics of hope, such symbols disclose a world in front of themselves that I may inhabit, those disclosing of moral freedom. But I am suggesting that these religious symbols articulate the structure of lived reality when and if they are confirmed and give direction to primal sensibilities. Stated otherwise, "creation" articulates the moral space of life not merely in terms of a possibility we may enter but in which we in fact dwell. It is creation, the goodness of being, that instigates the moral life rather than human fault and violence. We are enjoined before we hope.

That insight is not the whole story, of course. There is in fact violence in the world and any realistic ethics must not only specify the ontological reach of value, as just argued, but also how the brokenness and violence of the world can and ought to be met. Once we have grasped the connection between creation and love of enemy, then we enter the domain of morality in the narrow sense in that we move reflection to the level of human interaction, responsiveness to others. Given the fact and possibility of violence, ascription of accountability is required. Without that demand, the love of enemy becomes immoral; the claim of justice is denied and ongoing fidelity to life truncated. In other words, the move from creative participation in a good but finite creation grasped through incarnate sensibilities and dispositions to the interaction between human agents and patients puts pressure to differentiate the language of responsibility. We can do so by distinguishing responsiveness and accountability. Responsiveness is about our relation to the worth of the other; accountability specifies the ascription of actions to agents with respect to norms governing the right use of our power to act in the world. Put differently, the right (accountability) is dependent on the good (responsiveness) for its intelligibility and validity; norms of rightness specify how we can and must respect and enhance the integrity of life. Yet this all remains within the structure of a responsibility ethics, since accountability rests on human responsiveness and also the right motive to abide by the moral law.

A differentiated idea of responsibility captures the kinds of passivity and activity implied in creation (humility/compassion/stewardship) and human interaction (agent/patient). It provides a conceptual structure for an ethics geared to the love of life mindful of evil and violence. Theological ethics interweaves the symbolics of creation with the conceptual richness of responsibility in order to reclaim an ontology of value on distinctly moral grounds.[45] Can we now travel from creation to new creation? Do the symbolics of creation and the idea of responsibility provide a context for understanding hope as the "form" new creation takes within the moral life?

Notice, as I stated at the beginning of this part of the inquiry, that we have reversed the direction of reflection taken in my reading of Ricoeur. He works from an account of the structure of thinking disclosed in the account of hope to clarify the moral meaning of the symbolics of creation. In this respect, his project remains within the general orientation of Kantian ethics. We can think religious ideas, and are warranted in so doing, insofar as those ideas (God, sin, redemption, eschatology) are provoked by the very limits of reason that philosophy charts and guards and required by what the moral law enjoins. In Ricoeur's terms, hope warrants the religious imagination in the face of evil and violence. Conversely, I have worked from the symbolics of creation toward hope and the structure of thinking.[46] I have unfolded a primary datum of the love of life presented in the symbolic richness of the creation narrative even in the face of brokenness. I have also had to attend to the prepositional content of the biblical claims about creation beyond the traditional logic of "dependence."

The argument has led us to see that thinking too is a response to something. That is to say, we do not exhaust the dynamics of thinking, even granting its limits, by specifying its legislative function (Kant) or open-ended direction (Ricoeur). The task of thinking is to articulate that to which we are already and always responding—namely, the complexity of the differentiated reality given in the symbolics of creation—and thereby responsibly to orient life. Articulation and orientation, if I can put it briefly, are primal acts of thinking that respect the distinction between explaining events and providing reasons for action without the separation implied in the Kantian agenda. But that having been said, in asking about hope we return to competing moral outlooks. We encounter again the conflict between the theology of hope and its censure of presence for the sake of promise and responsibility ethics focused on the concrete other.

I judge that the whole scope of eschatological and soteriological reflection—thinking about Christ, redemption, and God's reign—can and must be carried out within a realistic ethics in relation to a differentiated idea of creation.[47] I made the point by highlighting the connection between creation, God's act of loving mercy and redemptive action, and new creation as the regeneration of the self in response to divine action. Theologically construed, regeneration is a new birth, the revitalization of the self as the *imago Dei*, in and through the Christ scripturally presented. And this means, morally speaking, that one is enabled and empowered to dwell responsibly with and for others. The open-ended, active, and even hopeful structure of thinking as well as the coherence of the symbolic order of scripture can, and I think must, be read via creation–Christ–new creation if we are to articulate a realistic ethics of responsibility. But that said, I admit that, as Moltmann, Ricoeur, and others argue, one can see scripture, the moral meaning of creation, and the structure of thinking under the rubric of hope and eschatology. Does this mean that in the end there remains a fundamental rupture between hope and responsibility?

Perhaps we have uncovered an irreducible difference in moral convictions that foils all attempts at dialectical mediation. Perhaps a philosophy of hope, while it can account for responsibility to the other and also creation, articulates a moral stance that is fundamentally divergent from a realistic form of responsibility ethics. Perhaps the primary datum of hope in human life is morally different from a realistic love of life suffusing a sense of responsibility. Perhaps.

Granting different convictions and sensibilities, theological ethics must structure its hermeneutical and theoretic work through the idea of responsibility. Practical existence is unintelligible outside of things mattering, possessing worth, beyond our projects. The presupposition of the moral life is that existence has worth and evokes care and respect even in its brokenness and radical finitude. Without that conviction, all is reduced to our projects, the workings of the all-too-human will to power. The most radical point of the complex symbolics of creation is that divine goodness is not an act of brute power but a noncoercive acknowledgment and enhancement of the integrity of life. Whether one speaks of the God who is coming or the God who is, promise or presence, the moral meaning of faith is that reality itself, its intelligibility and purposes, transpires before a goodness beyond the will to power. Theologically considered, one says that to be is good simply and solely because God is. The claim of conscience is testimony to this divine goodness as an injunction to responsible existence. As theologians down the ages have known, our brokenness, vice, and even violence are not so deep nor so thorough as to efface the testimony of conscience. From out of the divine goodness arises the moral adventure of human life. In that goodness one hopes. Beyond a consent to destiny is a realistic and responsible love of life.

My argument is then fully dialectical in shape and justification. Of course, an ethics of hope can account for creation. However, in considering the dynamics of the moral life an ethics of responsibility enables us to articulate in a more complex way reasons for hope and also the depth and scope of the claim of life's goodness upon conscience. We are not left silent before the wonder and claim of life upon us, the starry heavens above and the moral worth of finite life testified within us. The work of theological ethics is to unfold the significance of that claim and wonder for the whole realm of human actions and relations.

Conclusion

In this essay I have examined hope and responsibility in Ricoeur's thought against the backdrop of current ethics and also the vexing question of the relation between being and goodness. Ricoeur's work moves in novel ways between other moral outlooks. More important, through the connection between religious symbols and morality, Ricoeur challenges the constrictions of the modern consensus in ethics. Yet I have argued that at the level of the structure of thinking, Ricoeur risks a return to the modern consensus under the lingering impulses of the philosophy and theology of hope. In order to avoid this ambiguity about value, I have exploited the symbolics of creation and new creation in outlining a hopeful but realistic theological ethics of responsibility.

I realize that advocates of the modern consensus will find odd and even nonsensical the use of religious symbols to articulate the full reach and implications of a nascent but enduring love of life. They cannot imagine that symbols and narratives invented in order to provide guidance for existence might nevertheless enable one through critical interpretation to discover something about the reach of the moral life. That should not surprise any of us. Thankfully, Paul Ricoeur is one philosopher who listens to religious discourse and dares to think within the realms of meaning disclosed by it. I have tried, accordingly, to think with and yet beyond Ricoeur about themes in contemporary ethics. In an age scarred by violence and facing planetary endangerment, it is time that we reclaim a sense of the goodness of life thereby to curtail and direct the power at our disposal. Beyond the modern consensus in ethics, that is the second naiveté now harkening us as responsible beings.

Notes

1. I want to thank W. David Hall, John Wall, and David E. Klemm for helpful comments on the argument of this essay.
2. On this see Louis Dupré, *Passage to Modernity: An Essay in the Hermeneutics of Nature and Culture* (New Haven: Yale University Press, 1993). One thinks also of the distinction, drawn by many scholars, between preaxial, axial, and postaxial religions. On that distinction the tension between a moral and cosmic order is long-standing indeed. The point was made forcefully within the modern context by Friedrich Nietzsche: " 'All gods are dead: now we want the Superman to live'—let this be our last will one day to the great noontide." Friedrich Nietzsche, *Thus Spoke Zarathustra: A Book for Everyone and No One*, trans. R. J. Hollingdale (New York: Penguin, 1961), p. 104.
3. This new direction of thought entails a different conception of the hermeneutical task within moral inquiry. In my account the task is not to trace connections internal to any text as constitutive of experience and moral identity, as so-called intertextual approaches do; it is also not the correlation between text and existence or a claim that these texts somehow "express" common human experiences. My position also does not center, as does Ricoeur's hermeneutics, on the disclosure of the world "in front of the text," although the disclosure of possible courses of action is always important. The approach taken herein is explicative or, as I have called it elsewhere, "mimetic": the interpretation of texts seeks to articulate or explicate the density of lived practical experience so that a critical understanding of the moral space of life is possible, but an understanding recognized as valid if and only if it is indeed explicative of reasons for action. In this way, the text is confirmed, lived

anew, or denied in actual life even as practical existence validates or negates the text's portrayal of life. The importance of this hermeneutic approach will become evident much later in our inquiry. On this account of interpretation, see William Schweiker, *Mimetic Reflections: A Study in Hermeneutics, Theology, and Ethics* (New York: Fordham University Press, 1990).

4. I have engaged Ricoeur's thought in other writings that inform the present essay. See William Schweiker, "Imagination, Violence, and Hope: A Theological Response to Ricoeur's Moral Philosophy" and "Hermeneutics, Ethics, and the Theology of Culture: Concluding Reflections," in *Meanings in Texts and Actions: Questioning Paul Ricoeur*, ed. David E. Klemm and William Schweiker (Charlottesville: University of Virginia Press, 1993), pp. 205–25, 292–313.

5. See Jürgen Moltmann, *Theology of Hope*, trans. J. W. Leitch (New York: Harper, & Row 1967), and *The Coming of God: Christian Eschatology*, trans. M. Kohl (Minneapolis: Fortress Press, 1996). Also see Johann Baptist Metz, *Faith in History and Society: Toward a Practical Fundamental Theology*, trans. D. Smith (New York: Crossroad/Seabury, 1980). One should note that in more recent work Moltmann has addressed matters of creation but still within an eschatological framework.

6. Paul Ricoeur, "Hope and the Structure of Philosophical Systems," in *Figuring the Sacred: Religion, Narrative, and Imagination*, trans. David Pellauer and ed. Mark I. Wallace (Minneapolis: Fortress Press, 1995), p. 207.

7. I am mindful that there is considerable debate about the possibility of the "gift." In this essay I leave this question aside insofar as for Ricoeur there is little doubt that gift exceeds reciprocity; it manifests its own logic of superabundance. On this problem, see the essays by Marcel Mauss, Jacques Derrida, and others in *The Logic of the Gift: Toward an Ethic of Generosity*, ed. Alan Schrift (New York: Routledge, 1977).

8. For a discussion of responsibility ethics, see William Schweiker, *Responsibility and Christian Ethics* (Cambridge: Cambridge University Press, 1995), esp. chapt. 4; and Gabriel Moran, *A Grammar of Responsibility* (New York: Crossroad, 1996).

9. See Emmanuel Levinas, *Otherwise Than Being or Beyond Essence*, trans. Alphonso Lingis (Boston: Kluwer, 1991).

10. See Hans Küng, *Global Responsibility: In Search of a New Global Ethic*, trans. John Bowden (New York: Crossroads, 1991).

11. Karl Barth, *Church Dogmatics*, ed. G. W. Bromiley and T. F. Torrence (Edinburgh: T&T Clark, 1957–70); Emmanuel Levinas, *Totality and Infinity: An Essay on Exteriority*, trans. A. Lingis (Pittsburg: Duquesne University, 1969); and H. Richard Niebuhr, *The Responsible Self: An Essay in Christian Moral Philosophy*, Library of Theological Ethics (Louisville, KY: Westminster/John Knox Press, 1999).

12. Marion Smiley, *Moral Responsibility and the Boundaries of Community: Power and Accountability from a Pragmatic Point of View* (Chicago: University of Chicago Press, 1992); Peter French, *Responsibility Matters* (Lawrence: University of Kansas Press, 1992); John Martin Fisher and Mark Ravizaa, *Responsibility and Control: A Theory of Moral Responsibility* (New York: Cambridge University Press, 1998).

13. See, for example, Seyla Benhabib, *Situating the Self: Gender, Community, and Postmodernism in Contemporary Ethics* (New York: Routledge, 1992).
14. Within Jewish and Christian moral inquiry, the modern rejection of metaphysics has never gotten far in that the good and right have been understood in relation to a reality, "God," not reducible to convention, preference, or communicative rationality. To be sure, theologians and philosophers have sought to avoid classical ontotheology and with it reduction of God, Good, or the Other to determinate states of affairs. The tendency now is to understand discourse about the divine in and through the strictures of moral demand and possibility. This fact makes the work of theological ethics crucial to the whole scope of contemporary moral inquiry.
15. Hans Jonas, *The Imperative of Responsibility: In Search of an Ethics for the Technological Age*, trans. Hans Jonas and David Herr (Chicago: University of Chicago Press, 1984), p. 90.
16. Ricoeur is correct to insist on the priority of dialectical thinking to the conceptual analysis of religious and moral ideas. See Paul Ricoeur, "Love and Justice," in *Figuring the Sacred*, pp. 315–30. On this correlational account of theological, if not ethical, reflection, see David Tracy, *The Analogical Imagination: Christian Theology and the Culture of Pluralism* (New York: Crossroad, 1981).
17. Paul Ricoeur, *Oneself as Another*, trans. Kathleen Blamey (Chicago: University of Chicago Press, 1992).
18. Ricoeur, as I read him, tends to understand Christian theology and ethics mainly in kerygmatic and scriptural terms. He speaks of "Christian ethics" as a "communal ethics in a religious perspective." Theological ethics, I believe, draws on the resources of a religious tradition—say, Christian thought and life—to articulate how we ought to live as moral agents. Theological ethics is the practical, dialectical mediation of philosophical and confessional ethics. We could call it Christian moral philosophy. It remains unclear to me that Ricoeur imagines theological ethics as a dialectical possibility in the structure of thinking. For the multidimensional structure of theological ethics, see William Schweiker, *Responsibility and Christian Ethics* (Cambridge: Cambridge University Press, 1995).
19. This approach can be called hermeneutical realism. See William Schweiker, *Power, Value, and Conviction: Theological Ethics in the Postmodern Age* (Cleveland, OH: Pilgrim Press, 1998).
20. John Lachs, *In Love with Life: Reflections on the Joy of Living and Why We Hate to Die* (Nashville, TN: Vanderbilt University Press, 1998), p. 21.
21. For helpful discussions about basic human goods and their place in moral theory, see Philippa Foot, *Natural Goodness* (Oxford: Oxford University Press, 2001); Martha C. Nussbaum, *Sex and Social Justice* (Oxford: Oxford University Press, 1999); Don Browning, *A Fundamental Practical Theology: Descriptive and Strategic Proposals* (Minneapolis: Fortress Press, 1996); John Finnis, *Fundamentals of Ethics* (Washington, D.C.: Georgetown University Press, 1983); Robin W. Lovin, *Christian Ethics: An Essential Guide* (Nashville, TN: Abingdon Press, 2000); and Schweiker, *Responsibility and Christian Ethics*.

22. See Ricoeur, "Hope and the Structure of Philosophical Systems," pp. 203–16.
23. On the idea of human capability basic to Ricoeur's philosophy, see his lecture that concludes this volume.
24. Ricoeur, *Figuring the Sacred*, p. 211.
25. Paul Ricoeur, "A Philosophical Hermeneutics of Religion: Kant," in *Figuring the Sacred*, p. 77. In line with Kant and Augustine—and behind them St. Paul (cf. Romans 7)—Ricoeur finds the paradox of evil to be that we are bound and yet free. Evil seems to happen to me, to take over my existence, and yet I also freely and willing engage in evil acts. In *The Symbolism of Evil* and other texts, Ricoeur investigates various depictions of evil in order to examine this doubleness.
26. Ricoeur, *Figuring the Sacred*, p. 206. But is this not simply to say that, philosophically speaking, as moral creatures we await a word to be spoken to us? As Paul Tillich might put it, we cannot answer the question that is our own being. "The answer cannot be derived from the question. It is said *to* him who asks, but it is not taken *from* him." The irony here is that while Ricoeur can specify the approximation to hope in regeneration as the heart of the structure of philosophical thinking, this must be sustained by listening to what is given to us. See Paul Tillich, "Aspects on a Religious Analysis of Culture" in his *Theology of Culture*, ed. Robert C. Kimball (Oxford: Oxford University Press, 1959), p. 49.
27. Ricoeur, *Figuring the Sacred*, p. 206.
28. Recall that in *Oneself as Another* Ricoeur insists on a distinction between "ethics" concerned with the good life and "morals" that focuses on relations of duty and justice. His point is that what is morally right must be grounded in the ethically good, but the good must also be tested by the claims of morality. Ricoeur makes the same point in the lecture that concludes this volume. I certainly agree that any form of ethics must be related to the good and the right and that the "right" is unintelligible without some connection to the good. That being said, I prefer to retain the term *ethics* for the enterprise of critical moral inquiry and retain *morals* for actual life. For the sake of this essay I have followed Ricoeur's terminological distinction.
29. Paul Ricoeur, "Ethical and Theological Considerations on the Golden Rule," in *Figuring the Sacred*, p. 295.
30. Ibid., p. 293.
31. Hans Dieter Betz and William Schweiker, "Concerning Mountains and Morals: A Conversation about the Sermon on the Mount," *Criterion* 36, no. 2 (1997): 23. On this topic one must see Hans Dieter Betz, *The Sermon on the Mount* (Minneapolis: Fortress Press, 1995).
32. Ricoeur, "Ethical and Theological Considerations on the Golden Rule," p. 294.
33. Ricoeur, *Oneself as Another*, p. 354.
34. See, for example, Alan Gewirth, *Reason and Morality* (Chicago: University of Chicago Press, 1978).
35. Ricoeur's argument means, in terms of motivation, that affection, desire, and want—the whole field of virtue theory—must be reconsidered beyond its rejection in much modern ethics. However, because we are interested in a very specific problem of regeneration, and not an account of human action in general, I leave aside a consideration of virtue theory.

36. Ricoeur, "Ethical and Theological Considerations on the Golden Rule," p. 298.
37. One should recall that Ricoeur has long held that "feeling" as a second-order intentional structure, is the way in which people make "schematized thoughts our own.... Feelings, furthermore, accompany and complete imagination as *picturing* relationship." In this way, religious sensibility completes the poetic or imaginative function of religious texts and symbols (like the creation story) while remaining, so I am arguing, within the structure of thought defined by hope. See Paul Ricoeur, "Metaphorical Process as Cognition, Imagination, and Feeling," in *On Metaphor*, ed. Sheldon Sachs (Chicago: University of Chicago Press, 1979), pp. 154–55. For a further discussion of this point, see Schweiker, *Mimetic Reflections*, esp. chapt. 3.
38. Ricoeur, *Figuring the Sacred*, p. 298.
39. Ibid., p. 299.
40. Ricoeur, *Oneself as Another*, p. 355.
41. In the lecture that ends this volume, Ricoeur seems to move in the direction of my argument; he even notes the need for a closer relation between theology and philosophy. While that might be his current judgment, a happy development I believe, it is clear that in his writings to date the problems I have noted are present. One should also note that Ricoeur, in the concluding lecture, also is interested in expanding the range of morally important "feelings," but this also suggests that distinctly religious claims are not explored ontologically.
42. Ricoeur, "Ethical and Theological Considerations on the Golden Rule," pp. 297–98.
43. Stated even more provocatively, the biblical insight seems to be that ontological claims are always situated within a moral order established by the divine: nature makes sense only within creation. This is why Christian moralists, and thinkers in other religious traditions as well, have been uneasy with the modern consensus in ethics. Yet making this point does not require, as far as I can see, a reversion to the supposed "religious synthesis" between the moral and natural order. On this point, see William Schweiker, "Time as a Moral Space: Moral Cosmologies, Creation, and Last Judgment," in *The End of the World and the Ends of God*, ed. John Polkinghorne and Michael Welker (Harrisburg, PA: Trinity Press International, 2000), pp. 124–40.
44. Michael Welker, *Creation and Reality*, trans. John F. Hoffmeyer (Minneapolis: Fortress Press, 1999), p. 13.
45. My point here is that there is no simple "correlation" between symbol and concept as if a concept gives full and adequate translation of a "symbol," and the "symbol" somehow makes up for lack in our concepts. Consistent with the mimetic or explicative hermeneutics noted before, I am "overlaying" or "interweaving" cognitive-discursive forms (symbols, narrative, ideas, concepts, theories) in order to articulate the moral space of life.
46. I realize that in making this judgment I read Ricoeur's work in a more Kantian frame than do many of the other authors included in this volume.
47. I should note again that Ricoeur seems to gesture in this direction in the lecture that concludes this volume and may, in this respect, be responding to my argument and that of other authors as well. If that is the case, it is a development within his work that I, for one, wish to applaud!

8
The Site of Christian Ethics
Love and Justice in the Work of Paul Ricoeur
W. DAVID HALL

Introduction

Near the end of the essay entitled "Ethical and Theological Considerations on the Golden Rule," Paul Ricoeur states, "What is called 'Christian ethics,' or, as I would prefer to say, 'communal ethics in religious perspective,' consists, I believe, in the tension between unilateral love and bilateral justice, and in the mutual interpretation of each of these in terms of the other."[1] My purpose in this essay is to take seriously Ricoeur's claims about the ethical possibilities of biblical witness. To this end, my thesis is twofold. First, I suggest that Ricoeur's comparatively recent interest in a dialectical engagement between a theology of *creation* and a theology of *redemption* presses his thinking about religion in new directions that are crucial for theological and ethical reflection. Second, and in relation to this first claim, I suggest that Ricoeur's understanding of the creative tension between love and justice is itself critically important for Christian ethics in particular and for ethical theory in general. The depth of this importance resides in the possibility of giving some systematic structure to a set of Ricoeur's occasional writings.

The analysis will proceed in three stages. First I will address the dialectical engagement that Ricoeur establishes between a theology of redemption and a theology of creation. The bulk of Ricoeur's theological writings have been devoted to articulating a theology of hope or redemption, à la Jürgen Moltmann. However, the theology of redemption raises problems for the possibility of affirming ethical value because it tends to conceive a creation devoid of the good, due to the ubiquity of evil, from which we hope to be redeemed at the eschaton. Comparatively recently in his career, however, Ricoeur has become interested in the resources that a theology of creation might contribute to ethical reflection. In the first section, I will address Ricoeur's interest in both of these strands of theological speculation and the manner in which he views the relationship between the two.

This analysis of Ricoeur's theological writings opens immediately upon the second section, which deals with the theological orientation of this ethical theory. In this section, I will attempt to offer some structure to Ricoeur's presentation, in a series of seemingly unrelated occasional essays, of the relationship between an ideal of love and an ideal of justice. This structure allows us to begin to think systematically about theological ethics in a Christian perspective within the creative tension between these two ideals. Ricoeur's insights into the dynamics of this confrontation offer some tantalizing possibilities for those interested in Christian ethics, but these insights have not been systematically drawn out either by Ricoeur or his commentators. I will explore this creative tension at three distinct but related levels: the confrontation between a logic of equivalence and a logic of superabundance; the competing orientations of the Golden Rule and the love command; and the creative tension between the ideas of autonomy and theonomy. Finally, I will analyze the manner in which Ricoeur seeks a deepened understanding of both love and justice through mutual interpretation.

In conclusion, I will argue that we can and ought to ask what this account of theological ethics from a Christian perspective offers to our understandings of ethical reflection in general. Is Christian ethics a discipline sui generis, or is it possible for an ethics that finds its explicit foundations in a particular religious witness to lend itself to and be informed by ethical reflection in general? Debate rages over this question, and this essay does not attempt to give a definitive answer. I will suggest, however, that there is reason to claim that within Ricoeur's corpus there are points of crossing between theology and philosophy, and that ethics is one of the principal sites for such a crossing.

With this itinerary in mind, let me state my twofold thesis again: First, I am claiming that the turn to the dialectic between a theology of creation and a theology of redemption has wrought a new and important direction in Ricoeur's thinking about religion and ethics. Second, I am arguing that the creative tension between an ideal of love and an ideal of justice is crucial for our understandings of Christian ethics in particular and ethical theory in general. That is to say, my thesis is both an interpretation of Ricoeur's religious thought and an argument about ethics.

The Theology of Redemption and the Theology of Creation

Ricoeur has always followed Immanuel Kant in marking the entrance to the philosophy of religion with the recognition of the paradoxical and radical nature of moral evil. What makes moral evil so paradoxical is the fact that it resides in the foundation of freedom. Any particular evil choice finds its ultimate foundation in a choice that precedes any discrete determination of freedom. But the leap from the possibility to the actuality of an evil foundation in the will, or, in Ricoeur's terms, from fallibility to fault, is itself inscrutable. This signals the ultimate incapacity of freedom to extricate itself from the dilemma of radical evil, and freedom despairs over this incapacity.

And yet despair is not the last word. Rather, despair opens onto hope, and this opening onto freedom's hope is simultaneously an opening onto the question of religion, both for Kant and for Ricoeur. In this sense, the question of religion places freedom at the crossroads of despair and hope. Addressing the crisis of freedom, Ricoeur claims:

> Now, evil is a problem for the philosopher only inasmuch as it belongs to the problematic of the actualization of freedom; evil makes of freedom an impossible possibility. . . . A real liberty can be hoped, beyond this speculative and practical Good Friday. We are nowhere so close as here to the Christian kerygma: hope is hope of resurrection, of resurrection from among the dead. In philosophical terms: evil requires a nonethical and nonpolitical transformation of our will, which Kant calls regeneration; it is the task of "religion within the limits of reason alone" to elaborate the condition of possibility of this regeneration, without alienating freedom either to a magical conception of grace and salvation or to an authoritarian organization of the religious community.[2]

In other words, the despair of freedom marks the point of entrance into the philosophy of religion and the configuration of hope in freedom's possibility.

The problem of moral evil, therefore, signals a gap in the purely philosophical account of ethical existence that necessitates a turn toward decidedly religious themes. Ricoeur's account of biblical witness functions in two directions. With regard to the question of evil, biblical witness serves to articulate a proposed end that poetically reconfigures the paradox of voluntary servitude. By interpreting the gospel kerygma along the trajectory of a theology of redemption, following theologians such as Karl Barth, Rudolf Bültmann, and Jürgen Moltmann, biblical witness offers the promise of a restoration of freedom and goodness beyond the presence of evil. However, Ricoeur has more recently begun to address the possibility of a theology of creation that points to a recognition of the fundamental value of the created order. Following thinkers such as Gerhardt von Rad, Jon Levinson, and, most especially, Franz Rosenzweig, he has relocated the process of redemption itself within the account of an origin that grounds the value of creation in the power of a benevolent God. Thus, along this twofold path of a theology of redemption and a theology of creation, of the end and origin of human possibility, I will explore Ricoeur's account of the world the biblical witness presents to the possibility of ethically meaningful existence.

For reasons of limited space, I will not address Ricoeur's adoption of the theology of redemption in detail. Rather, I place my emphasis on the problems that this theological perspective raises for ethics. The fundamental problem that the theology of redemption raises for ethical reflection is the question of value—that is, the question of where we are to "place" the good. The theology of hope is unable to affirm the good of creation because it places the good outside of creation. How is this the case?

We can begin by analyzing the antithesis that the theology of hope establishes between a religion of promise and a religion of presence. The God it preaches, and with this God, the ultimate reality to which it points, is "not yet," not present but coming. The kerygmatic content of biblical witness proclaims a reality not yet a reality. Ricoeur continues, "It is then not only the Name that must be opposed to the idol, but the 'He is coming' of Scripture must be opposed to the 'It is' of the Proem of Parmenides. This dividing line is henceforth going to separate two conceptions of time and, through them, two conceptions of freedom."[3] In this reading, the core of the kerygma is the issuance of a promise by a God who recedes from history, who in effect disclaims the process of history.

Now, why is this antithesis important for our understanding of the good? The theology of redemption takes as its point of origin the recognition of the reality and radicality of evil. It is the despair over evil that calls for a final reconciliation and that gives the promise its profound significance. Yet this reconciliation is "not yet." It is promised at the eschaton; the restoration of the good, configured poetically as universal resurrection, is nonhistorical, atemporal. This is an important claim about the relationship of the good to creation. To the degree that the good resides at the end of history—that is, signals the conclusion of creation—the good is fundamentally outside of creation; it is "not yet." Given this "not yet" of the good, the only response open to freedom is hope in the proclaimed promise.

We find some indication of a shift in Ricoeur's perspective in his attempt in later work to reestablish relations between two ideas that were severed above—that is, to establish a mediated relationship between a hermeneutics of proclamation and a phenomenology of manifestation and, by means of this, a mediated relationship between the two dimensions of the religious as such: the kerygmatic and the sacred, promise and presence. Indeed, Ricoeur argues that while the process of demythologization may have been correct in calling into question the residues of a "degenerate sacred," the scientific-technological ideology that fueled this process itself presents problems. He suggests that, in fact, both may be symptoms of a "common cultural configuration":

> And this cultural configuration is that of nihilism. The scientistic illusion and the retreat of the sacred into its own particular phantoms together belong to the forgetfulness of our roots. In two different yet convergent manners the desert is spreading. And what we are in the midst of discovering, contrary to the scientific-technological ideology, which is also the military-industrial ideology, is that humanity is simply not possible without the sacred.[4]

The Site of Christian Ethics

In what sense is the theology of hope bound up in this enterprise of nihilism? To the extent that the theology of hope seeks to divest the present of divine significance, it places the good outside of time. Hence, history itself becomes meaningless; hope paradoxically waits for a nontemporal future.

My argument for a shift in perspective is further strengthened by the fact that Ricoeur adopts the very Greek christologies that he criticized above to establish the mediation between proclamation and manifestation.[5] Once the word is reconciled with the manifest, once proclamation is a proclamation of the sacred, then the kerygma becomes an affirmation of the present.

The relocation of the constitutive word has radical implications for our understanding of freedom within the context of Christian witness. If we can take as established, at least tentatively, that the kerygma is no longer for Ricoeur simply the proclamation of promise and fulfillment, but also the testimony to a word, spoken in time, that is fundamentally constitutive of the self, then freedom's orientation is not only hope in a final resurrection, but also response to that word. This discussion points to the idea of a second trajectory in Ricoeur's account of biblical witness. I believe that Ricoeur's continuing interest in the work of Franz Rosenzweig points decisively in this direction.

Ricoeur's principle interest in addressing Rosenzweig is the distinction that Rosenzweig draws between commandment and law, a distinction that will be extremely important in the next section. However, the position that the idea of the commandment holds in the complex structure of *The Star of Redemption* forces us to draw a broader significance. This work is a philosophical-theological treatise on the interconnection of the ideas of creation, revelation, and redemption. Creation and redemption cross in revelation, and the commandment is the figure of revelation. Redemption is made possible by the command "Love me!"; redemption resides in love actualizing itself in love of creation, and the self is given form through this process of redemption. Rosenzweig is profoundly important for Ricoeur's articulation of the relation of the transcendent to the temporal by virtue of Rosenzweig's configuration of the triad of creation-revelation-redemption. Within the Star of Redemption, creation serves as an enduring origin within which revelation and redemption configure their own particular temporality. "Rosenzweig is careful," Ricoeur argues, "to emphasize this: 'Creation; or, The Ever-Enduring Basis of Things.' "

> In one sense, creation does not cease to lie behind us. The beginning is not a surpassed commencement but, in a sense, an unceasingly continued beginning.... The immemorial past in some way underlies the present of revelation and, if I may put it this way, the future of the expectation of the kingdom, rather than being before the present of the one and the future of the other.... In relation to chronology, the moment or instant—in a quasi-Kierkegaardian sense of the term—arrives at any moment; it is the occuring moment that opens toward an ever-enduring.[6]

Thus, Rosenzweig's configuration of creation-revelation-redemption moves biblical narrative out of a linear conception of temporality into what Ricoeur at points calls a "profound temporality." In this account, creation, revelation, and redemption are three fundamental, intersecting modes of temporality: creation is the ever-enduring origin of existence; revelation is the ever-enduring birth of the soul to its relationship to the divine and to the world; redemption is the ever-enduring future possibility of the coming kingdom of God. Creation signals our dependence with respect to the origin of existence. Redemption signals our responsibility with regard to the reconciliation of the world. Revelation signals the birth of the self's recognition of this twofold relationship.

Thus, a theology of redemption and a theology of creation are not competing strategies. Neither are they trajectories that can be collapsed into each other, however. Ricoeur argues that "we can affirm that the theology of Creation constitutes neither an appendix to the theology of Redemption nor a separate theme. The always-already-there of Creation does not make sense independently of the perpetual futurity of Redemption. Between these two is intercalated the eternal now of the 'you, love me!' "[7] In the obverse direction, we can argue, as well, that the theology of redemption cannot exist independently of the theology of creation without losing sight of the value within creation that redemption seeks to increase.

At the end of this all too brief exploration, I am arguing that Ricoeur's understanding of the biblical configuration of existence is twofold. With respect to the end of existence, we are oriented by a theology of redemption that seeks final reconciliation of the self with itself, with the divine, and with the world. With respect to the origin, we are oriented by a fundamental value within the created order through which we are sustained in existence and toward which we are responsible. These two orientations meet in the moment at which the divine manifests itself to the individual soul.

Now, this exploration of the dialectical relationship between a theology of redemption and a theology of creation opens onto a set of ethical concerns that places us in the midst of the confrontation between the opposing ideals of love and justice. Our point of entry into theological discourse was the problem of moral evil; the theology of redemption presented us with the hope for freedom's deliverance from evil. On the other hand, the theology of creation reorients the task of redemption toward service to the value that is inherent in the created order. If redemption is the task of authentic selfhood, that task is carried out in service to creation. We will explore this ethical demand more fully in the next section.

Love and Justice

As I claimed, Ricoeur's writings on the relationship of love and justice have not received the kind of systematic treatment that they deserve. The purpose of this section is to offer a systematic structure to these writings. Most broadly construed, the exploration of the encounter between justice and love involves the confrontation of an ideal of reciprocity characteristic of justice and an opposing ideal of generosity that orients love. I will address the relationship between love and justice along three distinct but related lines that I designate the logic of equivalence versus the logic of superabundance, the Golden Rule versus the love command, and autonomy versus theonomy. The progression through these levels of analysis takes us from the level of logical structures, through the configuration of our confrontation with the other (both as other person and as the divine) in ethical concern, to the self's constitution in freedom's response to the word spoken.

Once again, the works that I focus on in this section are occasional writings that have not received the kind of treatment that Ricoeur has directed to his more philosophical endeavors. In this section, I am attempting both to systematically engage these ideas and, in doing so, to impose some kind of systematic structure upon what otherwise appear to be a set of disconnected insights. However, I am attempting to offer this structure without doing violence to the ideas themselves. Rather, the structure I offer is intrinsic to the ideas themselves, or so I am claiming. In all cases, I follow Ricoeur in the endeavor to explore the tensions between opposing ideals with the hopes of establishing a mutual reinterpretation that deepens our understandings of both justice and love.

The Logic of Equivalence versus the Logic of Superabundance

At the level of basic structures the confrontation between justice and love involves the juxtaposition of opposing logics of equivalence and superabundance. Now, the logic of equivalence that governs justice is predicated on a particular conception of the nature of society that Ricoeur unfolds through an examination of John Rawls's *A Theory of Justice*.

Rawls asserts that society is both a cooperative and a competitive venture: cooperative because the members of society recognize that life holds more promise in community; competitive because each prefers a greater to a lesser share of social goods. Given this conception of society, the need for justice arises out of what Rawls calls the circumstances of justice. Objectively, the circumstances of justice entail a condition of moderate scarcity of goods. Corresponding to this objective condition is the subjective condition of mutual disinterest in the interests of others by all competing for a share of those scarce goods. This is not to say that individuals concerned to promote their own welfare are necessarily selfish or egoistic. Rather, given the scarcity of goods, each is concerned to advance his or her interests regardless of the interests of others. Thus, Rawls asserts that the circumstances of justice obtain whenever mutually disinterested individuals advance conflicting claims to the division of social goods and advantages under conditions of moderate scarcity. Principles of justice are intended to secure equal opportunities and equal protections for all members in the distribution system.[8]

Within the distributive context, the logic of equivalence is formulated by the dictum "to each his or her due." That is, the distribution of goods, rights, privileges, and so on is governed by what the participants in the system of distribution can reasonably expect as their rightful share; disputes over distribution are settled on the basis of what one deserves as a member in the distribution system. In a punitive context, the logic of equivalence demands that the punishment must fit the crime: "An eye for an eye and a tooth for a tooth." If the logic of equivalence seems intuitively sound, it is because it most basically represents our human response to others in light of the circumstances of justice. Under the figure of law, equivalence configures human relationships on the basis of a rule of justice that is constantly threatened by the possibility of injustice.

This understanding of the rule of justice hinges on a conception of society as a space of confrontation between rivals for a moderately scarce set of goods. The rule of justice, therefore, represents a social practice that regulates conflicts over these goods. Adherence to formulated principles of justice is expected to uphold, or perhaps enforce, a dimension of social cohesion that prevents mutual disinterest in the interests of others from devolving into outright hostility or violence. That is to say, a rule of justice provides prudential grounds for recognizing the equal claim of others to liberty and opportunity. My interests are advanced to a greater extent by the equivalence that justice institutes between my claims to the distribution of social goods and those of others.

Now, it is precisely the logic of equivalence that seems so basic to human response that the logic of superabundance calls into question. The paradigm case of this logic is the extreme sayings attributed to Jesus in the Sermon on the Mount. The demands to turn the other cheek, to offer the cloak as well as the coat, to walk the second mile, to lend without expectation of return seem to contradict the concern for equivalence and reciprocity. This confrontation is amplified by the verses that introduce these sayings: "You have heard that it was said, 'An eye for an eye and a tooth for a tooth.' But I say to you . . ."[9]

In order to gain some insight into the logic employed here, Ricoeur turns to the work of biblical scholar Robert Tannehill. Tannehill suggests that the strategy employed here, and in other such extreme statements, is that of simply reversing our natural tendencies in such situations. He argues that these extreme commands function as focal instances that direct attention toward patterns of behavior. As such, these sayings are characterized (1) by their specificity and (2) by their extremity. First, these sayings do not propose a priori principles to guide behavior, but rather focus attention on specific situations. To derive general principles from these specific commands, Tannehill argues, is to miss their point. Second, the extremity of the sayings causes a radical disorientation with regard to general modes of behavior and judgments of the correct response given the situation. It is precisely in the tension between the extremity of the command and the typical response that the command takes on meaning and functions to reorient imagination toward a different way of being.[10]

In what sense is this reorientation a logic of superabundance? Is it not rather a logic of extremity, or better, a logic of reversal that is instituted here? A more penetrating look reveals that there is more at issue than a simple reversal, however. If these extreme commands do not generate general principles, they nonetheless elicit a general pattern of behavior that Ricoeur characterizes as giving more. He claims that "each response gives more than that asked by ordinary prudence.... Not just this, but even that! It is this giving more that appears to me to constitute the point of these extreme commands."[11] Ricoeur finds the echo of the same logic in the *how much more* of grace in Paul's Epistle to the Romans.[12]

This second aspect of the logic of superabundance raises the stakes by leveling an ontological claim about the cosmos and our place in it. In much the same way as the logic of equivalence is predicated on a particular set of circumstances—that is, moderate scarcity and mutual disinterest—the logic of superabundance rides on a claim about the nature of things. We find some indication of this in the overall drift of the Sermon on the Mount that surrounds Jesus' extreme commands. The text announces a realm of abundance and security assured by the providence of a benevolent God. This idea reaches its highest pitch in the metaphorical connection that Jesus draws between human life and "the birds of the air." The text counsels us not to be anxious, "But strive first for the kingdom of God and his righteousness and all these things will be given you as well."[13]

I want to turn once again to Tannehill in order to gain some perspective on what is being presented here. What this passage serves to do is to shock us out of the structures of concern that anxiously direct us toward our own security. Tannehill argues:

> [w]e may point out that the birds are also concerned with food; indeed, they spend most of their day seeking it. Even so, the contrast remains between man's elaborate structures of care and the comparatively simple, direct supplying of needs in the life of other creatures, and it is on this contrast that the text wishes us to meditate.... We experience a heightened awareness and the disturbing impingement of another reality. This opens a new possibility for life, a possibility which the text describes as seeking the Kingdom.[14]

I want to mark this ontological claim here and return to it later. I will turn now to the moral demands that arise out the structural confrontation between these two logics.

The Golden Rule versus the Love Command

The competing logics of equivalence and superabundance find fruition in two equally competing ethical orientations: the Golden Rule and the love command. I follow Ricoeur in choosing the Golden Rule as the principal expression of the ideal of justice, first, on the basis of his arguments for its comprehensiveness over rival principles; for example, Kant's second formulation of the categorical imperative. Second, the proximity of the Golden Rule to the love command in the Gospel passages highlights the tension between the two principles in enlightening ways.

The Golden Rule is expressive of the ideal of reciprocity characteristic of justice in two senses. First, the Golden Rule highlights the fundamental asymmetry of action, the fact that action involves both an agent and a patient. This recognition is guaranteed by the tension between "doing unto others" and "as oneself." Opposed to a conception of the situation of action solely in terms of the confrontation between two agents, this presentation of action recognizes both an actor and another who is a potential victim. The merit of the Golden Rule is its acknowledgment, at the level of grammar, of both the one who acts and the one who is acted upon. Second, the Golden Rule sets both agent and patient on the same footing relative to the deliberation over action. An equivalence is established in the application of the Golden Rule to discrete situations; both myself and others are potential aggressors or potential victims.

However, the equivalence established by the Golden Rule is called into question in significant ways by the love command. How is this the case? Does not the command to love one's neighbor as oneself establish the same equivalence by the qualification *as oneself*? The love command enters a logic of extremity once we address the question of who the neighbor is. If we take as an example Luke 6:27–31, the compass of love is extended to include even one's enemies. If this command to love one's enemies does not directly contradict the equivalence of the Golden Rule, it nonetheless radically disorients the manner in which it is typically applied. Indeed, the tension between the Golden Rule and the love command is heightened within the Lukan text itself: verses 27 to 28, which introduce the passage, command, "Love your enemies, do good to those who hate you, bless those who curse you, pray for those who abuse you." Verse 31, which concludes the passage, commands precisely the Golden Rule: "Do to others as you would have them do to you."

The conjunction of these two ideals produces some moral vertigo, to say the least. First, we are commanded to forgo reciprocity, then to uphold it. Yet the disorientation does not signal contradiction. Rather, it disorients in order to reorient; what is reoriented is our very understanding of the Golden Rule. What love demands is that we not reciprocate evil for evil, that we exercise a generosity of spirit toward others, even in the advent of evil. The Golden

The Site of Christian Ethics

Rule is inclined away from a reactive interpretation of strict reciprocity—that is, do to others what they do to you—toward a proactive orientation that takes generosity as its keystone.

But the introduction of generosity into our dealings with others raises the stakes of moral obligation, and here we touch, once again, on the ontological claim that was witnessed above. Ricoeur argues that the love command, placed as it is within the logic of extremity, introduces what he calls the hyperethical orientation of the economy of the gift.[15] The logic of this economy is well expressed a little further on in Luke: "Be merciful, just as your Father is merciful."[16] The orientation of love, structured as it is by the economy of the generosity, results in the paradoxical reciprocity of escalating generosity: love as you have been loved, give as you have been given, forgive as you have been forgiven. The mercy that has been proffered by the divine cannot be reciprocated in any way other than an orientation of continued mercy toward others. In this way, the logic of extremity, with which the command to love our enemies strikes us, is reintroduced to a logic of superabundance that makes the gesture of openness to the enemy understandable.

Here we stand at the boundary of the final dimension of the confrontation between love and justice: the creative tension between the ideas of theonomy and autonomy. Both of the previous levels of the argument have closed with an ontological claim about our place in the cosmos, a claim that can be broadly characterized as a feeling of dependence upon and receptivity to a creative ground of being. In addressing the competing logics of equivalence and superabundance, I concluded with the sense of abundance to which the writer of Matthew appeals in drawing the metaphorical connection between human existence and the "birds of the air." Echoing this, Paul's witness to the church at Rome of the "how much more" of grace further defines the experience of dependence upon which the sense of abundance hinges.

Addressing the confrontation between the competing orientations of the Golden Rule and the love command, I concluded with the idea in the Lukan texts of an economy of generosity that arises out of the demand to reciprocate mercy for mercy. I suggested that this is a paradoxical reciprocity because the mercy that has been given by the divine can be reciprocated only through extension to others. The economy of generosity has already been recognized in an experience of receptivity and dependence that challenges with a moral claim of mercy.

Turning to the final dimension of the argument, I will directly address this hyperethical economy under the figures of creation and redemption. It will become apparent that the seemingly opposed ideas of autonomy and theonomy are actually involved in a complex dialectic whereby theonomy institutes autonomy rather than cancelling it. From the symbols of creation and redemption we can begin to explore what Ricoeur calls the "traits" of theonomy that allow us to place the idea in dynamic confrontation with that of autonomy.

Autonomy versus Theonomy

The confrontation between autonomy and theonomy represents the point of highest tension between the ideals of justice and love to the degree that the formation of a principle of justice is conceived within the bounds of freedom's self-legislation. This juxtaposition represents one of the many places where Ricoeur wrestles with the Enlightenment legacy deriving principally from Kant. He states: "At least at first blush, the idea of a legislation of divine origin must appear as a form of heteronomy, diametrically opposed to the presumed autonomy of moral consciousness."[17] The tension between love and justice reaches its highest pitch here precisely in the fact that the economy of generosity, which arises out of a demand that seems to overstep the dictates of what is reasonable, finds its foundation in a divine command. The admission of a divine command as the ground for ethics is what Kant placed out of bounds in placing the self-sufficient, self-legislating capacity of autonomy in the position of moral foundation. However, this impasse is non-negotiable only so long as it is posed in terms of the antinomy of autonomy and heteronomy. Ricoeur seeks to avoid this by conceiving the idea of theonomy not in opposition to autonomy, but as its foundation. He questions the self-sufficient foundation of autonomy, but not its self-determining, self-legislating character.

As I suggested, the confrontation between the ideas of autonomy and theonomy finds its first foothold in the notion of the economy of generosity understood in terms of creation and redemption. Here my ethical analysis meets up with the previous analysis of the dialectical engagement between a theology of redemption and a theology of creation. The articulation of this economy from the angle of the idea of creation follows two lines, both of which characterize its hyperethical character. First, the idea of creation is expressive of the experience of dependence on a higher power that precedes us, envelops us, and sustains us. For Ricoeur, the symbol that gives meaning and direction to this experience is that of an original but always ongoing creation. This symbol of creation as ever-renewed foundation characterizes the supraethical quality of generosity in its profoundest dimension. Yet, if the experience of radical dependence constituted by the symbol of ongoing creation is supramoral in quality, Ricoeur argues that it is not amoral, inasmuch as the idea of power is immediately joined with that of a goodness to which we are receptive. This second aspect of the articulation of the economy of generosity from the angle of creation emphasizes the confirmation of the goodness of the creation that follows every creative act, culminating in Genesis 1:31: "God saw everything that he had made, and indeed, it was very good." The conjunction of the power of the creative act and the predicate "good," which designates God's ongoing creative project, constitutes the symbol of creation under the aegis of the economy of generosity.

The Site of Christian Ethics

This hyperethical claim serves to reorient us not just toward others, but toward reality as such; it is, in this sense, an ontological claim that levels a moral demand. Ricoeur argues:

> No doubt, this symbol sets human beings in the place of honor, but within a cosmos created before them and that continues to shelter them. Each of us is not left face-to-face with another human being, as the principle of morality taken in isolation seems to imply. Rather nature is between us, around us—not just as something to exploit but as an object of solicitude, respect, and admiration. The sense of our radical dependence on a higher power thus may be reflected in a love for the creature, for every creature, in every creature—and the love of neighbor can become an expression of this supramoral love for all creatures.[18]

The supramoral character of the sense of dependence, which makes the love of neighbor an expression of love for all creatures, compels love to its greatest extreme, even to the enemy.

It may be objected, however, that this characterization of God as loving creator presents only one side of the coin. Is God not also portrayed as harsh judge and, often, as destroyer of what has been created? Is God not also the one who threatens the chosen with destruction, who rewards the unjust and visits suffering on the just? These aspects of the tradition stand as obstacles to a representation of divine activity solely in terms of its giftlike character. Yet Ricoeur argues that these instances must not be isolated from the matrix of religious symbolism that surrounds them; God is, after all, the one we deem, or perhaps more accurately, the one whom the text reveals as being worthy of praise, veneration, and love. This concern opens onto the second line of inquiry in the articulation of the economy of generosity, that of redemption. Ricoeur offers two instances in support: the giving of the Torah and the Christological doctrine of Atonement: "The gift of the Torah is recounted narratively as a founding event, as we read in Exod. 20:1.... In this way, the law becomes an integral part of a history of liberation and becomes the expression of a gift. As for the Christian doctrine of 'satisfaction,' to the extent that it is accepted, it must not eclipse the giftlike character attached to the symbols of the cross."[19] The aspect of redemption—revelation of God as liberator at Sinai, revelation of Jesus as the suffering Christ—places the symbols of divine legislation back within the economy of generosity.

This initial exploration helps to orient us toward what Ricoeur calls the "traits" of theonomy. The idea of receptive dependence addresses the confrontation between autonomy and theonomy through the notion of being "before God" that arises initially out of the establishment of the covenant. The idea of covenant is useful here because it serves to reorient our understanding of the issue of divine command. It is not the case that God imposes a law on human relations; rather, God seeks covenantal relations with a people who then become God's own. While it must be admitted that this covenantal relation is not a relation among equals, it nonetheless takes on a remarkable quality of reciprocity in the form of an exchange of promises. This double promise of the covenant establishes the two sides of the category "before God": first, God is revealed as the one who follows the chosen through their history of trial and tribulation, the one who offers protection and comfort. The Other is not utterly other. At the same time, however, the experience of being before God, the recognition of the promise of support and protection, entails a promise of obedience. Ricoeur concludes, "Here is the other side of the coin of the 'before God' category: free consent is sought within a nonetheless unequal relation."[20] It is in this sense that covenant issues in legislation.

The issue of the law is not a simple one, however. Ricoeur argues that the law is subject to a "twofold pulsation": on the one hand, there is a thrust toward a fundamental level of legislation that seeks to gather together and unify the various codes toward a common purpose; on the other, there is the tendency toward complexity and multiplication into "ever finer layers of legislation." This same tension works its way throughout the legislation of the Pentateuch. A unifying impulse asserts itself most profoundly in the commandments to love God and neighbor, an impulse to complexity in the Deuteronomic and Levitical codes. While the former compose the core content of the law, the latter interpret what this core content means and how to achieve it. Now, this core content establishes the idea of theonomy in its crowning glory. With the commandment to love, we reach both the depths and heights of theonomy.

There is reason, however, to pause and contemplate the paradoxical nature of this commandment. Indeed, can love be commanded? Is love not rather an affection that is either present or not present, fundamentally beyond the dictates of law? Addressing this enigma, Ricoeur turns to Franz Rosenzweig's *The Star of Redemption*, the cornerstone of which is the revelatory character of the love command. Describing God as "the lover," Rosenzweig claims: "The commandment to love can only proceed from the mouth of the lover. Only the lover can and does say: love me! . . . In his mouth the commandment to love is not a strange commandment; it is none other than the voice of love itself. The love of the lover has, in fact, no word to express itself other than the commandment."[21] In the immediacy of the moment, when God directly addresses the individual, the love command takes on its imperative overtones.

Ricoeur argues that Rosenzweig employs a *poetic* use of the imperative. As such the love command makes use of the whole poetic matrix of the biblical text, most immediately poetic praise, in a way that makes it irreducible to a simple imperative of duty. The poetic imperative is irreducible to an imperative of duty because it serves not only to orient our ethical obligation; it also serves as an ontological foundation for the self as such. Prior to the moment of address from the divine, the self is blind to itself because it does not recognize itself as bound to the unfolding fabric of creation. Thus, the imperative tone of the love command refers back to the ontological claim of dependence. The call of love opens the self to itself in the recognition of its responsibility. In turn, all claims to responsibility issue from the command of love.

This is most profoundly the case with love of neighbor. Rosenzweig argues that love of neighbor is only possible in the advent of the commandment, which secures the soul as beloved of God beyond any declaration of love. The clarity of purpose in the love of neighbor, outstripping, as Rosenzweig argues, any willing "in general," is fundamentally directed by the commandment that proceeds from the lover. He states: "[Love of neighbor] originates in the directed freedom of the character, and this commandment needs a presupposition beyond freedom. *Fac quod jubes et jube quod vis* means that God's 'ordaining what he will' must, since the content of the present ordinance is to love, be preceded by God's 'already having done' what he ordains. Only the soul beloved of God can receive the commandment to love its neighbor and fulfill it."[22] Who is the neighbor? We have already placed this concept within the logic of extremity by extending love even to the enemy. Rosenzweig extends this logic even further to include whatever is love's nearest representative. In the extreme case, the nearest representative is potentially life as such, life conceived in its broadest possible sense—the "coming into being" of the world.

I have followed Ricoeur in this path from the idea of receptive dependence through covenant and commandment in order to pose the relationship between autonomy and theonomy in a way that skirts the antinomy of autonomy and heteronomy. To witness to the idea of a receptive dependence that obliges us to loving concern for the well-being of others is not to stake a claim against autonomy as self-determining will. Quite the opposite, the claim that love obliges—that is to say, the recognition that being loved issues in a moral claim to love others—opens the way to self-legislating freedom. If the idea of dependence challenges the claim of the self-sufficiency of autonomy, it does not challenge the claim to self-determination, but rather places it in a different light. To paraphrase Rosenzweig, the free outpouring of love for neighbor resides in a presupposition beyond freedom, a presupposition that he characterizes as being beloved of God.

This said, I turn to the critical rapprochement of the claims of love and justice. The wager is that a reexamination and mutual reinterpretation will yield a deepened understanding of both.

Mutual Reinterpretation, Deepened Understanding

The first point to be made in the critical rapprochement of the ideals of love and justice is that love requires more, and not less, than justice. It is precisely this character of love to demand *more-than-justice* that marks it as supraethical. At the same time, this character preserves the supraethical from devolving into the amoral, or, worse, the immoral. The fact that love demands more than justice means that love, in many circumstances, demands a dimension of self-sacrifice, most notably in the form of renouncing a strict reciprocity. Nonetheless, this demand for self-sacrifice in particular instances is not equivalent to a demand for complacency in the face of injustice nor to a demand for self-negation. Rosenzweig suggests, in fact, that the love command is constitutive of the self as such. Beyond this, however, the more-than-justice of love marks out the intersection of the ideals of love and justice in its depth. Ricoeur argues, in fact, that "justice is the necessary medium of love."[23] That is to say, the poetic imperative initiated by the praise of love is drawn in the direction of an authentic interpretation only so long as it remains within the compass of its relationship with the ideal of justice. What, then, is the character of the more-than-justice that love demands?

We can trace certain perverse interpretations to which the Golden Rule, left to its own, is not immune. These take two principal forms. First, the Golden Rule might be interpreted in terms of a reactive reciprocity: do to others what they do to you. This orientation links the Golden Rule to what might be called an economy of retribution. Second, and perhaps more insidious, the Golden Rule can be interpreted in terms of a kind of instrumental reciprocity: I give so that you will give. Ricoeur argues that posing the Golden Rule and love command along the lines of dynamic encounter, rather than static opposition, offers some corrective to these dual tendencies. The case for a dynamic encounter is pressed, in large measure, by the very proximity of the two commands in the passage in the Gospel of Luke that I cited. In a sense, the hyperethical category of love, paradoxically, preserves the moral from a fall into the immoral and saves reciprocity from its perversion into retribution or utility. This creative tension strikes deeply at our understanding of justice as a logic of equivalence. It is precisely out of the more-than-justice that love calls for justice. But this is a call for justice, as Ricoeur states, "reared in the economy of gift."

This economy confronts our understanding of justice at a deeper level, however. With Ricoeur, I have advanced the argument that the generosity engendered by the love command is the only thing that saves reciprocity from its fall into retribution and utility, a fall that turns the striving for justice into a perverse form of injustice. In this instance, the ideal of love places in question what Ricoeur labels the "hubris of justice"—that is, the ambition of justice to found itself on its own terms. But this argument redirects attention back to the foundational claims encountered in the examination of theonomy and its relation to autonomy. The idea of receptive dependence takes on moral overtones once it is introduced to the workings of the love command and the idea of a loving obedience. I have followed Ricoeur in the endeavor to conceive theonomy in such a way that it does not contradict autonomy, but

The Site of Christian Ethics

rather engenders it, even if autonomy must finally dissociate its lot from self-sufficiency. But in what direction is autonomy engendered?

In posing the idea of theonomy, I also posed the idea of a fundamental receptivity in the event whereby the divine addresses itself to the soul in the form of command. The "Love me!" of the commandment demands a response; my reliance on Rosenzweig led me to claim that the response to the word is realized in responsibility to, responsibility *for*, the world. Ricoeur seems to concur when he states:

> I would emphasize that a loving obedience arouses us to responsibility with regard to the other, in the sense in which Emmanuel Levinas says it of the face, whose injunction compellingly invites me to care for the other to the point of bending me to the posture of hostage and the act of substitution. In this sense, theonomy, understood as the call to a loving obedience, generates autonomy, understood as call to responsibility. Here we touch on a delicate point, where a certain foundational passivity joins with an active acceptance of responsibility.[24]

Theonomy, therefore, is generative of autonomy in the sense that response to the word issues in responsible spontaneity on behalf of the world.

Having reached the end of this itinerary, a final question remains: To what extent does this theologically oriented ethics lend itself to ethical reflection in general? It is difficult to assess Ricoeur's views on the degree to which theology and philosophy can authentically approach each other. He has claimed to be a philosopher who listens seriously to the Christian witness, and the wealth of his writings on various religious topics testifies to the fact that his listening is seriously engaged. At the same time, he has argued that philosophy and theology are separate and autonomous discourses. In the last section of this essay, I will address what I take to be several premier places where moral philosophy and theological ethics in fact do speak to each other. I will not attempt to reduce one to the other. However, I will argue that there is more room for a critical rapprochement than Ricoeur has often suggested, and that his own formulations of some key problems open the path to such a rapprochement.

Moral Philosophy and Theological Ethics

There are, in Ricoeur's work, three principal points where moral philosophy and theological ethics speak to each other across the boundary that separates them: the paradox of moral evil, the question of moral responsibility, and the possibilities for an understanding of conscience. I will not attempt to give a complete account of the shape of this rapprochement, but rather will briefly offer some lines of possibility.

The problem of moral evil is an immediate and abiding point of contact between philosophy and theology. As we saw, Ricoeur follows Kant in placing the entrance into religious concern in the recognition of the paradoxical and radical character of moral evil. Moral philosophy comes up against its practical limit in the paradox of the voluntary servitude of the will. Theological discourse does not resolve this paradox, but rather reconfigures it under the productive sign of hope. Under the figure of the promise, the theology of redemption bolsters freedom in the hope for its own reconciliation. This point of crossing has received the most attention both from Ricoeur and from his commentators. The second point of crossing, however, has received very little attention.

I addressed some of the problems that the theology of redemption presents for the question of moral responsibility. Because of the tendency of the theology of redemption to banish value from the created order, it becomes difficult to locate anything within the world that ought to elicit our responsibility. But this is a problem within moral philosophy as well. One of Ricoeur's principal criticisms of Kant's second formulation of the categorical imperative is that it directs respect not toward individual persons, but toward the abstract ideal of humanity. Another more vexing problem concerns the formation of a rule of justice as this is set out by John Rawls. Ricoeur argues that "the highest point the ideal of justice can envision is that of a society in which the feeling of mutual dependence—even of mutual indebtedness—remains subordinate to the idea of mutual disinterest.... The idea of mutuality is by no means absent from this [Rawls's] formula, but the juxtaposition of interests prevents the idea of justice from attaining the level of a true recognition and a solidarity such that each person feels indebted to every other person."[25] Paradoxically, the formation of a rule of justice that every reasonably self-interested person can agree upon is precisely what shields individuals from any sense of moral responsibility toward others. As a member of the discussion in the original position, I am fundamentally disinterested in the interests of my counterparts. The formation of the rule of justice is a purely prudential concern.[26]

In significant ways, the outline of a theology of creation offers a change of heart at the levels of both moral philosophy and the theology of redemption. What the theology of creation serves to do is ground value in the ongoing process of creation. In this sense, the created order itself becomes an object of my solicitude. More important, if we consider Rosenzweig's understanding of redemption as human action on behalf of the world, then the process of redemption itself is redirected toward the active increase of value within creation. Creation is not something that we must suffer in our hopeful anticipation of the eschaton. Rather, the created order, including individual persons, is that which solicits our active response, our *responsible spontaneity*, even as we recognize our fundamental dependence on the creation. As well as opening us to a recognition of moral value in the other, this theology of creation offers profound possibilities for ecological ethics.

But it is perhaps with regard to a deepened understanding of the idea of conscience that moral philosophy and theological ethics stand in closest proximity. In the concluding section of *Oneself as Another*, Ricoeur attempts to negotiate a path between Heidegger's "demoralized" account of conscience, which risks evacuating self-attestation of any ethical and moral concern, and Levinas's "deontologized" account, which risks reducing the phenomenon of conscience to the otherness of other persons. He states:

> To these alternatives—either Heidegger's strange(r)ness or Levinas's externality—I shall stubbornly oppose the original and originary character of what appears to me to constitute the third modality of otherness, namely being enjoined as the structure of selfhood.... To Heidegger, I objected that attestation is primordially injunction, or attestation risks losing all ethical or moral significance. To Levinas, I shall object that the injunction is primordially attestation, or the injunction risks not being heard and the self not being affected in the mode of being-enjoined.[27]

But it is precisely in steering this philosophical path that Ricoeur encounters a similar kind of impasse on the side of philosophy. From whence comes the injunction? Ricoeur concludes, "Perhaps the philosopher as philosopher has to admit that one does not know and cannot say whether this Other, the source of the injunction, is another person whom I can look in the face or who can stare at me, or my ancestors for whom there is no representation, to so great an extent does my debt to them constitute my very self, or God—living God, absent God—or an empty place."[28] This silence on the part of Ricoeur the philosopher is another point of crossing between philosophy and theology for Ricoeur the listener.

The voice is the metaphor that Ricoeur adopts to explore the phenomenon of conscience, and, in his more theologically oriented writings, he has explored this idea of the voice as the word that is constitutive of the self. Indeed, in at least one place, he has drawn the connection between the figure of the summoned self in the narratives of the prophetic call and self-attestation in the voice of conscience. At the end of "The Summoned Subject in the School of the Narratives of the Prophetic Vocation," Ricoeur advances a theological interpretation of conscience, following Gerhard Ebeling, claiming that "in the *bona conscientia*, the Christian is thereby as much protected against despair as warned against presumptuousness, that the 'true self' lies in this reconciliation."[29] However, as enlightening as this interpretation is, it seems to turn into a theological interpretation of Heidegger's strange(r)ness; conscience is once again deflected away from the moral injunction.

There is one avenue, however, that Ricoeur does not explore in the journey that leads from the prophetic call to the voice of conscience: Rosenzweig's interpretation of the love command. This is not overly surprising; Rosenzweig rarely, if ever, touches on the topic of conscience, and the idea of a direct confrontation with the divine that confronts the soul in the form of a direct address is problematic from Ricoeur's perspective.[30] Yet still, the possibilities that Rosenzweig's account offers to the idea of "being-enjoined as the structure of selfhood" are tantalizing to say the least.

Once again, these final statements are intended to be exploratory in nature. It is hoped that they will open new possibilities for continued engagements with the work of one of the great listeners of our time.

Notes

1. Paul Ricoeur, "Ethical and Theological Considerations on the Golden Rule," in *Figuring the Sacred: Religion, Narrative, and Imagination*, ed. Mark I. Wallace and trans. David Pellaur (Minneapolis: Fortress Press, 1995), p. 301.
2. Paul Ricoeur, "Hope and the Structure of Philosophical Systems," in *Figuring the Sacred*, p. 215.
3. Paul Ricoeur, "Freedom in Paul Ricoeur, 'Ethical and Theological Considerations on the Golden Rule,' in Light of Hope," in *The Conflict of Interpretations*, ed. Don Ihde and trans. Robert Sweeney (Evanston, IL: Northwestern University Press, 1974), pp. 406–7.
4. Paul Ricoeur, "Manifestation and Proclamation," in *Figuring the Sacred*, p. 64.
5. Ibid., p. 65.
6. Paul Ricoeur, "The 'Figure' in Rosenzweig's *The Star of Redemption*," in *Figuring the Sacred*, pp. 102–3.
7. André LaCocque and Paul Ricoeur, *Thinking Biblically: Exegetical and Hermeneutical Studies*, trans. David Pellauer (Chicago: University of Chicago Press, 1998), p. 67.
8. John Rawls, *A Theory of Justice* (Cambridge, MA: Harvard University Press, 1971), pp. 126–28.
9. Matthew 5:38–42.
10. Robert Tannehill, *The Sword of His Mouth* (Philadelphia: Fortress Press, 1975), p. 72.
11. Paul Ricoeur, "The Logic of Jesus, the Logic of God," in *Figuring the Sacred*, p. 281.
12. Romans 5:6–11.
13. Matthew 6:33.
14. Tannehill, *The Sword of His Mouth*, pp. 63, 66.
15. What Ricoeur continues to call the "economy of the gift" I will consciously call, throughout this examination, the "economy of generosity." I employ this change in terminology for several reasons. First, the concept of *the gift* is exceedingly ambiguous, as Marcel Mauss and Jacques Derrida, among others, have shown. Indeed, Ricoeur's own use of the term, in conjunction with the idea of *economy*, serves to heighten the ambiguities already associated

with the idea of a gift. Whether or not this is one of Ricoeur's characteristically veiled ironic twists is hard to tell, but my hope is that the idea of generosity might circumvent some of these ambiguities. A second reason is more germane to this particular examination, though it is linked to my initial concerns. While the logic of superabundance does strike the imagination in the form of the giftedness of existence, the introduction of the idea of covenant, which will appear in the next section of this analysis, reintroduces the same ambiguities. The gift does not come without an obligation, hence it is not really a gift. For these reasons, among others, I will employ the term *generosity*, which, though perhaps less poetically interesting, nonetheless more readily offers itself to this discussion.

16. Luke 6:36.
17. Paul Ricoeur, "Theonomy and/or Autonomy," in *The Future of Theology: Essays in Honor of Jürgen Moltmann*, ed. Miroslav Volf (Grand Rapids, MI: Eerdmans, 1996), p. 284.
18. Ricoeur, "Ethical and Theological Considerations on the Golden Rule," pp. 297–98.
19. Ibid., p. 299.
20. Ricoeur, "Theonomy and/or Autonomy," p. 287.
21. Franz Rosenzweig, *The Star of Redemption*, trans. William W. Halo (Notre Dame, IN: University of Notre Dame Press, 1985), p. 176.
22. Ibid., pp. 214–15.
23. Paul Ricoeur, "Love and Justice," in *Figuring the Sacred*, p. 329.
24. Ricoeur, "Theonomy and/or Autonomy," p. 296.
25. Ricoeur, "Love and Justice," pp. 323–24.
26. In *Oneself as Another* (trans. Kathleen Blamey [Chicago: University of Chicago Press, 1992]), Ricoeur argues that the rule of justice, which hinges on the idea of mutual disinterest in the interests of others, is predicated on a prior *sense* of justice, taken from Hannah Arendt. This sense of justice itself rides on the idea of mutual indebtedness that binds citizens together in the exercise of power in common.
27. Ricoeur, *Oneself as Another*, pp. 354–55.
28. Ibid., pp. 354–55.
29. Paul Ricoeur, "The Summoned Subject in the School of the Narratives of the Prophetic Vocation," in *Figuring the Sacred*, p. 274.
30. "Christian faith does not simply consist in saying that it is God who speaks in our conscience. This immediateness professed by Rousseau in his 'The Profession of Faith of a Savoyard Priest' ('conscience! conscience! divine voice . . .') misconstrues the meditation of interpretation between the autonomy of conscience and the obedience of faith" (ibid., p. 274).

9
Veils and Kingdoms
A Ricoeurian Metaphorics of Love and Justice
GLENN WHITEHOUSE

Introduction

Paul Ricoeur is above all the thinker of *mediation*. In one subject area after another, he has risked the wager of thinking together different theoretical and disciplinary positions that bear every appearance of incompatibility. Over and over again, his considerable intellectual gifts have been applied to the task of uncovering the unrecognized kinship between the procedures of two different methods of inquiry, or of identifying the subject matter around which stubborn intellectual adversaries can become partners in a fruitful conversation. But Ricoeur is the thinker of mediation only because he is also the thinker of *distanciation*. In line with his conviction that hermeneutics should not divorce truth from method, he has directed our attention to the ways in which human understanding is schematized through texts, rules, and institutions. His painstaking analyses of the *detours* of understanding put the brakes on any premature synthesis between different points of view, insisting that we first explore the internal logic of a particular mode of discourse before asking the question of how a dialogue can open between that discursive system and another. In this way, Ricoeur has helped the contemporary intellectual world understand both the closure of discourse and its openings, the borders that are necessary for understanding to articulate any definite meaning, and the refiguring that can occur when a mode of understanding opens itself to its other in dialogue.

Among the most important encounters that Ricoeur has sought to mediate in recent years has been the meeting of philosophy and religious studies, the two areas in which his own constructive contributions have been most significant. Perhaps here especially, though, we see his characteristic caution against mixing genres of thinking assert itself. "If I defend my philosophical writing against the accusation of crypto-theology," he tells us in the introduction to *Oneself as Another*, "I also refrain, with equal vigilance, from assigning to biblical faith a crytophilosophical function."[1] One can understand the source of this vigilance. While Christian faith finds its bearings by responding to the manifold ways that God is named in the genres of the biblical text,[2] philosophy must always reposit any meaning *it* receives in the responsibility of autonomous thought. As a thinker who is oriented more toward biblical exegesis than philosophical theology,[3] Ricoeur has sought above all to make sense of Christian religious identity as the response to a gift of meaning that proceeds from the reading and preaching of a text. He has been reluctant to follow the path of those theologians who bring the categories of philosophical systems directly into religious thought, fearing the reductionism that often accompanies this enterprise. Likewise, he has defended himself against the charge that his philosophical anthropology rests on unacknowledged theological presuppositions, insisting that hermeneutics' detour of self-understanding implies and requires no particular faith in God.[4] Nonetheless, in recent years Ricoeur's thought has cautiously sought ways to think beyond the division between autonomous secular philosophy and heteronomous biblical religion, to point toward a *theonomous* thinking that dwells in the dialogue between the two.[5]

It is in the field of *ethics* more than any other that Ricoeur has sought to work out this theonomy, exploring the intersection of philosophical and religious ethics in such essays as "Ethical and Theological Considerations on the Golden Rule" and "Love and Justice."[6] Ricoeur remains cautious about a premature synthesis that would assume ready commensurability between *love*, which is figured through the poetic discourse of praise, and *justice*, which is schematized through procedures of juridical argumentation.[7] Ricoeur will state that "Biblical *agape* ... [possesses] a metaethical character, which makes me say that there is no such thing as a Christian morality ... but a common morality ... which biblical faith places in a new perspective, in which love is tied to the 'naming of God.' "[8] Still, this "new perspective" is not without a practical effect on the structures of secular morality. When the believing subject becomes open to seeing herself as part of an "economy of the gift" based on love, her moral imagination will come to be refigured in such a way that her interpretation and application of the precepts of secular ethics will be decisively transformed. In the aforementioned essays, Ricoeur has explored both the refiguring of moral imagination through love and the accompanying transformation of practice that go together to make up the theonomy specific to the ethical domain.

The ambition of this essay will be to add constructively to Ricoeur's attempt to think the unity of love and justice. My own wager is that we can gain deeper insight into the *refiguration* of justice by love if we pay attention to the *figurative language* through which both justice and love are thought. This will require that we pay close attention to the *metaphors* that Ricoeur utilizes in his analyses of religious faith and philosophical ethics. I will locate the heart of a Ricoeurian approach to ethical theonomy in the relation between two metaphors that play a key role in his writings: the veil and the kingdom. My thesis is that a deeper metaphorical relation between justice in secular society and love in the religious community will be revealed in the juxtaposition of these two images. In order to unpack this relation, it will be helpful to extend the evocative power of these metaphors through a disciplined improvisation on the images of veil and kingdom as used in Ricoeur's texts. In order to give this improvisation its fullest possible scope, it will be necessary not only to examine where Ricoeur uses these metaphors, but also to notice where he does *not* use them. In this extension of the metaphorics of the veil and the kingdom, we will find a distinctive way of thinking love's poetry together with the prose of justice. Although this way of proceeding may speak where Ricoeur is silent and may dwell longer in the tension of metaphor than he would want to, I offer it as an example of how a critical appropriation of Ricoeur's texts may provide a fruitful way to think the central categories of Christian religious ethics and philosophical ethics together.

As a preliminary to this exercise, it will be useful briefly to recall the general importance of metaphor in Ricoeur's work. At its most basic level, Ricoeur's approach to metaphor focuses on the link between *semantic innovation* and *productive imagination*.[9] The former term refers to the idea that a metaphor is best understood as a *twist* in the meaning of a sentence produced by the "semantic impertinence" of a literally absurd combination of words, such as "time is an arrow."[10] In such a statement there is a *tension* created between the declarative assertion that these words are true, and the judgment that must be passed about the literal truth of the sentence: time both is and is not an arrow. The latter term recalls Kant's reference to the imagination as the function that mediates between concepts and sense intuition to synthesize the objects of the everyday perceptual world. Imagination can do this because of its capacity to produce a schema of relation between the conceptual and sensible components of knowledge. Now Ricoeur claims that imagination's operation of grasping the similar between different sources of knowledge is the very function that also makes it capable of schematizing the reference of poetic language—of creating a figurative meaning on the basis of a literal one. The impertinent predication of metaphor that "twists" literal language will now be associated with a twist in the understanding that is now able to see through the "is" and the "is not" to an "is like" in which time is *seen as* an arrow. In this respect, metaphor is constantly functioning to bring new levels of reality to human understanding, allowing the *reference* of discourse to extend beyond the literal level.[11]

The semantic innovation of metaphor is thus intimately linked to the capacity of the imagination to see what is *new* and different from ordinary understanding. This makes metaphor an ingredient not only of poetic lan-

Veils and Kingdoms 167

guage, but also of the speculative language of philosophy. Although philosophical discourse takes on the responsibility of constructing a proper conceptual language to express its insights, it nonetheless depends for those insights on the capacity of our understanding to schematize new objects of meaning beyond the physical reality of the world. According to Ricoeur, "it can be shown that . . . speculative discourse has its condition of *possibility* in the semantic dynamism of metaphorical utterance."[12] Though Ricoeur remains critical of a Nietzschean or Derridean attempt to deconstruct philosophy based on the metaphorical origin of its language, he does give some support to the strategy of approaching speculative thought with its metaphorical condition of possibility in mind. Such an approach is in fact central to the project of hermeneutics, inasmuch as "Interpretation is . . . a mode of discourse that functions at the intersection of two domains, metaphorical and speculative. . . . On one side, interpretation seeks the clarity of the concept; on the other, it hopes to preserve the dynamism of meaning that the concept holds and pins down."[13] It is this notion of *interpretation* that will be the guide and justification for the approach of this essay. If interpretation stands between the concept and the metaphor, then the proper method for investigating the intersection of a biblical religion based on figurative language and a philosophical discourse that articulates its insights in conceptual language, will be an *interpretive* process that seeks to restore the dynamism and direction of both kinds of discourse. By dwelling at the intersection of image and concept, we should be able to gain a glimpse into the process by which the concepts of philosophy are poeticized and the poetics of the biblical text are conceptualized, in the *event* of encounter between love and justice.

The Veil and the Kingdom

Let us now turn our attention to the way in which Ricoeur incorporates the metaphors of the veil and the kingdom into his ethical writings. As we will see, each metaphor has a specific role to play within the mode of discourse in which it is found, philosophical ethics or biblical religion, respectively. We will then turn a critical ear toward Ricoeur's silences, and take note of ready uses of these metaphors that he *declines* to exploit. We will find that where Ricoeur's words associate the veil with philosophical ethics and the kingdom with biblical religion, his silences suggest an opposite association of the kingdom with philosophy and the veil with religion. The four-term structure that arises from this analysis will then be used as the scale on which to play out the constructive improvisation of the third part.

The metaphor of the veil enters Ricoeur's reflection on justice through his interest in the contracturalist theory of John Rawls, who uses the idea of a "veil of ignorance" behind which the members of society choose the principles of justice.[14] One might object that this is Rawls's image rather than Ricoeur's, but it should be remembered that Ricoeur's insights are typically worked out in and through his engagement with other thinkers. A brief account of Rawls's veil of ignorance will serve to orient our look at Ricoeur's appropriation of the image in *Oneself as Another.*

For Rawls, the veil of ignorance forms a vital part of the *procedure* through which his quasi-Kantian *Theory of Justice* finds its justification. Rawls's use of the image blends the contracturalist tradition of social theory together with the Kantian notion of persons as autonomous agents who self-legislate the universal moral laws to which they are held accountable. Without a ready way to conceive autonomy at the intersubjective level of society, Rawls uses the fiction of a veil of ignorance as a method to think a hypothetical *original position* of society, such that the *procedure* of setting up that original scene will guarantee the *fairness* of those principles that agents will choose in the original position. The veil of ignorance is part of that original position because Rawls, like Kant, locates the major source of unfairness in those particular, contingent preferences that will impel each agent to choose laws that will benefit themselves at the expense of others. As a remedy to this "mask of self-conceit," Rawls proposes a veil of ignorance in which agents will be deprived of all knowledge of their position in society, their special talents or weaknesses, and even of their personal goals and notions of the good life. In this situation, Rawls proposes, all agents would freely choose those principles that guarantee the maximum basic liberties possible for everyone, and that tolerate social inequalities only to the extent that they are distributed fairly and ultimately work to the benefit of all.[15] Using this fiction of the veil of ignorance to justify his Kantian moral convictions, Rawls believes he has succeeded in substituting a *purely procedural* concept of justice for any teleological theory based on people's common convictions about the good life. Though he goes on to elaborate his principles of justice in great detail, it is this fable of a veil of ignorance that is the symbol as well as the keystone of Rawls's procedural approach to justice.

Ricoeur challenges Rawls's claim that his theory provides a justification for the principles of justice that is based solely on rational procedure to the exclusion of teleological convictions about the good. Calling attention to Rawls's own contention that there must be a circle of "reflective equilibrium" between the theory of justice and our own considered convictions about what is just, Ricoeur contends "that a procedural conception of justice provides at best a rationalization of a sense of justice that is always presupposed."[16] This procedure of rationalization clarifies, systematizes, and balances, but does not *replace* a teleological notion of justice based on the good. Ricoeur even goes so far as to suggest that without the connection to an intuitive sense of justice that is articulated *outside* the veil of ignorance, the application of those principles chosen behind the veil bears the danger of falling into just the sort of utilitarian calculation that Rawls is trying to argue against in *A*

Theory of Justice. "Detached from the context of the Golden Rule the maximin rule [by which Rawls's hypothetical agents calculate the distribution of social goods in such a way as to maximize the minimum share within a necessarily unequal distributive system] would remain a purely prudential argument characteristic of every exchange relation."[17]

Despite these critiques, Ricoeur will make Rawls's fiction of the veil of ignorance an integral part of the dialectic of ethical theories he fleshes out in the "little ethics" of *Oneself as Another*. This "little ethics" is structured around two organizing principles: (1) the division between teleological and deontological approaches to ethics, which defines a three-step dialectic from the ethical aim (teleological), to the moral norm (deontological), to practical wisdom that mediates the two in concrete decisions; and (2) the grammatical progression of the three morally relevant senses of "self" running from the solitary self, to face-to-face relationships with others, to life in the institutions that define communities.[18] Within this structure, Rawls's procedural approach to justice has a definite role to play. As a deontological theory of moral rules closely linked to Kant, Rawls's procedural theory functions as a critical "sieve" through which the ethical sense of justice must pass, if it is not to fall prey to the evil of personal and social prejudice, which can virtually destroy the sense of social bond that defines a community. The strategy of purifying oneself of such personal preferences by erecting a veil of ignorance provides the needed means for universalizing and equalizing the distributive system of society, and hence for *protecting* the social bond on which the communitarian teleological sense of justice depends. At the same time, however, the veil of ignorance *separates* the formal principles of justice from the actual concrete contexts in which they will have to be applied. In order then to resolve the conflicts that result from a hidebound application of formal rules, a society must lift the veil of ignorance and balance the procedures of fairness with a recollection of the actual ethical goods that are at stake, in order to produce a wise practical decision in the third stage of Ricoeur's ethical dialectic.

As for Ricoeur's analysis of three senses of moral selfhood, Rawls's procedural theory of justice would obviously fit in the place of the ethical third person—the institution. Here it is worth noting that in using Rawls to talk about the deontology of social justice, Ricoeur is breaking a pattern established in his chapter on the ethical aim, inasmuch as there he focused on Aristotle in his discussion of all three ethical "persons." When he then turns to the stage of the moral norm, he draws directly from Kant to discuss the first person, the autonomous agent, and the second person, respect for rational agents. Why now the turn from master to disciple when we reach the institutional level? Ricoeur states that Rawls's fiction of a veil of ignorance is the most adequate projection of the Kantian notion of autonomy in the institutional realm. But it is crucial to note that he makes this concession only on the condition that we remember the *fictional* character of the model, which contrasts with Kant's direct foundation of the moral law in selfhood: "while autonomy can be said to be a fact of reason, . . . the contract can only be a fiction . . . because the republic is not a fact, as is the consciousness born of the confused yet firm knowledge that a good will is unconditionally good."[19] The veil of ignorance, then, serves as a compensation for the forgetfulness of the original social bond or will to live together. If "immoral society" first shows us the face of evil rather than the intention toward the good, the fiction represented by the veil of ignorance functions as a kind of place-holder that attempts to ground and heal that social bond so that the original will to live together can eventually be restored on the basis of equality rather than domination. Rawls's metaphor of the veil of ignorance therefore serves two crucial functions in Ricoeur's treatment of justice. First, by virtue of its connection with the process of purifying ourselves of particular interests, it serves to represent the critical distance that Ricoeur claims is a limited but crucial part of the process of ethical decision-making. Second, by virtue of its status as a fiction, it allows moral theory to think a counterfactual situation—a just and equitable society.

The second metaphor we are interested in—that of the kingdom—finds its home in Ricoeur's religious writings. Ricoeur's contribution to the exegesis of New Testament texts has focused largely on the question of how the Kingdom of God is revealed to human understanding through certain "extravagant" forms of biblical discourse, especially the parable. Ricoeur will base his biblical hermeneutics on the claim that human understanding can approach the Kingdom of God only through being refigured by the appropriation of scriptural language that has a metaphorical structure to it. In discussing the New Testament parables, Ricoeur says of the "Kingdom of God" (as he elsewhere says of "God" and "Christ") that it functions as a qualifier or "enigma expression" that frames the different genres of biblical discourse while receiving content from them.[20] When Jesus says "The Kingdom of God is like this . . ." and then proceeds to tell a parable, then the enigma expression of the "kingdom" both gives direction to the meaning of the parable and receives content from it.

The parable itself is a conjunction of *narrative form* and *metaphorical process*—a metaphorized narrative.[21] Ricoeur analyzes parables as a special kind of metaphor in which the "twist" operates through the plot of a story rather than in the predication of a simple sentence. The plot exhibits this twist by having an element of "oddness" or "extravagance" that transgresses the ordinary expectations of the narrative genre:[22] If narrative is the literary form that schematizes the unity of human practical existence in time,[23] then a narrative will be counted odd or extravagant when it appears to subvert or burst any normal practical quest to make a whole of one's existence. The effect of this odd predication is to call into question the listener's *own* attempt to make a coherent whole of her life—to subvert it in such a way that one is ready to refigure one's life in response to the *event* of encounter with the divine.[24]

The process by which ordinary life and language are refigured in the direction of this "enigma expression" indicate some further senses in which the image of "kingdom" serves as the central metaphor of biblical faith for Ricoeur. For one thing, the image of the *kingdom* of God (more so than the symbol "God") emphasizes that the ultimate referent of biblical discourse is *human experience as refigured* through the encounter with the divine mediated through the text.[25] What is figured in the parable is a kingdom, a realm, an existential location I can inhabit even if it reverses my normal expectations of living. The political image of a kingdom likewise connotes the idea of a law that would be the ruling principle of that kingdom. What is figured through the extravagant discourse of the biblical text is as much as anything a new *logic* of existence that challenges our mundane ways of calculating the interactions of human social life. Whereas human law and ordinary prudential calculation are based on a logic of *equivalence* ("this for that"), the new law of the Kingdom of God will be based on a logic of *superabundance* ("how much more . . .") that refigures our interactions in the direction of generosity, transformation, or justification.[26] Another way to speak of religious transformation in connection with the metaphor of "kingdom" is through the idea of the "economy of the gift," a phrase Ricoeur has associated with the Kingdom of God in recent writings. In line with the "kingdom" metaphor, if economics is how a society *distributes* goods, then under the kingship of God, goodness is distributed superabundantly. This refers not only to the goodness of grace or forgiveness added on to my life, but also to the goodness inherent in the act of creation itself, including the creation of people as creatures capable of imitating divine generosity. The transformation in self-understanding wrought by seeing one's own self as a gift brings with it a redirection of the principle of distribution, from "give in order that you may receive," to "Since it has been given you, give."[27] In all these ways, the image of a "kingdom" gathers together the different senses in which the divine overturns or explodes the normal structure of human social and practical life to reveal a new way of living. At the same time, the tensional structure of the metaphor "kingdom" also indicates continuity with our familiar ways of living by referring to the familiarity of an ordinary human political arrangement—as the subject matter of the parables remind us, the extraordinary *is like* the ordinary.[28]

The image of a "kingdom" of God is also linked to the notion of *love* as the central ethical expression of religious faith. Love for Ricoeur is only adequately understood to the extent that one sees it as part and parcel of the Kingdom of God. Its relation to the justice of the earthly world can only be indirect—that is why Ricoeur insisted that agape is *meta*ethical in the passage I indicated above. The metaphor of "kingdom" serves to express that difference through the image of a social realm structured in accordance with the extraordinary "economy of the gift." What we call love is really just the expression of the logic of action in the Kingdom of God where that economy of generosity reigns—and the image of this ethical superabundance as a separate kingdom serves to remind us that love stands at a distance from the language and logic of our earthly kingdom; only the knowledge that the extraordinary is encountered *in* the ordinary gives us the indication that love will have to be related to earthly justice. But this problem is best explored in what follows.

We have seen how the metaphors of "veil" and "kingdom" occupy central places in Ricoeur's constructive contributions to the areas of philosophical ethics and biblical theology. Each image functions as a focus that concentrates many of the central ideas of his thought. Now it will be useful to dwell briefly on Ricoeur's silences—the places where he *declines* to emphasize each of these images. It would of course be highly questionable to argue from silence if we were primarily interested in *explaining* the formal structure either of Ricoeur's philosophical writings or of his religious works. But since we are attempting to uncover the intersection of the two through an *interpretation* that aims both to respect the structure of conceptual systems and to reactivate the dynamism of the metaphors presupposed within these systems, it is legitimate to investigate the full range of possible significations that these metaphors may have in Ricoeur's thought.

On the side of secular justice, we found that it was the fiction of a "veil of ignorance" that served to schematize the ethical process of setting critical limits on the action of social institutions in Ricoeur's *Oneself as Another*. It is worthwhile to think about the move Ricoeur chose *not* to make when he constructed his ethical dialectic, however. In the study "The Self and the Moral Norm" from that work, Ricoeur used Kantian ethical theory as the paradigm for the deontological "sieve" that puts the teleological wish to live well to the test. Extending the function of moral critique through the different kinds of ethical selfhood, Ricoeur uses the Kantian notion of autonomy to represent the first person, and at the stage of the second person, he makes reference again to a central concept of Kant's ethics, respect for persons. When the time comes to speak of justice at the third-person level of social institutions, however, Ricoeur chooses to switch conversation partners and focus on Rawls's image of the veil of ignorance. We discussed above how this appeared to be motivated by the conviction that the *fiction* of the veil was needed to compensate for the forgotten *fact* of reason linking agency to rationality, which is still evident in the first and second persons, but has been covered over at the level of the institution. But what if Ricoeur had elected to remain with Kant through his discussion of all the types of moral selfhood? How does Kant's categorical imperative apply to the ethical third person, the institu-

Veils and Kingdoms

tion? It does so through appeal to another fiction, the metaphor of a *Kingdom of Ends*. This "very fruitful concept," as Kant describes it, arises by extending the imperative to treat rational beings as ends in themselves to the idea of a totality of all rational beings: "Hereby arises a systematic union of rational beings through common objective laws, i.e. a kingdom that may be called a kingdom of ends (certainly only an ideal), inasmuch as these laws have in view the very relation of such beings to one other as ends and means."[29] Kant realizes that the image of a totality or kingdom of agents who all follow the moral law is "only an ideal." Nonetheless, he finds the image a useful way to justify the fundamental dignity of *persons* in their plurality, to the extent that people can be conceived as participating *legislators* in such a potential Kingdom of Ends.[30] The basic ethical convictions of respect for the dignity of persons are clarified and rationalized through the positing of a counterfactual society in which the laws (plural) that regulate interactions are the product of an ideal legislative activity on the part of its members. Only here with Kant, that theoretical move is figured through the metaphor of the *kingdom* rather than the veil. Ricoeur, as we noted, had reasons for shifting the focus to Rawls, but it is at least worthwhile for us to keep in mind that there is a kingdom on the philosophical side that may possibly be able to serve as an analogy to the religious Kingdom of God.

On the side of biblical faith, we saw how Ricoeur uses the image of the Kingdom of God as a way to emphasize the differences between our mundane ways of living and the overturning of those ways that occurs when the self is born again into the new world of the biblical text. But there is another very powerful image that figures the separation between mundane society and the things of God that Ricoeur does *not* utilize: that is the veil or curtain that separates the human community from the Holy of Holies in Israelite religion, as well as the veil that conceals the face of Moses after his trip to the mountain. This image brings with it a different set of associations than that of the kingdom, but what they seem to express in common is the barrier to any direct translation between the extraordinary logic of God and the ordinary logic of humanity. No one may approach God directly; the "shaking of foundations" that occurs when God is encountered is so radical that cautionary steps must be taken so that a direct "face-to-face" vision of God's nature does not occur. Moses's veil and the curtain in the Temple function as if to emphasize the impossibility of a direct glimpse into the divine Kingdom from the side of mundane reality—they are "veils of ignorance" in that respect. Still, the *language* in which the divine is figured *can* be spoken through this veil. The connection of this image to the category of love comes through the New Testament. In the Christian tradition the passion of Christ has rent the veil that divides humanity from the glory of God. Placing this in connection with other Christian images, it is this tearing that would allow the light of love to shine directly through to the human community. This is ultimately what can justify an equation of "God" and "Love" with each other in 1 John 4, an equation that transforms the meaning of each term and ultimately refigures the relation between law and grace in human life.[31] Nonetheless, a torn veil is not the same as no veil at all, so Ricoeur's caution against endorsing a straightforward "ethics of love" would still be compatible with such an image.[32] Though it is more of a visual metaphor than Ricoeur, with his concern for divine *discourse,* tends to emphasize, the image of the veil does seem as if it could serve to support some of Ricoeur's ideas about the qualitative difference between secular concerns and the "new being" brought by the encounter with God.

Each of these alternative uses of the metaphors of "veil" and "kingdom" represents a road not taken in Ricoeur's ethical writings. Inasmuch as he carefully develops and defends those metaphors he does use, pointing out the silences hardly constitutes grounds for criticism. But since we are attempting to use Ricoeur's ideas constructively to interpret the intersection between love and justice, the appearance of a four-term metaphorical structure in which the philosophical and religious sides are *each* associated with a veil and a kingdom may constitute a promising start as we try to rethink and restore the dynamism of the encounter between the discourses of love and justice. It is to this constructive task that we now turn.

The Symbolism of Love and Justice

Taking a cue from the hermeneutical maxim that the symbol gives rise to thought, the task is now to *use* the four-term metaphorical structure set up in the above section to liberate new insights into the meeting place of the discourses of love and justice. What I have in mind here is a disciplined improvisation on the metaphorics of veil and kingdom, one that alternates between being receptive to the gift of meaning suggested by these two metaphors, and seeking conceptual clarification of this gift in terms of Ricoeur's characterization of the relation between love and justice.

The four metaphors taken together constitute a kind of scenario in which the intersection of love and justice can be visualized in various ways. Instituting justice in secular society requires that we be able to see ourselves as members of a Kingdom of Ends. But this kingdom can only exist behind the veil of ignorance that is needed to make self-legislation rational and universalizable. In order to move on to apply justice in concrete practical life, the veil must be lifted in some way. When we consider the relation of ordinary social life to religious faith, however, the human community will still find itself facing another veil. On the other side of the veil that separates us from God's glory is a Kingdom of God, a kingdom that we may hear about but not see. In the messages from the other side of the veil we may gain insight into what it would mean to live in that kingdom, a way of life we associate with the term *love*. If we follow the Christian equation of God with love, we may even be illuminated by the light of that kingdom in a more direct way. One thing is sure, however, and that is that any "theonomous" unity between love and justice will be the outcome of a dialogue that we can metaphorize as a traversing of the space between the two veils. What kind of trip this is will depend on which of the meanings associated with "veil" and "kingdom" we choose to emphasize in a particular reading. Let us try out some variations on these images, building on the previous readings as we move through our improvisation. In each case, it will be a variation on the connotation of "veil" that initiates a new stage of interpretation.

In the first variation, we will stay close to Ricoeur's own use of the metaphors, and consider what comes to mind when we figure the veil as a *text*—a piece of paper. In a certain regard, this variation simply reinforces aspects of Ricoeur's hermeneutical theory that we have already treated above, but it will nonetheless be useful to think through this image in order to clarify some of the conditions for traversing the space between the Kingdom of God and the Kingdom of Ends.

To consider the veil as a text is to consider the role of *distanciation* in the creation of meaning. Ricoeur is a thinker whose dialectic between different domains of human understanding has been premised on a careful consideration of the way in which the communication of meaning constantly takes detours by being schematized through distinct kinds of discourse. *Texts* hold a special status in this process because texts are the place where discourse is *fixed* in such a way as to abstract language from the immediate situation of interlocution and give it a potentially universal scope of application.[33] To *read* a text can therefore take two forms: "We can, as readers, remain in the suspense of the text, treating it as a worldless and authorless object; in this case, we explain the text in terms of its internal relations, its structure. On the other hand, we can lift the suspense and fulfill the text in speech, restoring it to living communication; in this case we interpret the text."[34] These possibilities of reading are what give Ricoeur's hermeneutics its characteristic dialectical movement between explanation and interpretation. When applied to the two veils in our scenario, these modes of reading will bear on how we conceive the kingdoms that lay behind them.

On the side of biblical faith, we have already hinted at how the Kingdom of God is only glimpsed through the veil of the *parable* or some other extravagant mode of religious discourse. The parable as Ricoeur understands it is a perfect example of the kind of transformation that can happen to discourse when it is fixed in a text. As a *metaphorized narrative* the parable can work its transformative power on the imagination only to the extent that the ordinary narrative unity of life becomes *configured* in the text in a special and extraordinary way. To understand the parable, it is not enough to know the formal principles of this configuration; we must rather complete the intention of the parable and enter the *world* of the text. The *Kingdom* of God can therefore be considered as the world of a specific kind of text. This notion is certainly commensurate with the idea of the kingdom as a separate realm possessing its own extraordinary logic and economy. We would then encounter this realm through the messages brought to us from it. The veil worn by Moses becomes a scroll that he holds in front of his face—outward, for our benefit. But we should be careful not to equate this encounter with the appropriation of just any fictional text, where the world of the text is played off against the world of the reader and appropriated as one of her possibilities.[35] Unlike the text of a fictional or historical narrative, the world of the biblical text is not a world I can appropriate—at least not on my own terms. This is a text-world with a king—hence a realm that claims authority over the way I appropriate it. To encounter the Kingdom of God through the parable will not be to gain a new possibility for my self-understanding. Rather, it will be to receive a new self—a new subjectivity as a *subject* of the Kingdom of God. The veil of the text reminds us of the extraordinary and baffling character of this transformation. We may have a new relation to the King of creation, but as is customary for monarchs, we can't gaze on him directly.

Turning to the philosophical side, we can view the veil of ignorance as a text when we recognize its status as a philosophical *allegory*.[36] The entire purpose of the veil of ignorance for Rawls is, after all, to enable construction of a version of the original position that will confirm our intuitive sense of justice. Like any text, the veil of ignorance serves to configure, organize, and structure our intuitions, but it does not, as in the case of parable, "twist" them around. Rather, the genre of allegory serves as a useful figure for philosophy's activity of examining and giving clarity to our everyday convictions without necessarily changing them. What is of interest in this case is the extent to which the philosophical allegory associated with the veil of ignorance encourages a mode of reading that remains within the suspense of the text without necessarily relating its structure back to the everyday world. The contractarian version of justice theory promoted by Rawls is most interested in *extending* the suspension of our ordinary knowledge represented by the veil of ignorance, in order to use it as the basis for elaborating a complex "moral geometry" out of an analysis of the decisions made behind the veil.[37]

An important parallel to the religious side comes out when we compare Rawls's strategy with Kant's image of the Kingdom of Ends, understood as the ideal community described in the allegory. For Kant, there are two ways to belong to the Kingdom of Ends: as member or as sovereign. Each is legislative, but the sovereign is independent and unlimited so as not to be subject to the will of any other rational agent, whereas a member *is* so subject.[38] Rawls certainly intends his allegory of the veil of ignorance to describe an association of *members* of a Kingdom of Ends, people who would democratically legislate the principles of justice to which they themselves would be subject. But by removing all sense of individual perspective and interest from his legislating agents, Rawls in a curious sense also removes everything that would ever cause people's wills to be at odds with one another. He thus elevates his agents to a position where the actual conflicts they can expect lie only on the other side of a curtain that, in *A Theory of Justice* at least, never falls. For the purposes of formulating the principles of justice, then, Rawls's agents are effectively sovereigns of the Kingdom of Ends. Ricoeur makes the shrewd observation that Rawls is attempting to work out a kind of earthly solution to the paradox of the perfect legislator from Rousseau's *Social Contract*, in which the legislators' knowledge of but detachment from human concerns leads Rousseau to compare them with gods.[39] The juxtaposition of the image of kingdom thus suggests a certain figuration of moral agents as God in Rawls's allegory of the veil of ignorance. The fact that there is a plurality of agents is not significant for this allegory; under the conditions behind the veil, they all express a single Will. It is significant in this regard that Rawls envisions a consensus of *all* the inhabitants of the original position on the principles of justice—as in the story of the translation of Septuagint, the conditions of ignorance give way to a unanimous translation of the edict of the divine Sovereign.

It should be noted that this perverse figuration of the legislating subject as equivalent to God is a danger only if the theory of justice remains at the stage of critical distanciation indefinitely, if it is *purely* procedural in nature. Ricoeur, of course, will place the procedural notion of justice in the middle position of a dialectic whose ultimate goal will be to return to and refigure the intuitive sense of justice that started the process in the first place. So placed, the philosophical allegory of the veil of ignorance can serve as a necessary corrective against the evil that taints human social relations. One must remember to lift the veil, however, by reading the text of the moral law in the context of applying it to the concrete circumstances of practical decisions. Isolated from that application, the *calculation* of those principles that will provide the best protection against evil too easily turns into a perverse image of the divine moral governance of the universe. Between Rawls's rational calculation of distributing goods according to the "maximin" principle (maximizing the minimum share), and Leibniz's theodicy in which God balances good and evil to create the best of possible worlds,[40] there is at least a family resemblance. The difference, of course, is that while God calculates the best possible moral order in full knowledge of the particular characteristics of the universe, the human legislator calculates the best principles of the social order in willful ignorance of those particulars. The abstracting move that allows the human legislator to calculate the moral law places this choice in the suspension of an ethical allegory/text, the veil of ignorance. Remembering that it is the Kingdom of Ends that lies behind this veil, we remain on guard against an insidious tendency to treat the body of moral principles chosen behind the veil *as* another kind of text—the edict of a divine Sovereign.

At this initial stage of considering the veil as a text, then, we see the way in which the Kingdom of God on the one hand or the principles of justice on the other are schematized through the veil of a text that defines the way in which our understanding can grasp and appropriate them. We also see the way in which the isolation of the two kingdoms behind their respective veils can lead the notions of faith and philosophy in a direction by which they become alienated both from each other and from the ordinary human experience they are supposed to be transforming. We should keep these dangers in mind, then, and seek new variations that will allow us to imagine how the gap between faith and philosophy, love and justice could be traversed. Perhaps this encounter can be figured in images of travel between one kingdom and the other. Depending on the direction of travel, the relation of our two domains could be described as *love seeking justice*, or as *justice seeking love*.

To explore the idea of *love seeking justice,* we will take up a new variation on our metaphorics, in which the veil is refigured as a *wedding veil*. The image of a wedding is meant to evoke the transformation that is supposed to occur when the passion of Christ tears the veil separating the human community from God, and floods the world with the illumination of the heavenly kingdom. How shall we now think about the relation between these two realms, given that the earthly world and the Kingdom of God are still distinct, but the barrier separating them is now permeable? One traditional image draws off the analogy between Christian agape and erotic love,[41] to figure the relation between Christ and the human community as a marriage. The human community transformed into subjects of the Kingdom of Heaven is the ideal description of the *church,* which in turn is traditionally imagined as *the bride of Christ*. The workings of Christian love in this world can therefore be imagined in terms of a partnership, between a heavenly and an earthly spouse, in which the bride is transformed by her new relation to the groom. She wears the veil that represents her own status as an ambassador between two worlds—clothed in the very barrier that defines the border between the Kingdom of God and earthly society. As in any good marriage, she and her partner will both retain a sense of their own prior identity *and* grow into a new sense of shared selfhood. But how is the bride of Christ supposed to relate to her spouse in the world? She is illuminated by the love that her partner exhibits as an inhabitant of the superabundant Kingdom. Among the instructions she gets is one that indicates that she is encountering her elusive groom wherever there is an opportunity to bring the generosity of love to others in the world: "As you do to the least of these, so you do to me." The human community is transformed into the bride of Christ exactly to the extent that it in turn works to transform the world in accordance with the economy of the gift.

If one thinks about Christian love being reflected in the world through the actions of the bride of Christ, some parallels to the veil of ignorance and the Kingdom of Ends suggest themselves. For one thing, the image of a partnership that becomes active whenever one encounters a creature in need of the gifts of love makes the marriage veil of the church begin to look a little like Rawls's veil of ignorance. The bride, like the inhabitant of Rawls's original position, does not know how to recognize the particular object of her desire—does not know which of her fellow creatures represent her beloved groom. She only knows that to love Christ in the world, she must extend the generosity that *gives more* of herself, even—and especially—to those who appear to reflect God's glory the *least*. The principles of *justice* chosen behind the veil of ignorance bear *some* formal similarity to this superabundant benevolence of *love*. After all, these principles call for the *greatest* extension of basic liberties, the *greatest* possible minimum share, and so forth. Moreover, the *distribution* of these shares is carried out without reference to merit or desert, and even with special attention to those whose native assets are deficient.[42] In this respect, anyway, the distribution of goods in the original position bears a similarity to the gratuitous economy of divine love, which dispenses *undeserved* grace. In all these respects, the metaphor of the marriage veil points toward some likeness between the original position that grounds the principles of justice and the economy of the gift that is the expression of Christian love.

This likeness at the level of key metaphors does not mean that Christian love and secular justice are the same thing—far from it. The principles of justice are based on an assumption of a mutual disinterest between rational agents, while the generosity of love extends my interest to *everyone*. Nonetheless, an interaction between love and justice is indicated here in that love can work at the metaethical level of transforming the presuppositions of ethical agency. Love does not turn into justice, but love does appear to be capable of transforming the *sense of justice* that lies at the basis of systems of justice. Ricoeur suggests that our sense of justice "moves back and forth between two levels.... At the lower level ... is a feeling of mutual disinterest.... At the higher level [is] ... a desire for mutual dependence, even for what we can call mutual indebtedness. Is it not then the function of love to help this sense of justice to reach the level of mutual recognition wherein each and everyone feels indebted to all the others?"[43] Rawls's theory of justice masks any sense of mutual indebtedness through the veil of ignorance, so as to build its principles only on the weak assumption of mutual disinterest. One might wonder, though, whether the benevolent effects of combining mutual disinterest with the veil of ignorance in Rawls's system are really stable. Ricoeur notes in a number of writings that the logic of equivalence characteristic of secular justice is susceptible to a perverse utilitarian interpretation that goes in the direction of "give to get."[44] This self-interest may work to the benefit of all *behind* the veil of ignorance, but what motivates the erection of the veil in the first place? What impels the "haves" to accede to a kind of moral reflection the end result of which will almost certainly be to limit and even redistribute their resources?

Christian love can educate the moral sense by figuring the self as a *gift*. In marriage, I give myself to my partner, and the giving works to embody an economy of gift—because it has been given, one gives in return. It is this mutual benefit that, as 1 Corinthians suggests, creates a sense of *mutual indebtedness* that is nonetheless beyond any *accounting* of debt. To the extent that secular justice can come to see its veil of ignorance as the expression of such a "marriage ethic," it will be protected against the slide into self-serving interpretations and may even succeed in becoming love's partner. It is of course a strange marriage suggested by a veil of ignorance in which I do not know the qualities of my partner—an arranged marriage perhaps. But this is exactly the situation of the bride of Christ, who must see the image of her bridegroom in every face she sees. For Christian love, this indifference about to whom love is extended does not however convert into an indifference *to* that person, in their particular situation of need and want. The marriage image moves us in the direction of a universal love that *does* see the particular faces of other people, where I am called to have the empathy and compassion that create a spousal sense of shared selfhood in all my relations. "Is it not up to love's imagination and singularizing regard to extend the privilege of the face-to-face relation to include all those other relations with (faceless) others?"[45] To the extent that the sense of justice can be educated by love, then, it will move justice to consider the application of its principles to *singular* others. There may be ways to say this within the language of justice: the sense of mutual indebtedness educated by love prevents the veil of ignorance from obscuring the Kingdom of Ends. Because we do not *see* ends behind the veil of ignorance (though we know people have them), the republic of justice is too easily reduced to a kingdom of *means* in which justice becomes a matter of calculus. To see the similarities between our veil of ignorance and the marriage veil is to see *through* the abstraction of the formal calculus of rules to the kingdom of concrete human beings who live according to those rules, just as the bride sees through the formality of the ceremony and the standardized vows to the real relationship that is *guided* by those vows and sealed by that ceremony.

We asked then what relation between love and justice would be figured by the image of love seeking justice in a kind of marriage ceremony. It might be appropriate in this case to speak of love as *parabolizing the allegory* of justice. Inasmuch as our relation to the Kingdom of God is schematized in narratives that not only configure but transform our selfhood, and our relation to the Kingdom of Ends is schematized through an allegory that configures and systematizes but does *not* transform the basic intent of our practical existence, we can see an interaction between love and justice to the extent that love transforms—even "twists"—the sense of justice in the direction of mutual indebtedness. After this transformation, we are able to see the original position as one of solidarity and the principles and practice of justice as the expression of that solidarity.

How shall we refigure our metaphors to explore the opposite movement—that of *justice seeking love*? I will suggest that to consider this interaction we should regard the veil alternately as *funeral shroud* and as *swaddling cloth*. Where do these significations come from? To see the veil of ignorance as a kind of funeral shroud is to consider the relationship between philosophical ethics and *death*. Ricoeur at times appeals to Franz Rosenzweig's claim that "All cognition of the All originates in death, in the fear of death."[46] The constant tendency and temptation of interpretation is to follow philosophy in its attempt to think the totality of reason and reality. But, as Hegel knew, this thinking of totality only occurs in retrospect, at the dusk where the forms of life one is considering have had their day and are at the point of death.[47] The Kingdom of Ends that lies behind the veil of ignorance is also based on cognition of totality. It is not *absolute knowledge* in Hegel's sense, inasmuch as the systematic union of rational beings under the law remains an *ideal* and not an actualized reality. Nonetheless, we have seen the tendency of the idea of a Kingdom of Ends to join with that of a veil of ignorance to produce a body of moral law that is close to claiming the status of divine edict. This tendency is linked with death in two senses. On the one hand, the type of moral theory that so seeks to calculate the totality of principles of justice depends on a reading of the allegory of the veil that remains in the suspension of the text of this allegory, without lifting the veil to consider the application to actual existence. In this regard the principles of justice become a *dead letter* (in a Pauline and hermeneutical sense), never to be fulfilled in the living reality of existence. Second, the analogy we suggested above between the calculating rational agent of Rawls's allegory and God's moral governance of the universe as figured by Leibniz reveals the principles of justice as a *law of death*. The law originates in the fear of death arising out of the evil of social oppression. But it can curb evil only through a desperate imitation of the governing power of the Lord of Life. The inability of this law to see all the particular faces whose concrete needs it will have to regulate once the veil is lifted shows that the rational abstraction that philosophy applies to life is of a fundamentally limited character. To the extent that this limitation is not accepted, however, we tend defiantly to figure ourselves as the sovereigns of our moral world.

Alternately, we can figure the other veil dividing ordinary human reality from the Kingdom of God as a *swaddling cloth*. The connection of this metaphor to Christ's nativity is obvious enough. To the extent that the Christian not only weds Christ but imitates him, though, this image also connotes the second birth that grants a new self and a new sense of human community. Here, we conceive the divine reality as shining *directly* on the face of the transformed Child, in accordance with the notion that "all of us, *with unveiled faces*, seeing the glory of the Lord as though reflected in a mirror, are being transformed into the same image from one degree of glory to another."[48] Ethically, this reflection and change can be figured as the light and transforming power of love, symbolized well enough by the image of parent and child. The child receives, reflects, and grows through the love radiated by the parent. To the extent that the Christian community is called upon to live life in imitation of Christ, then, it also comes to receive the love of the divine parent and accordingly to grow into a new kind of community that is capable of reflecting and displaying that love in return.

The Christian symbol system is ready enough to think the connection between these two significations of the veil. In order to be born again, after all, must one not first die to one's old self? To receive the light of God's love and grace, must one not first try (and fail) to justify oneself by the law? One can consider the movement here as that of a man who embodies the kind of disinterested objectivity of the original position and who seeks to apply the principles of justice in the world. Not knowing, though, that his philosophical wisdom is only retrospective and that he is facing backward, he becomes entangled in the veil of ignorance, falls to the ground, and dies. Later, he finds his shroud lifted as he beholds in childlike wonder the loving face of God. He has become a new person, seeing the world and being seen for the first time, seeing things as they really are, with an unveiled face that enables him to see the world *as* God's kingdom and others *as* fellow children of God. Certainly, this is a legitimate image of Christian life and of the transformation of personal and communal existence that it brings. When I die to my old self and take on a new one in the loving arms of God, it appears that I am enabled to see beyond and even to live on the other side of the barrier that separates humanity from God. If I am born again, am I not born again *into* God's kingdom? True enough, but I am still *bound* by the swaddling cloth that covers my body, a cloth that is representative not only of the veil separating humanity from God, but of the veil that I brought with me in passing out of the original position. My face may be uncovered to behold the glory and Kingdom of God, but my body, my limbs, the means by which I *act* in the world, are still wrapped in the cloak of the law, in the veil of ignorance that holds my action to laws of justice. It is therefore worth considering the image of the swaddled child as indicative of the transitional status of the Christian individual who is partially liberated and partially bound, inhabited with a new spirit but still clothed in the flesh of the old, dead self. We find that as justice seeks love by dying to itself and being reborn as this child, both justice and love are affected.

For one thing, a transformation of the *sense* of justice similar to what we described in the marriage metaphor above will occur when the anonymity of the veil of ignorance is replaced by the *vision* of love that is revealed to the child in the face of its parent. Whereas the legislative scheme of the veil of ignorance required only mutual *disinterest*, Ricoeur, as we saw earlier, sees the sense of justice as oscillating between disinterest and mutual indebtedness, depending on the extent to which that sense has been educated by love. How better can love so educate justice than by replacing mutual disinterest with the *family* feeling suggested by the image of parent and child? Who is more mutually indebted than the members of a family? And who is more solicitous of the singular needs of a child than its parent? Even more so than the marriage image, perhaps, this metaphor indicates the potential of love to refigure the basic *intent* behind the practice of justice. But the image of the child's limbs still bound by the law and the veil of ignorance suggests some continuity in *action* between life under the law of justice and life as a member of the loving family of God. It is worthwhile to explore why this continuity would still obtain for a new society peopled by God's children.

If the idea of autonomous self-legislation behind the veil of ignorance was susceptible to the perverse interpretation in which the human agent was equated with the divine sovereign of the Kingdom of Ends, it is also true that love and singularizing regard of the divine parent for the children of God can be interpreted in perverse ways. As we have discussed, the grace of God that is extended to us as undeserved recipients of divine favor places us within the "economy of the gift" according to which the Kingdom of God is structured. But the receipt of the gift of parental favor can be taken in at least two ways. One would be the command of love discussed before: "Because it has been given to you, give in return." The child accepts the gratuitous love of the parent and through it grows into a generous person who is herself capable of extending the singularizing regard of love to others. The other way would be to take the gift of love as a sign of the *singular* favor in which I am held by the heavenly father. However much we are reminded of the undeserved character of the grace that transforms us, the message that we are God's favored ones has the potential to turn us into spoiled brats. The legacy of religious bigotry around the world should be enough to make us cognizant of the human potential to interpret the gift in a distorted way.

It is this potential for gratuitous love to be distorted into *injustice* that should underline the continuing relevance of secular *justice* to religious life. God does not after all keep us in the house all day long. We are sent out into the world to play with the other children, and hopefully in so doing to reflect the love in which we were brought up. And we are not sent out naked and wild either. We remain clothed in the principles of a just society and are held accountable to them. In this need to clothe love in justice, we can see the continuing relevance for Christian ethical life of a reflection on justice such as Rawls provides. Against the perverse interpretation of divine love as exclusive divine *preference*, the veil of ignorance that is still our most intimate clothing provides a way to imagine how best to be faithful images of God's love. God after all extends love gratuitously, by a principle we cannot fully understand, but at any rate without reference to individual merit. However much love calls us to unveil our faces and behold the faces of others, it may be through something like the veil of ignorance that we can discern the best *human* way of imitating this love, by seeking to extend our benevolence to all persons equally and fairly. The principles of justice *educated* by love will be a part of this imitation of God, to the extent that we take our best, and most generous, interpretation of the just *human* order as the *rules* that bind us as free and equal but occasionally unruly children of God. If we imagine the task of justice as that of imitating the rules that a divine parent might impose on children who are learning to reflect the love they have been given but who must still be admonished and taught to play well with others, we see a more *charitable* interpretation of the image of a human legislator as the imitator of God. Educated by love, the human activity of instituting justice becomes part of the divine economy of action by which we are called to imitate Christ. Thus not only does love educate justice, but *justice educates love*, since every human reflection of love's generosity must be acted out in cognizance of the scarcity of goodness and compassion in human life, a scarcity that justice seeks to remedy by calculating principles of distribution.

When *justice seeks love*, then, by dying to its old world and being born again as one of God's children, the relation of love and justice is affected by the clothing that justice brings with it and that continues to cover the *acting* parts of its body. Reversing what we said in the last section, we can see the movement between justice and love as involving an *allegorizing of the parable* of love. In other words, however much love turns my face, transforms my self and intentions, and educates justice, we should still keep in mind Ricoeur's caution that love provides only a new perspective on a common ethic and not a brand-new ethic. If we are to understand how love affects ethics, we must look at how the new being of love, like that of hope, has the power to *reorganize* and reorient the systems of autonomous philosophical thought it encounters.[49] Love may alter systems and theories of justice by transforming the ethical intuitions that are the basis of those systems. But the important thing to note is that in affecting human ethics love refigures and does not replace justice. The parable, according to which I was granted a new self and turned in the direction of love, must itself be turned in the direction of allegory that seeks systems, rules, and conceptual clarifications that will allow our ethical insights to be preserved, taught, and practiced in the human world.

Throughout this metaphorics of the veil and the kingdom, then, we have seen that the resources of Ricoeur's thought justify a way of thinking about love and justice that both respects their differences and places them in a meaningful and transformative relation with one another. As with any mediating thinker, there will be those from each side who complain that Ricoeur goes too far, or not far enough, in mediating the encounter between philosophy and religious faith. But I would contend that we should read Ricoeur the hermeneut primarily as a guide for a responsible *interpretive* activity in our own imaginations that seeks to work out the dialogue between these two partners both as careful analysis and as the dynamic possibility of new meaning. If we follow his lead, we are invited to be partners in a conversation in which love and justice negotiate the terms of their meeting, both retaining their own distinct problems and liberating new insights about each other. Dwelling in this conversation, we can appropriate possibilities for refiguring our own lives within the middle space between the two kingdoms that claim our allegiance: who has words and imagination, let him interpret!

Notes

1. Paul Ricoeur, *Oneself as Another*, trans. Kathleen Blamey (Chicago: University of Chicago Press, 1992), p. 24.
2. Paul Ricoeur, "Naming God," in *Figuring the Sacred: Religion, Narrative, and Imagination*, ed. Mark Wallace and trans. David Pellauer (Minneapolis: Fortress Press, 1995), pp. 217–35.
3. André LaCocque and Paul Ricoeur, *Thinking Biblically*, trans. David Pellauer (Chicago: University of Chicago Press, 1998), p. xv.
4. Cf. Ricoeur's response to Christian Bouchindhomme, in Christian Bouchindhomme and Ranier Rochlitz, eds., *Temps et récit de Paul Ricoeur en débat* (Paris: Cerf, 1989), pp. 210–12.
5. Especially in "Thou Shalt Not Kill: A Loving Obedience," in André LaCocque and Paul Ricoeur, *Thinking Biblically*, trans. David Pellauer (Chicago: University of Chicago Press, 1998), pp. 111–38.
6. In *Figuring the Sacred*, pp. 293–302, 315–29.
7. Paul Ricoeur, "Love and Justice," in *Figuring the Sacred*, pp. 317, 321.
8. Paul Ricoeur, *Oneself as Another*, trans. Kathleen Blamey (Chicago: University of Chicago Press, 1992), p. 25.
9. Paul Ricoeur, *From Text to Action*, trans. Kathleen Blamey and J. B. Thompson (Evanston, IL: Northwestern University Press, 1974), p. 173.
10. Paul Ricoeur, "Biblical Hermeneutics," *Semeia* 4 (1975): 74f.
11. Paul Ricoeur, *The Rule of Metaphor*, trans. Robert Czerny (Toronto: University of Toronto Press, 1977).
12. Ibid., p. 296.
13. Ibid., p. 303.
14. John Rawls, *A Theory of Justice* (Cambridge, MA: Harvard University Press, 1971), pp. 136–42.
15. Ibid., p. 60.
16. Paul Ricoeur, "Is a Purely Procedural Theory of Justice Possible: John Rawls's *Theory of Justice*," in *The Just*, trans. David Pellauer (Chicago: University of Chicago Press, 2000), p. 50.

17. Ibid., p. 56. Ricoeur reiterates this same point in "After Rawls's *Theory of Justice,*" in *The Just,* pp. 66–67.
18. Ricoeur, *Oneself as Another,* pp. 170–72.
19. Ibid , p. 229.
20. Paul Ricoeur, "The Bible and the Imagination," in *Figuring the Sacred,* p. 164.
21. Ricoeur, "Biblical Hermeneutics," p. 30.
22. Ibid., p. 99.
23. Paul Ricoeur, *Time and Narrative,* 3 vols., trans. Kathleen Blamey and David Pellauer (Chicago: University of Chicago Press, 1984–88).
24. Paul Ricoeur, "Listening to the Parables of Jesus," in *The Philosophy of Paul Ricoeur,* ed. Charles Reagan and David Stewart (Boston: Beacon Press, 1978), p. 241.
25. Ricoeur, "Biblical Hermeneutics," p. 34.
26. Paul Ricoeur, "The Logic of Jesus, the Logic of God," in *Figuring the Sacred,* pp. 279–83.
27. Ricoeur, "Love and Justice," p. 325.
28. Ricoeur, "Listening to the Parables of Jesus," p. 239.
29. Immanuel Kant, *Grounding for the Metaphysics of Morals,* 3rd ed., trans. James Ellington (Indianapolis: Hackett Publishing Company, 1993), pp. 39–40.
30. Ibid., p. 43.
31. Ricoeur, "Thou Shalt Not Kill" p. 118.
32. Ricoeur, "Love and Justice," pp. 315–29.
33. Ricoeur, *From Text to Action,* pp. 145–50.
34. Ibid., p. 113.
35. For the details of Ricoeur's theory of reading, see especially Ricoeur, *Time and Narrative,* vol. 3.
36. Ricoeur, *Oneself as Another,* p. 230.
37. Rawls, *A Theory of Justice,* p. 121.
38. Kant, *Grounding for the Metaphysics of Morals,* p. 40.
39. Ricoeur, "Is a Purely Procedural Theory of Justice Possible," p. 40.
40. Paul Ricoeur, "Evil, a Challenge to Philosophy and Theology," in *Figuring the Sacred,* pp. 254 f.
41. On the justification for considering the different significations of love together, see Ricoeur, "Thou Shalt Not Kill," p. 125.
42. Rawls, *A Theory of Justice,* p. 100.
43. Ricoeur, "Thou Shalt Not Kill," pp. 126–27.
44. Ricoeur, *Figuring the Sacred,* pp. 300, 328.
45. Ricoeur, "Thou Shalt Not Kill," p. 132.
46. Franz Rosenzweig, quoted in Paul Ricoeur, "The 'Figure' in Rosenzweig's *The Star of Redemption,*" in *Figuring the Sacred,* p. 105.
47. G. W. F. Hegel, *Philosophy of Right,* trans. T. M. Knox (London: Oxford University Press, 1967), p. 13.
48. 2 Corinthians 3:18, quoted in Paul Ricoeur, "The Summoned Subject in the School of the Narratives of the Prophetic Vocation," in *Figuring the Sacred,* p. 267.
49. Paul Ricoeur, "Hope and the Structure of Philosophical Systems," in *Figuring the Sacred,* pp. 203–16.

10
Jacques Derrida, Paul Ricoeur, and the Marginalization of Christianity
Can the God of Presence Be Saved?

LINDA M. MACCAMMON

Over the last several decades, the postmodern critique of contemporary culture has effected a paradigm shift away from the traditional presuppositions, concepts, and beliefs of the Enlightenment worldview toward a "new Enlightenment" that is characterized by a radically historical outlook and a deconstructive critical agenda. In dismantling the foundations of Enlightenment thinking, postmodern theorists have attempted to open up and to reform social and political institutions that have become static, limiting, exclusionary, and oppressive. As Seyla Benhabib observes, "If there is one commitment that unites postmodernists from Foucault to Lyotard to Derrida it is this critique of western [sic] rationality as seen from the perspectives of the margins, from the standpoint of what and whom it excludes, suppresses, delegitimizes, renders mad, imbecilic or childish."[1] The result has been a wide-ranging and diverse critique of culture that celebrates difference, indeterminacy, inclusivity, and pluralism. Yet for Christian theologians and ethicists these positive developments have also produced a negative side effect. For in deconstructing traditional notions of reality, truth, objectivity, morality, and religion the postmodern critique has virtually eliminated the possibility of any genuine engagement between Christianity and culture.

This turn of events is more than a little ironic, since in recent years religion has made a remarkable comeback. Nietzsche's proclamation of the death of God did not result in a rush toward humanistic atheism. On the contrary, with a few notable exceptions (Richard Rorty being the most prominent) the Enlightenment critique of Western ontotheology has led to a rethinking of religion from a postmodern perspective. Postmodern thinkers such as Jacques Derrida, Mark C. Taylor, Emmanuel Levinas, John D. Caputo, and others have realized the importance of religious reflection for grasping the "experience of the impossible" that sparks the human imagination and the passions of the heart. Thus, they have revisited the biblical God, developing alternatives to the Christian "God of presence" that focus on God as Wholly Other and as a wholly future possibility.[2] But while religion has enjoyed something of a renaissance, Christianity has become increasingly marginalized as both a religion and as a source for ethical reflection. The reason for this is simple: while God as Wholly Other is no longer denied, the God of Jesus Christ is denied, because the Wholly Other cannot be present in history—the Logos is an impossible possibility that cannot be realized without falling into idolatry and an oppressive fundamentalism. Based on this premise, the marginalization of Christianity as a religious and moral source is both unavoidable and necessary.

This in a nutshell is the challenge that postmodernism presents to Christianity. The question for Christian theologians and ethicists is, How do we respond to it? I believe that the first thing we must do is get a clear understanding of the issues at stake: Precisely what is being gained and lost by the rejection of the God of presence? And then we must respond to the challenge with an alternative that addresses postmodern concerns without dispensing with the Christian God. This essay will undertake these twin tasks through a comparative study of the philosophical and religious writings of Jacques Derrida and Paul Ricoeur.

Derrida is an obvious choice for this study, not only because he introduced deconstruction to philosophy, but also because his "faith without religion" thoroughly rejects the Christian God of presence and all historical forms of religion associated with the bible. In contrast to Derrida's deconstructive faith, Ricoeur refuses to dispense with the Christian God entirely. Instead, his biblical hermeneutics rethinks biblical revelation and the way we interpret the biblical God. Comparing their work will show that while Derrida's deconstructive program is an important source for illuminating some of the problems associated with Enlightenment thought, his deconstruction of the Judeo-Christian tradition goes too far, effectively transforming deconstruction into a quasi-religion that distorts the nature of faith, especially in respect to the faith-ethics relation. Ricoeur's work, on the other hand, shows that it is indeed possible to address the problems associated with ontotheology while retaining the Christian God and the revelatory content that is crucial to understanding how biblical faith informs ethics.

The study will unfold in four parts: the first part will examine Derrida's deconstructive project and his "faith without religion," focusing on Derrida's critique of Western metaphysics and on his understandings of justice, the religious concept of "the gift," and the faith-ethics relation. The second part will present a critical assessment of his project followed by a brief discussion of the similarities and differences between Derrida and Ricoeur with respect to their philosophical perspectives and methodology. The third part will present Ricoeur's work as a viable alternative to Derrida's scheme, focusing on his understandings of justice, the biblical God, and the "economy of the gift," which retains the Christian God of presence, albeit in a modified form. The precise manner in which faith informs ethics will be illustrated through Ricoeur's analysis of the relationship between biblical agape and the Golden Rule, as preached in the sermons of Jesus. The study will conclude with a brief consideration of the prospects for retrieving the Christian God of presence in a postmodern age.

Derrida's Deconstructive Project

Jacques Derrida pioneered and introduced deconstruction (a term he personally dislikes) in the 1960s and it has been both praised and condemned ever since. No doubt some of the criticism has stemmed from confusion about the precise nature of deconstruction. Derrida maintains that "deconstruction is not a method or some tool that you apply to something from the outside."[3] Deconstruction is rather an internal critique that suspects, interrogates, and challenges the presuppositions and traditional concepts of a given conceptual system, whether that system be a text, a discipline, an institution, a society, a religion, or even history itself. A brief discussion of the central ideas of deconstruction and Derrida's critique of Western metaphysics will set the necessary context for his religious writings.

Deconstruction as Internal Critique

As an internal critique, the purpose of deconstruction is to illuminate critical or prophetic elements within a system that will open up new possibilities that will prevent any one principle, rule, or ideology from becoming fixed, dominant, and abusive. According to Derrida,

> What is called "deconstruction" . . . has never, never opposed institutions as such, philosophy as such, discipline as such. . . . Because, however affirmative deconstruction is, it is affirmative in a way that is not simply positive, not simply conservative, not simply a way of repeating the given institution. I think that the life of an institution implies that we are able to criticize, to transform, to open the institution to its own future. The paradox of the instituting moment of an institution is that, at the same time that it starts something new, it also continues something, is true to the memory of the past, to a heritage, to something we receive from the past, from our predecessors, from the culture. If an institution is to be an institution, it must to some extent break with the past, keep the memory of the past, while inaugurating something absolutely new.[4]

For Derrida, inaugurating something absolutely new requires a series of careful and layered deconstructive readings that privilege the operation of difference over classicist notions of unity and totality, moving from more traditional readings to more heretical ones, permitting inconsistencies, aporias and nontraditional elements to play within the system. But despite all the playfulness, deconstruction is serious business with a serious goal in mind. Derrida's critique of Western metaphysics is a good case in point.

In deconstructing the philosophical writings of Plato (especially the *Phaedrus* and *Timaeus*), Derrida proposes a radical break with the ontological models of presence that have grounded Western philosophy and Christian theology. He argues that conceptual unities, such as essence, existence, substance, subject, and so on, are illusory. They are simply verbal constructs that deny otherness and that prevent the free play of oppositions within the system, thus preserving the system's pretense of certainty, power, authority, and self-immediate truth. For Derrida, difference is primary. Difference is prior to any attempt to form a unity and, therefore, must be considered the origin (nonorigin) of inquiry.

The significance of this shift in priority cannot be overstated. Unity is suddenly displaced as origin and now becomes a goal. But it is a goal that is never realized, because the priority and play of difference forever defer the goal of fixed origin or meaning. Using the timely example of cultural identity, Derrida describes how deconstruction establishes the precedence of difference over unity and the impact this move has on the relationship between the self and the other and on an ethics of responsibility.

> We often insist nowadays on cultural identity—for instance, national identity, linguistic identity, and so on. Sometimes the struggles under the banner of cultural identity, national identity, linguistic identity are noble fights. But at the same time the people who fight for their identity must pay attention to the fact that identity is not the self-identity of a thing, a glass, for instance, . . . but implies a difference within identity. That is, the identity of a culture is a way of being different from itself; a culture is different from itself; language is different from itself; the person is different from itself. Once you take into account this inner and other difference, then you pay attention to the other and you understand that fighting for your own identity is not exclusive of another identity, is open to another identity. And this prevents totalitarianism, nationalism, egocentrism, and so on. . . . [It is] a duty, an ethical and political duty, to take into account this impossibility of being one with oneself. It is because I am not one with myself that I can speak with the other and address the other. That is not a way of avoiding responsibility. On the contrary, it is the only way for me to take responsibility and to make decisions.[5]

Thus, contrary to the assessment of many of his critics, Derrida maintains that the goal of deconstruction is not to destroy the system, but to ensure that the system is open to its own future and that it is "just with justice"; that is, that responsibility for the other is placed before the rights of the self.

Jacques Derrida, Paul Ricoeur, and the Marginalization of Christianity

Derrida's shift in priority is significant for another reason. By eliminating the notions of fixed origins and overarching or ruling categories, he opens the way for a new understanding of existence that shifts from the stasis of ontology to the fluidity and dynamics of language. Vincent Leitch provides a good summary of Derrida's understanding of the textuality of the world and how deconstruction as an internal critique continually works to destabilize our presuppositions, our perceptions, and our truth claims about reality.

> Since language serves as ground of existence, the world emerges as infinite Text. Everything gets textualized. All contexts, whether political, economic, social, psychological, historical or theological, become intertexts; that is, outside influences and forces undergo textualization. Instead of literature we have textuality; in place of tradition, intertextuality. Authors die so that readers can come into prominence. In any case, all selves, whether of critics, poets, or readers, appear as language constructions—texts. What are texts? Strings of differential traces. Sequences of floating signifiers. Sets of infiltrated signs dragging along ultimately indecipherable intertextual elements. Sites for the freeplay of grammar, rhetoric, and (illusory) reference. What about the truth of the text? The random flights of signifiers across the textual surface, the disseminations of meaning, offer truth under one condition: that the chaotic processes of textuality be willfully regulated, controlled, or stopped. Truth comes forth in the reifications . . . of reading. Truth is not an entity or property of the text. No text utters its truth; the truth lies elsewhere in the reading. Constitutionally, reading is misreading. Deconstruction works to deregulate controlled dissemination and celebrate misreading.[6]

The end result of this process of purposeful misreading is a form of deconstructive discourse that has no final or proper meaning, but that is in a continual state of transition and wandering. Presence is not eliminated as an element within the system but is continually deferred, thus ensuring that it does not take the form of an abusive rule, principle, or totalizing ideology.

Deconstruction and Textual Reference

Although Derrida's theory of textuality has found a receptive audience, his understanding of textual reference has met with some resistance because of its implications for understanding the relationship between language and existence. Contrary to what many critics claim, Derrida does not deny textual reference, but he does severely limit its parameters. In his view, when we read a text, what we are really doing is producing a signifying structure; consequently, we "cannot legitimately transgress the text toward something other than it, toward a referent (a reality that is metaphysical, historical, psychobiographical, etc.) or toward a signified outside the text whose content could take place, could have taken place outside of language, that is to say ... outside of writing in general."[7] Thus, Derrida's famous claim, that *there is nothing outside the text,* means that reference can only apply to signifiers within the text.

Such a claim is controversial because it effectively closes the door on most forms of realism, which presumes that our speech acts (whether religious or nonreligious) signify an objective reality that grounds our notions of truth, objectivity, and meaning. Derrida's rejection of traditional notions of reference reflects his deep suspicion of any language that claims to be the language of reality itself. For Derrida, we are always working within contextual and conceptual frameworks—we can neither escape them nor use language to reach the "things themselves" outside of them. Thus, in contrast to the Enlightenment penchant for definition and fixed meanings, Derrida's deconstructive approach strives to keep us ever vigilant and ever suspicious of claims about reference, meaning, and truth that emanate from institutional structures. Derrida prefers instead to let the shock of alterity continually open up new forms of expression that lie hidden within them.

Derrida's philosophical perspective and deconstructive approach have been highly influential in the development of contemporary thought. Caputo's radical hermeneutics and Drucilla Cornell's recent work on sexual freedom and the "imaginary domain" are just two examples of the positive contributions deconstruction can make to ethics and social theory.[8] But when applied to the Judeo-Christian tradition, Derrida takes his deconstructive agenda too far, deconstructing the Christian God from a vantage point outside the Judeo-Christian tradition. The result is a faith that becomes little more than a motive force for the deconstructive process.

Derrida's Faith without Religion

Although Derrida considers himself to be an atheist, he is not lacking in religious sensibility. In recent years, he has written and lectured extensively on the possibility of "faith without religion," which rejects the dogmatic systems of what he calls "historical messianisms." Derrida's faith finds its source in a universal "structure of messianicity" that is illuminated in the fundamental speech act of promise.

> Each time I open my mouth, I am promising something. When I speak to you, I am telling you that I promise to tell you something, to tell you the truth. Even if I lie, the condition of my lie is that I promise to tell you the truth. So the promise is not just one speech act among others; every speech act is fundamentally a promise. This universal structure of the promise, of the expectation of the future, for the coming, and the fact that this expectation of the coming has to do with justice—that is what I call the messianic structure.[9]

For Derrida, the promise carries the spark of divine immanence that ignites the "passion for the impossible" in the historical messianisms of Judaism, Christianity, and Islam. But Derrida argues that these "religions of the Book" are problematic, because as soon as "you reduce the messianic structure to messianism, then you are reducing the universality and this has important political consequences. Then you are accrediting one tradition among others and a notion of an elected people, of a given literal language, a given fundamentalism."[10] As human history attests, the result of this kind of radical particularity has been hatred, violence, oppression, and death on a grand scale. To sidestep this problem, Derrida's nonreligious messiah is understood as "the gift" that is always expected, but that never makes an appearance in history. Here we see a direct link between human subjectivity, deconstruction, and religion: the deconstructive impulse is fueled by a universal messianic structure that ignites the passion for the impossible. This intense sense of longing keeps the system open to the impossible, to the incoming of the impossible gift. But what exactly is the gift? And how does an impossible gift inform ethics?

The Gift and the Faith-Ethics Relation

The gift is an elusive category in Derrida's work and it is meant to be. Two observations can be made: First, although the gift is acknowledged as a category within the system, it has no phenomenality because it never appears—it is always deferred. In fact, Derrida makes the startling and fascinating suggestion that despite our urgent prayers and tears for the Messiah to come, we really do not want him to arrive because his nonappearance is the necessary condition for us to go on asking questions and living. For Derrida, this paradox reveals "some ambiguity in the messianic structure. We wait for something we would not like to wait for. That is another name for death."[11]

Second, the gift can inform ethics only by "thinking" gift. For Derrida, the idea of gift is implied in the promise—it is a passion for what is to come and as such it is "totally foreign to the horizon of economy, ontology, knowledge, constanstive statements, and theoretical determination and judgment."[12] While the gift does not exist per se, that does not mean that there is no gift. Rather the gift is something that is thought, and in thinking the gift, the gift carves out a space for what is to come. As such, the gift has no specific content—it simply translates into a call (an ethical demand) to give whatever is lacking in the historical "economic" circle, where notions of exchange, calculation, and debts prevail. In this respect, the gift acts as a prophetic mechanism that elicits action in the here and now. It demands that we give, but without specifying what is to be given and without the taint of reappropriation. Derrida explains this movement, forging a strong tie between the gift and justice.

> A gift is something that is beyond the circle of reappropriation, beyond the circle of gratitude. A gift should not even be acknowledged as such. As soon as I know I give something ... I just canceled the gift. I congratulate myself or thank myself for giving something and then the circle has already started to cancel the gift.... If the gift is given, then it should not even appear to the one who gives it or to the one who receives it, not appear as such. That is paradoxical, but that is the condition for a gift to be given....That is the condition the gift shares with justice. A justice that could appear as such, that could be calculated, a calculation of what is just and what is not just, saying what has to be given in order to be just—that is not justice. That is social security, economics. Justice and gift should go beyond calculation.[13]

Thus, the gift informs ethics by opening it up to something that lies beyond the practical prescriptions and specifications of ethics and the law. That something is the Wholly Other, the "relationless relation" that is the condition for the gift, for justice, for peace, for ethics, for revolution, for progress, for future possibilities. Derrida is not suggesting, however, that we abandon calculations and criteria altogether; rather, he is insisting that if we are to be truly free and responsible, then criteria cannot be used to determine the moment of decision.

> If I had criteria, a set of norms, that I would simply apply or enforce, there would be no decision. There is a decision to the extent that even if I have criteria, the criteria are not determining, that I make a decision beyond the criteria, even if I know what the best criteria are, even if I apply them, the decision occurs to the extent that I do more than apply them. Otherwise it would be a mechanical development, a mechanical explicitation, not a decision.[14]

Thus, following Kierkegaard's analysis of Abraham in *Fear and Trembling,* Derrida maintains that the gift as the opening to the Wholly Other does not complement or enlarge ethics as much as it suspends ethics in the moment of decision. Alluding to Abraham in *The Gift of Death* he writes:

> From the moment that I am in relation with the other, with the look, the request, the love, the order, the call of the other, I know that I am able to respond to it only by sacrificing ethics, that is to say, by sacrificing that which obliges me to respond also and in the same way, in the same instant, to all others. I offer the gift of death, I betray, I do not need to raise the dagger over my son on top of Mount Moriah to do this. Day and night, in each instant, on all the Mount Moriahs of the world, I am doing this, raising the dagger over what I love and ought to love, over the other, such or such an other to whom I owe absolute fidelity, incommensurably.[15]

Thus, like Kierkegaard's solitary knight of faith, Derrida's deconstructive faith is a singular commitment to the Wholly Other (to what is to come). It is a commitment that cannot be calculated (via ethics or law) or communicated (via ideology or theology); it can only be practiced in each moment of decision.

Critical Assessment and Comparison of Derrida and Ricoeur

This brief overview of Derrida's understanding of faith offers interesting insights and provocative ideas that open up new ground for the religious imagination and for religious inquiry. His description of promise, for example, establishes vital connections between religion, human subjectivity, and culture—something that was often denied by Enlightenment humanists. For Derrida, faith is a universal structure that continually drives deconstruction toward reforming institutions and illuminating possibilities for a better future. In this sense, deconstruction becomes a kind of quasi-religious impulse that is akin to that of the prophets of the Judeo-Christian tradition, but without the dogmatic and theological baggage that has brought division, exclusion, and oppression. Nevertheless, these positive aspects are more than offset by what is lost after the smoke of deconstruction clears.

Contrary to Derrida's stated agenda, it would appear that he is moving outside the Judeo-Christian "institution," using his theory of textuality to establish a deconstructive faith that retains the messianic dynamic while "depersonalizing" God. But for those of us who uphold the priority of scripture in revealing religious consciousness, such a move raises some severe problems. The first involves his understanding of the divine-human relation. Can we deny the God of presence given the fact that throughout the bible God is proclaimed and is experienced as both present and absent? Contrary to the assessments of Derrida and Kierkegaard, Abraham's ability to make the leap of faith at Mount Moriah was not achieved in a vacuum. The Abraham saga depicts a loving, stormy, and incredibly complex relationship between Abraham and Yahweh—a concrete faith relation that lasted for many years and that made it possible for Abraham to believe in the impossible and to raise the knife. Abraham's story suggests that faith is not simply a belief in what you cannot see or logically prove, nor is it something that suddenly appears at a moment of existential crisis. Faith is derived in part from the trustworthiness of relationships that are experienced as present. Given this biblical insight, can we legitimately abandon the God of presence as a religious and theological category without also losing the content that is the basis for biblical faith?

Another problem has to do with Derrida's understanding of the gift in relation to ethics. For the Christian, one of the central biblical claims is that human beings are situated between the "already" of Jesus Christ (the gift of the gospel) and the "not yet" of the eschaton (the gift to come). Together the person and teachings of Christ are the good news that informs ethics and that shapes Christian morality. For Derrida, the radical obligation to the other, which is the condition for the gift, does not complement or enlarge ethics as much as it suspends it. But again this interpretation contradicts the biblical account. As will be discussed presently, the sermons of Jesus present the gift of the gospel as breaking into the ethical order, radicalizing the law rather than suspending it. The possibilities for justice are made actual through a rethinking and reapplication of the law. Jesus affirms this idea when he tells the crowd, "Do not think that I have come to abolish the law or the prophets. I have come not to abolish but to fulfill" (Matthew 5:17). Thus, in the form of the gospel, the gift is a present reality that makes justice a practical possibility, something that *can* appear in history if only in fleeting moments. The full measure of justice will be realized only in the future gift of the coming kingdom.

The distortion that arises with Derrida's deferral of justice and the gift also affects how the reader experiences biblical revelation, which raises the thorny issue of textual reference. As a revelatory text, the bible recounts lived experiences that are shared to some degree by most human beings, such as alienation, temptation, reconciliation, compassion, hope, suffering, joy, and so on. Readers of the bible consider it to be truthful and authoritative precisely because it speaks truthfully and authoritatively about these fundamental experiences. Derrida's understanding of reference severs the existential tie between the Wholly Other, the text, and the reader, thus severing a principal source of religious hope. Hope contains an element of presence, a sense of belonging to something that once was and that could be again. Derrida's claim that justice and the gift never appear in history places the source of hope solely in the *idea* of gift, the *idea* of justice. Such formality provides little comfort and even less practical guidance. Richard Kearney summarizes and articulates the content issues well when he asks,

> If *tout autre* is indeed *tout autre*, what is to prevent us saying yes to an evil alien as much as to a transcendent God who comes to save and liberate? Is there really no way for deconstruction to discriminate between true and false prophets, between bringers of good and bringers of evil, between holy spirits and unholy ones? How do we tell the difference, even if it's only more or less? How do we decide—even if we can never *know* (for certain), or *see* (for sure) or *have* (a definite set of criteria)? Blindness is all very well for luminary painters and writers, for Homer and Rembrandt, but don't most of the rest of us need just a *little* moral insight, just a few ethical handrails as we grope through the dark night of postmodern spectrality and simulacritude toward the "absolute other," before we say "yes," "come," "thy will be done"? Is there really no difference, in short, between a living God and a dead one, between Elijah and his "phantom," between messiahs and monsters?[16]

Kearney's questions point to the central weakness in deconstruction generally and in deconstructing the God of presence in particular. In purely practical terms, deconstruction prevents us from moving beyond the moment of deconstructive criticism and moving toward some kind of content that can be affirmed now and confirmed later. Caputo minces no words when he says, "To be sure, deconstruction does not affirm what *is*, does not fall down adoringly before what is *present*, for the present is precisely what demands endless analysis, criticism, and deconstruction."[17] But it seems to me that something is indeed being affirmed; namely, the deconstructive process itself. Deconstruction becomes the alpha and omega of inquiry, for as soon as we set down on any kind of certainty, deconstruction shifts the ground under our feet, keeping us in a continual state of anticipation, looking for something that never arrives, whether that something be justice or the presence of the divine gift. Ultimately, the "already" of ethical and religious experience is continually negated or deferred for the "not yet" of justice and the gift, leaving us with no stable content from which to develop practical and consistent standards for moral and religious judgments; hence Kearney's pointed questions.

In contrast to Derrida's deconstructive faith, Ricoeur's biblical hermeneutics offers an alternative scheme that addresses postmodern concerns about the idols of fundamentalism without having to resort to the complete rejection of the God of presence as a religious and theological category. Before discussing his work, however, it will be helpful to present the fundamental differences in philosophical perspective and approach to inquiry that distinguish Ricoeur's hermeneutical project from Derrida's deconstructive one.

A Comparative Summary of Derrida and Ricoeur

As a contemporary philosopher, Ricoeur subscribes to many of the basic tenets of postmodernism. He affirms, for example, the radically historical and textual nature of human existence, he insists on the necessity of religious reflection for understanding human subjectivity, and he is critical of the idealism of Western metaphysics and the ontotheology of Christianity. But he also parts company with postmodernism in several fundamental ways.

The most obvious difference lies in the basic presupposition that guides Ricoeur's work. In contrast to Derrida's emphasis on difference, Ricoeur's phenomenological and hermeneutical studies presuppose a unity that underlies the divisions and conflicts that characterize the human condition. Following Martin Heidegger's analysis in *Being and Time*, Ricoeur acknowledges the presence of a primordial sense of *belonging-to* that precedes the subject-object relation of epistemology and that enables us to know anything at all. This ontology of understanding would seem to place Ricoeur back into the fold of the discredited metaphysics of presence (a criticism lodged against Heidegger). But he manages to avoid this trap through the use of hermeneutic phenomenology, a reflective method that focuses on meaning in symbolic languages and that allows him to recover human subjectivity without falling into idealism. Kearney describes Ricoeur's project in relation to Heidegger and Hans-Georg Gadamer:

> Together with Heidegger and Gadamer, Ricoeur considers interpretation not on the basis of a psychological self-consciousness, but against the historical horizon of a finite being-in-the-world. But while Heidegger takes the "short route" to Being, where interpretation culminates, Ricoeur and Gadamer opt for the "long route" which examines the various inevitable detours which interpretation undergoes through language, myth, ideology, the unconscious and so on—before it arrives at the ultimate limit of Being. Man's final project is indeed a being-towards-death whose fundamental encounter with "nothingness" provokes the question of Being. But between birth and death, human understanding is compelled to traverse a range of hermeneutic fields, where meaning is dispersed, hidden, withheld or deferred.[18]

In reflecting upon and elucidating the meanings hidden within the symbolic texts of culture (principally the texts of Freud and Hegel, and the bible), Ricoeur discovers a fundamental ontology, but it is not the original fixed presence that Derrida and other postmodern thinkers reject; rather, it is a "being-interpreted." This means that the presence of the subject to itself is always mediated and is always subject to (de)constructive criticism and to the conflict of interpretations that invariably arise among the various hermeneutic disciplines (for example, psychoanalysis, the social sciences, religion) that interpret the human condition. Thus while Ricoeur accepts conflict and embraces the need for deconstructive criticism, he also stresses—contra Derrida—that they are never final. The significance of conflict and criticism lies in their ability to reveal the essential unity of human existence, a unity that finds its ultimate ground in the Wholly Other and its ultimate expression in sacred symbolism.

Another fundamental difference between Derrida and Ricoeur lies in their understanding of textual reference. In contrast to Derrida, Ricoeur's "long route" of interpretation presupposes that written language does indeed refer to something beyond the text. According to Ricoeur, written discourse moves beyond the author's reference to particular situations or things to an array of nonsituational, nonhistorical references that open up a world to the reader.

> [W]e speak about the "world" of Greece, not to designate any more what were the situations for those who lived them, but to designate the nonsituational references that outline the effacement of the first and that henceforth are offered as possible modes of being, as symbolic dimensions of our being-in-the-world. For me, this is the referent of all literature; no longer

the *Umwelt* [world around us] of the ostensive references of dialogue, but the *Welt* [being-in-the-world] projected by the nonostensive references of every text that we have read, understood, and loved. To understand a text is at the same time to light up our own situation or, if you will, to interpolate among the predicates of our situation all the significations that make a *Welt* of our *Umwelt*. It is this enlarging of the *Umwelt* into the *Welt* that permits us to speak of the references *opened up* by the text—it would be better to say that the references *open up* the world. Here again the spirituality of discourse manifests itself through writing, which frees us from the visibility and limitation of situations by opening up a world for us, that is, new dimensions of our being-in-the world.[19]

This description of reference reflects Ricoeur's belief that when language functions as discourse a fundamental change takes place. Language is no longer a system of signs, but is encountered as functioning, as *saying*. This change implicates an intentional speaking subject; in Ricoeur's famous phrase, *someone says something to someone about something*. This common experience of language, in both oral and written forms, is the medium through which we express ourselves and express things, whether the things are objects in the world or possible modes of being-in-the-world. Ricoeur's language theory upholds external realism because it presupposes a world that exists apart from our representations of it. John R. Searle provides a helpful explanation:

[When we make statements] the assumption we are making is that there is a normal way of understanding utterances, and that when performing speech acts in a public language, speakers typically attempt to achieve normal understanding. The point . . . is that for a large class [of utterances] a condition of intelligibility for the normal understanding of these utterances is that there is a way that things are that is independent of human representations. The consequence is that *when we attempt to communicate to achieve normal understanding with these sorts of utterances we must presuppose external realism.*[20]

This means that texts can make truth claims about the world and can support a correspondence theory of truth, which gauges whether there exists a correlation between sense (what the text means) and reference (what the text is about). The linkage between language and experience also means that in Ricoeur's religious scheme justice and the gift are not ideas that are continually deferred, but are present within the practical economy of exchange, debt, and gratitude that characterizes human experience. Interpreting philosophical and religious texts gives us access to them.

Finally, while Ricoeur is also critical of the ontotheology of Christianity, he is not willing to follow Derrida in completely rejecting the God of presence.

In his hermeneutical analysis of God's self-presentation in Exodus 3:1–6, he admits that the enigmatic nature of that event "does force us to think in another way about the verb being, but it does not force us to eliminate it from our translation."[21] Further evidence of his desire to retain some degree of presence can be found in his earlier writings on the naming of God and on the economy of the gift, which will be discussed presently. In both cases, Ricoeur's analysis reveals God as both present and absent, a tension that is central to the nature of biblical revelation and to the faith-ethics relation.

As these comparisons make clear, whereas Derrida's deconstructive project emphasizes difference, otherness, and deconstruction, Ricoeur's exploration of human subjectivity emphasizes unity, ontological rootedness, fundamental meanings, and the connection between language and experience. Exploring his analyses of morality, biblical revelation, and the faith-ethics relation will show that these differences enable Ricoeur (1) to develop very different understandings of justice and the relationship between the self and the other, (2) to retain the God of presence without falling into the trap of idolatry, and (3) to clarify how biblical faith informs ethics.

Ricoeur's Descriptions of Morality, Biblical Revelation, and the Faith-Ethics Relation

Ricoeur's phenomenological descriptions of the foundations of moral philosophy reveal that practical freedom presents itself to the world as a complex network of essential relations that he calls the "ethical intention." Expressed verbally as the "I can," the ethical intention is a fundamental drive or belief that enables human freedom to be actualized in the world, regardless of historical location. In Ricoeur's words, the ethical intention is "this movement . . . of actualization, this odyssey of freedom across the world of works, this proof-testing of the being-able-to-do-something . . . in effective actions which bear witness to it. Ethics [is the product of] this movement between naked and blind belief in a primordial 'I can,' and the real history where I attest to this "I can.' "[22]

As freedom moves along the path of self-actualization, it encounters other freedoms with the same agenda. The encounter between individual freedoms in the world—between the self and the other—requires mediation through neutral third terms, or "institutions," of increasing complexity: from value, to norm, to imperative, to the Kantian concept of law. Ricoeur argues that although these mediating terms are the result of historical processes of evaluation, they are not wholly relative to their historical-cultural contexts, because embedded in these essential structures are common meanings (the social bond) that serve as a basis for making consistent moral judgments over time. The value of justice, for example, ultimately means "that you may be free." Its meaning arises in a moment of recognition in which the "I can" recognizes the other as another self—as another "I can." And with this recognition comes the awareness of the supreme value of the other's freedom for actualizing freedom generally. It is at this moment that moral obligation is born, when the essential freedom of the other must be allowed "to be." But, as Ricoeur explains, moral obligation is not derived from difference (a point Hobbes's *Leviathan* makes very clear); rather it comes from a self-affirmation that is prior to difference.

> We truly enter into a problem of morality when we posit freedom in the second person, as the willing . . . of the other's freedom, the willing that your freedom might exist. Then and only then are we on the trail of a real obligation, and . . . a law. But it was necessary to begin with the self-affirmation of freedom . . . [because] there can be no problematic of the second person if I do not know the meaning of "I" and of "ego." The other is indeed another me, an "alter ego"—*alter*, yes, but alter *ego*. If I did not understand what it means for me to be free, and to have to really become free, I could not will it for others. Actually, if in moments when my belief collapses, I doubt that I am free, if I experience myself as crushed by determinisms of every sort, then I can no longer believe in the freedom of the other person and I can no longer help him to be free. If I believe myself not to be free, I also believe the other person is not free.[23]

What Ricoeur is claiming here is that there is a primary affirmation of being (an ontological preunderstanding) that is prior to the encounter with the other and that grounds the demand for justice. The problem of morality arises at the moment the self acknowledges the other as another "I can." But that does not mean that justice is reduced to an instant of recognition. Ricoeur's description of the function of justice as a mediating term reveals the ongoing connection between justice and experience.

> Justice . . . is not an essence, which I reach in some atemporal heaven, but the institutional instrument by means of which several freedoms may coexist. Therefore, it is a mediation of coexistence. If I want to be free, justice, we could say, is the schema of actions to be done to make institutionally possible the community and communication of freedom. In still other terms, the desire for an analogue of freedom as another freedom receives support from a group of institutionalized actions whose meaning is justice. Justice therefore ultimately means "that you may be free."[24]

Thus, justice is not simply recognition or an idea that is continually deferred; rather, it is part of historical processes of proof testing and evaluation that attend freedom's drive toward self-actualization. Over time the meanings of justice function as a schema or model that has a fundamental meaning ("that you may be free") and that is used as a basis for sustaining justice within the practical economy. In this sense, justice is a value that is continually present and experienced in history—however partial it may be. Ricoeur's analysis of the processes of practical freedom thus establishes that there is experiential content from which to develop consistent standards for judgment both in individual communities and in cross-cultural dialogue.

The fundamental relationship between experience and language is also central to Ricoeur's understanding of biblical revelation. For Ricoeur, biblical revelation displays an "economy of the gift" that contains a variety of divine names. It is in this variety that Ricoeur discovers the intertextual mechanisms that destroy the idols of fundamentalism while affirming the God of presence.

Ricoeur's Analysis of Biblical Revelation

According to Ricoeur, the religious language of scripture follows the dynamics of written discourse but with an important difference. Biblical discourse has a poetic function that is distinguished by its split reference, which is the ability of language to suspend descriptive reference (which refers to objects of the world) so that other, more affective dimensions of human existence may be dramatically revealed. As noted previously, the bible speaks about the human encounter with the Wholly Other (and with evil) through common human experiences, such as alienation, temptation, reconciliation, compassion, hope, suffering, joy, and peace. For Ricoeur, these lived experiences refer to more primordial modes of being and of belonging-to that escape the methods and discourses of ethics and the sciences. The truth claims of biblical revelation, therefore, are affective and experiential rather than factual, and thus require a different understanding of truth.

> To reveal is to uncover what until then remained hidden. Now, the objects of our manipulation dissimulate the world of our originary rootedness. Yet in spite of the closed-off character of our ordinary experience, and across the ruins of the intraworldly objects of everyday reality and science, the modalities of our belonging trace out their way. Revelation, in this sense, designates the emergence of another concept of truth than truth as adequation, regulated by the criteria of verification and falsification: a concept of truth as manifestation, in the sense of letting be what shows itself.[25]

Scripture's ability to manifest these affective modes of being is made possible through its internal structure, which establishes a context that permits multiple dimensions of meaning to be reinforced simultaneously. Ricoeur observes that like the individual poem the bible is a structured space in which "language is in celebration." Grasping the internal dynamics of scripture requires a very different approach to interpretation, one that distinguishes Ricoeur's hermeneutics from the historical-critical method and from Derrida's deconstructive readings.

Jacques Derrida, Paul Ricoeur, and the Marginalization of Christianity

> [My investigation] must of course take into account the historical-critical method, but it cannot be reduced to it . . . . [T]he reading I am proposing begins from the fact that the meaning of the recounted events and the proclaimed institutions has become detached from its original *Sitz-im-Leben* by becoming part of Scripture, and this Scripture has so to speak substituted what we may call a *Sitz-im-Wort* for the original *Sitz-im-Leben*. My reading shall begin from here, from the *Sitz-im-Wort* of events, actions, and institutions that have lost their initial roots and that, as a consequence, now have a *textual* existence. It is this textual status of the narratives, laws, prophecies, wisdom sayings, and hymns that makes these texts contemporary with one another in the act of reading. This synchronic reading is called for to complete the diachronic approach of the historical-critical method. This synchronic reading is at the same time an intertextual reading, in the sense that, once they are apprehended as a whole, these texts of different origins and intentions work on one another, displacing their respective intentions and points, and they mutually borrow their dynamism from one another . . . . My reading, in short, seeks to grasp this labor of the text upon itself through an act of reconstructive imagination.[26]

As this passage makes clear, Ricoeur's biblical hermeneutics welcomes the free play of signifiers, but within a global context that orchestrates the labor of the text upon itself. Biblical revelation is thus understood as a unified phenomenon in which the diverse images and literary genres of scripture poetically combine to open up a biblical world—an economy of the gift—that is kept in constant motion and perpetual mystery by the indirect and multiple namings of God.

The Economy of the Gift

The economy of the gift contains a whole range of symbolic expressions that participate in naming God. At one end of the spectrum are forms of expression that symbolize an original and ongoing creation—a gift that is deemed good by the Creator. At the other end of the spectrum are symbolic forms that express the end of existence: God appears as a God of hope, as a God of future possibilities—a gift of salvation. Ricoeur contends that the God of creation and the God of hope is one and the same God situated at both ends of the economy of the gift. In between these two terminal points, God is named symbolically as legislator, judge, servant, and so on. Ricoeur argues that these diverse forms of discourse constitute a living dialectic that displays their interferences with one another.

> Thus God is named in diverse ways in narration that recounts the divine acts, prophecy that speaks in the divine name, prescription that designates God as the source of the imperative, wisdom that seeks God as the meaning of meaning, and the hymn that invokes God in the second person. Because

of this, the word "God" cannot be understood as a philosophical concept, not even "being" in the sense of medieval philosophy or in Heidegger's sense. The word "God" says more than the word "being" because it presupposes the entire context of narratives, prophecies, laws, wisdom writings, psalms, and so on. The referent "God" is thus intended by the convergence of all these partial discourses. It expresses the circulation of meaning among all the forms of discourse wherein God is named.[27]

The God-referent not only reveals how the diverse forms of biblical discourse interact, but also indexes their incompleteness, because in each case, something is revealed and something remains hidden. Essentially, religious language fuses together analogy and negation: "God is like . . . , God is not . . ." For example, in the episode of the burning bush, Ricoeur argues that the declaration "I am who I am" does not institute a positive ontology that may be completed in the narratives and other namings. Instead, it "protects the secret of the 'in-itself' of God, and this secret, in turn, sends us back to the narrative naming through the names of Abraham, Isaac, and Jacob, and by degrees to the other namings."[28]

As with his understanding of justice, Ricoeur likens the various ways in which God is named to a schema. The diverse forms of biblical discourse (for example, narrative, hymn, prophecy) provide images and meanings for the divine Name. The images of the monarch, the judge, the father, the suffering servant, the Christ, the Logos, and so on are not abstract ideas, but are images rooted in human experience, expressing God's relationship to God's people and to the world. Although these schemas are quite diverse and are themselves incapable of forming a conceptual "system," they do have a tendency to become objectified; that is, to become anthropomorphic representations. To counteract this idolatrous tendency, Ricoeur insists that the functioning of the models must be understood within a dialectic of the idol and the Name.

> The name works on the schema or model by making it move, by making it dynamic, by inverting it into an opposed image. (Thus God assumes all the positions in the figures of the family: father, mother, spouse, brother, and finally Son of Man.) Just as, according to Kant, the Idea requires the surpassing of not only the image but also the concept, in the demand to "think more," the Name subverts every model, but only through them.[29]

What Ricoeur is suggesting here is that the overarching presence of the word *God* in the biblical economy surpasses any particular name for God. This means that while each name is valid, none can become wholly definitive. This internal dynamic thus counteracts the idolatrous tendencies inherent in each name while sustaining the meanings revealed through them. Thus, *Jesus Christ* as Word, as Logos, can be retained but cannot be considered definitive.

For Ricoeur, the decentering dynamics found in the biblical world correspond to the way in which biblical revelation informs the reader's ethical intention. The existential condition that prompts the "leap" to symbols of the sacred is the reality of evil, which presents a fundamental paradox for ethical reflection. Simply put, the paradox is that as autonomous creatures, we assert that we are free and yet when we encounter evil we admit that we are enslaved. How do we deal with this paradoxical reality? For Ricoeur, the answer lies in the poetic texts of scripture. For in admitting the limits of human knowledge and power, we are ready to make the leap to sacred symbolism that enables us to overcome the pathologies of evil and to progress toward the authentic actualization of our freedom. This is done through reanimating the whole structural network of the ethical intention. In confronting the paradox of evil in all its manifestations, biblical revelation does not suspend ethics, as Derrida suggests, but places ethics in a new perspective that effects a conversion of the ethical intention.

The Faith-Ethics Relation

The radical shift in perspective is the result of the exchange between the poetic properties of scripture and the productive imagination of the human subject. In the act of reading, the tensive interplay among the diverse texts of scripture poetically combine to challenge and to replace the reader's blind self-interest with a compassionate vision—a new way of "seeing as" that *demands* a moral response. The ethical demand finds its source in the economy of the gift, which manifests within human consciousness the awareness that because God has given the gifts of creation, mercy, peace, love, forgiveness, and hope, disciples *ought to give to others* with the same degree of compassion and generosity.

This sense of givenness raises the issue of reappropriation that Derrida finds so troubling. Ricoeur does not address this issue directly, nor, as far as I know, has he participated in recent debates about the nature of gift.[30] What can be inferred from his writings is this: when we enter the biblical world, we have to enter it with a "second naiveté," with an openness to perceiving what is manifested there. The biblical world presents itself to the reader as a world of givenness—something Derrida refuses to accept in his appropriation of scripture. But for Ricoeur the awareness of what has been given is the biblical truth that enables human beings to overcome the ethical paradox. The visions of innocence, regeneration, compassion, and reconciliation manifested in the biblical economy illuminate new ways of actualizing freedom in the world that break the sense of alienation and bondage that accompanies the insatiable will-to-power of the "I can." Within the biblical economy, a sense of unity and solidarity with others is reborn. The focus of human activity suddenly shifts from the self to the other; from what we can do for ourselves to what we can do for our neighbor. The biblical model for this kind of discipleship is surely the Good Samaritan (Luke 10:29–37), who sees an injured man alongside the road and is compelled to perform extraordinary actions on his behalf, actions that escape the taint of reappropriation and that go far beyond the accepted requirements of justice. Givenness, therefore, has a very practical function within the biblical economy that cannot be eliminated without severely blunting the revelatory power of scripture.

Scripture's unique ability to heal the ethical intention and to cultivate the kind of compassionate vision that compels moral action is what distinguishes the Christian moral life from other historical "forms" of morality. But it is important to reiterate that for Ricoeur a morality informed by scripture is not specifically Christian; rather, it reflects what it means to be *fully human* in spite of the evil that afflicts all human beings. His analysis of the sermons of Jesus on the relationship between the radical command to love one's enemies and the Golden Rule illustrates this point.[31]

Love and Justice

As a fundamental principle of morality, the Golden Rule has a central place in both the Sermon on the Mount ("So whatever you wish that men would do to you do so to them; for this is the law and the prophets" [Mark 7:12]) and the Sermon on the Plain ("And as you wish that men would do to you, do so to them" [Luke 6:31]). Both articulations of the rule presuppose a principle of reciprocity between persons that characterizes justice. Ricoeur argues, however, that this demand for reciprocity has a dark side. The Golden Rule remains within the parameters of the *lex talionis*; that is, an eye for an eye, a tooth for a tooth. Within this context, the Golden Rule simply says, "I give *so that* you give." But Jesus fights against such self-interested interpretations. He warns: "If you love those who love you, what credit is that to you?' For even sinners love those who love them . . . . But love your enemies, do good and lend, expecting nothing in return" (Luke 6:32–35).

Many Christian theologians have interpreted these "hard sayings" as inaugurating a wholly new and radical morality, but Ricoeur argues that the command to love and the Golden Rule are placed in a dialectical relation. On the one hand, the demand of Jesus to love one's enemies brings about a *conversion* of the rule from its penchant toward self-interest to a welcoming attitude toward the other. Its radicality challenges the reader to "think more," to consider alternative ways to apply the Golden Rule that exceed the accepted requirements of justice ruled by a "logic of equivalence." The self-interest and "eye for an eye" mentality that shadow the Golden Rule are transformed by a "logic of generosity." This logic does not replace or add to the rule, but illuminates the deeper, more essential meaning of justice, as well as the creative possibilities of justice in a world that is limited and broken by the reality of evil. On the other hand, the Golden Rule tempers the radical demands of the love command, preventing it from veering over into nonmoral and even immoral results. For example, the command to "do good and lend, expecting nothing in return" could very well lead to social chaos. In Ricoeur's judgment, "This . . . is the fundamental reason why the new commandment does not and cannot eliminate the golden rule or substitute for it. What is called 'Christian ethics,' or, as I would prefer to say, 'communal ethics in a religious perspective,' consists, I believe, in the tension between unilateral love and bilateral justice, and in the interpretation of each of these in terms of the other."[32] This ongoing tension is the biblical realism and biblical truth that inform the ethical intention and shape human praxis. This is why Ricoeur insists that reflection on scripture is essential for self-understanding and for the full realization of social justice. It is essential because the biblical economy illuminates practical possibilities that transcend the standards set by moral philosophy. Put another way, if justice ultimately means "that you may be free," scripture reveals what that could mean in its fullest and most complete sense.

Conclusion

This study has tried to present a clear picture of what would be gained and lost if the Christian God of presence were abandoned. Clearly, Derrida's concerns about the idols of fundamentalism are justified, but I believe this study has shown that abandoning the God of presence altogether is both problematic and unnecessary. Ricoeur's biblical hermeneutics indicate that scripture is a deconstructive text that celebrates the diverse names of God while preventing any one name from becoming definitive.

Can the Christian God of presence be saved? Not only do I believe that it can be saved, but I believe this study has shown that it must be saved. The real challenge for all "disciples of the Word" is to transfer scripture's structural tension into historical traditions so that the traditional category of Logos no longer dominates and limits theology. In this respect, the current move to deconstruct and develop new understandings of "God without Being" is vitally important. Exploring God as the impossible gift, as love, as process, as mystery illuminates dimensions of the divine that have always been present in scripture, but that have been overlooked or forgotten by Christian theology. At the same time, Ricoeur's fundamental ontology as "being-interpreted" offers Christian theology possibilities for developing a more nuanced understanding of being, one that is more dynamic, historical, and open-ended. I believe we can move beyond the deconstructive moment toward a common goal: an authentic biblical faith that can bring Christianity back from the margins.

Notes

1. Seyla Benhabib, *Situating the Self: Gender, Community, and Postmodernism in Contemporary Ethics* (New York: Routledge, 1992), p. 14. Prominent figures in this cultural movement include Jean-François Lyotard, Michel Foucault,

Jacques Derrida, and Richard Rorty. Some feminist writers who have been influenced by the movement are Judith Butler, Iris Young, and Drucilla Cornell. For an overview of the diverse voices in the movement, see Joseph Natoli and Linda Hutcheon, eds., *A Postmodern Reader* (Albany: State University of New York Press, 1993); and Steven Best and Douglas Kellner, *The Postmodern Turn* (New York: Guilford Press, 1997).

2. For an overview and excellent sampling of current work in this area, see John D. Caputo and Michael J. Scanlon, eds., *God, the Gift, and Postmodernism* (Bloomington: Indiana University Press, 1999). See also Emmanuel Levinas, *Ethics and Infinity* (Pittsburgh: Duquesne University Press, 1985); and Mark C. Taylor, *About Religion: Economies of Faith in Virtual Culture* (Chicago: University of Chicago Press, 1999).
3. See John D. Caputo, *Deconstruction in a Nutshell: A Conversation with Jacques Derrida* (New York: Fordham University Press, 1997), p. 9.
4. Ibid., pp. 5–6.
5. Ibid., pp. 13–14.
6. Cited in Richard Kearney, *Modern Movements in European Philosophy* (Manchester: Manchester University Press, 1986), p. 123.
7. Jacques Derrida, *On Grammatology* (Baltimore: Johns Hopkins University Press, 1974), p. 158.
8. See John D. Caputo, *Radical Hermeneutics: Repetition, Deconstruction, and the Hermeneutic Project* (Bloomington: Indiana University Press, 1987); and Drucilla Cornell, *At the Heart of Freedom: Feminism, Sex, and Equality* (Princeton: Princeton University Press, 1998).
9. Caputo, *Deconstruction in a Nutshell*, pp. 22–23.
10. Ibid., p. 23.
11. Ibid., p. 25.
12. See Richard Kearney, "On the Gift: A Discussion between Jacques Derrida and Jean-Luc Marion," in *God, the Gift, and Postmodernism*, p. 59.
13. Caputo, *Deconstruction in a Nutshell*, pp. 18–19.
14. See Richard Kearney, "Desire of God," in *God, the Gift, and Postmodernism*, p. 134.
15. Cited in John D. Caputo, "Abraham's Gift," in *The Prayers and Tears of Jacques Derrida*, (Bloomington: Indiana University Press, 1997), p. 204.
16. Kearney, "Desire of God," p. 127.
17. See John D. Caputo, "Deconstruction in a Nutshell: The Very Idea (!)," in *Deconstruction in a Nutshell*, p. 41.
18. Kearney, *Modern Movements in European Philosophy*, p. 100.
19. Paul Ricoeur, "The Model of the Text: Meaningful Action Considered as a Text" in *From Text to Action*, (Evanston, IL: Northwestern University Press, 1991), p. 149.
20. See John R. Searle, *The Construction of Social Reality* (New York: Free Press, 1995), p. 184.
21. Paul Ricoeur, "From Interpretation to Translation," in André LaCocque and Paul Ricoeur, *Thinking Biblically: Exegetical and Hermeneutical Studies* (Chicago: University of Chicago Press, 1998), p. 360.
22. Paul Ricoeur, "The Problem of the Foundation of Moral Philosophy," *Philosophy Today* (fall 1978): 177.

23. Ibid., p. 178.
24. Ibid., pp. 182–83.
25. Paul Ricoeur, "Naming God," in *Figuring the Sacred: Religion, Narrative, and Imagination*, ed. Mark I. Wallace and trans. David Pellauer (New York: Fortress Press, 1995), p. 223.
26. Paul Ricoeur, "Biblical Time," in *Figuring the Sacred*, pp. 170–71.
27. Ricoeur, "Naming God," pp. 227–28.
28. Ibid., p. 228
29. Ibid., p. 233.
30. One of the interesting debates about the gift recently took place between Jacques Derrida and Jean-Luc Marion at the conference "Religion and Postmodernism" held at Villanova University on September 25–27, 1997. The content of their exchange can be found in Caputo and Scanlon, eds., *God, the Gift, and Postmodernism.*
31. See Paul Ricoeur, "Love and Justice," in *Figuring the Sacred*, pp. 315–29.
32. Paul Ricoeur, "Ethical and Theological Considerations on the Golden Rule," in *Figuring the Sacred*, p. 301.

PART III:

Moral Practice, Responsible Citizenship, and Social Justice

11
Ethics and Public Life
A Critical Tribute to Paul Ricoeur

FRED DALLMAYR

Both in theory and in practice, ethics today is in disarray. In the famous opening pages of his *After Virtue*, Alasdair MacIntyre depicted a grim scenario of devastation where ethical memories—especially the great ethical teachings of the past—had been obliterated by a debacle akin to a nuclear holocaust. Although perhaps overly dramatized, the scenario seems not far off the mark. On the level of social practice, an age marked by genocide and ethnic cleansing cannot credit itself with a high degree of ethical sensibility. Partly as a result of the practical malaise, ethical theorizing in many ways presents a Babel of tongues, with protagonists of the most diverse paradigms competing for attention: from rational cognitivism and moral imperativism to noncognitivism, skepticism and (even) antiethics.[1] To some extent, the clamor of voices can be simplified or streamlined by turning attention to the presumed source of moral concerns, a source located either in the individual or else in society or a public community. In this respect, the recent Cold War still throws its long (and disorienting) shadow over contemporary debates, by pitting against each other champions of individual freedom—self-styled as defenders of the "free world"—against socialists and social communitarians. While the former exalt private autonomy—sometimes to a point indistinguishable from license—the latter accentuate social obligations (which often turn out to be obligations to a dominant regime or ruling doctrine). The demise of the Cold War has only rearranged and broadened these intellectual front lines. Today liberal defenders of the "free world" (meaning the West) are confronted by the upsurge of numerous nonindividualistic cultural traditions in the rest of the world—which demonstrates that ethics today has necessarily a global or cosmopolitan cast.

Venturing into the thicket of contemporary ethical debates requires courage and intellectual stamina; attempting to make headway in that thicket also demands sobriety, perseverance, and a good dose of fair-mindedness—

qualities or virtues that nowadays are in short supply. Fortunately, our age is not entirely devoid of guideposts or guiding mentors; one of the more competent and reliable guides is Paul Ricoeur. Although frequently sidelined by changing "fashion trends" in his native France, Ricoeur over the decades has proven himself to be one of the most trenchant and perceptive analysts of contemporary social-political dilemmas as well as one of the most sober and clear-minded voices in the complex (and often overheated) controversies of our time. Steeped deeply in "continental" philosophy—especially the writings of Edmund Husserl, Martin Heidegger, Karl Jaspers, and Gabriel Marcel—but also attentive to Anglo-American "analytical" reasoning, his publications betray a breadth of intellectual scope that militates against any kind of parochialism. In the field of ethics, including public or political ethics, his work stands as an impressive counterexample to MacIntyre's scenario by recollecting and vividly bringing back to life the classical, *polis*-centered teachings of Aristotle's ethics as well as the modernist "groundwork" of autonomous moral self-legislation celebrated by Kant. By correlating and carefully calibrating these diverse legacies, his approach makes a major contribution to (among other things) the festering "liberalism versus communitarianism" debate and also to the "tradition versus modernity" conundrum. Nowhere is this contribution more powerfully evident than in *Oneself as Another*, the chef d'oeuvre of his later years that will be the main focus of the following discussion. The aim here will be to highlight and applaud Ricoeur's accomplishments—but to do so in a critical vein (which alone befits a philosopher); paying him such a critical tribute, in any case, seems to accord well with his own emphasis on "critical solicitude" seen as the preeminent form of practical wisdom.[2] The presentation will be tripartite. The first section recapitulates the main arguments regarding ethics and its role in the public domain, while the second part raises a number of critical queries or reservations. The point of the final section is to explore the relevance of Ricoeur's ethics for contemporary politics and public life, especially in the context of the emerging "global village" or cosmopolis.

The Theme of Ethics and Public Life

The theme of ethics and public life is a central concern of *Oneself as Another*, but it is approached somewhat circuitously: namely, through an analysis of "selfhood" in its different modalities. This approach seems to insert Ricoeur's text into a broadly familiar framework: that of the "subject" seen as the source of moral norms and obligations. This impression, however, is unwarranted. As is well known, and as he himself repeatedly insists, Ricoeur is not a "philosopher of the subject" or of the "cogito," but rather a hermeneuticist—moreover, the proponent of a hermeneutics enriched or amplified by borrowings from linguistic analysis, depth psychology, and poststructuralist efforts to "decenter" the ego. This decentering has been a hallmark of his thought from the beginning. Thus, although Ricoeur was a profound student of René Descartes and Husserl, some of his early writings had called into question the foundational role of subjectivity in favor of a notion of situated and embodied selfhood (indebted in many ways to Marcel). Somewhat later, his investigation of depth psychology vindicated a complex "hermeneutics of suspicion" as opposed to the straightforward grasp of semantic meanings. Roughly at the same time, his analysis of "willing" and "freedom of will" complicated the linearity of rational intention through recourse to a quasi-mythical "symbolism of evil." Congruent with these precedents, the selfhood invoked in *Oneself as Another* is not a fixed or self-contained ego, but rather a flexible "emergent" being discovering itself in a variety of situated engagements; differently phrased: "self" is not a stable substance but rather a practical category (amenable only to "practical" philosophy). Reflecting this practical accent, the text examines in sequence these basic questions: "Who is speaking? Who is acting? Who is recounting [narrating] about himself/herself? Who is the moral subject of interpretation?"—thus passing successively in review the speaking, the acting, the narrating, and the moral-ethical self (with the latter serving as a capstone of the entire series).[3]

What renders the theme of ethics and public life central or pivotal in *Oneself as Another* is the fact that only here the "other" or "other-than-self" comes specifically into focus. Although, in Ricoeur's account, selfhood is never devoid of other-relation, this relation only now becomes the distinct target of inquiry. In exploring this relation, Ricoeur's text advances a novel and startling theory of ethics, and of ethics in public life, which is marked both by a circumspect balance and a definite weighting of accents in one direction. In large measure, this weighting derives from the premise of a situated selfhood and the critique of the ego. What this premise renders dubious is the theory of moral self-legislation anchored in "noumenal" consciousness; what it renders attractive is the assumption of an ethical bond preceding and undergirding normative stipulations. Although indicating an order of preference, however, the text does not simply reject or negate the first option in favor of the second. In a manner distantly echoing G. W. F. Hegel, Ricoeur maintains the respective legitimacy of both "morality" and "ethics"—where ethics deals with "the *aim* of an accomplished life," while morality stands for normative legislation characterized by the "claim to universality" and an "effect of constraint." As he adds, the two terms are stand-ins for two traditions of ethical teaching: namely, an Aristotelian heritage "where ethics is characterized by its teleological perspective" and a Kantian heritage "where morality is defined by the obligation to respect the norm, hence by a *deontological* point of view." Combining the two traditions with his weighted preference scheme, *Oneself as Another* formulates a series of basic propositions that remain guideposts for the entire study:

(1) the primacy of ethics over morality; (2) the necessity for the ethical aim to pass through the sieve of the norm; and (3) the legitimacy of recourse by the norm to the aim whenever the norm leads to an impass in practice.... [Thus] morality is held to constitute only a limited, although legitimate and even indispensable, actualization of the ethical aim, and ethics in this sense would then encompass morality.[4]

In line with these propositions, the text moves from a discussion of teleological ethics in the Aristotelian vein via a Kantian or quasi-Kantian deontology to a final recuperation of ethics under the rubric of situated *phronesis* or practical wisdom. Reformulating the respective philosophical traditions, Ricoeur posits as the aim of teleological ethics the achievement of "self-esteem," while deontology is said to obey the principle of "self-respect"; the key category of a recuperative ethical praxis, finally, is found to reside in ethical "conviction," the term taken not in the sense of private opinion but rather in that of a reflective "attestation" bearing witness to competing demands in the public area. Elucidating the meaning of teleological ethics, the text offers a capsule phrase that highlights its central ingredients: ethics on this level, we read, means "*aiming at the 'good life' with and for others, in just institutions*." Decomposing the phrase into its constituent components, Ricoeur first focuses on the notion of leading a "good life" or "living well." As he notes, goodness along Aristotelian lines is always a "good for us"—not in the sense of an instant possession, but in that of something constantly (and unendingly) yearned or striven for. The question that arises here immediately is whether goodness is the mark of a particular action taken by itself, or whether the latter is only a means to a more distant end (which perhaps can never be fully specified). Taking a leaf from the writings of MacIntyre, Ricoeur distinguishes between particular actions or practices and broader, more encompassing "life plans" that allow the integration of singular acts into a "narrative unity of life" governed by intrinsic "standards of excellence." By adopting this perspective, goodness can be shown to be the intrinsic measure both of individual actions taken by themselves and of the "good life" taken in the sense of a whole life "lived well"—thus lending credence and support to the teleological argument of *Nicomachean Ethics*: "The action-configurations that we are calling life plans stem, then, from our moving back and forth between far-off ideals, which have to be made more precise, and the weighing of the advantages and disadvantages of the choice of a given life plan on the level of practice."[5]

Ethical goodness, however, cannot be a private monopoly; hence a "good life" is not one lived in isolation, but a life "with and for others." To characterize the aspect of living-with or co-being Ricoeur chooses the term *solicitude* (full of Heideggerian resonances). As he emphasizes, just as the "self" should not be construed as an ego, self-esteem as the aim of the good life cannot be divorced from solicitude; in fact, the latter is not "something added on to self-esteem from the outside" but rather an intrinsic quality unfolding "the dialogic dimension of self-esteem." As an emblem of co-being, solicitude is deeply shaped by reciprocity or mutuality—the kind of mutuality that Ricoeur sees as the hallmark of Aristotelian friendship. In Aristotle's account, (genuine) friendship involves neither an appropriation of the other nor a self-effacement in favor of the other, but rather a balance between self-love or self-care (*philautia*) and a self-transgression where the other is loved "for his or her sake," as "the being he/she is." Akin to friendship, solicitude thus emerges as an interchange between self and other, as "the midpoint of a spectrum" located between "giving and receiving." Arguing against Emmanuel Levinas's privileging of the "other" (at the expense of self-initiative), Ricoeur faults this approach for failing to establish an interhuman relation "to the extent that the other represents absolute exteriority with respect to an ego defined by the condition of separation." Moreover, Levinas's elevation of morality to the level of "first philosophy" tends to bury ethical sensibility under norms (the "summons to responsibility") while sidestepping the role of ethical solicitude as a "benevolent spontaneity." Most important, ethical sensibility for Ricoeur extends beyond interpersonal or face-to-face encounters to the field of "institutions," a public domain basically governed by the category of "justice." By institutions the text means structures of shared life, or else "bonds of common mores" permeating a historical community. Like solicitude, justice occupies a kind of midpoint: namely, between interpersonal care and the externality of legal constraints. As an ethical category, justice involves the proper distribution of shares among members of a community, where shares include not only material goods but also roles, advantages, and forms of life.[6]

Having thus defended the "primacy of ethics" (in a more or less Aristotelian manner) Ricoeurs recalls his second basic proposition, according to which ethics, or the ethical aim, must "pass through the sieve of the norm"—that is, through the sieve of deontological morality. The way in which ethics is tested by morality is chiefly through the principle of "universality" (or universalization) expressed preeminently in the universal maxims of Kantian moral theory. In the Kantian tradition, this accent on universality is closely linked with the idea of "noumenal" self-legislation whereby contingent desires or inclinations are strictly subordinated to "duty"—a self-legislation that is ultimately grounded in radical human freedom or "autonomy" (from nature). In Ricoeur's account, Kant's categorical imperative is precisely designed to pass the test of universalization—although the different formulations of the imperative give rise to quandaries. The text at this point refers to a number of problems or aporias in Kant's theory—to which it will be necessary to return later, but that can be flagged briefly here. These problems all have to do with the return of a certain moral affectivity (presumably exiled by self-legislation), giving rise to questions like these: Does the derivation of autonomy from a "fact of reason" not jeopardize the former's purity? Does Kant's admission of radical evil not rebound on the postulated freedom of will? Does the central category of "respect" for others not circumscribe a sovereign self-rule? Pursuing the last point, Ricoeur finds in respect a certain "dialogic structure" that approximates it to solicitude (in teleological ethics) and in any case to the traditional "Golden Rule" with its demand for reciprocity. In his words, respect owed to persons (as ends in themselves) "is, on the moral plane, in the same relation to autonomy as solicitude was to the good life." Here again, however, a certain problem or tension emerges: namely, that between respect owed to "humanity" at large and respect owed to persons in their singularity, "The notion of humanity has the effect of lessening, to the point of elimination, the otherness that is at the root of this diversity" (of persons). To round out this discussion of morality, the text turns finally to the theme of justice as seen under deontological or proceduralist auspices. The prime example of the latter approach is John Rawls's *A Theory of Justice,* with its blending of Kantian and contractarian premises— with the Kantian legacy being evident especially in the assumptions of the "original position" and the "veil of ignorance."[7]

As announced in the third basic proposition, deontological morality cannot stand on its own or have the last word: by virtue of its intrinsic dilemmas or limitations, moral reflection is prompted to return to "the initial intuition of ethics"—now under the rubric of "moral judgment in situation" or "practical wisdom." Surprisingly, the return occurs again circuitously: namely, through the detour of tragedy or "tragic action." The basic point of the detour is to ward off any thought of a final reconciliation or synthesis, especially a Hegelian-style synthesis in which the preceding steps would be "sublated" (*aufgehoben*). In Ricoeur's words, tragedy—above all Sophocles' *Antigone*— teaches "something unique about the unavoidable nature of conflict in moral life"; it offers viewers a glimpse of "the agonistic ground of human experience," of the "interminable confrontation" of men and women, individual and society, humans and gods. The only way to mitigate or mediate these conflicts is through cultivation of practical wisdom (nurtured by tragic wisdom). In *Oneself as Another*, the return to ethics moves in the opposite or reverse direction from that outlined previously: the path now leads from institutions via respectful solicitude to the ground of self-legislation in moral autonomy. In the field of institutions, the study presents a careful critique and reformulation of Hegel's political philosophy, especially of his notion of the modern "state" as the embodiment of "objective spirit," and of the category of *Sittlichkeit* seen as the ultimate resolution of moral conflicts. For Ricoeur, rather than clinging to the letter of Hegel's work, it seems preferable to "shift Hegelian *Sittlichkeit* in the direction of Aristotelian *phronesis.*" Once this is done, *Sittlichkeit* would no longer denote "a third category, higher than ethics and morality," but would designate "one of the places in which practical wisdom is exercised, namely the hierarchy of institutional mediation through which practical wisdom must pass if justice is truly to deserve the name of fairness." The benefits of a turn to *phronesis* are illustrated by Ricoeur on three levels of public debate. In the case of everyday debates about concrete policies, Aristotle's notion of deliberation warrants and supports the modern-liberal demand for open discussion in a public forum (*Öffentlichkeit*). On the level of debates about preferable regimes or constitutional arrangements, *phronesis* helps to guard against simplistic recipes by appealing to the wisdom of practical experience. Finally, on the level of the basic legitimation of regimes, *phronesis* aids in combating the "crisis of legitimacy" by marshalling the "overlapping consensus" of diverse traditions.[8]

Moving on to the theme of respect/solicitude, Ricoeur repeats and sharpens a dilemma he had previously noted in Kantian morality: namely, the tension between respect for humanity at large and respect for singular persons (seen as ends in themselves). For Ricoeur, this is another area calling for the intervention of prudential judgment. In Kant's formulas, he writes, "respect tends to split up into respect for the [universal] law and respect for persons." Under these conditions, "practical wisdom may consist in giving priority to the respect for persons, in the name of the solicitude that is addressed to persons in their irreplaceable singularity." For Kant, every deviation or exception from universality was necessarily a moral lapse; the situation changes, however, once the demand for respect is radicalized. At this point, "the genuine otherness of persons makes each one an exception"; practical wisdom here means pursuing a course that "will best satisfy the exception required by solicitude"—without arrogantly nullifying universal rules as such. Proceeding, in a final step, to the topic of self-legislation grounded in autonomy, Ricoeur recapitulates some of the quandaries previously alluded to, especially the role of the "fact of reason" and of the pervasive affectivity infiltrating rational obligation. In Ricoeur's pointed words, "An autonomy that is of a piece with the rule of justice and the rule of reciprocity can no longer be a *self-sufficient* autonomy." Similar quandaries beset the principle of universality or universalization—which Ricoeur prefers to replace with the standard of "constructive coherence" (as found in judicial reasoning, especially in common-law countries). Reservations of this kind spill over into the assessment of more recent, neo-Kantian approaches, especially formulations of communicative or "discourse" morality as propounded by Habermas and Karl-Otto Apel. Although appreciating the communicative focus, Ricoeur deplores here the underdevelopment of practical judgment. "My thesis is," he writes, "that this undertaking is fully authorized if it is kept along the regressive path of [normative] *justification*, thereby leaving uncovered the conflictual zone situated along the progressive path of *actualization*." The problem is that the justification of norms tends "to conceal the conflicts that lead morality back toward practical wisdom whose place is that of moral judgment in situation."[9]

The discussion of ethics and public life, in *Oneself as Another*, is rounded out by some general comments on the relation, or rather correlation, between universal principles and historical or cultural contexts. As the preceding step-by-step review has indicated, this correlation is surely a central concern of the entire study—apart from constituting a prominent issue in contemporary ethical and political thought. As Ricoeur himself remarks, all the arguments presented in previous chapters "find an echo and the focal point of their reflection, as it were, in the conflict between universalism and contextualism." The issue clearly impinges on Rawls's theory of justice, given that a "fair" distribution of social goods depends on historically and culturally shaped understandings of the meaning of "goods"—with the result that "no system of distribution . . . is universally valid." The issue also affects the Habermasian program of a universal discourse morality (or discourse ethics). Without in any way endorsing cultural or historical relativism, Ricoeur detects in this program the legacy of Kantian dualisms. "What I am criticizing in the ethics of argumentation," he writes, "is not the invitation to look for the best argument in all circumstances," but rather the recourse to an absolute rational validation resembling the Kantian "strategy of purification." While in Kant this strategy was directed against inclination or desire, Habermas directs his energies against "everything that can be placed under the title of *convention*"—an opposition congruent with his sharp break between tradition and modernity (the former being demoted to prejudice). Paralleling his reformulation of Hegelian *Sittlichkeit*, Ricoeur at this point proposes a replacement of the reason/convention dualism by the more subtle dialectic between "*argumentation* and *conviction*." In this dialectic, argumentation allows itself to be inserted into a multiplicity of different (though not incommensurable) language games, thereby gaining historical and cultural richness and profile. At the same time, social contexts permit themselves to be seasoned by critical reasoning, the latter operating not as the enemy of tradition but as a "critical agency operating *at the heart* of [historically sedimented] convictions," thereby carrying them to the level of "considered convictions" or what Rawls calls "reflective equilibrium." As Ricoeur concludes, "It is just such a reflective equilibrium between the requirement of universality and the recognition of contextual limitation affecting it that is the final issue in situational judgment" or the exercise of practical wisdom.[10]

Critical Solicitude

Having followed the book's intellectual journey, the reader is likely to be stunned by the vastness of its scope and the subtlety of its insights. Placed in its own context, *Oneself as Another* surely deserves to be ranked as one of the great philosophical works of our century. The virtues of the study are too numerous to be fully enumerated, but a few should be highlighted. One of the primary virtues resides in the boldness of the first proposition, which sets the basic tenor of the study: the affirmed "primacy of ethics over morality" (or of the good over the right). With this affirmation, Ricoeur sets his face against one of the dominant but thoroughly disorienting assumptions of modernity: that of a presocial, autonomous human existence outside of community bonds (as postulated by the contractarian tradition from Hobbes to contemporary liberal proceduralism). What this assumption ignores is that being human is not something "given" (by nature or reason), but rather a practical task requiring steady cultivation in social contexts. Differently phrased: human nature or "humanity" is not a fixed endowment but the fruit of a process of "humanization" involving sustained interactive solicitude. Ricoeur on this point is not reluctant to show his cards—that is, his intellectual indebtedness to Aristotle and his notion of *zoon politikon*. Referring to *Oneself as Another*, he describes it as a study "whose tone is Aristotelian from start to finish." In the same context, he takes a stand against the contractarian doctrine of a state of nature (replete with "natural rights"), stating: "This hypothesis of a subject of law, constituted prior to any societal bond, can be refuted only by striking at its roots. Now the root is the failure to recognize the *mediating* role of others."[11]

To be sure, as indicated, Aristotle is not the sole mentor (although he certainly provides the key tonality). In *Oneself as Another*, he shares the limelight with two prominent figures not usually associated with him: Kant and Hegel. The linkage of Aristotle and Kant, and especially the treatment of Kant as a necessary gateway from Aristotle to a viable modern ethics, is surely a unique and startling idea. Proponents of Aristotle are usually averse to Kantian teachings, and the reverse holds equally true; hence both sides are disinclined to mutual learning. (Probably one of the weakest parts of MacIntyre's *After Virtue* is his cursory dismissal of Kantian morality.) Here Ricoeur boldly breaks the pattern by giving broad room to Kantian universalism and categorical maxims; what primarily motivates this break is the recognition of Kant as a thinker of human freedom and self-legislation—aspects that our age cannot and should not hastily renounce. The presence of Kant is further complicated by the additional invocation of Hegel, which testifies to a remarkably tolerant scope of intellectual horizons. In this respect, Ricoeur also breaks some established patterns, especially the fashionable and almost ritualistic denunciation of Hegel as proponent of "totalization" (read: totalitarianism) as found in recent French (poststructuralist) philosophy. Although critical of Hegel's metaphysics of "spirit" (*Geist*), Ricoeur is far removed from sharing these simplistic denunciations (reminiscent of Popperian invectives). As he admits frankly, Hegel's philosophical project "remains very close to my own views, to the extent that it reinforces the claims directed against political atomism"; in this respect at least, the notion of *Sittlichkeit* "has never ceased to instruct us." The remarkable triad of mentors is summed up by Ricoeur in these words:

> This "little ethics" [developed in *Oneself as Another*] . . . suggests that the practical wisdom we are seeking aims at reconciling Aristotle's *phronesis*, by way of Kant's *Moralität*, with Hegel's *Sittlichkeit*. . . . Between the "naïve" *phronesis* of our first pages and the "critical" *phronesis* of our final pages extends, first, the region of moral obligation, of duty . . . and, more particularly, the demand that the suffering inflicted on humans by other humans be abolished. . . . In this way, "critical" *phronesis* tends, through these mediations, to be identified with *Sittlichkeit*. The latter, however, has been stripped of its pretention to mark the victory of Spirit over the contradictions that it itself provokes. Reduced to modesty, *Sittlichkeit* now joins *phronesis* in moral judgment in situation.[12]

Intellectual amplitude or generosity extends also to some prominent contemporary figures, including Habermas and Levinas (though for very different reasons). Although critical of his practical deficit—his sidelining of practical judgment—Ricoeur readily endorses Habermas's "linguistic turn," or his turn to argumentation. In this respect, *Oneself as Another* takes sides against certain contextualist (or "communitarian") detractors of Habermas who—perhaps too quickly—are ready to abandon broader horizons in favor of self-enclosed language games. What these critics neglect, in Ricoeur's view, is the linkage between argumentation and an open-ended public arena and hence the former's relevance for nonexclusive democratic politics; under these auspices he willingly concedes that, in our time, the "demand for universality" finds its "most adequate expression in the morality of communication" along Habermasian lines. In a very different register, Ricoeur's text grants a hearing to the Levinasian inversion of ethics—provided that the privileging of the "other" is seen simply as an antidote to, or compensation for, rampantly egocentric approaches prevalent in modernity. As an astute reader of Kant, Ricoeur cannot fail to be apprehensive about such Levinasian formulas as radical "exteriority," "dissymmetry," and "heteronomy"—suspecting them as new forms of human self-alienation and authoritarian tutelage. On this score, his text deviates from another intellectual mood or fashion—namely, the tendency to elevate his compatriot's work into a cult object. While appreciating a certain transcendental élan, Ricoeur is unwilling to suspend critical judgment. By installing the other as "master of justice," he notes, the self is liable to be reduced to a passive recipient or object: "summoned" to responsibility, "it is in the *accusative* mode alone that the self is enjoined"—which means that the summons targets "the passivity of an 'I' who has been called upon." The critique of Levinas is carried forward and expanded in the book's final chapter or epilogue, dealing with the metaphysics (or ontology) of self and other. There, appealing to the dialectic-dialogical character of solicitude, Ricoeur chides both Husserlian "egology" and Levinasian "exteriority." The self-other nexus, he insists, cannot and should not be constructed "in a unilateral manner"—regardless of whether one attempts "with Husserl, to derive the alter ego from the ego" or whether "with Levinas, one reserves for the Other the exclusive initiative for assigning responsibility of the self." In the case of Levinas, the "exteriority of the Other" can no longer be expressed at all in the language of a relation; rather, "the Other absolves itself from relation, in the same movement by which the Infinite draws free from Totality."[13]

These critical strictures, however, do not amount to complete rejection. Underneath overt denials, there is an undercurrent of covert complicity, signaling an indebtedness to Levinasian discourse and, more broadly, to poststructuralist accents on "otherness." Sensitive to these accents, Ricoeur is unwilling to subscribe to any unitary metaphysics (or ontology) that would submerge the diversity of particulars to a grand synthesis (or totalization). This aversion colors the reception of his mentors. Thus, in the case of Aristotle, the ethical aim of leading a "good life," both individually and collectively, no longer obeys a unitary formula, but is decentered into different types of goodness (which sometimes are in tragic conflict). In the case of Kant, the maxim of treating humans as ends is decomposed into respect for humanity in general and for persons in their singularity, with a distinct preference given to the second formulation. As the text notes, behind Kant's sweeping imperatives there appears "the intuition, inherent in solicitude, of genuine otherness at the root of the plurality of persons." The most resolute decentering, however, affects Hegelian philosophy where *Geist* is subordinated to *phronesis* and *Sittlichkeit* is transformed into practical judgment in concrete situations. Apart from its philosophical importance, this decentering clearly has far-reaching political implications—to the extent that Hegel's philosophy is seen as a bulwark of the modern state. Ricoeur is adamant on this point. What he finds "inadmissable" in Hegel's work is the concept of the "objective mind" and, as its corollary, "the thesis of the state erected as a superior agency endowed with self-knowledge." As a recipe for "demystifying the Hegelian state" he recommends the turn to "political practice" in concrete contexts (although the point is not further pursued). Basically, what these comments suggest is a turn from the "state" to the domain of "civil society"—the latter seen not so much (or not only) as an arena of economic competition but as a space for the unfolding of different "life plans" on the part of individuals and groups. Relocated on the level of a decentralized civil society, *Sittlichkeit* would mean the cultivation of respect for, and willingness to learn from, a variety of narrative trajectories (many of them nurtured by cultural or religious traditions).[14]

Having highlighted some—by no means all—of the fruitful and promising features of *Oneself as Another*, it is time to make room for "critical solicitude."

Reservations arise at a number of points—one being precisely the treatment of Hegel. A central motive behind Ricoeur's critique of the Hegelian state derives from the horrible experiences of our time. As he writes, people who have moved through "the monstrous events of the twentieth century tied to the phenomenon of totalitarianism" can no longer be sanguine about the state; when social community is perverted "to the point of feeding a deadly *Sittlichkeit*," only recourse to heroic individuals (perhaps imbued with Kantian morality) can bring relief. Here one may wish to remonstrate against the equation of the Hegelian state with political perversion or corruption. Pace Popper, the Hegelian state is a rational-ethical "idea" and as such not reducible to contingent, empirical structures; by the same token, a "deadly *Sittlichkeit*" can no longer count as ethical but precisely as *unsittlich*. Hegel himself was by no means unaware of these issues; after all, political perversion is not an invention of our century. As he observes in the *Philosophy of Right*, the state is "no ideal work of art" but "stands in the world and so in the sphere of caprice, chance and error"; hence, "bad behavior can disfigure it in multiple ways." However, for Hegel, disfigurement should not be taken as the essence or "idea" of the state, nor can it be derived from this essence in a linear fashion. What this means is that Hegelian thought probably cannot be criticized, and certainly cannot be dislodged, by purely empirical rejoinders pointing to the "way of the world." Fittingly for a philosophical discourse, a basic theoretical or metaphysical idea can be countered only by a "better argument"—that is, by the development of a more adequate or more nuanced idea (liable to its own empirical disfigurement). In its main tenor, Ricoeur's study precisely pursues such a course, namely by articulating the notion of a decentered or nonunitary *Sittlichkeit* illustrated by respect for persons in their singularity and by pursuit of the "good life" in different modalities.[15]

Next to Hegel, the treatment of a number of other figures elicits critical qualms. Among more contemporary thinkers, Charles Taylor deserves brief mention. As students of Taylor surely will have noticed, there are multiple parallels linking him with Ricoeur's arguments: prominent among these are the privileging of the "good" over the "right," the reconstruction of "selfhood," and the remolding of Hegel's legacy in the direction of a viable public ethics in our time. Despite some furtive compliments, however, the Canadian receives only scant attention in the text; occasionally he is linked with contextualist "communitarians" disdainful of universal rights—in neglect of Taylor's own complex mediation of universalism and historical context on the ethical plane.[16] Probably the least coherent or persuasive treatment in the text is accorded to Heidegger—whose voice meanders intermittently through its pages, but receives distinct contours only in the epilogue. Despite the clear connection between "solicitude" and Heidegger's notion of "care" (*Sorge*), the relation is initially left unexplored and tackled only late in the book, in a somewhat roundabout way. The Heidegger that emerges in the conclusion is basically Heidegger the interpreter and adapter of Aristotle, with *Being and Time* said to perform three central interpretive moves: namely, from Aristotelian *praxis* to "care"; from Aristotelian *phronesis* to "conscience" (*Gewissen*); and from Aristotelian *energeia* to being-in-the-world as "facticity." Leaving aside the aspect of conscience, these moves—as presented in the text—clearly involve a kind of positivist (or ontic) adaptation neglecting the more disturbing and even "nihilating" dimensions of Heideggerian "care" and being-in-the-world—a positivism evident in the treatment of *praxis* as action (versus passion) and also in Ricoeur's own preferred restyling of *energeia* as *conatus* (a term borrowed from Spinoza's metaphysics of life and power). Regarding conscience, the text charges Heidegger with offering only a pale description obtuse to the role of moral injunctions or "summoning." By focusing on "*being*-guilty" instead of thematizing moral guilt, he is said to "abolish the primacy of ethics" while being unable to travel back "from ontology toward ethics"—comments that are hard to reconcile with *Being and Time* and especially with the phrase in the "Letter on Humanism" that a thinking "which ponders the truth of being as the primordial abode of humans, is in itself the original ethics."[17]

The discussion of Heidegger brings into view an aspect that is perhaps the most problematical feature of *Oneself as Another*: namely, Ricoeur's preference for detours and circuitous byways in lieu of a more direct rethinking or reformulation of basic issues. As it happens, this feature is a long-standing trait of Ricoeur's corpus. His *Conflict of Interpretations* chided Heidegger for taking a "short route" in blending hermeneutics with phenomenology—in contrast to a recommended "long route" leading through the detours of epistemology and (transcendental) reflection. Similarly, his *Rule of Metaphor* charged Heidegger with leaping headlong into poetic metaphor instead of pursuing the longer path through conceptual/speculative discourse.[18] In *Oneself as Another*—explicitly self-styled as a "philosophy of detours"—the argument tends to proceed in quasi-Hegelian fashion from one side to the opposite side, with practical wisdom finally brought onto the stage as deus ex machina. On the level of general ethical theory, the text juxtaposes an Aristotelian ethics of virtue to a Kantian deontological morality, presenting both as equally necessary stepping stones to *phronesis*. Similarly, in discussing public ethics and justice, the study pits Rawlsian deontology of rights as well as Habermasian universalism (of validity claims) against communitarian skeptics, depicting the former as a necessary detour to moral praxis. One may ask, however, how two questionable positions can yield a viable theory. In the case of Aristotle, given a multiplication of goods, how much of teleology remains standing? In the case of Kant, does the enumeration of paradoxes and aporias—from the "fact of reason" to the inroads of affectivity and radical evil—still permit recourse to deontological morality as a necessary detour? The same reservations obviously apply also to the treatments of Rawls and Habermas; in the case of the latter, can one still uphold as "exemplary" his "universalist thesis" while deploring his deficit on the level of praxis (or "actualization")? Would it not be desirable to rethink the universalism/contextualism conundrum—perhaps along the lines of Merleau-Ponty's "lateral universals"?[19]

The preference for detours takes its heaviest toll in the domain most central to the book's concerns: the relation of self and other. Here detour may mean precisely derailment; for clearly, if the "other" is merely a detour on the road from self to self (presumably from naive self to reflective self), the book's announced theme of "oneself *as* another" is foiled. This problem is not obviated by Ricoeur's distinction between two types of selfhood, *idem*- and *ipse*-identity—the former referring to a stable self-nature, the second to authentic singularity—because the road to *ipse*-selfhood still remains circuitous (despite occasional disclaimers).[20] This circuitous or detourlike approach is glaringly manifest in the epilogue, dealing with the "ontology" of self and other. Here, Ricoeur steers a precarious course between Husserl and Levinas—that is, between a constitution of the other by the self and a constitution of the self by the other's summons. However, the basic tenor of the entire discussion is closer to Levinas, in the sense that the "other" remains in principle "other than the self" and thus is experienced as an inroad in the mode of "passivity." The conclusion discusses this other-experience under three headings, labeled the "triad of passivity and hence, of otherness." There is, first of all, the passivity represented by "the experience of one's own body" (or one's own "flesh"), where the body appears as a kind of alien agent. Next, there is the "otherness of other people"—that is, passivity involved in the relation of self to the "foreign" or "other (than) self." Finally, there is the "most deeply hidden passivity," located in the relation of the self to itself, a relation disclosed in "conscience" (*Gewissen*). Thus, there are for Ricoeur "three great experiences of passivity" undergone by the self at the hands of otherness—but nowhere (or so it seems) an experience of "oneself *as* another." Perhaps another borrowing from Merleau-Ponty would have been advisable, this time from his posthumously published manuscripts. As is well known, Merleau-Ponty in those manuscripts developed the intriguing notion of "reversibility," sometimes termed "lateral reversibility" or "chiasm," between self and other. As he observed, it is only through reversibility that there is passage from self to other; for, in reality, "there is neither me nor the Other as positive, positing subjectivities—there are two caverns, two opennesses, two stages where something will take place."[21]

Solicitous Appreciation

Having made room for some critical reservations, it seems appropriate to conclude these pages on a note of solicitude or solicitous appreciation. There are many aspects of Ricoeur's work that deserve praise; some have been mentioned before. Overshadowing all other features in importance is the asserted primacy of the "good" over the "right"—that is, the affirmation of a basic goodness of life prior to any "rights" talk and also prior to any theoretical formulation of ethics or metaethics. Covertly or indirectly, this primacy is acknowledged even by its critics, including proponents of deontological morality. With regard to Rawls, for example, Ricoeur legitimately raises the question of whether his theory of justice "does not in a certain way call upon the ethical sense of justice" that it spurns. Ricoeur's own (quite plausible) thesis is that deontology "provides at best the formalization of a sense of justice that it never ceases to presuppose." This, to be sure, leaves open the question of how to proceed from a primary sense to a viable theoretical conception—a question that raises again the vexed problem of "detours"—that is, the progression from teleology via deontology to practical *phronesis*. In a sense, even the notion of detours may be proper or justifiable—provided the term does not signal a zigzag movement between opposite positions (along thesis-antithesis lines), but rather the path of a complex learning process involving trials and errors (and also *Holzwege*). Clearly, for inhabitants of modern Western societies, none of the great episodes of modernity—from Renaissance and Reformation to Enlightenment and industrialization—can be simply expunged (without causing psychic and mental traumas). This means that even staunch opponents of Enlightenment still have to come to terms with, or offer a response to, developments they reject. By the same taken, the notion of history as a learning process also implies a movement of sedimentation or accretion—which entails that earlier phases still reverberate in later accretions, thus placing the "tradition versus modernity" issue under the aegis of continuity more than of rupture.[22]

In terms of contemporary public life, one of Ricoeur's most incisive contributions resides in his resolute effort to move beyond the stale oppositions between liberalism and communitarianism, and also between universalism and contextualism. As previously indicated, one of the central aims of *Oneself as Another* is to find a "reflective equilibrium" between "the requirement of universality and the recognition of contextual limitations"; a crucial thesis advanced in this respect is that an open political arena demands the maintenance of both claims, the universalist and the contextualist, "each in a place" without amalgamation or mutual exclusion. It is here that Ricoeur's argument regarding multiple kinds of goodness reveals its present-day political significance. Clearly, in an age marked by multiculturalism or the upsurge of multicultural diversity, the maintenance of a public space requires both the cultivation of (individual or group) differences and the "solicitous" search for a shared framework, perhaps an "overlapping consensus," through interactive dialogue and contestation. In this contemporary situation, older ethical paradigms—like restrictive communitarianism stressing a unitary goal or liberal contractarianism focused on narrow self-interest—are no longer attractive or persuasive. What Ricoeur's public ethics recommends, instead, is a tolerantly open public space encouraging respect for persons or groups in their "singularity" without losing sight of the requirement of justice or a general rule of law. Such an ethics maintains a shared horizon of "truth" and "goodness" but allows for multiple, even conflicting interpretations of these terms—without lapsing into a debilitating relativism; it honors a sense of universalism that Ricoeur at one point (too briefly) describes as "universals in context" or else "potential or inchoate universals."[23]

The contemporary salience of this kind of public ethics is particularly manifest in light of the unfolding global scenario—that is, the emergence of a global community differentiated along multiple (cultural, ethnic, religious) lines. What this scenario clearly requires is cultivation of respect for difference, for the diversity of cultures and traditions—without succumbing to particularistic myopia anchored in self-enclosed language games. *Oneself as Another* remonstrates strongly against the latter type of relativism: against the claim, as Ricoeur says, that "cultures are ultimately multiple" and incommensurable—where "culture" is taken in a narrowly ethnographic sense "far removed from that of instruction in the ways of reason and liberty" (favored by modern *Bildung*). At the same time, the goal of *phronesis* would not be served by a simple neglect of cultural diversity—an issue that is well illustrated by the controversy surrounding the alleged "ethnocentrism" of supposedly "universal" human rights. As Ricoeur notes, such rights—enshrined in the Universal Declaration of Human Rights (of 1948)—have in fact been ratified or endorsed by the vast majority of countries in the world. Yet, "the suspicion remains that they are simply the fruit of the cultural history belonging to the West, with its wars of religion, its laborious and unending apprenticeship of tolerance." Particularly in terms of application and legislative enforcement, rights talk seems to be part of "a singular history that is broadly that of Western democracies." In this situation, *phronesis* demands a complex negotiation of claims—through dialogue and argumentation—that steers clear both of hegemonic universalism and contextual incommensurability:

> On the one hand, one must maintain the universal claim attached to a few values where the universal and the historical intersect, and on the other hand, one must submit this claim to discussion, not on a formal level, but on the level of the convictions incorporated in concrete forms of life. Nothing can result from this discussion unless every party recognizes that other potential universals are contained in so-called exotic cultures. The path of eventual consensus can emerge only from mutual recognition on the level of acceptability, that is, by admitting a possible truth, admitting proposals of meaning that are at first foreign to us.[24]

A highly intricate and erudite philosophical work, *Oneself as Another* thus reveals itself in the end as a major contribution to reflective political praxis (in the best Aristotelian, post-Hegelian, and Arendtian sense). Ricoeur is by no means a novice or a stranger to the political domain. In several of his previous writings, he had shown himself as both an astute observer of, and engaged participant in, the political agonies of our age. Thus, his *Political and Social Essays* (written during the decades following World War II) articulated a vision of politics or public life combining two central demands: first, creation of an open public space permitting the free pursuit of different modes of goodness (along broadly "liberal" lines), and second, cultivation of social solidarity and a sense of social responsibility, especially for the fate of underprivileged or disadvantaged groups. As he wrote at the time, the pursuit of "liberal politics" (devoted to human rights) must go hand in hand with the strengthening of social solidarity along the lines of democratic socialism—where "socialism" is seen not as a technique of control but rather as "the cry of distress, the demand and the hope of the most humbled men." This yearning for social justices, he added, cannot be divorced today from "solidarity with the most underprivileged fraction of humanity, with the misery of the underdeveloped peoples." Pursuing this line of thought, Ricoeur also commented on the process of globalization, on the emergence of a "planetary consciousness," highlighting both its promise and its perils. While potentially fostering greater solidarity and shared respect among humanity at large, this globalizing process—especially under the rubric of "mondialization"—can also lead to increased uniformity and streamlining of cultures under the pressure of economically and technologically hegemonic powers. In this context, a commitment to social democracy, projected onto the global scale, implies resistance to the division of the world into "haves" and "have-nots," into North and South, and to the systematic exploitation of one part of humanity by another. Nothing less is demanded by distributive justice and by the reflective equilibrium of *phronesis*. As Ricoeur writes suggestively and engagingly in *Oneself as Another*, "the 'good life' is for each of us [and hence for humanity at large] the nebulus of ideals and dreams of achievements with regard to which a life is held to be more or less fulfilled or unfulfilled." What we are summoned to think here is the idea of a highly complex "finality" (*telos*) of humankind that can and should never cease to be the "internal mainspring" of human praxis.[25]

Notes

1. For an overview of ethical theories in our time, see Steven M. Cahn and Joram G. Haber, *Twentieth Century Ethical Theory* (Englewood Cliffs, NJ: Prentice-Hall, 1995); T. Henderich, ed., *Morality and Objectivity* (London: Routledge and Kegan Paul, 1985); William D. Hudson, *Modern Moral Philosophy* (Garden City, NY: Anchor Books, 1970); also my "Introduction" to Seyla Benhabib and Fred Dallmayr, eds., *The Communicative Ethics Controversy*

(Cambridge, MA: MIT Press, 1990), pp. 1–20. Compare also Alasdair MacIntyre, *After Virtue: A Study in Moral Theory,* 2nd ed. (Notre Dame, IN: University of Notre Dame Press, 1984), pp. 1–2; and John D. Caputo, *Against Ethics: Contributions to a Poetics of Obligation with Constant Reference to Deconstruction* (Bloomington: Indiana University Press, 1993).

2. Paul Ricoeur, *Oneself as Another,* trans. Kathleen Blamey (Chicago: University of Chicago Press, 1992), p. 273.
3. Ibid., p. 16. As he himself emphasizes (p. 19), "The philosophy that comes out of this work deserves to be termed a practical philosophy." For some of Ricoeur's earlier writings, see *Gabriel Marcel et Karl Jaspers* (Paris: Temps Present, 1948); *Freud and Philosophy: An Essay on Interpretation,* trans. Denis Savage (New Haven, CT: Yale University Press, 1969); *Freedom and Nature,* trans. Erazim Kohák (Evanston, IL: Northwestern University Press, 1966); *Husserl: An Analysis of His Phenomenology,* trans. Edward G. Ballard and Lester E. Embree (Evanston, IL: Northwestern University Press, 1967); *The Symbolism of Evil,* trans. Emerson Buchanan (New York: Harper and Row, 1967); *The Conflict of Interpretations,* ed. Don Ihde and trans. Willis Domingo et al. (Evanston, IL: Northwestern University Press, 1974); *Time and Narrative,* 3 vols., trans. Kathleen McLaughlin and David Pellauer (Chicago: University of Chicago Press, 1984–88).
4. Ricoeur, *Oneself as Another,* p. 170. As Ricoeur adds (pp. 170–71), "There will thus be no attempt to substitute Kant for Aristotle, despite a respectable tradition to the contrary. Instead, between the two traditions, I shall establish a relation involving at once subordination and complementarity, which the final recourse of morality to ethics will ultimately come to reinforce."
5. Ibid., pp. 172–77.
6. Ibid., pp. 180–83, 188–90, 194, 197, 200.
7. Ibid., pp. 204–7, 209, 212–19, 222–23, 229. See also John Rawls, *A Theory of Justice* (Cambridge, MA: Harvard University Press, 1971).
8. Ricoeur, *Oneself as Another,* pp. 243, 256–61. As Ricoeur elaborates (p. 261), "There is nothing better to offer, in reply to the legitimation crisis . . . than the memory and the intersection in the public space of the appearance of the traditions that make room for tolerance and pluralism, not out of concessions to external pressures, but out of inner conviction, even if this is late in coming. . . . If, and to the extent that, this 'good counsel' does prevail, Hegelian *Sittlichkeit* . . . proves to be the equivalent of Aristotle's *phronesis*: a plural, or rather public, *phronesis* resembling the debate itself."
9. Ibid., pp. 262, 265, 269, 275–77, 280.
10. Ibid., pp. 284–88.
11. Ibid., p. 281.
12. Ibid., pp. 254–55, 290. Regarding denunciations of Hegel in recent French philosophy, see my "Effective History: Hegel's Heirs and Critics," in *G. F. W. Hegel: Modernity and Politics* (Newbury Park, CA: Sage, 1993), pp. 233–38. Compare also Karl Popper, *The Open Society and Its Enemies,* rev. 5th ed. (London: Routledge and Kegan Paul, 1966).
13. Ricoeur, *Oneself as Another,* pp. 189, 281, 284, 331, 336. As Ricoeur recognizes, this critique is primarily addressed at Levinas's *Totality and Infinity.*

He also comments, however, on a subsequent radicalization, in *Otherwise Than Being*, whereby the recipient subject is transformed hyperbolically into a hostage (p. 338): "The paroxysm of the hyperbole seems to me to result from the extreme—even scandalous—hypothesis that the Other is no longer the master of justice here, as is the case in *Totality and Infinity*, but the offender who, as an offender, no less requires the gesture of pardon and expiation." See Levinas, *Totality and Infinity: An Essay on Exteriority*, trans. Alphonso Lingis (Pittsburg: Duquesne University Press, 1969); and *Otherwise Than Being or beyond Essence*, trans. Alphonso Lingis (Dordrecht: Kluwer, 1991).

14. Ricoeur, *Oneself as Another*, pp. 225, 256. For a development of an argument along these lines, see my "Rethinking the Hegelian State," in *Margins of Political Discourse* (Albany: State University of New York Press, 1989), pp. 137–57. Regarding civil society, compare especially Jean L. Cohen and Andrew Arato, *Civil Society and Political Theory* (Cambridge, MA: MIT Press, 1992); and John Keane, ed., *Civil Society and the State* (London: Verso, 1988).

15. Ricoeur, *Oneself as Another*, p. 256. See G. W. F. Hegel, *Hegel's Philosophy of Right*, trans. T. M. Knox (Oxford: Oxford University Press, 1967), par. 258 (addition), p. 279.

16. Ricoeur, *Oneself as Another*, pp. 179, 181, 280n67. See Charles Taylor, *The Ethics of Authenticity* (Cambridge, MA: Harvard University Press, 1992).

17. Ricoeur, *Oneself as Another*, pp. 308–17, 348–49. On the question of conscience, Ricoeur in the end wants to mediate between Heidegger and Levinas, stating (p. 354): "To the reduction of being-in-debt to the strange(r)ness tied to the facticity of being-in-the-world, characteristic of the philosophy of Martin Heidegger, Emmanuel Levinas opposes a symmetrical reduction of the otherness of conscience to the externality of the other manifested in his face.... To these alternatives... I shall stubbornly oppose the original and originary character of what appears to me to constitute the third modality of otherness, namely *being enjoined as the structure of selfhood*." Compare Martin Heidegger, *Being and Time*, trans. Joan Stambaugh (Albany: State University of New York Press, 1996), esp. pp. 247–77; and "Letter on Humanism," in *Martin Heidegger: Basic Writings*, ed. David F. Krell (New York: Harper and Row, 1977), pp. 234–35. Regarding the ethical dimension of Heidegger's thought see also my "Heidegger on Ethics and Justice," in *The Other Heidegger* (Ithaca, NY: Cornell University Press, 1993), pp. 106–31.

18. See Paul Ricoeur, *The Conflict of Interpretations: Essays in Hermeneutics*, ed. Don Ihde (Evanston, IL: Northwestern University Press, 1974), pp. 6–11; *The Rule of Metaphor: Multi-Disciplinary Studies of the Creation of Meaning in Language*, trans. Robert Czerny (Toronto: University of Toronto Press, 1977), pp. 293–312. For critical comments on both studies, see my *Language and Politics: Why Does Language Matter to Political Philosophy?* (Notre Dame, IN: University of Notre Dame Press, 1984), pp. 120–23, 139, 161–65, 179–82. For some earlier comments pointing in the same critical direction, see my "Tale of Two Cities: Ricoeur's Political and Social Essays," in *Twilight of Subjectivity: Contributions to a Post-Individualist Theory of Politics* (Amherst:

University of Massachusetts Press, 1981), p. 269: "The predilection for tensions and antinomies sometimes impales arguments on the proverbial horns of dilemmas, while mediations acquire overtones of weak compromise."

19. Ricoeur, *Oneself as Another*, pp. 17, 212–18, 223–27, 236–39, 284–85. Regarding "lateral universals," see Maurice Merleau-Ponty, "From Mauss to Claude Lévi-Strauss," in *Signs*, trans. Richard C. McCleary (Evanston, IL: Northwestern University Press, 1964), p. 120.

20. On this distinction, see Ricoeur, *Oneself as Another*, pp. 2–3, 118–19. The task announced in the title is on occasion lucidly stated, but without serious effect on the overall argument. Thus, we read (p. 3): "A kind of otherness that is not (or not merely) the result of comparison is suggested by our title, otherness of a kind that can be constitutive of selfhood as such. *Oneself as Another* suggests from the outset that the selfhood of oneself implies otherness to such an intimate degree that one cannot be thought of without the other."

21. Ibid., pp. 318, 355. Compare Maurice Merleau-Ponty, *The Visible and the Invisible*, ed. Claude Lefort and trans. Alphonso Lingis (Evanston, IL: Northwestern University Press, 1968), pp. 160, 263. For a more detailed review, see my "Interworld and Reversibility: Merleau-Ponty," in *Twilight of Subjectivity*, pp. 103–7.

22. Ricoeur, *Oneself as Another*, p. 236. In line with this insight, Ricoeur criticizes Habermas's "continually pejorative use of the idea of tradition, following his long-standing confrontation with Gadamer." As one of the more dubious or "sensitive" points of the ethics of argumentation he singles out "its tendency to overevaluate the break of modernity, to confirm secularization not only as a fact but as a value, to the point of excluding from the field of discussion, either tacitly or openly, anyone who does not accept as a prior given the Nietzschean profession of the 'death of God' " (p. 287n79).

23. *Oneself as Another*, pp. 274, 288–89. For a similar correlation of universalism and contextualism, effected through the connection of "blind" universal justice and concrete "seeing-eye" justice, see my "'Rights' versus 'Rites': Justice and Global Democracy," in *Alternative Visions: Paths in the Global Village* (Lanham, MD: Rowman and Littlefield, 1998), pp. 253–76.

24. Ricoeur, *Oneself as Another*, pp. 286, 289. In this context (p. 289n83), Ricoeur speaks of "those inchoate universals whose genuine moral tenor will be established only by the subsequent history of the dialogue between cultures."

25. Ibid., p. 179. See also Ricoeur, *Political and Social Essays*, ed. David Stewart and Joseph Bien (Athens, OH: Ohio University Press, 1974), pp. 213, 241.

12
Ricoeur and the Tasks of Citizenship

BERNARD P. DAUENHAUER

The condition of being a citizen in a stable, reasonably well ordered political society and living according to its requirements has historically enjoyed a predominantly favorable assessment in the West. To be a citizen of such a state is to have political rights and some voice in its governance. These are no small goods. But the ethical defensibility of the institution of state citizenship, and indeed of independent states themselves, has never been without its critics. Many of these critics have argued for some version of world citizenship or cosmopolitanism that would supercede, or even entirely replace, state citizenship.[1]

Reinhold Niebuhr, in his now classic critique of what he called the "paradox of patriotism," gave voice to the most typical sorts of objections to state citizenship that critics have voiced over the centuries. For him,

> The paradox is that patriotism transmutes individual selfishness into national egoism. Loyalty to the nation is a high form of altruism when compared with lesser loyalties and more parochial interests. It therefore becomes a vehicle of all the altruistic impulses and expresses itself, on occasion, with such fervor that the critical attitude of the individual toward the nation and its enterprises is almost completely destroyed. The unqualified character of this devotion is the very basis of the nation's power and the freedom to use the power without moral restraint. Thus the unselfishness of individuals makes for the selfishness of nations.[2]

Thus for Niebuhr, state citizenship leads in practice (1) to a denial of the common humanity that binds each of us to all other persons, (2) to infringement upon the citizen's autonomy, and (3) to the suspension of the citizen's critical judgment about the state and its policies and programs. The only remedy for these maladies is a robust cosmopolitanism.

Recently, and apparently for reasons much like Niebuhr's, Vaclav Havel forecast with enthusiasm the ethically progressive transformation in the next century of most states "from cultlike entities charged with emotion into far simpler and more civilized entities, into less powerful and more rational administrative units that will represent only one of the many complex and multilayered ways in which our planetary society is organized."[3]

The cosmopolitan critiques of state citizenship are obviously nontrivial. Nevertheless, there is strong evidence that for the foreseeable future states and their institutions are practical necessities for political life. States are not only the principal sites of their members' loyalty and the political authority they recognize. They also contain the primary structures for formulating political policies and fashioning the command system for implementing them. Furthermore, states are practically alone in having the capability to make international agreements about military and ecological matters. And no other present or foreseeable institution has as much capacity as states do to deal with impending large-scale economic, technological, and demographic changes.[4] So there will be states, and if those states are reasonably well ordered there will be state citizens. But given the cosmopolitan objections, the moral defensibility of the institution of state citizenship remains an issue.[5]

In this essay, I want to show that Paul Ricoeur has articulated a particularly rich conception of citizenship, one that stands as a sound response to the cosmopolitan's objections. His conception does not reject all forms of state citizenship but it does demand that citizens constantly work to make their political life more inclusive. That is, the basic and interminable task of citizenship is to include those who either are or are in danger of being excluded from full political participation. His conception of citizenship rests on solid philosophical foundations. And the tasks that it assigns to citizens show its striking relevance to some of today's most difficult political issues.[6]

For Ricoeur, citizenship and the responsibilities connected with it are at the heart of political philosophy. In fact, he has said that he is "prepared to define political philosophy as a reflection on citizenship."[7] Furthermore, in his view "the most basic, and maybe the most ancient, component of our idea of right is the right to live in a state. That comes from the Greeks, from Aristotle."[8] Human beings, he says, are fully human only when they belong to a state in which they have some share in power. So to be a member of a state is a person's first right.[9]

The ultimate foundation for these claims is found in Ricoeur's analysis of the human capabilities for action. Their proximate foundation is in his conception of politics. Persons, he says, are fundamentally defined "by powers which achieve their full efficacy only under a system of political existence or, in other words, in the setting of a city. In this respect, a reflection on capable man seems to me to constitute the anthropological preface required by political philosophy."[10]

At bottom, the defining human capability is the capability for acting, broadly conceived. For Ricoeur, acting encompasses "saying inasmuch as it is a doing, ordinary action inasmuch as it is intervention into the course of things, narration inasmuch as it is the narrative reassembling of a life stretched out in time, and finally, the capacity to impute to oneself or to others the responsibility for acting."[11] For present purposes, I will focus on "ordinary action," the deliberate intervention into the course of things.

Every action, Ricoeur holds, is an event, but not vice versa. As event, an action is ascribable to some physical cause and has some physical consequence. But every action is also imputable to some agent as praiseworthy or blameworthy in some respect, for the agent deliberately initiates it for some specific purpose or reason. Accordingly, actions and their agents belong to two orders of causality, the physical and the intentional orders. Unlike the order of physical causality, in the order of intention or motivation there is a logical link between an action and its motivating intention. Human desire testifies to this twofold causality. On the one hand, desire is a force that moves or impels a person to perform some physical motion. But on the other hand, it is also a reason for the action, one that makes the doing intelligible and meaningful. Thus desire shows that the agent lives both in the order of nature, where desire impels, and in the order of culture, where actions make sense, both to the agent and to others who learn of it. "Human being," Ricoeur says, "is as it is precisely because it belongs both to the domain of causation and to that of motivation."[12]

To act is to exercise initiative and thereby to bring about a change in both the physical and the cultural worlds. The change brings about something new that would not otherwise have occurred when it did. For this to be possible, agents must both be bodily and live with other agents. Furthermore, they must also be participants in an ongoing history that is not wholly of their own making.

But initiative, in a strong sense, is not only a short-lived performance. It can also inaugurate a long-term commitment to one or more fellow human beings. It can inaugurate a way of abiding with them that involves persevering and enduring as well as initiating. By a strong initiative, I not only mindfully commit myself to a course of action that will alter my material and cultural circumstances, but I also commit myself to endure them as they themselves change in ways that I myself do not intend, or want, or even foresee.[13]

Furthermore, initiative takes place in a historical context constituted by predecessors' initiatives and their outcomes and their sedimented, institutionalized meanings. Without this rich historical context, I could do nothing meaningful. Reinhart Koselleck has called this context the space of experience. The space of experience is the past made present. It is the necessary condition of, as well as the point of departure for, my new action.

Besides this space of experience, initiative also presupposes what Koselleck calls a horizon of expectation. This is the field of unfolding possible projects that I can undertake, of openings that I can elect to explore. It is the future made present. And it too is something I receive from my material and cultural setting.

Present action preserves the dialectical tension between the space of experience and the horizon of expectation, without which tension there could be no subsequent genuine action. There could only be repetitions or reactions. But neither singly nor jointly do this space and this horizon wholly determine action. We are surely affected by a past that we have not made and by the picture of the possible future that we receive from our society. Nevertheless, we are indeed makers of history and affect ourselves in the process of doing so.[14]

Initiative, then, is both disjunctive and conjunctive vis-à-vis the world and its persons, including the initiators. It has "a disjunctive stage, the upshot of which is the recognition of the necessarily antagonistic character of the original causality of the agent in relation to other modes of causality; and a conjunctive stage, the upshot of which is the recognition of the necessity to coordinate in a synergistic way the agent's original causality with the other forms of causality."[15]

Thus all action is in multiple ways interaction. Every action, insofar as it belongs to a practice, bears a socially established meaning that is independent of its particular performer's intentions. The present action depends in this way on predecessors for its very possibility. Furthermore, part of every action's effective meaning depends upon its reception by the agent's contemporaries and successors.[16]

Here it is important to note that the recipients of actions often suffer from them. That is, my actions all too often impinge upon other persons in such a way that they reduce or block, at least for a time, their own capacity for acting. They experience this suffering not solely as physical or mental pain but as a violation of their own integrity.[17] This does not, of course, mean that every action necessarily violates someone else's integrity. But it does mean that "the opportunity for exercising violence lies within the very structure of human action—to act is to act upon another who undergoes my action."[18]

As this summary of Ricoeur's analysis of action intimates, that analysis is pregnant with a number of consequences for the responsible exercise of citizenship. But before I turn to them, let me introduce here a short report of Ricoeur's view of politics.

Following Eric Weil, Ricoeur has defined the state as "the organization of a historical community; organized into a state, the community is capable of making decisions."[19] The state's defining purpose is to enable its historical community not only to promote the community's survival but also to enable its members to act in concert and thus to be makers of their own history. It is to empower its people to exercise their freedom in such a way that they can accomplish together things that they could not accomplish singly. In short, the state's purpose is to produce a "power-in-common" among its citizens.[20]

But history shows, as Max Weber saw, that a distinguishing mark of all political institutions that we know about, including of course the state, is the presence of a relation of domination between the rulers and the ruled. In fact, "we can define the political [*le politique*] as the set of original practices relating to the distribution of political power, better termed domination."[21] Unsurprisingly, the regularly proffered justification for domination is either that it serves to support present power-in-common or that it will usher in power-in-common in the future. But the fact remains that political practice has always involved a struggle to gain or retain political dominance. It has always involved the granting of special, unmerited privileges and advantages to some dominant class. And rulers are always tempted to make ever greater impositions either upon those they already rule or on those whom they aspire to bring under their domination.[22]

Antithetical though they are, neither power-in-common nor domination is eliminable from actual political life. Indeed, the perpetual tension between them is constitutive of the domain of politics, and the handling of this tension is the political task par excellence. That this is so is the basic and theoretically unresolvable paradox of politics.

Hence, citizens are inescapably involved not only in the power-in-common but also in the relation of domination, either as dominators or as those who endure domination. It is this relation that gives purchase to some of the criticisms that cosmopolitans make against state citizenship.

Nonetheless, it makes no sense for a person to try to escape the paradox by opting out of politics. For today and for the foreseeable future "man cannot evade politics under penalty of evading his humanity. Throughout history, and by means of politics, man is faced with *his* grandeur and *his* culpability. One could not infer a political 'defeatism' on the basis of this insight. Such a reflection leads rather to a political *vigilance*. It is here that reflection . . . comes back to actuality and moves from critique to praxis."[23] Only citizens can have all of their capacities for action actualized.[24]

The basic task for citizens is to subordinate the domineering dimension of politics to the power-in-common dimension. The democratic project is "the set of measures that are taken . . . so that the horizontal bond of wanting to live together in general prevails over the irreducibly hierarchical bond of command and authority."[25] Because of the paradox of politics, this project can never be definitively completed. But the project remains the responsibility incumbent upon all citizens, not merely upon some political elite.[26]

As the basis for understanding what the democratic project concretely demands and hence for determining what responsibilities citizens have,

Ricoeur proposes a conception of liberal politics that can, for want of a better name, be called communitarian. This conception has its roots in his analysis of action and his conception of politics itself. Communitarian liberalism stands as a "third way" between political atomism and political holism. The former, as in individualistic liberalism, regards the individual, by reason of his or her innate capacity to act, as a full-fledged and autonomous agent basically independent of whatever communal relationships he or she participates in. On the other hand, political holism, exemplified by strong nationalisms, holds that there is a basically fixed communal identity into which individuals are born and which is a constitutive and determinate component of their personal identities.[27]

Ricoeur's conception of citizenship is liberal inasmuch as, with Weber, he holds that every action is imputable to a particular agent as his or her own individual performance. There are no higher-order agents.[28] But his liberalism is communitarian because it recognizes that

> without institutional mediation, individuals are only the initial drafts of human persons. Their belonging to a political body is necessary to their flourishing as human beings and in this sense, the mediation cannot be revoked. On the contrary, the citizens who issue from this institutional mediation cannot rightfully want anything other than that every person, like them, enjoy such political mediation, which when joined to the *necessary* conditions identified by a philosophical anthropology, become a *sufficient* condition for the passage from the man with capabilities to the real citizen.[29]

Communitarian liberalism therefore denies the individualistic liberal view that all of an individual's obligations to his or her community are contractual or dependent upon his or her always revocable consent. Indeed, it holds that a person can exercise his or her capabilities for action only if they are complemented by resources that the community supplies. As a consequence, an agent always has some precontractual obligations to his or her community. Accordingly, communitarian liberalism calls for individuals to acknowledge that they have debts to other persons and institutions that they have not contracted for. They ought therefore to admit a duty to preserve these institutions by keeping them available for others to participate in.

The debt in question here is historical. But history, strong nationalism to the contrary notwithstanding, is not a fate. Its present efficacious force, as space of experience, is open to revision by criticism and fresh action.[30] Thus communitarian liberalism need not and does not subscribe unreservedly to the legitimacy of just any historically established political regime and its institutions. Rather, it insists that to be a free agent one necessarily depends upon some institutionally established association with other free people. Consequently, these agents, in the interest of agency itself, ought to work to make their political society as a whole one that fosters the development and actualization of the capabilities that make each person, as liberalism of every sort rightly demands, someone who deserves esteem and respect.

But a politics of communitarian liberalism, no less than other sorts of politics, always involves domination. No less than any other sort of politics, its basic and endless task is to make power-in-common prevail as far as possible over domination. Ricoeur therefore explicitly rejects as a dream any "personalist communitarianism" that would seek to reconstruct the political bond exclusively on the models of an interpersonal bond exemplified by friendship and love.[31]

Let me emphasize that Ricoeur does not propose his communitarian liberalism as the definitive solution to the problem of politics, a solution from which one could derive without further ado the appropriate political practice. As I have said above, the paradox of politics admits of no definitive solution. Rather, the paradoxicality is something with which we must constantly cope. Ricoeur's conception of communitarian liberalism on the one hand lets us see why this is so. On the other hand, it provides an orientation for a course of action that holds good promise of making power-in-common prevail as far as possible over domination. A politics that does this is a good politics. A conception of politics that promotes such a politics is a good conception.

To see more fully the fruitfulness of Ricoeur's reflections on citizenship and its basis, consider now the history of political practice. This history, Ricoeur finds, shows that politics itself, as a distinctive domain of human endeavor, is intrinsically fragile. Though this fragility ultimately has its roots in politics' paradoxicality, it has multiple forms that themselves have a history. Here I want to discuss two forms of this fragility that have particular urgency today. One form of fragility appears as the susceptibility of the domain of politics to encroachment by other domains. Today, a striking manifestation of this susceptibility is the tendency to decide political issues on the basis of economic or technological considerations. A second form of fragility appears as the tendency to absolutize some determinate political institution or some canonical interpretation of it. Today one finds this tendency in some claims made about state sovereignty and political identity.

For Ricoeur, responsibility is the counterpart to fragility. Responsibility is "what one exercises toward someone or something fragile that has been entrusted to us."[32] My responsibility arises from having someone or something entrusted to my care or protection by some other in such a way that I can be held accountable.[33] Thus, what I am responsible for is something other than myself. Furthermore, when my responsibility extends over some notable period of time, it has the sense of an engagement. A person is engaged if his or her responsibility "is inseparable from the idea of a mission, in the sense of a specific task that is to be accomplished according to rules and that goes beyond the interests and preferences of the agent."[34] In short, to be responsible as an engaged person is "to be in charge of some zone of efficacy, where fidelity to one's word is put to the test.... A person is engaged if he or she feels himself or herself to be in a relationship of activity-passivity with someone or something entrusted to his or her care."[35]

Political responsibility, then, is the responsibility that citizens have for the well-being of their always fragile historical communities, including the state. Their responsibility, and corresponding potential political culpability, is of two sorts, namely moral and historical responsibility. I am morally responsible for what I myself do or refrain from doing. I am historically responsible as a participating member of a historical community for the institutionalized practices of the community as well as for the continued efficacy of the significant deeds of predecessors from which I benefit.[36] The recognition of one's historical responsibility is essential to the proper exercise of citizenship.

As I have said, one major respect in which political practice is fragile and vulnerable today springs from the tendency to decide political issues on the basis of economic or technological criteria or objectives.[37] This tendency has at its source two sorts of fragility ingredient in today's politics. First, technological capabilities and economic structures and operations are in principle, and apparently increasingly in fact, global. It is commonplace today to speak of a global market, where rationality itself demands that efficiency be the overriding norm everywhere. But political communities are always multiple and diverse. Each has its own historical ways of life that give it its distinctiveness and call for preservation. Given the strength of global economic considerations, citizens and their rulers regularly find themselves pressed to make political decisions more on the basis of economic standards such as market share, gains in technological expertise, or efficiency rather than on the basis of political criteria, the aim of which ought to be the "creation of spaces of freedom"[38] and thereby the promotion of the participation of all its citizens in a good life together. A basic task for citizens is to ensure that political criteria are ultimately primary in determining the state's policies and practices. They cannot prudently disregard technological and economic considerations. But they should not allow them the last word. For "a society where the economic dominates the political (and in the economic, competition dominates the calculation [*calcul*] of and the appetite for gain, which is the very definition of a market economy) is a society that creates indefensible inequalities."[39] Inequalities generated in this way undermine power-in-common and hence politics itself.

A second sort of political fragility that arises from its ties to economics and technology is observable in the differences between the histories of politics and economics. The history of economics shows a progressive and cumulative increase in the sophistication of the techniques and tools available for commerce and industry. There is no comparable progressive, cumulative growth in the political domain. Unlike in rationalized economics and technology, in politics there can be sustained regression as readily as progression. Furthermore, there is no way to measure or quantify political progression as one can do in economics. In short, "history—as history of power—is uncertain. It is the collection of chances and perils, the possibility of gaining everything or losing everything."[40]

Politics' lack of cumulative progress makes it fragile precisely because it can therefore seem to be impervious to rational thought. Serious people are tempted to treat politics as not worth their best efforts. Without measurable accomplishments that belong to a progressive sequence of comparable accomplishments, politics often appears to be sterile or even futile by contrast with the secure and fertile accomplishments made in the technicoeconomic domain. Those who argue that political considerations ought to play a leading role in determining how the society's members engage in and assess economic practice expose themselves to the charge of curtailing reason rather than of promoting a more complex exercise of it. Citizens have the responsibility to understand the kind of reason that is in play in good politics and to take part in the discourse that makes its importance clear.[41]

A second prominent form of political fragility is the tendency to adopt an exclusionist politics, a politics that works to exclude as far as possible some group of persons from participating in political decision-making. Sometimes in domestic politics, a group of people is relegated to an inferior status or is effectively blocked from having their voices heard on at least some matters. In international politics, absolutist conceptions of state sovereignty serve as warrant for disregarding the interests of those who are not citizens of the exclusionist state. The proffered basis for exclusionist policies are such doctrines as racism, nationalism, and historical fatalism.

Ricoeur has addressed both domestic and international exclusionism. Here I will focus on the international side and then briefly indicate the domestic relevance of his reflections.

Today, the internationalization of so many important parts of public life foredooms any attempt to achieve absolute state sovereignty. No state can handle problems of national security, ecology, finance, or technology all by itself. For a people to aim for or claim absolute sovereignty is a form of escapist utopianism. To insist upon one's state's right to pursue its own "national interest" regardless of consequences for other states and peoples is to adopt a distorted and distorting ideology. To oppose these two forms of exclusionist politics, Ricoeur calls for the development of political entities that cut across state lines to forge new institutions for cooperation among peoples. These entities are to emphasize the common humanity of all peoples rather than the particularity of one group over and against others.[42] He does not call for the abolition of present states in favor of these new entities. But he sees that to be responsible today a state's citizens must care about the well-being of other states and their peoples.

Ricoeur does not pretend to have a grand plan for the formation of these new political entities. But he does hold that the solution to the problem of exclusionism is not likely to be achieved by simply replicating on a larger scale the structures of federal states like the United States or Switzerland. He has no global "world state" in view. Rather, a successful response to the fragility brought about by internationalization will require a fresh and sustained reflection on the ethical and spiritual conduct of individuals. This reflection must take place in learned societies, religious communities, and other institutions of civil society as well as in the established political forums. The satisfactory transfer of some sovereignty to these new political entities requires not only changes in existing political and legal institutions but also changes in the mentality and ethos of the individual citizens. Without these latter changes, the new entities that would emerge would not be truly democratic.[43]

To foster an appropriate renovation of European political institutions, Ricoeur recommends that citizens employ in their political discourse three models for communicating with foreigners, namely the models of translation, of the exchange of memories, and of forgiveness. Here I will focus on the latter two of these models.

The model of the exchange of memories calls for individuals and peoples to be hospitable to the memories foreigners have that are constitutive of the identity and uniqueness of their respective cultures. These common, or collective, memories, expressed in their customs, elementary convictions, and practices, are told in the stories that recount a people's narrative identity. They make up a people's heritage.

Our heritage, without which we could not be who we are, is the weight of our past on our future. It obligates us, in historical responsibility, not only to take our past into account in what we do today and tomorrow but also to respect and preserve it. It is indeed a burden but it is also an indispensable resource for our future action.[44]

This heritage or tradition recounts the triumphs and the endured hardships of our predecessors. But as we have come to understand, the expressions of this heritage have all too often either neglected or distorted the impact of our predecessors' actions on other peoples. The expressions have also not infrequently misrepresented the responsibility other people are said to have for the sufferings our predecessors had to endure.

Accordingly, heritages are in need of regular reconsideration. Fortunately, they are always open to it. The material and cultural circumstances in which we are to pay our debts to our heritages are not the same today as they were yesterday. It is in the nature of stories of narrative identity that they are always in principle revisable. Furthermore, it is always possible, within limits, to tell more than one story about the same set of events.

Major resources for the constructive reconsideration of the narratives of a heritage are the stories of other heritages. Even cursory reflection shows that all the narratives of identity that we know of are inextricably tied to stories of identity of other peoples. Linked together, they give rise to second-order stories, each of which is also intertwined with still other stories. The works of critical historians regularly articulate these connections. And it is the task of the responsible political educator to make use of these resources to refashion his or her heritage with an eye to fulfill in present and future deeds the benevolent but previously unfulfilled promises embodied in it.[45]

The relevance of this model to the renovation of European political institutions is easy to see. If people rethink their own stories of identity by hospitably attending to the stories of others, they can together arrive at a new and more benign way of interacting. Only by this kind of renovation can a heritage remain a positive source for its inheritors' well-being, for, as Ricoeur puts it, "The unfulfilled future of the past forms perhaps the richest part of a tradition. The liberation of this unfulfilled future of the past is the major benefit that we can expect from the crossing of memories and the exchange of narratives."[46]

A necessary condition for the successful application of the model of the hospitable exchange of memories is a second model for political renovation, namely the model of forgiveness. Forgiveness is a distinctive kind of renovation of the past, one aimed at overcoming the exclusions that the past has produced. It is concerned with the suffering that a culture has had inflicted upon it by outsiders. This kind of forgiveness has to begin by having a people first put itself in the shoes of another people and thus paying heed to that people's suffering. Only then can it properly rethink its own sufferings.

Regrettably the history of Europe, whatever else it may be, is a history of violence and cruelty. It is a history of "wars of religion, wars of extermination, subjugation of ethnic minorities, expulsion or reduction of religious minorities to slavery."[47] Very often, this cruelty has sprung from an inordinate pride in one's cultural identity. If there is to be reconciliation and peace, then we must make our own the sufferings of others, even of those others who have made us suffer. For they too have sometimes been victims.

Unlike the usual political categories that have to do somehow with justice, forgiveness or pardon is a gift given out of generosity by victims to their victimizers. No victimizer has a right to pardon. To ask for it is to admit that it can rightfully be refused.

Nonetheless, the giving of forgiveness "has immense curative value, not only for the guilty . . . but also for the victims."[48] Among the examples that Ricoeur invokes are Chancellor Willy Brandt kneeling in penitence in Warsaw and President Anwar Sadat's penitential visit to the Israeli Knesset in Jerusalem. The strong protests against these gestures on grounds that the offenses in question were unpardonable shows how fragile repentance is when the crimes have been great. But these protests do not show that there are any wrongs that are wholly unforgivable.[49]

Ricoeur's models for reforming European political life are not designed to be directly applicable to every part of the world. But given the history of conquest, slavery, and colonization that has touched practically every corner of the earth, his model of forgiveness is applicable well beyond European boundaries. And given the internationalization of so many parts of public life, his model of the exchange of memories holds significant promise not only to ward off new atrocities but also to enhance the quality of life for all peoples who would participate in it.

For example, I believe that Ricoeur's models hold promise for dealing well with the vast, complex, and urgent matter of forcible intervention in the political life of a foreign people. This matter, as Haiti, Somalia, Rwanda, Bosnia, Kosovo, and so on have made all too plain, is extremely hard to think well about. The intervening agencies, governmental and nongovernmental, have been of various sorts with various objectives.[50] And the question of who can properly authorize interventions is at best tangled. Ricoeur's models do not provide a way to resolve all the issues raised by the question of intervention. But they do, I believe, give important guidance with a number of them.[51]

Consider which states ought to enjoy immunity from intervention. Some French jurists have reasonably proposed that a state that observes principles of hospitality and security enjoys this immunity. These principles require that a state do all that it can to provide for the safety and security of all persons living within its borders, citizens, resident aliens, and transients alike. Such a state's political institutions may leave much to be desired. But it is not a candidate for intervention.[52]

Consider next who is to decide (1) whether a state is immune from intervention; (2) whether, if it is not immune, an intervention is feasible; (3) who the interveners are to be; and (4) what the specific objectives of the particular intervention ought to be. Today and for the foreseeable future, the institution with the most comprehensive authority to make these determinations is the United Nations. Other institutions, such as NATO and the Organization of African States, have been involved with some legitimacy in making these determinations. But in principle the United Nations should have the last word about any interventions.

But it is widely recognized that the United Nations, in its present form and condition, is less than ideally equipped for this role. Among its problems are a Security Council whose membership no longer reflects geopolitical realities and the widespread paralysis that is a result of the broad range of issues subject to the veto. Hence the United Nations needs substantial reformation if it is to fulfill its stated goals. That reformation will have to include giving it the wherewithal to deal effectively with the problem of intervention.[53]

In broad outline, Ricoeur's models of exchange of memories and forgiveness are relevant to the question of intervention in at least two ways. First, before, during, and after intervention, the interveners must recognize that their actions are most likely to have some bad consequences. Hence they must be receptive to criticism. This criticism can and should draw on a historical record that includes violent conquest and colonialism as well as reasonable and benign aspirations that we can confidently expect to be found in the traditions of every historical community. That is, there is reason to believe that everyone has something beneficial to contribute to a conversation among peoples. Both the interveners and the intervened upon have reason to draw upon this record of memories to bring the need for intervention to as rapid an end as possible.

Second, an intervention ought to be conducted in such a way that, at its end, there are good grounds for mutual forgiveness. Forgiveness does not entail an amnesty that would claim to wipe the slate clean.[54] But the only defensible ultimate objective of intervention is the eventual reconciliation, through mutual forgiveness, of the interveners and the intervened upon.

Furthermore, a good case can be made that, mutatis mutandis, these two models are well suited to promote domestic well-being, particularly in those pluralistic societies riven by long-standing antagonisms between substantial numbers of members of competing linguistic, religious, or ethnic groups. Consider for example the antagonisms between Protestants and Catholics in Northern Ireland, the Anglophones and Francophones in Canada, the Flemish and the Waloons in Belgium, and the several ethnic groups in Spain. The adoption and implementation of policies and programs based on Ricoeur's models would hold strong promise either of preventing secessions or political devolutions or at least of reducing the hostility so often connected with these ruptures or rents in a state's political fabric. So too would these models hold great promise for dealing with the ethnic and racial antagonisms that have so long been part of political life in the United States.

Overcoming these hostilities is of great importance not only for the peoples of the state in question. It is also a weighty matter for other states and their citizens. Healing them would, among other things, reduce the number of refugees, reduce the danger of rash fragmentation into economically nonviable political entities, and strengthen the capacity of the healed state to help other peoples in times of distress.

Ricoeur's models of course cannot guarantee the fruitfulness of policies or programs based on them. Nor could one claim that these models are sufficient, without supplementation, to deal effectively with all violent conflicts among peoples or states. But it is hard to imagine any alternative models that would render Ricoeur's otiose.

In sum, in my view, Ricoeur's account of the irreducibility of the fragility inherent in politics and the responsibility that follows upon this fragility is soundly anchored in his analysis of human action. So too are his conceptions of politics and its paradoxicality on the one hand, and his conception of communitarian liberalism on the other. To the extent that people ignore or disregard the fragilities and corresponding responsibilities, their politics will be, in an Aristotelian sense, an antipolitics. Genuine politics, in his view, is always good politics.

Furthermore, in my view, Ricoeur's political thought as such rightly avoids either prescribing or proscribing specific political policies or programs. He does insist upon a politics that is concerned with the well-being of all people. And he calls for a redistribution of economic wealth to ameliorate the condition of the poor and the weak. But at bottom what he gives us is a cluster of critical questions about how one ought to engage in politics, whether as citizen or officeholder. These are questions that one ought to raise before endorsing or rejecting particular proposals. They in effect mark off the boundaries within which policies and programs must fall to deserve endorsement. Political philosophy, if it is attentive to the thoroughgoing historicality of politics, ought to go no further.

Finally, I admit, as he would, that Ricoeur has not developed a comprehensive, systematic political philosophy, one that addresses every major political issue. Indeed, there is good reason to think that he would be deeply suspicious of any attempt to produce such a system. But his political thought is not devoid of anchoring principles that give rise to a genuine unity. Its limitations and lacunae notwithstanding, his achievement is remarkably rich and fertile.

Notes

1. For a helpful guide to the history of thought about citizenship, see Derek Heater, *Citizenship: The Civic Ideal in World History, Politics, and Education* (London: Longmans, 1990); and his *World Citizenship and Government* (New York: St. Martin's Press, 1996). As will become apparent, I do not share Heater's enthusiasm for any version of world government that would render states idle.
2. Reinhold Niebuhr, *Moral Man and Immoral Society* (New York: Charles Scribner's Sons, 1949), p. 91.
3. Vaclav Havel, "Kosovo and the End of the Nation-State," trans. Paul Wilson, *New York Review of Books* 46, no. 11 (1994): 4.
4. See Paul Kennedy, *Preparing for the Twenty-first Century* (New York: Random House, 1993) p. 336.
5. For a more extended discussion of the present debate about citizenship, see my *Citizenship in a Fragile World* (Lanham, MD: Rowman and Littlefield, 1996), pp. 17–46.
6. For a good collection of contemporary views of citizenship, see Ronald Beiner, ed., *Theorizing Citizenship* (Albany: State University of New York Press, 1995); and Ronald Beiner, ed., *Theorizing Nationalism* (Albany: State University of New York Press, 1999).
7. Paul Ricoeur, "Ethics and Politics," in *From Text to Action*, trans. Kathleen Blamey and John B. Thompson (Evanston, IL: Northwestern University Press, 1991), p. 330.

Ricoeur and the Tasks of Citizenship

8. Paul Ricoeur, in a videotaped interview with Jonathan Rée, produced by Films for the Humanities and Sciences in association with the Oxford Amnesty Lectures, 1992.
9. Ricoeur, in his interview with Rée.
10. Paul Ricoeur, "Morale, éthique, et politique," *Pouvoirs: Révue francaise d'études constitutionelles et politiques* (1993): 5.
11. Paul Ricoeur, "De l'ésprit," *Révue Philosophique de Louvain* 92, no. 2 (1994): 248. See also Paul Ricoeur, "Autonomie et vulnerabilité," unpublished lecture given at the Séance inaugurale du Seminaire de l'IHEI, November 6, 1995, esp. pp. 5–6; and Paul Ricoeur, "Le destinaire de la religion: L'homme capable," unpublished paper given in Rome in January 1996. In Ricoeur's view, his conception of action corresponds with Heidegger's conception of care as the basic way in which persons exist and inhabit the world. See Paul Ricoeur, *Critique and Conviction*, trans. Kathleen Blamey (New York: Columbia University Press, 1998), pp. 74–75.
12. Paul Ricoeur, "Explanation and Understanding," in *From Text to Action*, p. 135; see also p. 133; and Paul Ricoeur, "Événement et sens," in *L'événement en perspective*, ed. Jean-Luc Petit (Paris: Éditions de l'École des Hautes Études en Sciences Sociales, 1991), pp. 41–56.
13. Paul Ricoeur, *Oneself as Another*, trans. Kathleen Blamey (Chicago and London: University of Chicago Press, 1992), pp. 109–11; and Paul Ricoeur, "Initiative," in *From Text to Action*, pp. 214–17.
14. Paul Ricoeur, "Entre mémoire et histoire," *Projet*, no. 248 (1996): esp. pp. 13–14. See also Ricoeur, "La marque du passé," *Révue de métaphysique et de morale*, no. 1 (January–March 1998): esp. pp. 18–31.
15. Ricoeur, *Oneself as Another*, p. 102. My modification of the translation.
16. Ricoeur, *Oneself as Another*, p. 156. Acknowledging a debt to Hegel here, Ricoeur says: "The way the work has of taking its meaning, its very existence as work, only from the other underscores the extraordinary precariousness of the relation between the work and the author, the mediation of the other being so thoroughly constitutive of its meaning." See also Ricoeur, "Le destinaire de la religion," esp. p. 4.
17. Ricoeur, *Oneself as Another*, p. 190.
18. Paul Ricoeur, "Entretien," in *Éthique et responsibilité Paul Ricoeur*, ed. Jean-Christophe Aeschliemann (Neuchâtel: Baconniere, 1994), p. 16. See also Paul Ricoeur, "Interviews," in Charles E. Reagan, *Paul Ricoeur* (Chicago and London: University of Chicago Press, 1996), pp. 113–14. Recall also Hannah Arendt's remarks on the transgressive character of action in *The Human Condition* (Chicago and London: University of Chicago Press, 1958), esp. pp. 240–41.
19. Eric Weil, *La philosophie politique* (Paris: Vrin, 1984), p. 131, cited in Ricoeur, "Ethics and Politics," p. 330. For the development of Ricoeur's view of the state and its function, see François Dosse, *Paul Ricoeur: Les sens d'une vie* (Paris: La Découverte, 1997), pp. 166, 188, 586–87.
20. Ricoeur, *Oneself as Another*, pp. 194–95; Paul Ricoeur, "Éthique et Morale," in *Lectures I* (Paris: Editions du Seuil, 1991), p. 259; Paul Ricoeur, "De la philosophie au politique, in *Lectures I*, pp. 17–18.

21. Ricoeur, *Oneself as Another*, p. 257.
22. Paul Ricoeur, "The Political Paradox," in *History and Truth*, trans. Charles A. Kelbley (Evanston, IL: Northwestern University Press, 1965), esp. pp. 248, 259. This essay, written in 1956 shortly after the Soviet invasion of Hungary, is, Ricoeur says, seminal for all his subsequent political thought. See Ricoeur, *Critique and Conviction*, pp. 95–96. For very helpful remarks about "The Political Paradox" and its context, see Dosse, *Paul Ricoeur*, pp. 231–38.
23. Ricoeur, "The Political Paradox," p. 261. My modification of the translation. See also Paul Ricoeur, "State and Violence," in *History and Truth*, p. 244.
24. Ricoeur, "Morale, éthique, et politique," p. 257.
25. Ricoeur, *Critique and Conviction*, p. 99. My modification of the translation.
26. Paul Ricoeur, "Fragility and Responsibility," *Philosophy and Social Criticism* 21, no. 5/6 (1995): 15–22. A somewhat longer version of this essay appeared as "Fragilité et responsabilité," in *Eros and Eris*, ed. Paul Van Tongeren et al. (Dordrecht: Kluwer, 1992), pp. 295–304. The intrinsic incompletability of any democratic political project is at the root of my criticism of John Rawls's *Political Liberalism* (New York: Columbia University Press, 1993), in my "A Good Word for a Modus Vivendi," in *The Idea of Political Liberalism: Essays on Rawls*, ed. Victoria Davion and Clark Wolf (Lanham, MD: Rowman and Littlefield, 2000) pp. 204–20.
27. It is worth noting that, as Ronald Beiner points out, the logic of individualistic liberalism moves in the direction of cosmopolitanism. See Ronald Beiner, "Introduction," in *Theorizing Citizenship*, pp. 16–18. Furthermore, nationalism is interpreted in many ways. My characterization of it here is extracted from Bhiku Parekh, "The Incoherence of Nationalism," in *Theorizing Nationalism*, esp. pp. 303, 309. Parekh rejects all nontrivial versions of nationalism.
28. Paul Ricoeur, "Practical Reason," in *From Text to Action*, p. 204.
29. Paul Ricoeur, "Who Is the Subject of Rights?" in *The Just*, trans. David Pellauer (Chicago and London: University of Chicago Press, 2000), p. 10. My modification of the translation. See also Paul Ricoeur, "Langage politique et rhétorique," in *Lectures I*, pp. 162–63. Ricoeur takes it that his position on the necessity of institutional mediation for genuine agency agrees with Charles Taylor's.
30. For Ricoeur's rejection of historical fatalism on the one hand and strong nationalism on the other, see his "Le pardon peut-il guerir?" *Esprit*, no. 210 (1995): 80; and his "Memory, Forgetfulness, and History," in *History, Memory, Action*, published by the Israel Academy of Sciences and Humanities, pp. 14–16. This essay is reprinted from *The Jerusalem Philosophical Quarterly* 45 (July 1996): pp. 237–48. See also Ricoeur, "La marque du passé," pp. 28–29.
31. Ricoeur, "Who Is the Subject of Rights?" p. 7.
32. Ricoeur, "Entretien," p. 25.
33. For more detail on the "other" that entrusts something political to me, see my *Paul Ricoeur*, pp. 266–70.
34. Ricoeur, "Entretien," p. 30.
35. Ibid., pp. 30–31. For a fuller analysis of the concept of responsibility, see Paul Ricoeur, "The Concept of Responsibility," in *The Just*, pp. 11–35.

36. Ricoeur, *Oneself as Another*, p. 107; and Paul Ricoeur, "Le sentiment du culpabilité: Sagesse ou nervrose?" in *Innocente culpabilite*, ed. Marie de Solemne (Paris: Editions Devry, 1998), pp. 15–17. See also Paul Ricoeur, *Time and Narrative*, vol. 1, trans. Kathleen Blamey McLaughlin and David Pellauer (Chicago and London: University of Chicago Press, 1984), p. 260n11.
37. For Ricoeur's analysis of the multiple ways in which politics is fragile, see in particular his "The Fragility of Political Language," *Philosophy Today* 31, no. 1 (1987): 35–44; and his "Langage politique et rhétorique," in *Phénomenologie et politique* (Bruxelles: Editions Ousia, 1989), pp. 479–95.
38. Paul Ricoeur, "Ethics and Politics," in *From Text to Action*, p. 334.
39. Ricoeur, "Le sentiment de culpabilité," p. 26. All of pp. 26–29 is relevant here.
40. Paul Ricoeur, "The Tasks of the Political Educator," *Philosophy Today* 17, no. 2 (1973): 145.
41. Ricoeur, "Ethics and Politics," p. 329.
42. Ricoeur, "Fragilité et responsabilité," p. 302. This is a view that Ricoeur has long held. One of its sources is Ricoeur's commitment to biblical principles. See, in this connection, Dosse, *Paul Ricoeur*, pp. 292–93.
43. Paul Ricoeur, "Reflections on a New Ethos for Europe," *Philosophy and Social Criticism* 21, no. 5/6 (1995): 27–31; and his "Fragilité et responsabilité," p. 303. In these two pieces, Ricoeur is clearly referring to the development of the European Union. Stanley Hoffmann, among others, has worried about the European Union's "democratic deficit." The danger that he sees is that the European Union will be the work of technocrats who never gain popular support for what they have done. See his "Goodbye to a United Europe?" *New York Review of Books* 41, no. 10 (1994): 27–31.
44. Ricoeur, "La marque du passé," esp. pp. 27–29. See also Ricoeur, "History and Rhetoric," *Diogenes* no. 168, 42, no. 4 (1994): 23.
45. Ricoeur, "La marque du passé," pp. 30–31.
46. Ricoeur, "Reflections," p. 8. See also Ricoeur, "Entretien," pp. 13–15, 19–20; and Dosse, *Paul Ricoeur,* pp. 678–79, 769–70.
47. Ricoeur, "Reflections," p. 9.
48. Ricoeur, *Critique*, p. 125. See also Ricoeur, "Le pardon," pp. 77–82; Ricoeur, "Fragilité et responsabilité," pp. 303–4, Ricoeur, "Sanction, Rehabilitation, Pardon," in *The Just*, pp. 133–45; and esp. Paul Ricoeur, *La memoire, l'histoire, l'oubli* (Paris: Seuil, 2000) pp. 593–656.
49. Ricoeur, "Reflections," pp. 10–11.
50. Interventions, by definition, are always against the wishes of the powers that be in the state in question.
51. I find support for what I say about intervention in Paul Ricoeur, "L'intervention entre la souffrance des victimes et la violence des secours," *Esprit*, no. 199 (1994): 155–59; and in remarks he made to David Pellauer and me in a conversation in Chicago, October 23, 1999. Of course Ricoeur is not responsible for the use I make of that conversation.
52. A state could observe the principles of hospitality and security and still not be one that Rawls would consider well ordered. See John Rawls, "The Law of Peoples," in *On Human Rights,* ed. Stephen Shute and Susan Hurley (New York: Basic Books, 1993), pp. 60–68.

53. For an example of a useful critique of some recent interventions, see Brian Urquhart, "Mission Impossible," *New York Review of Books* 46, no. 18 (1999): 26–29. For a good analysis of the sort of reformation that the United Nations needs, see "Global Governance: Defining the United Nations' Leadership Role," the report of the Stanley Foundation's United Nations of the Next Decade Conference, 1999.
54. On the differences between forgiveness and amnesty, see Ricoeur, "Sanction, Rehabilitation, Pardon," pp. 143–45; and Ricoeur, *La mémoire*, pp. 585–89, 650–56.

13
Ricoeur and Practical Theology

DON BROWNING

In the last fifteen years, there has been a worldwide revival and redefinition of a field of theology called practical theology. Because of these changes, this discipline has moved from the sidelines of the theological enterprise to a more central place in the religious academy. It has been given seats at consultation seminars in government and business both in the United States and abroad and has received a place in the funding programs of major foundations. In this essay, I will briefly characterize this reformulation of practical theology and how the turn to what is often called "practical philosophy," especially the work of Paul Ricoeur, has contributed to the transformation of this discipline.

Pannenberg tells us that the term *practical theology* was first used in Roman Catholicism at the 1215 Lateran Council to refer to the theological ordering of the penitential.[1] In Protestant circles, however, practical theology was defined in the nineteenth-century encyclopedias as theological reflection on the practices of the ordained minister, namely preaching (homiletics), worship (liturgics), pastoral care (poimenics), and social service (diaconia). As Edward Farley has aptly characterized it, this was practical theology within the *clerical paradigm*; it was primarily a theology about the activity of the ordained minister.

Gradually, however, this subdiscipline broadened its self-definition to the *ecclesial paradigm,* which saw practical theology as theological reflection on the practical ministry of the entire confessing church.

By the 1970s and 1980s there had arisen calls for a thoroughly public definition of practical theology that, as Alastair Campbell suggested, would define it as critical theological reflection on the entire ministry of the church-in-the-world.[2] In this later definition, often referred to as the *public paradigm*, the clerical and ecclesial models were not lost but subsumed to the broader view of practical theology as a kind of public theology.

These new definitions have been seen by some parts of the theological community as overly expansionist if not triumphalist moves by ambitious new voices in the field of practical theology. Some of us have spoken of a "fundamental practical theology" that absorbs all of theology into the contours of practical thinking. When theology is conceived as practical through and through, the traditional practical disciplines of preaching, worship, care, and service must be viewed as culminations of a theological-reflective process that is practical from the very beginning.[3] Even respected systematic theologians such as Farley have argued that what we call systematic or constructive theology today was once viewed as a *habitus*—an existentially engaged and practical search for the saving knowledge of God.[4] Furthermore, liberation theology has urged that theology shift its attention away from dogmatics to orthopraxis; that is, to a theology of right practice rather than one that concentrates primarily on orthodox belief. Hence, from the quarters of both practical theology and systematic theology, there has emerged a new preoccupation with the category of *praxis* as a model for theological thinking.

The emergence of the practical as a model for theological reflection has raised the crucial question of the relation of practical theology to theological ethics. In some nineteenth-century theological encyclopedias, theological ethics was seen as a subdiscipline of practical theology—indeed its normative core. Somewhat in keeping with this older model, the question of the relation of practical theology to theological ethics has been the topic of two recent international symposia held at the Wissenschaftsforum at the University of Heidelberg, one held in autumn 1998 and the other in October 2000. In short, the new redefinition of practical theology is associated with a worldwide inquiry into the proper boundaries and relations of all the theological disciplines. This is a project symbolized, in many respects, by Farley's and Barbara Wheeler's 1991 edited volume of essays titled *Shifting Boundaries* and the recently published German volume titled *Christentum und Spätmoderne*.[5]

There are many social, historical, and conceptual sources for this ferment in practical theology. The processes of modernization and differentiation of secondary institutions have put new pressures on theology both to describe and address increasingly complex social patterns. Accelerated rates of social change have demanded that theology give accounts, evaluations, critiques, and at least some guidance to these new societal disruptions and differentiations.

But the main reason for the new boldness of practical theology has been its awareness of the turn in philosophy to what is often called "practical philosophy."[6] By this I mean the rather widespread trend in modern philosophies to give *phronesis* or practical reason a renewed place of honor. According to Richard Bernstein, this movement toward the practical can be found, for example, in Ludwig Wittgenstein's ordinary language analysis, Hans-Georg

Gadamer's philosophical hermeneutics, American pragmatism, Marxism, Jürgen Habermas's discourse ethics, and Ricoeur's critical hermeneutics.[7] More specifically, *phronesis* as the practical attempt to establish and implement the norms of life is being viewed by many as giving contextual significance to both *theoria* (theoretical reason) and *techne* (technical reason).

To understand the influence and contributions of practical philosophy to the reformulation of practical theology, it is useful to notice what Ricoeur calls in *Oneself as Another* (1992) the "three-step rhythm" of any hermeneutics of the self and its actions; that is, the steps of describing, narrating, and prescribing.[8] This is one of the many happy formulas that Ricoeur provides to unify the complex texture of his thought and guide us through several methodological detours. It should be understood in light of his other famous and useful formulas, such as the early rule in *Freedom and Nature* (1966) that "the voluntary is by reason of the involuntary while the involuntary is for the voluntary."[9] To understand this threefold movement fully, one would also want to interpret it in close relation to his famous formula in *Oneself as Another* for defining ethical intentions "*as aiming at the 'good life' with and for others, in just institutions.*"[10] It is this threefold rhythm understood in close relation to these other formulas that opens for Ricoeur an understanding of the self in relation to its world. It is the rhythm of describing, narrating, and prescribing that reveals the nature of the self as a practical thinker, both within the context of philosophy and, as I will claim, within the context of theology. This formula also reveals the special role of narrative in linking the self in the process of describing with the self in its task of prescribing.

These three movements are parallel to the four movements found in some contemporary expressions of practical theology. These analogues divide theology as a whole into descriptive theology, historical theology, systematic theology, and strategic practical theology. Parallel to Ricoeur's threefold rhythm that places narrative between describing and prescribing, these new practical-theological perspectives envision the middle moments of historical and systematic theology as having the special task of interpreting the guiding narratives of the Christian faith. In turn, these narratives are viewed as linking the descriptive and the prescriptive/strategic moments of practical-theological reflection.[11]

The Central Message

This parallel between Ricoeur's three-step hermeneutics of the self and the four reflective moments of the new practical theology is no accident. Gadamer and Ricoeur are chief sources for the methodologies of the new practical theology. This is true not only for my own work, but for the important and widely recognized work of Hans van der Ven of the University of Nejmegen, Gerben Heitink of the Frei Universität in Amsterdam, and

Friedrich Schweitzer of the University of Tübingen.[12] In many ways, however, Ricoeur is more important for this movement than Gadamer. This is because Ricoeur finds a place in human understanding for both ideology critique and the distanciating methods of science in ways that elude Gadamer. Using Ricoeur, rather than Gadamer alone, makes it possible for practical theology to become a critical discipline. It also equips it to use the social sciences in its descriptive moment and in all succeeding steps without losing unique identity as a religiously contextualized form of *phronesis*.

In the following paragraphs, I will amplify this statement by showing briefly where Gadamer and Ricoeur agree, where they diverge on the role of method or science, and some differences these points make for practical theology. I will conclude by discussing certain ambiguities in Ricoeur's view of the role of "distanciation" for understanding and what this concept means for the descriptive and the prescriptive tasks of a hermeneutics of the self as well as a viable practical theology. Among the many observations I will make, my central claim is this: as Ricoeur's thought has developed, there has been at least one important loss. There has been a blurring of the meaning of the highly important concept of "diagnosis," a crucial concept in the early Ricoeur for showing how the objectifying attitudes of science can contribute to an understanding of the self. I will argue that Ricoeur's significant contribution to ethics can be heightened if the concept of diagnosis is used to clarify the teleological goods implicit in both his proposed "deontological" test and the test of "practical wisdom." I will attempt to clarify this admittedly dense formulation of my central message.

Gadamer and Ricoeur

There are important parallels between Gadamer and Ricoeur, and Ricoeur would be the first to acknowledge the impact of Gadamer on his thought, in spite of their important differences. I draw attention to their similarities and differences in order to unpack the meaning of Ricoeur's injunction to describe, narrate, and prescribe.

First, to describe. Both Gadamer and Ricoeur believe that human understanding is primarily a historically situated dialogue or conversation exhibiting the features of question and answer.[13] To describe is first to understand the situated dialogue in which one is already embedded—the dialogue that also already makes up the self. Hence, description, even social-science description, is not primarily an objective process of standing outside one's historically located dialogue. Rather, it is first a matter of accounting for what has shaped us in the unfolding situation we are attempting to describe. Both Gadamer and Ricoeur believe that the prejudgments or prejudices implicit in our questions are crucial for the understanding process.[14] They are shaped by the continuing presence in our experience of the "effective histories" of the past, especially the classic texts and monuments that have shaped our civilization.[15] These prejudgments must be brought to light as referents in relation to which we understand new experience.

Gadamer's idea of the classic and Ricoeur's idea of narrative constitute the link between description and prescription. Gadamer speaks more about classics than narratives: Ricoeur writes about both but ends by suggesting that classics really come in the form of narratives. The point for both men is this: when we describe something, the normative horizons of our effective histories inevitably and rightly cast a fringe of meaning over the object of description. But the same is true, rightly and necessarily, for the self's act of prescription. Our practical actions and strategies are shaped, although not necessarily totally dictated, by our individual and cultural narrative backgrounds. But Gadamer and Ricoeur see the process of understanding, including understanding the classics or narratives that help shape our selfhood, as a practical or applicational process through and through. Our practical situations and questions shape our construal of the normative horizons of our effective histories just as these horizons in turn shape our description of situations. Gadamer wrote, and Ricoeur would affirm, the following words that invoke the authority of Aristotle: "We, too, determined that application is neither a subsequent nor a merely occasional part of the phenomenon of understanding, but co-determines it as a whole from the beginning."[16]

In the above paragraph, you may have noticed me say that our classics or central narratives shape, but do not necessarily totally determine, our prescriptive and strategic actions. This qualification, I believe, is more in accordance with the sensibilities of Ricoeur than with those of Gadamer. Ricoeur steers a delicate course between the respect for tradition found in Gadamer and appreciation for the critique of tradition found in the Frankfurt *Schule* and the thought of the German social theorist Habermas. Ricoeur eschews foundationalism (the attempt to base knowledge and ethics on objective science, sense data, or transcendental phenomenology), whether in scientific epistemology or in ethics. Foundationalism in its various guises has an alienating disregard for tradition—that is, the histories that have formed us and, therefore, to which we already belong. In one essay he writes, "History precedes me and my reflection: I belong to history before I belong to myself."[17]

On the other hand, Ricoeur readily acknowledges the place for what he calls cognitive distanciation in both epistemology and ethics. But he views whatever cognitive distanciation that is possible as a submoment within a more basic background of historical belonging. Hence, rather than celebrating either the hyperdistanciating pretensions of objective science or an uncritical embeddedness in tradition, Ricoeur asks, "Would it not be appropriate . . . to reformulate the question in such a way that a certain dialectic between the experience of belonging and alienating distanciation becomes the mainspring, the key to the inner life, of hermeneutics?"[18] Hence, for

Ricoeur, truth and method are not viewed, as they are for Gadamer, as a matter of either/or; he sees truth and scientific method not as "a disjunction but rather a dialectical process."[19]

This interlude opens us to the central theme of this essay—the potential role of distanciation and explanation in describing, narrating, and prescribing; that is, the three moments of self-understanding that I have said are so important for the contemporary field of practical theology. In short, there is for Ricoeur a subordinate role for distanciation and explanation in each of these three moments. This, finally, is why Ricoeur more than Gadamer has been so useful for practical theology's struggle to control its use of the social sciences in all its various submoments, but especially its descriptive and prescriptive/strategic ones.

Ricoeur's Moral Philosophy

The readers of this volume are probably familiar with the outlines of Ricoeur's moral philosophy. I will summarize it briefly, primarily to illustrate how it is presently being used in contemporary practical theology to critique the entire field of moral education. I will then conclude by showing how the concept of diagnosis, as Ricoeur understands this idea, may have a role in analyzing and criticizing confusions about conflicting goods in the first and last moments of Ricoeur's threefold view of moral reflection—the moment of what he calls ethics and the moment of what he terms practical wisdom.

Let us recall Ricoeur's formula for the moral life as "*aiming at the 'good life' with and for others, in just institutions.*" This formula tells us that Ricoeur sees moral reflection beginning with the teleological quest for the good life and the various discrete goods that make up this life. Ricoeur teaches that these goods are discovered indirectly through our inherited and multidimensional social practices. Practices as viewed by Ricoeur are multi-layered or thick; they consist of many different dimensions—such as the push and pull of our basic desires, goal-oriented instrumental actions, more encompassing rules of the game, ideals of the good life, and finally integrating narratives about life that subordinate and contextualize the dimensions mentioned earlier.[20] To *describe* the goods we desire and think we need— which is, as you recall, the first step in a hermeneutics of the self—is to interpret them within the full thickness of the social practices that encode them.

The dominant narratives that surround our practices and their embedded goods provide the self, in its exercise of *phronesis*, with a plot that gives some unity to the discordant goods we experience. This narrative also provides a home within which the self can experiment with solutions to the tensions of life.[21] Telling stories is an act of *phronesis*; it is a way of rehearsing the meaning and consequences of various possible plots for one's life. In Ricoeur's view, the interpretation and retrieval of the narrative or narratives that inform our practical actions is a primary task for moral reflection. This is why acting morally, as we have seen, entails first *description* and then *narration*—the rhythms that also roughly correspond to the first moments of the new practical theology. Description in its fullest expression is about describing our ethical practices—the various ways we pursue the goods of life. Narration, on the other hand, is about retelling the stories that we use to make sense of the various levels and conflicts in our ethical practices.

The third moment of practical wisdom and prescription is, for Ricoeur, actually divided into two parts—the so-called deontological test (a variation on Immanuel Kant's *Moralität*) and the test of practical wisdom (a variation on G. W. F. Hegel's *Sittlichkeit*).[22] It is conflict, violence, or tragedy between teleological goods in the ethical quest for the good life that requires the test of morality. Our pursuit of the goods of life, no matter how morally contributory in a prima facie sense, may be problematic when these goods conflict with other goods, both within ourselves and between ourselves and others. Hence, the good that can also be considered morally right must pass the test of universalization. But Ricoeur's categorical imperative, in contrast to Kant's, is not disconnected from teleology, just as his theory of respect is not sundered from esteem for the self's capacities and an analogous solicitude for the capacities of others.[23] In the end, Ricoeur redefines the categorical imperative in light of Hillel's view of the Golden Rule; that is, "Do not do unto your neighbor what you would hate him to do to you."[24] Ricoeur believes that this injunction against hate by implication opens the teleological issues associated with the stage of ethics—our pursuit of practices that lead to values one finds satisfying and away from disvalues that one finds harmful. As a consequence, Ricoeur believes that the Golden Rule bridges Aristotelian teleology with Kantian formalism by including the former within the tests of the latter. In effect, Ricoeur's deontological test is a mixed formula. It tells us to *do good to the other as you would have the other do good to you*.[25] The formal aspect of the Kantian rule, as we have seen, is retained, but a concern with the goods of life is made intrinsic to the formula.

But for Ricoeur, the deontological moment does not by itself constitute a sufficient test. One must return to the original ethical situation (the *Sittlichkeit*) to determine what this abstract test means for the pursuit of the original conflicting goods first described in the descriptive moment of moral understanding.[26] This is why description in moral philosophy, just as it is in practical theology, is not a trivial aspect of practical moral reflection. Without describing the original practices and their encoded yet conflicting goods, there is no adequate way to return to that situation and fulfill the test of wisdom. Description is essential for the exercise of practical wisdom.

Ricoeur's model of moral reflection is highly suggestive, but it is not without problems. Before turning to these, I want to show how his views already are being used in contemporary practical theology. The versatile

Roman Catholic practical theologian van der Ven, in his important book *The Formation of the Moral Self* (1998), uses Ricoeur's moral philosophy to critique and reformulate the entire field of moral education and moral psychology.[27] In fact, he analyzes and reconstructs seven different and competing models of moral education. These models variously emphasize discipline, socialization, transmission, cognitive development (associated with Lawrence Kohlberg), value clarification, emotional formation (Freudian perspectives), and finally, what he calls education for character. Once again, the threefold rhythm of description, narration, and prescription and the parallel division of moral philosophy into ethics, morality, and practical wisdom are incorporated into his practical-theological critique of the whole field of moral education.

I only have space to illustrate his use of Ricoeur with regard to one of these seven models—Kohlberg's cognitive model of moral development. Kohlberg focused his research on a single aspect of moral development—what he called the line of moral thinking. He saw moral thinking as moving through three stages as a person grows to moral maturity—a preconventional and essentially egocentric stage, a conventional and essentially conformist stage, and a postconventional or autonomous stage. Van der Ven points out that Kohlberg's view of moral development unfortunately ends in implying that individuals who give conventional justifications for their moral decisions (for example, that morally right action is a matter of following the guidance of family, community, or religion) are not really fully moral, no matter how admirable their actual conduct.[28]

To correct this implication, van der Ven uses Ricoeur to argue that Kohlberg's third stage, rather than being called "postconventional," should more properly be called "convention-critical."[29] This phrase communicates the possibility that good moral reflection might build on tradition and convention while at the same time submitting them to the deontological test and the critical review of practical wisdom. Some conventional behavior is morally good and right even though it has not yet passed the tests of deontology and practical wisdom. These tests do not as such make the action moral, they simply show or critically demonstrate that it is moral. But the action is not immoral or morally inferior simply because it has not yet explicitly passed these moral tests. Hence, there is no good reason to disparage tradition and convention-based morality as such simply because it has not yet been tested critically. This critique of Kohlberg would apply equally to Habermas, who, in his use of Kohlberg and his appreciation for critical theory, sometimes distances morality too completely from the treasures of convention and tradition.[30]

A Modest Critique

Ricoeur's contributions are extremely important for moral philosophy, moral theology, and, as I have argued, for the new practical theology. But both Ricoeur and van der Ven overlook difficulties that emerge in the prescriptive moment of moral understanding, especially the move into the last stage of practical wisdom. The test of practical wisdom—the return to the original ethical situation of conflicting goods—is bereft in Ricoeur of a clear discussion of how one might weigh or hierarchize the clash of goods in specific contexts. The test of universalization, even when formulated to include teleological goods, is too abstract and inconclusive to provide any prioritization of conflicting concrete goods in specific contexts.

Ricoeur is aware of this and has invoked Alan Donagan's theory of fundamental human goods to refine his own reformulation of the Golden Rule. Taking his cue from Donagan, Ricoeur has recently rendered the Golden Rule to read: "Act so that the optative goods to which your practice aims conform with the normative goods entailed by the Golden Rule."[31] But what are these normative or fundamental goods, and how does Ricoeur derive them? They are certainly more than Kant's empirical desires ruled by the hypothetical imperative. Fundamental or normative goods for Ricoeur doubtless include but are more concrete than John Rawls's social goods of liberty, opportunity, and wealth or Rawls's natural goods of health and intelligence.[32] In one place, Ricoeur refers to these fundamental goods as "interests" that we must respect in our solicitude for the other's pursuit of the good life.[33]

Ricoeur does give hints as to how one might evaluate and prioritize conflicting goods. Clearly, the hermeneutic retrieval of a tradition would be the first step, because traditions themselves are carriers of hierarchies of goods. As far back as his *Freud and Philosophy* (1970), when Ricoeur's turn to hermeneutic philosophy was well in place, he argued that knowledge of our desires and needs is always mediated through language and the traditions that give us our linguistic systems.[34] Although Ricoeur gives us little discussion of precisely how teleological goods are prioritized for specific situations, we must assume that he believes that the traditions ensconced in our classic narratives carry indices and scales of human needs that must be satisfied by fundamental or generic goods.

I want to conclude this essay, however, by suggesting that Ricoeur does open a supplemental and subordinate procedure for the discovery and evaluation of the goods pursued in our ethical practices. This is the path of "diagnosis." This concept is closely associated with the two concepts of explanation and distanciation, two ideas more fully developed in Ricoeur's later thought. The concept of diagnosis is prominent in *Freedom and Nature* (1966) and *Freud and Philosophy*. My understanding of Ricoeur's concept of diagnosis entails the following elements. Diagnosis is designed to uncover the involuntary yet pervasive regularities of the human will. It functions analogously to the process of diagnosis in medicine in which the doctor first approaches the body of the patient through the selfhood of the patient, seeing the embodied consciousness of the ailing person as the first line of inquiry for gaining insight into the states, needs, and symptoms of the body.[35] But then, just as the doctor uses her instruments to supplement, corroborate, or qualify the intentional reports of the patient, Ricoeur in these early works used scientific psychology, psychoanalysis, and biology in correlation with his phenomenological descriptions of intentionality. As he writes in *Freedom and Nature*, "This is why our method will be most receptive with respect to scientific psychology, even though it will make only diagnostic use of it."[36] He could have included in this sentence the disciplines of biology and psychoanalysis as well.

The diagnostic use of these distanciating disciplines offers two sets of learning: (1) the recovery of structures of intentionality that are assumed, but often ignored or unthematized, by so-called objective studies of our motivations and needs; and (2) the clarification of opaque aspects of our involuntary needs that escape the full lucidity of consciousness.[37] For instance, the field of biology known as genetics may clarify aspects of my experienced body that are too obscure for the cogito to discern, but then its significance rests in what my genetic heritage means to me; that is, how this diagnosis is assimilated by the embodied cogito. To sum up, Ricoeur's concept of diagnosis allows him to correlate what we know about our fundamental needs and goods through the indirect route of hermeneutics with what we can learn about them through a diagnostic use of the distanciating disciplines of biology and psychology.

Although I cannot elaborate these points in detail, a more energetic use of the concept of diagnosis in his moral philosophy might give Ricoeur ways to make more fine-tuned evaluations of conflicting goods in the moment of practical wisdom. Ricoeur's use of the diagnostic moment would not give us a systematic index of basic human needs or capabilities and their connection with abstract human goods. In his hands, we would not come up with a systematic list of needs and capabilities of the kind assumed by twentieth-century documents on human rights or found in Martha Nussbaum's powerful list of the human capabilities that ground her theory of human rights.[38] Although Ricoeur has at times expressed skepticism about the normative use of the category of needs because of his perception of their cultural relativity, in *Oneself as Another* and *The Just* (2000), he invokes the concept of "capacity."[39] Ricoeur tells us that our self-esteem, partially mediated through the regard of others, is precisely esteem for our basic capacities.

But what are these capacities? Ricoeur's language of capacity is primarily about "being-able-to-do" and being able to impute one's actions to oneself—that is, own one's personal narrative.[40] But does not the question of capacities open the issue of underlying regularities of human needs and basic capabilities that must both be satisfied, exercised, and prioritized if we are to live well with others in just institutions? And in order to apply the test of practical wisdom, don't we need a more differentiated and articulate language of these needs, capacities, and capabilities than Ricoeur presently provides?

I believe that such a language is needed and that Ricoeur himself hints at the necessity of it. Whatever progress Ricoeur might make on this issue, he would doubtless turn first to the long route of hermeneutics—identifying needs, capacities, and capabilities from the perspective of traditions of interpretation and using the distanciating features of diagnosis in only a secondary way. His list of needs and capacities, as a consequence, would be more heuristic and tentative—used more as stimulants to dialogue than as measuring rods for determining the adequacy of our various societies and cultures. In the end, these refined insights would not constitute definitive resolutions of conflicting goods. They would, however, help test our convictions and move them from being naive beliefs to more critically tested attestations.

In recent years, Ricoeur's early concept of diagnosis has tended to merge into his theory of explanation in his famous dialectic of understanding-explanation-comprehension. Furthermore, the idea of explanation in his later thought has been associated closely with the structural analysis of texts, a perspective that he claims is meaningful only when placed within a text's wider semantic and narrative frameworks.[41] Hence, the hermeneutic realism or naturalism of his early thought—for instance, in *Freud and Philosophy*—seems less visible in his later writings. Retrieving the concept of diagnosis within his hermeneutics of human goods would enable him to develop firmer indices of human needs and capacities and the fundamental human goods required to support them. This could happen, I believe, without losing the cultural sensitivity of his hermeneutic beginning point. This modest amendment would strengthen Ricoeur's critical hermeneutics and its important contributions to both moral philosophy and the new practical theology.

Notes

1. Wolfhart Pannenberg, *Theology and the Philosophy of Science* (Philadelphia: Westminster Press, 1976), p. 426.
2. Alastair Campbell, "Is Practical Theology Possible?" *Scottish Journal of Theology* 25, no. 2 (May 1972): 217–27.
3. Don Browning, *A Fundamental Practical Theology* (Minneapolis: Fortress Press, 1991), p. 57.
4. Edward Farley, *Theologia* (Philadelphia: Westminster Press, 1983), p. 35.
5. Barbara Wheeler and Edward Farley, *Shifting Boundaries: Contextual Approaches to the Structure of Theological Education* (Louisville, KY: Westminster/John Knox Press, 1991); Wilhelm Grab, Gerhard Rau, Heinz Schmidt, and Johannes A. van der Ven, *Christentium und Spätmoderne* (Stuttgart: W. Kohlhammer, 1999).
6. Ricoeur refers to the complex set of studies as "practical philosophy." See his *Oneself as Another* (Chicago: University of Chicago Press, 1992), p. 19.
7. For careful characterizations of these philosophical perspectives as types of practical philosophy, see Richard Bernstein's *Praxis and Action* (Philadelphia:

University of Pennsylvania Press, 1971); *The Reconstruction of Social and Political Theory* (Philadelphia: University of Pennsylvania Press, 1978); *Beyond Objectivism and Relativism* (Philadelphia: University of Pennsylvania Press, 1983).

8. Ricoeur, *Oneself as Another*, p. 20.
9. Paul Ricoeur, *Freedom and Nature* (Evanston, IL: Northwestern University Press, 1966), p. xv.
10. Ricoeur, *Oneself as Another*, p. 172.
11. Browning, *A Fundamental Practical Theology*, pp. 49–53.
12. Johannes A. van der Ven, *Entwurf einer Empirischen Theologie* (Kampen: Weinhim, 1990); *Ecclesiology in Context* (Grand Rapids, MI: Eerdmans, 1996); *Formation of the Moral Self* (Grand Rapids, MI: Eerdmans, 1998); Gerben Heitink, *Practical Theology* (Grand Rapids, MI: Eerdmans, 1999); Friedrich Schweitzer, *Die Religion des Kindes: Zur Problemeschichte einer religions-pädagogishen Grundfrage* (Gütersloh: Gütersloher Verlaghaus Gerd Mohn, 1992).
13. Paul Ricoeur, *Hermeneutics and the Human Sciences* (Cambridge: Cambridge University Press, 1981), p. 62; Hans-Georg Gadamer, *Truth and Method* (New York: Crossroad, 1982), pp. 330–31.
14. Ricoeur, *Hermeneutics and the Human Sciences*, pp. 66–67, 76–78; Gadamer, *Truth and Method*, pp. 238–40.
15. Ricoeur, *Hermeneutics and the Human Sciences*, pp. 73–76; Gadamer, *Truth and Method*, pp. 267–74.
16. Gadamer, *Truth and Method*, p. 289.
17. Ricoeur, *Hermeneutics and the Human Sciences*, p. 68.
18. Ibid., p. 90.
19. Ibid., p. 93.
20. Ricoeur, *Oneself as Another*, pp. 153–63; Ricoeur, "Teleological and Deontological Structures of Action: Aristotle and/or Kant?" ed. A. Phillips Griffiths in *Contemporary French Philosophy* (Cambridge: Cambridge University Press, 1987), pp. 99–103.
21. Ricoeur, *Oneself as Another*, p. 164.
22. Ibid., pp. 250–63.
23. Ibid., pp. 181–89.
24. Ibid., p. 219.
25. Ibid., p. 219; Ricoeur, "Teleological and Deontological Structures of Action," pp. 107–9.
26. Ricoeur, *Oneself as Another*, pp. 241, 250–55.
27. Hans van der Ven, *The Formation of the Moral Self* (Grand Rapids, MI: Eerdmans, 1998).
28. Ibid., pp. 226–27.
29. Ibid., p. 227.
30. Ibid., p. 224.
31. Ricoeur, "Teleological and Deontological Structures of Action," p. 18.
32. John Rawls, *A Theory of Justice* (Cambridge, MA: Harvard University Press, 1971), p. 62.
33. Ricoeur, "Teleological and Deontological Structures of Action," p. 110.

34. Paul Ricoeur, *Freud and Philosophy* (New Haven: Yale University Press, 1970), pp. 15–16, 395–405.
35. Ricoeur, *Freedom and Nature*, pp. 12–13.
36. Ibid., p. 13.
37. Ibid., pp. 12–13, 87–88.
38. Martha Nussbaum, "Non-Relative Virtues: An Aristotelian Approach," in *The Quality of Life*, ed. Martha C. Nussbaum and Amartya Sen (Oxford: Clarendon Press, 1993), pp. 263–65.
39. Ricoeur, *Oneself as Another*, p. 181; Paul Ricoeur, *The Just* (Chicago: University of Chicago Press, 2000), p. xvi.
40. Paul Ricoeur, "Reply to Ted Klein," "Reply to Peter Kemp," in *The Philosophy of Paul Ricoeur*, ed. Lewis Hahn (Chicago: Open Court, 1995), pp. 367, 397.
41. Paul Ricoeur, *Interpretation Theory* (Fort Worth: Texas Christian University, 1976), pp. 80–86.

14
Ricoeur on Tragedy
Teleology, Deontology, and *Phronesis*

MARTHA C. NUSSBAUM

Among the many areas in which Paul Ricoeur's distinguished philosophical work has achieved worldwide recognition, the area of moral and political philosophy is perhaps the most recent. It would be quite mistaken, however, to suggest that Ricoeur has only recently turned his attention to the great problems of social justice, and to the difficulty of relating the just to the good. As he relates in the interviews translated under the title *Critique and Conviction*, he was passionately involved in discussions of social justice at least from the time of his participation in the socialist youth movement in the early 1930s. And he records that he understood at that time that the religious imperatives that had always guided his thought would not suffice to chart the course of a nation seeking justice—"a mistake," he says, "to which many Christian socialists are prone." There is need for a theory of economic justice, which cannot be deduced directly from the maxims of the Gospels. It is no surprise, then, that Ricoeur has turned to the question of justice as a major topic of his recent work and thought: in *Oneself as Another*, with its wonderful sections on the good and the just; in many articles and essays; and, most recently, in a collection of essays published in French under the title *Le Juste*—with a most illuminating foreword, in which Ricoeur describes the evolution of his thinking about justice and law, and places himself in relation to distinguished philosophers of the Anglo-American tradition. At the same time, he has played the role of leading public philosopher in many ways: in his impressive edited volume on toleration, and in his discussions of public issues, from Nazism to the structure of contemporary higher education in France and in the United States. (To those who have an interest in our "culture wars," I strongly recommend the interview in *Critique and Conviction*, which perceptively contrasts French and U.S. higher education, commenting on such diverse issues as affirmative action, the multicultural curriculum, the relations between faculty and students—all of this interspersed with fascinating reminiscences of his time at the University of Chicago "school of religious sciences," as Ricoeur told his interviewer our divinity school really ought to be called.)

Because Ricoeur is one of our most important thinkers about all these social and political issues, a brief talk could not engage with his views in any depth. The choice seems to be either to lay out an overview of his thinking, without substantive engagement and critique, or else to choose just one issue and to focus on that one in greater depth, with more opportunity for critique. I have chosen the latter course, focusing on an area where my work crossed the path of Ricoeur's some time ago. This is the topic of tragic conflicts, a topic that plays a very important role in *Oneself as Another*.

I shall proceed as follows: I shall lay out the problem of tragic conflict, giving two examples. I shall then describe (all too briefly) the complex way in which Ricoeur uses this issue to illuminate the limits of deontology and to forge a (yet more) complex relationship between deontology and teleology at the level of Aristotelian *phronesis*. I shall say why I think this approach is superior to two extremely prominent and influential approaches, those characteristic of Kantian deontology and of utilitarianism. I shall then pose some questions to this view, suggesting that it is possible that even singular judgments made in the spirit of Aristotelian *phronesis* do not remove the problem of tragic conflict, and that it is very good for judges to acknowledge the limits even of *phronesis*, if judgment, as Ricoeur poignantly says in *Le Juste*, has as its ultimate goal the achievement of social peace.

I shall begin with an example from the classical Indian epic *Mahabharata*, because it reveals the structure of the problem very clearly; but I shall not ignore Greek tragedy, and I shall also deal with the *Antigone*, which is Ricoeur's own central example.

Tragic Predicaments[1]

Arjuna stands at the head of his troops. A huge battle is about to begin. On his side are the Pandavas, the royal family headed by Arjuna's eldest brother, legitimate heir to the throne. On the other side are the Kauravas, Arjuna's cousins, who have usurped power. More or less everyone has joined one side or the other, and Arjuna sees that many on the enemy side are blameless people for whom he has affection. In the ensuing battle he will have to kill as many of them as possible. How can it be right to embark on a course that involves trying to bring death to so many relations and friends? How, on the other hand, could it possibly be right to abandon one's own side and one's family duty?

> Arjuna saw his closest kinsmen, related to him as father or grandfather, uncle or brother, son or grandson, preceptor as well as companion and friend, on both sides. Overcome by this sight, he said in sorrow and compassion, "O Krishna, when I see my own people ready to fight and eager for

battle, my limbs shudder, my mouth is dry, my body shivers, and my hair stands on end. Furthermore, I see evil portents, and I can see no good in killing my own kinsmen. It is not right and proper that we should kill our own kith and kin, the Kauravas. How can we be happy if we slay our own people? . . . O Krishna, how can I strike with my arrows people like the grandsire Bhisma and the preceptor Drona, who are worthy of my respect?" . . . Having said these words, Arjuna threw away his bow and arrows, and sat down sorrowfully on the seat of his car.[2]

Arjuna poses himself not one but two questions. The first question, which I shall call the obvious question, is the question of what he ought to do. That question may be difficult to answer. It may also be difficult to identify the best method for arriving at the answer. In this case, Arjuna and his advisor Krishna differ sharply about method, Krishna recommending a single-minded pursuit of duty without thought for the unpleasant consequences, Arjuna proposing a careful consideration of all the foreseeable consequences.[3] What is not difficult, however, is to see that it is a question that has to be answered, since some action must be taken, and even inaction is, in such a situation, a kind of action. In that sense, the question is obvious; it is forced by the situation. Arjuna cannot be both a loyal, dutiful leader of his family and at the same time a preserver of lives of friends and relations on the other side. He has to choose.

The other question is not so obvious, nor is it forced by the situation. It might easily have eluded Arjuna. I shall call this the "tragic question." This question is whether any of the alternatives available to Arjuna in the situation is morally acceptable. Arjuna feels that this question must be faced, and that when it is faced, its answer is "no." Krishna, by contrast, either simply fails to see the force of the question altogether, or recommends a policy of deliberately not facing it, in order the better to get on with one's duty.

The tragic question is not simply a way of expressing the fact that it is difficult to answer the obvious question. Difficulty of choice is quite independent of the presence of moral wrong on both sides of a choice. In fact, in this case as in many tragic dilemmas, it is rather clear what Arjuna should do: much though he is tempted to throw away his arrows, that would accomplish nothing, resulting simply in the deaths of many more on his own side, and possibly the loss of their just cause, while countless lives will still be lost on the other side. So he should fight. The tragic question registers not the difficulty of solving the obvious question, but a distinct difficulty: the fact that all the possible answers to the obvious question, including the best one, are bad, involving moral wrongdoing. In that sense, there is no "right answer."

How does Arjuna determine that the answer to the tragic question is "no"? Not, clearly, by merely assessing the costs and benefits on both sides. That he has done already in considering what he ought to do. (That was, in effect, his method, a quite reasonable one in the circumstances.) To answer the tragic question, he appears to consult an independent (quite deontological) account of ethical value, according to which murdering one's own kin, especially when they are blameless, is a heinous wrong; but deserting one's family when one is their leader and essential supporter is also morally wrong. Ethical thoughts independent of the "what to do" question, thoughts about respect, kinship, and the right, enter in to inform him that his predicament is not just tough, but also tragic.

What is the point of the tragic question? When we think about Arjuna's situation, it might easily seem that Krishna has a point. The real question is the obvious question, and the tragic question is just a useless distraction. "O Arjuna," he says, "why have you become so depressed in this critical hour? Such dejection is unknown to noble men; it does not lead to the heavenly heights, and on earth it can only cause disgrace." Quite right, one may think: when one has seen where one's duty lies, one ought to get on with it, without tragic moaning and groaning. We don't want military leaders who self-indulgently wring their hands about the blood they are about to shed, or throw away their arrows to sit sorrowfully on the seats of their cars. It does no good for them to think this way, and it may well do harm, weakening their resolve and that of their troops.

On the other hand, one can argue that Arjuna is a better model of deliberation than Krishna: even in a case like this, where the tragedy does not look like one that could have been avoided by better political planning, there is a point to the tragic question. It keeps the mind of the chooser firmly on the fact that his action is an immoral action, which it is always wrong to choose. The recognition that one has "dirty hands" is not just self-indulgence: it has significance for future actions. It informs the chooser that he may owe reparations to the vanquished, and an effort to rebuild their lives after the disaster that will have been inflicted on them. (Michael Walzer has written eloquently on this issue, using as his example Truman's decision to drop the bomb at Hiroshima.) Most significantly, it reminds the chooser that he must not do such things henceforth, except in the very special tragic circumstance he faces here. Slaughtering one's kin is one of the terrible things that it is always tragic to pursue. In that way, facing the tragic question reinforces moral commitments that should be reinforced, particularly in wartime.

Asked to lecture on tragic dilemmas to the undergraduates at West Point, I had one of the best classroom discussions I've ever had, because these students knew that tragedy was not just a myth, it was their own future. And they recognized that the tragic question should be faced, again and again. Most of them thought that not deadening one's mind to the fact that (for example) one was taking an innocent life was among the first virtues of a good military leader. Clearly the officers in charge of the ethics program thought this as well: that was why the program was there, and why I was invited to address this topic. The topic of Lieutenant Calley and the My Lai incident kept recurring in my informal conversations with the officers. One might say that they saw the purpose of the ethics program as the prevention of such unthinking acts of brutality. Not only higher-ups, but all officers, should have a sense of tragedy, which will contain and limit their aggression.

But there is a further way in which the tragic question brings illumination. Sometimes a tragic predicament arises because of background human error: foolishness, greed, sloppiness, sheer bad social planning. In such cases, a different arrangement of the relevant values might have prevented the catastrophe.

Consider Sophocles' *Antigone*.[4] Creon tells the entire city that anyone who offers burial to the traitor Polynices is a traitor to the city, and will be put to death. Antigone cannot accept the edict, because it asks her to violate a fundamental religious obligation to seek burial for her kin. As G. W. F. Hegel correctly argued, each protagonist is narrow, thinking only of one sphere of value and neglecting the claim of the other. Creon thinks only of the health of the city, neglecting the "unwritten laws" of family obligation. Antigone thinks only of the family, failing to recognize the crisis of the city. We may add that for this very reason each has an impoverished conception not only of value in general but also of his or her own cherished sphere of value. As Haemon points out, Creon fails to recognize that citizens are also members of families, and that therefore a protector of the city who neglects these values is hardly protecting the city at all. Antigone fails to note that families also live in cities, which must survive if the survival of the family is to be ensured. A person who thought well about Antigone's choice would see that it is genuinely a tragedy: there is no "right answer," because both alternatives contain serious wrongdoing. Burying a traitor is a serious wrong to the city, but for Antigone not to bury him involves a serious religious violation. Because neither sees the tragedy inherent in the situation, because neither so much as poses the tragic question, both are in these two distinct ways impoverished political actors.

And this makes a huge difference for the political future. The drama depicts a very extreme situation, which is unlikely to occur often. In this extreme situation, where the city has been invaded by a member of its own ruling household, there may be no avoiding a tragic clash of duties. But a protagonist who faced the tragic question squarely would be prompted to have a group of highly useful thoughts about governance in general. In particular, noting that both the well-being of the city and the "unwritten laws" of religious obligation are of central ethical importance, he or she would be led to want a city that makes room for people to pursue their familial religious obligations without running afoul of civic ordinances.[5] In other words, he or she would want a city such as Pericles claims to find in democratic Athens, when he boasts that public policy shows respect for unwritten law. Just as Americans believe that we can create a public order that builds in spaces for the free exercise of religion, in which individuals are not always tragically torn between civic ordinance and religious command, so ancient Athens had an analogous anti-tragic thought—as a direct result, quite possibly, of watching tragedies such as Sophocles' *Antigone*.

It was here, indeed, that Hegel found, plausibly, the political significance of tragedy. Tragedy reminds us of the deep importance of the spheres of life that are in conflict within the drama, and of the dire results when they are opposed and we have to choose between them. It therefore motivates us to imagine what a world would be like that did not confront people with such choices, a world of "concordant action" between the two spheres of value. In that sense, the end of the drama is written offstage, by citizens who enact these insights in their own constructive political reflection. "The true course of dramatic development consists in the annulment of *contradictions* viewed as such, in the reconciliation of the forces of human action, which alternately strive to negate each other in their conflict."[6]

Now in one way Hegel's approach to tragedy is too simple, for it ignores the possibility that some degree of tragedy is a structural feature of human life.[7] Many distinct spheres of value claim our attention and commitment. As Greek polytheism expresses the insight, there are many gods, all of whom demand worship. But the gods do not agree. Therefore the contingencies of life make it almost inevitable that some disharmony will materialize among our many commitments. The only alternative to the permanent possibility of tragedy would appear to be a life so impoverished in value that it neglects many things that human beings should not neglect. And of course such a life does not really avoid tragedy: it just fails to see the tragedy involved in its own neglect of genuine values.

In another way, however, Hegel gives us the best strategy to follow, especially in political life. For we really do not know whether a harmonious fostering of two apparently opposed values can be achieved—until we try to bring that about. Many people in many places have thought that a harmonious accommodation between religion and the state is just impossible. Athens tried to prove them wrong. Modern liberal states—grappling with the even thornier problem of the plurality of religions, and of secular views of the good—all in their own ways try to prove them wrong. To a great extent, a political regime like ours does enable citizens to avoid Antigone-like tragedies. That is what is meant by saying—as the U.S. Supreme Court said until *Employment Division v. Smith*, and as Congress said in passing the Religious Freedom Restoration Act (RFRA)—that the state may not impose a "substantial burden" on an individual's free exercise of religion without a "compelling state interest."[8] Creon, presumably, had such an interest, and so too will quite a few other state actors. Consequently, there will be a residuum of tragedy left even in the Hegelian nation. But we proclaim that we do our best to keep tragedy at bay. We do so because we understand the force of the tragic question: understand, that is, that to require an individual to depart from a religious commitment is not just to impose an inconvenience, it is to ask something that goes to the heart of that person's being. It is to deprive them of a sphere of liberty to which, as citizens, they have an entitlement based upon justice.

Often we do not know what arrangements we are capable of making, until we have faced the tragic question with Hegel's idea in view. We could multiply examples, but I particularly like to think about the tragic choices women frequently faced in previous eras, and often face now, choices between family obligation and the pursuit of a career. In many such cases, bad social arrangements were to blame for the fact that women were tugged tragically in two directions. Better social supports for the care of children, and more flexible structuring of career paths, can make it possible for people to pursue both of these important goods. But we would not have seen that if we hadn't seen the tragedy first, and seen it as a tragedy.

To summarize: I would hold that it is useful to pose the tragic question for four reasons. First, to do so clarifies the nature of our ethical alternatives, informing us about important differences between self-interest and commitment, prudential and moral values. Second, to recognize the existence of a tragic dilemma, in those cases where the answer to the tragic question is "no," reinforces commitments to important moral values that should in general be observed. Third, to recognize tragedy and our own "dirty hands" motivates us to make appropriate reparations for conduct that, while in a sense inevitable, was also unethical.[9] Finally, the Hegelian point: the recognition of tragedy leads us to ask how the tragic situation might have been avoided by better social planning; tragedy thus provides a major set of incentives for good social reflection.

Notice that our examples reveal a persistent human tendency to neglect the tragic question in favor of the more straightforward obvious question, a question that can hardly be avoided if action is in the offing. Krishna gives advice that is deeply equivocal in the context of the epic, where he is portrayed as a deceiver, and not at all a simply admirable character. Nonetheless, a lot of people like this advice, as evidenced by the fact that the *Bhagavad-Gita* (the section of the poem in which Krishna gives his advice) has acquired a life of its own, becoming one of the most influential texts of the history of philosophy, while Arjuna's very sensible response to his dilemma is not revered in this way, or, frequently, even considered part of the same discussion. Again, Creon and Antigone prefer the simple focus on issues of choice and action to a more complex reflection on the plurality of conflicting values and the need to arrange things so that they conflict less tragically. Focusing on the moment of choice requires only some decision strategy, and one can always choose in an arbitrary way if a sounder decision strategy does not suggest itself. Asking the tragic question requires, first of all, assuming a possible burden of guilt and of reparative effort, something people, and especially leaders, do not always enjoy doing. Asking it in the Hegelian way requires more: a systematic critical scrutiny of habit and tradition, in search of a reasonable *Aufhebung* of the contending values. And this scrutiny requires of us nothing less than a comprehensive account of justice and central human goods.

Ricoeur on Tragedy

In order to approach the subject of Ricoeur's views on tragedy, I will need to do some summarizing. For we can only appreciate the role of the tragic in Ricoeur's thought if we understand first the relationship he maps out between the teleological and the deontological. This relationship must not be understood in an oversimple way, as a simple opposition. For Ricoeur in *Oneself as Another*, the central ethical question is a question about the *good*. The question is, in essence, Aristotle's: How shall I attain a complete good human life? But already in the posing of this question, other people and their interests are included. For Ricoeur as for Aristotle, the person who wishes for a good life does not wish for a solitary life, but rather for a life lived with and toward others. Moreover, for Ricoeur as for Aristotle, the institutional aspect of this life is already included in the wish for the good: the agent's wish is to live a complete good life with others *in just institutions*. It is very important for Ricoeur that this is so: justice enters morality on the same level as the wish for a good life for oneself. It is in the first instance an object of teleological wishing. As he says in *Le Juste*, it makes its presence felt as an optative before it is present as an imperative.

But for Ricoeur, unlike Aristotle, the teleological perspective proves incomplete. The reason for this is that action in society involves power, and the existence of power (of one agent over another, of institutions over agents) always involves the possibility of violence and force. The fact that both individuals and institutions use force requires us to think about what it is in the human being that limits the use of force, and also what might possibly legitimate it in certain circumstances. These problems lead, Ricoeur argues, to a need for the Kantian idea of *universal law*, and the closely related idea of the *human being as an end*. Taking up the Kantian perspective, the agent uses the notion of *obligation* where formerly she had used the idea of *good*.

But the deontological level never attains a complete independence from the level of the good: for justice must be concerned with the distribution of something, and we have to be cognizant of these things as goods. Justice in that way can never be purely procedural, as Ricoeur has several times observed in discussing the work of John Rawls: it always has a content, is about getting good things to people. Furthermore—and here lies Ricoeur's central objection to Rawls—the goods considered by political institutions are plural, heterogeneous, and incommensurable. (Here he draws on Walzer's idea of distinct *spheres of justice*.)

Because the good things are plural and incommensurable, tragic conflicts arise. The needs of one sphere conflict with those of another. In Antigone's case, for example, the needs of family religion conflict with those of civic safety. Ricoeur holds that "this tragedy says something unique about the unavoidable nature of conflict in moral life."[10]

Ricoeur notes that in a certain sense the deontological morality characteristic of modernity makes the painful character of these conflicts clearer than did predeontological moralities: these "conflictual situations would be stripped of their dramatic character if they did not stand out against the backdrop of a demand for universality."[11] Thus, although the Aristotelian teleological project already presupposes justice as a goal, deontology is needed in the more complete articulation of that goal. When we arrive at the tragic conflict, however, deontology no longer helps us decide what to do.

At this point, Ricoeur holds, we need to move on to a third level of thought, a level already implicit in the "tragic wisdom" of *Antigone*. This level is the level of *phronesis*. What is the lesson taught us by the play's concluding appeal to practical wisdom (*to phronein*)? How can there be "good deliberation" in a situation in which all the alternatives involve doing violence to an important value? The first thing that tragic *phronein* shows us, for Ricoeur as for Hegel, is the one-sidedness or partiality of the competing principles. "The source of conflict lies not only in the one-sidedness of the characters but also in the one-sidedness of the moral *principles* which themselves are confronted with the complexity of life."[12] To this one-sidedness, the solution is a *phronesis* that is contextual, situational, sensitive to the conflicting demands of reality, willing to choose in the full knowledge of reality's conflictual character. "From tragic *phronein* to practical *phronesis*: this wll be the maxim that can shelter moral conviction from the ruinous aternatives of univocity or arbitrariness."[13]

Ricoeur's approach to the problem of tragic conflict moves well beyond that of Kant, who simply denied that such conflicts ever arise. One or the other apparently conflicting duties will turn out not to be a genuine duty, and our only moral difficulty is to sort things out correctly, deciding which duty is the real duty. Kant took this plainly inadequate line, it seems, because he could not bear the idea that the contingent demands of reality should ever put the moral agent in the position of being false to a genuine duty. And it lands him in an untenable position. In the famous example of whether I should lie to a murderer who comes to my door asking for the whereabouts of the person he wants to murder, Kant simply sees one duty only, that of not lying; he simply refuses to recognize another duty exerting its claim, namely that of saving my friend's life. This deontological approach is plainly inadequate to the complexities of life.

Equally inadequate is another approach that now determines most of the public policy that gets made in this nation and in many others: that is, the approach characteristic of utilitarian cost-benefit analysis. This approach doesn't even bother denying that there is a conflict of duties; it simply never gets to that question at all, probably because it really doesn't recognize a deontological level distinct from the teleological. For the public practitioner of cost-benefit analysis, then, the only question to be asked in such a situation is what I've called the obvious question: What shall be preferred to what? This question is approached by reckoning up the costs and benefits of each of the alternatives to the parties concerned—usually by some plainly crude stratagem, such as asking people what they are willing to pay to avoid each of the evils in question. This approach, though rarely seriously challenged in our public life, is far more inadequate than the Kantian approach, since it doesn't even get to the point of recognizing the existence of right and obligations.[14]

Notice, then, that Ricoeur has given us a proposal that goes well beyond the two dominant approaches to tragic predicaments characteristic of modernity. His solution is not entirely unprecedented—I think, for example, that Cicero in *On Duties* takes a similar line. But he lays the solution out with a clarity and theoretical precision of which Cicero was not capable, at least not in the final months of his life while on the run from assassins. And of course he is able to relate his solution to the distinction between the teleological and the deontological in a way that no premodern writer would have been able to do.

There remains in my mind, however, a question about how far the turning to *phronesis* should go. Suppose, recognizing a conflict of obligations, I turn to *phronesis* to get a concrete decision, peculiar to the situation, about what is best to do. I make my choice. What remains? Does the obligation that lost out continue to exert any claim at all? Am I, for example, obliged to make reparations to those who have suffered by my choice, even though I made the best decision possible in the circumstances? (Walzer argues, concerning the bombing of Hiroshima, that I most certainly am.) And am I, in Hegelian fashion, even more deeply obligated to ponder the genesis of the tragedy, asking how a different arrangement of social institutions might eliminate such conflicts for citizens in the future? Surely Hegel thought that this was the deepest wisdom of tragedy—and I will not attain that wisdom if I too quickly rest content with my fine-tuned situational judgment. In the Antigone case, for example, I will, as Creon, choose the best way I can in the circumstances. But I must also ask what kind of a city could bring about a harmonious reconciliation of public safety and family religion.

It is certainly true that any modern society contains separate spheres of value; but these can be better or less well adjusted to one another, so that they pose citizens with more or fewer tragic dilemmas. Women of my mother's generation had to make an all-or-nothing choice between motherhood and career, which was frequently tragic for them. In our era, a different arrangement of public institutions has not altogether removed conflict, but it has made it less perpetual. Even in cases in which a state simply cannot eliminate a tragedy any time soon, wise Hegelian thinking, over and above *phronesis,* may guide the way to a better future.

Consider a case familiar to me from my international development work, the case of compulsory education in India. All Indian states require primary education; in many cases, secondary education is compulsory as well. But literacy rates remain low: about 35 percent for women, 65 percent for men in the nation as a whole. Economic necessity is clearly involved in this distressing pattern: poor parents need to rely on the labor of their children, whether in the home or outside it. As I have noted above, many families would be at risk of going under completely if they were to send all their children to government schools. And yet there are also signs that intelligent planning can make a difference. The state of Kerala, a relatively poor state, has an adolescent literacy rate of 99 percent for both boys and girls. The difference has a great deal to do with state policies: aggressive campaigning in favor of literacy; incentives to poor parents, in the form of a nutritious school lunch that goes some way to offsetting the losses to parents in child labor; and flexible multisession school hours.[15] If we look to states where literacy is particularly low, we find, correspondingly, an absence of intelligent planning. In some rural areas (in Andhra Pradesh, for example), there aren't any schools or teachers, since state government is corrupt and inefficient and has not bothered to make things happen. In many others areas, government schools fail to offer flexible hours that make schooling possible for working children; NGOs sometimes fill the gap, but sometimes they don't.

All this suggests that there is some point to going beyond the best *phronesis* that we can exercise, and adopting a currently unrealizable constitutional goal that specifies a basic education right for all citizens. This is in fact what India is now doing: a proposal to amend the constitution's list of fundamental rights to include a fundamental right of primary and secondary education has been introduced, and has broad support.[16] Obviously enough, amending the constitution does not all by itself change the conditions I have described. But it does give education a new moral and legal emphasis: it is now a fundamental entitlement of all citizens, the deprivation of which constitutes a tragic cost. It will also be possible to litigate against states or other public actors that deprive children of this fundamental right through deficient planning. If political actors had *simply* turned to *phronesis,* not pressing into the future the demands of the losing claim, we would have missed a profound element in political justice. Tragic dilemmas may have a natural element, but they usually also have an element of human greed or neglect or lack of imagination. We should not treat the greed as a given; we should exercise imagination in a free Hegelian spirit, asking what steps might be taken to produce a world that is free of some life-crushing contradictions.

* * *

Ricoeur on Tragedy

So I have some unresolved questions about what Ricoeur's proposal for the turning to *phronesis* involves. I believe it probably does not require us to forgo the further thinking and planning that I have just described, and I would simply suggest that this further element might be seen as a most important part of *phronesis* itself, if *phronesis* is a kind of wisdom in the service of public peace. But whatever the answer to these questions is, we must applaud Ricoeur for courageously going against both of the major ethical traditions of modernity, to recognize a central feature of the ethical life.

Notes

1. I have written extensively about these predicaments, both in *The Fragility of Goodness: Luck and Ethics in Greek Tragedy and Philosophy* (Cambridge: Cambridge University Press, 1986), chapts. 2, 3; *Love's Knowledge: Essays on Philosophy and Literature* (New York: Oxford University Press, 1990), especially in the essay "Flawed Crystals"; and, finally, in "Tragic Conflicts," *Radcliffe Quarterly* (March 1989). *Fragility* contains a detailed account of the tragic dilemmas in Aeschylus's *Agamemnon* and *Seven against Thebes* and in Sophocles' *Antigone*, with many references both to scholarship on those works and to the contemporary philosophical literature on moral dilemmas. Most recently, I have addressed the question in "The Cost of Tragedy: Some Moral Limits of Cost-Benefit Analysis," *Journal of Legal Studies* (spring 2000). In the modern philosophical literature, I have found most helpful: Ruth Barcan Marcus, "Moral Dilemmas and Consistency," *Journal of Philosophy* 77 (1980): 121–36; Bernard Williams, "Ethical Consistency," in *Problems of the Self* (Cambridge: Cambridge University Press, 1993), pp. 166–86; John Searle, "*Prima Facie* Obligations," in Z. van Straaten, ed., *Philosophical Subjects: Essays Presented to P. F. Strawson*, ed. Z. van Straaten (Oxford: Clarendon Press, 1980), pp. 238–59; Michael Stocker, *Plural and Conflicting Values* (New York: Oxford University Press, 1990); Michael Walzer, "Political Action: The Problem of Dirty Hands," *Philosophy and Public Affairs* 2 (1973): 160–80.
2. *Mahabharata* (c. third century B.C.). This passage is quoted from the translation by Chakravarthi V. Narasimhan (New York: Columbia University Press, 1965), which translates only selections from the work, but renders fully those passages it does select (whereas many shortened translations are also reworkings). Van Buitenen's definitive unedited translation (see below) remains incomplete because of his death, and did not progress as far as this passage. The passage cited is from book 6, chapt. 23.
3. In the passage that has since become famous as the *Bhagavad-Gita*, Krishna advises Arjuna that he has "a right to action alone, but not to the fruits of action." Consequences should not be taken into account at all in choosing a course of conduct. "[M]en attain the highest good by doing work without attachment to its results."
4. My interpretation is defended with a lot of textual detail and full discussion of the scholarly literature in *Fragility*, chapt. 3.

5. In *Fragility* I note that this interpretation is shared by a number of critics, including I. M. Linforth, "Antigone and Creon," *University of California Publications in Classical Philology* 15 (1961): 183–260, at 257; Matthew Santirocco, "Justice in Sophocles' *Antigone*," *Philosophy and Literature* 4 (1980): 180–98, at 182, 194; Charles Segal, *Tragedy and Civilization: An Interpretation of Sophocles* (Cambridge, MA: Harvard University Press, 1981), p. 205. Linforth: "For all Athenians, the play offers a powerful warning to see to it that the laws they enact are not in conflict with the laws of the gods." Segal: "Through its choral song, the *polis* arrives at self-awareness of the tensions between which it exists. Embodying these tensions in art, it can confront them and work towards their mediation, even though mediation is not permitted to the tragic heroes within the spectacle itself. The play in its social and ritual contexts achieves for society what it refuses to the actors within its fiction. Its context affirms what its content denies."
6. G. W. F. Hegel, *The Philosophy of Fine Art*, vol. 4, trans. P. B. Osmaston, in *Hegel on Tragedy*, eds. A. and H. Paolucci (New York: Dover, 1975), pp. 68, 71.
7. This was the emphasis of my reading of *Antigone*; a similar view is defended in "Flawed Crystals," where I call moral dilemmas a secular analogue of original sin: you can't live a fully pure life, a life in which you are false to no value.
8. For my own discussion of the cases, and a proposal based on the language of RFRA, see *Women and Human Development: The Capabilities Approach* (Cambridge: Cambridge University Press, 2000), chapt. 3.
9. See Walzer, "Political Action"; Stocker, *Plural and Conflicting Values*.
10. Paul Ricoeur, *Oneself as Another*, trans. Kathleen Blaney (Chicago: University of Chicago Press, 1992), p. 243.
11. Ibid., p. 281.
12. Ibid., p. 249.
13. Ibid., p. 349.
14. See my "The Cost of Tragedy" for a detailed development of this position.
15. See Jean Drèze and Amartya Sen, *India: Economic Development and Social Opportunity* (Delhi: Oxford University Press, 1995). Kerala's relative poverty, Drèze and Sen argue, is due to its bad economic policies: permitting unions to drive wages up very high has caused employment to shift to neighboring states. On the other hand, health and education have been well promoted in the absence of robust economic growth. (They use this example, among others, to illustrate the fact that, even in the absence of economic growth, one may achieve progress in these areas; on the other side, focusing only on economic growth—as other states have done—does not achieve progress in these areas.)
16. See Archana Mehendale, "Compulsory Primary Education in India: The Legal Framework," *From the Lawyers' Collective* 13 (April 1998): 4–12.

Conclusion

Ethics and Human Capability
A Response[1]

PAUL RICOEUR

I intend to focus on two main topics: first, the place of my ethical and political contribution within the larger framework of my published work, as I understand it right now; and second, my recent attempts to reorient my thought, attempts that I now consider as basic to the ethical problems with which I have been concerned at large.

Human Capability

Let me say a few introductory words concerning the first topic about my thought as a whole, and, more specifically, the philosophical task to which I feel committed. I would not like to define my philosophy in terms of its speculative structure, not even of its methodology, but in terms of its basic problematics. This shift in emphasis in understanding my thought is all the more important in that at first sight my works may look scattered, according to a variety of limit-questions of which we were reminded by my close, my good friend David Tracy: voluntary, involuntary, finitude and guilt, meaning, the implication of Freud's psychoanalysis and the unconscious, fallibility, semantic innovation and poetic discourse around the metaphor, narrative and its linguistic configuration of the temporal experience, the concept and structure of selfhood, and more recently some political papers and my essays on justice.[2] According to a speculative structure, this work plainly looks scattered. But I insist that philosophical inquiry does not have to be monolithic. After all, these specific problems have a history of their own which calls for accurate scrutiny. Philosophers are, to my mind, first of all responsible for the exact formulation of specific problems. If I say so, I should not want to make any excuse for the heterogeneous aspect of my work. And what I intend to say now, concerning what I hold as a prevailing problematics of the whole set of my writings, is not intended to substitute for the acknowledged dispersion of my work.

When I try to cast a retrospective glance at my work, I agree that it is—for the sake of a discourse of the second order—a personal reinterpretation offered to my readers. And I must say that it is only recently that I felt allowed to give a name to this overarching problematics. I mean the problem of human capability, capability as the cornerstone of philosophical anthropology, or, to put it in more simple terms belonging to ordinary language, the realm of the theme expressed by the verb *I can*. I share this concern with Merleau-Ponty, whom I admired so much as a student and as a young instructor. The advantage of starting with this model verb *I can* is to be able to link it to a plurality of verbs implying some kind of actualization, a variety of potentialities or capabilities. Before I look at my work as an attempt to provide a survey of the capabilities, so to say, of the verb *I can* in terms of these complementary verbs, allow me to take as a leading thread my last systematic work, *Oneself as Another*. It can be read in terms of four verbs, which the "*I can*" modifies: *I can speak, I can do things, I can tell a story,* and *I can be imputed,* an action can be imputed to me as its true author.

As you shall see later, imputability will be the link between the descriptive and the prescriptive parts of my work. Under the three headings of philosophy of language, philosophy of action, and philosophy of narrative theory, I was able with the term *imputability* to reach the threshold between theoretical anthropology and ethics. Under the heading of language, I could restructure the field in terms of its triadic organization: the word, the sentence, the text, and each with their related units; in the field of action, to articulate together decision, motivation, and insertion of human intentions in the world; and at the level of narrativity, the parallel of reconfiguration of temporal experience in ordinary life in history and literature. And it is with the last stage, imputability, that the structuring function of the concept of capability came to my mind. Therefore, I see the concept of capability as having not only a structuring function but a cumulative function. To a further extent, each stage is the condition of the possibility for the next one. Language is not a capability among all of us, but is the condition of the possibility of all other meaningful human capabilities. To the extent that it is the mediating link, the mediator of action, action is symbolically mediated, as I used to say. And of course, at the level of narrative, storytelling and emplotment have their own linguistic structure. Imputability also has its own linguistic structure connecting, as Peter Kemp repeats, the narrative to ethical statements and commitments. In the second part of my remarks, I will try to show how imputability may provide the threshold leading to the triadic structure of the ethical. Before that, I want to move from the problematics to the methodology and the speculative organization of the whole inquiry.

Concerning the method: In what way does this cumulative problematics of the "I can" require a methodology of its own? I shall try to show that the complexity of the problematic has to be reflected in the complexity of the methodology itself. In this sense, I agree with Aristotle's saying that method is always under the sway of the problem, of the thing, of the object. And, therefore, I may provide a kind of survey of the methodological shifts which were required by the shift in problematics.

At the beginning, I thought that I could remain within the limits of a descriptive phenomenology in the sense of the first work of Edmund Husserl, his essential eidetics. My attempt was to expand eidetics from the field of perception and representation concerning such acts as memory, imagination, and conceptual thinking—that is, the field of representational acts—to practical and emotional fields. Such an extension was already a sort of significant improvement. But, when confronted with the problem of bad will and evil, I felt a need to enrich phenomenology by borrowing from a quite different field of discourse, that of exegesis, philology, jurisprudence, and the interpretation of texts at large. From these I proceeded to the analysis of the basic symbols of evil, myths, and the speculative fantasies that were built on this level and constituted together the symbolism of evil. This move implied a second methodological shift. I have to agree that in fact we have to do here with two opposite hermeneutics, a hermeneutics more or less reductive of its own intentional project, and the other one expanding, confirming, emphasizing what I had used in my *Symbolism of Evil*. That work led me to a rereading of the whole corpus of Freud. I had to come to grips with resistance to the claim of philosophy to put consciousness at the top of its own agenda. This was for me a real and conflictual situation, because the whole of modern philosophy, running from Descartes up to Husserl, was put to test, and even denied. Therefore, I tried to stabilize, so to speak, the conflict by elaborating a dialectics of force and meaning, of desire and purpose, which could be considered a hermeneutics of its own.

At the same time, my readings and my teaching in the United States, at Yale, Columbia, and then, since 1969, in Chicago, opened me to analytic philosophy and its highly logical requirements in the semantics and pragmatics of discourse. I had to take into account the propositional formulation of all the intellectual operations covered by phenomenology and hermeneutics. Here is found the most decisive step that governs the whole structure of *Oneself as Another*: namely, the need to articulate at each level an objective approach with a reflective one, according to the broad tradition of French reflexive philosophy exemplified by Jean Nabert and German post-Kantian reflexivity. This correlation between the objective mood of discourse and the reflective one governs the structure of *Oneself as Another*. I can put this correlation under a precept in the form of a slogan: "explaining more in order to understand better." This slogan conveys to the whole enterprise a workable articulation between two sides of each particular problematic: the linguistic and the reflective, the objective and the existential.

Each field in turn—language, action, narration, prescription—in *Oneself as Another* had to be construed according to the above-mentioned requirement.

For example, speaking of language, we have to take into account first the structure of statements as objectified expressions of language and then move from statements to speech acts, from speech acts to utterances, and from utterances to the utterer. I could survey the whole process as a way of appropriation joined to distanciation required by the objectifying approach. The same with the field of action, in which I start with Donald Davidson, at the level of his notion of events and therefore actions as kinds of events, but, on the other side, actions as the expressions of agency connected to an agent capable of acting. In the field of narrativity, I had to take into account, on the one hand, the structuralist approach, and connect it accurately, on the other hand, with narrative intentionality, the whole governed by the notion of plot and emplotment. We shall see later that the same could be said in the field of ethics, where a norm to a certain extent represents the objective side of the good life, and the wish for a good life represents the subjective side of ethical life.

To conclude this section on method, I could take into account the rhythmic constitution of the whole field, combining descriptive phenomenology on the one hand, and hermeneutical interpretation on the other hand: objectivity and reflexivity, distanciation and appropriation. That would be the main feature of the methodology governing the structure of *Oneself as Another*.

Now a word concerning the move from the problematics to method and from method to the speculative organization, or, better said, a move from epistemology to ontology. The decisive step in this regard was the attempt to correlate the basic concept of philosophical anthropology, namely that of capability (potentiality) to one of the most important ontological traditions which had been superseded in the history of Western thought because of its so-called substantialism: being as substance versus appearances. I am referring to Aristotle's *Metaphysics*, Epsilon, book V-2, with the famous saying, "being may be said in several ways," and among them being as actuality (*energia*) and potentiality (*dunamis*). I took the risk of putting my hermeneutical phenomenology under the heading of a philosophical anthropology governed by the concept of capability, and this, in turn, under the aegis of an ontology of actuality and potentiality. I find myself in the middle, not at the end, of an important philosophical stream which may be followed through Leibniz and Spinoza down to Schelling, Dilthey, and, to a certain extent, Heidegger and his concept of care, and to the power to be (belonging to my mind to the same tradition of being as actuality-potentiality) found in Paul Tillich, through Schelling, in his *The Courage to Be*. I could consider a hierarchical order read backward from thought to its basis, from being as *energia-dunamis*, capability as the basic concept of philosophical anthropology, and then the several phenomenological fields scattered along the lines of language, action, narration, imputability.

Allow me to say a few more words concerning my attempted ontological exercise, if I dare. My recourse to Aristotle's *Metaphysics*, Epsilon, V-2, is

Ethics and Human Capability 283

only the first one. Besides that, I took more seriously the last dialogues of Plato (*Theatetus, Sophist, Parmenides, Philebus*), which propose a somewhat different ontological excursus, namely the exploration of what Plato called the highest ideas: one and many, same and other, being and not being, motion and rest. This is the enumeration of *Philebus*, which provided the structure of what may be called a formal ontology governing the transcendental terms of any hierarchical discourse. Each philosophy at one stage or another makes use of one or several of these categories. Take as an example contemporary philosophy: we make use of the opposition between same and other. But it also belongs to *Parmenides*, to *Philebus*, and so on.

It was suggested to me to speak in this regard of the metafunction of discourse, which governs not only the concept of transcendental philosophy in the sense of Kant and the post-Kantians (for example, Fichte), but the highest structure of any hierarchical discourse, to the extent that it implies a nonreflected speculative tool, which needs a second or third order of reflection. And this attempt, in fact, brings us back to Parmenides and through Plato's *Parmenides* to Plotinus, Proteus, and others. Finally in this way we reach the *Ethics* of Spinoza.

Let me say one more word concerning my exploration of the grounds of a philosophical anthropology in ontology. I dare say now that some of my exercise in the field of biblical thought belongs to the same line of thought. When, with André Lacocque, we chose to use the term *thinking* concerning biblical literature, we had in mind the idea that it belonged to the broader field in which philosophy is only one part. It belonged to the same speculative level as Parmenides, Heraclitus, and so on. And this account of biblical thinking allowed me to attempt to reconnect the theological and the philosophical fields. Several speakers here have underlined my insistence on not mixing discourses. But now I feel freer to be attentive to the correlations and even to the unwrapping of the different fields of theology and philosophy.

Consider two examples from my work. My reflections are close to Rosenzweig's *Star of Redemption* concerning creation around the concept of origin, *Ursprung,* which has its correlates in Greek thought under the term *arche*. I tried to show that there is a dialectics between beginning and origin, beginning as a starting point in time and origin as the always-already-there of rising reality. This is an expression of Rosenzweig. To underline the difference between origin and beginning, I tried to show that the notion of origin has itself its own temporal development along the line of founding events transmitting the energy of the origin. I now think that there is a philosophical side to a theology of creation that allows us (maybe this would be the service of the philosopher?) to help the theologian not to cover over too quickly a theology of creation by a theology and christology of redemption. This reminds us that creativeness comes before law, guilt, and even redemption. And that would be a whole field of thinking on its own.

My second example, more classical, is my attempt to reformulate the whole problematic of Exodus 3:14: "I am who I am." I will not discuss the translation, because precisely I want to show that to translate is to conclude an operation of interpretation. The problem is whether this Hebrew expression may be held as an extension of the aforesaid polysemy of the Greek word for *enai, esse* or being, or whether it expresses something radically different. It is this option that governs the translatability of the word. If we say that in the tetragrammaton (YHWH) we have to do with the quite alien term which cannot be connected to the verb *to be*, then it is untranslatable. Of course, we may have some alternatives, but they are not real alternatives, such as *werden* in German, becoming, and so on. The plea for translatability is to say that the Hebrew term expands the polysemy of our word *being* and opens a window in the framework, the conceptuality of "being" according to the proposal by Aristotle in the *Metaphysics*.

The implications are huge. If no ontology is available in that field, then Emmanuel Levinas is completely right: ethics has to be completed without any ontology. But then we lose, to my mind, the root in a philosophical anthropology, because we are not allowed to use the terms *capability, imputability*, and the whole set of ideas around the "I can." This is, in fact, I think what is the courageous but maybe desperate attempt of Levinas to build an ethics without any recourse to any ontological discourse. And I should say that it has a counterexample in its own attempt, its indefinite fight with Heidegger, as if we could not get rid of this confrontation with ontology. But I leave this problem as an open problem.

To my mind, I would say that I am not ready for this sacrifice of any ontological foundation. And one reason for resisting such a temptation of an ethics without any ontological rooting is the possibility to think not only biblically but in any religious terms. For my part, I see a strong connection between a philosophical anthropology based on the idea of capability and the purpose of any religious thinking. Here I repeat my debt to Kant's *Religion within the Limits of Reason*, for the opening chapter on radical evil relates the trend toward evil to the originary goodness of the human being. As radical as evil may be, it will never be more originary than goodness, which is the *Ursprung* in the field of ethics, the orientation to the good as being rooted in the ontological structure of the human being, or in biblical terms: creation, createdness. I affirm it is important for the basic signification of religion at large and the possibility of comparative religion in the sense of Mircea Eliade. That is to say that all religions are different attempts in different language games to recover the ground of goodness, to liberate, so to say, the enslaved freedom, the enslaved capability. We have to look at the problem of evil in terms of some specific loss of capability as we have it in the symbolic mythical language of slavery, self-inflicted incapability. This does not suppress the mysterious character of evil, but puts it in the light of an encompassing ontology and theological anthropology. Then, the whole process of origin in the fourth chapter of Kant's *Religion* makes sense for a philosopher, after the rewriting of the myth in terms of this incapacitation of a free will. Then we have the rule of the schematization of liberation under the aegis of the Christian symbol of the perfect man ready to give his life for the sake of his friends, and the function of the religious community as the bearer of the teaching of this schematization.

So I stop here. Maybe I went too far, too quickly. But now I insist I am more interested in the interrelationship between the two fields, the different fields of philosophy and theology and on the basis of this free ontological excursus. As I said, Aristotle in his *Metaphysics*, Plato in the dialogues, the tradition of *arche* and the biblical concept of creation are related to it.

Ethics

Now, let me turn to the second part of my contribution. I want to say a few words concerning the revisions that I would now consider about the three chapters in *Oneself as Another* that I call, in a more or less ironic way, my *petite ethique, minima moralia*. First of all, I want to reconnect it more tightly with the previous chapters of *Oneself as Another*. It is not clear in the present presentation of the work, because the concept of imputability had to be put at the threshold of ethics and the ending point of the anthropological phemonenology. Therefore, I see the whole problematic of ethics as an exploration of one specific capability, the moral or ethical capability. I'll come in a moment to the alternatives: moral and ethical. This would be the first revision. But most important is an attempt to redistribute in new ways the several fields related to the competing concepts of ethics and morality. We need two terms. There were always two terms: *ethics* and *morality*. Why? There is no compelling reason in the etymology, because both terms have to do with the customs, the ethos. What is the need for two concepts?

I think that for the sake of clarity I suggest proceeding in the following way. To start from the moral level, that of obligation, as a level of reference of the whole investigation related to the use of the terms *ethics* and *morality*. And even if in the long run, at the end of the process, morality should appear as only an intermediary level, the level of testing programs, projects, maxims, as Kant has it, nevertheless morality constitutes the appropriate level of reference to the extent that it is here that two uses of the term *ethics* are required: a backwards, so to say, grounding of ethics on the one hand, and an ethics of practical wisdom on the other hand. This is, therefore, the bifurcation of the concept of ethics that will become the main problem, the most difficult problem, in this field.

Why? Let us start from common moral experience. To a large extent we may say that the moral philosophy of Kant is a kind of formalization of common experience—that is, the ordinary experience connecting together the two sides of the concept of imputability. On the one hand, imputability implies that an action has been already interpreted, evaluated, in terms of what is allowed and what is forbidden. This is the normative side of imputability. But it has its subjective side, the fact that it implies a subject who puts himself or herself under the rule of the norm. The connection between the normative and the existential side of imputability constitutes the basic moral experience. Whatever may be the contents of the norm, we know of no human experience that would ignore the relation to some norm, some evaluation and prescription concerning human action, the allowed and forbidden, connected with a subject capable of putting itself under the rule of this norm, whatever it may be. This seems to be the basic structure of common moral experience.

I must insist on one point before going further. When I speak of the "subjective side," I don't imply necessarily an individual subject. The dialectical structure of imputation is implied to the extent that imputation as such is already a dialogical act, either between two people or between a community and the individual, or as a kind of internalized dialogue according to the notion of the soul in Plato, which is in dialogue with itself. So we may call "the moral" also the deontological, if you will, at this level. We must also try to show that we should not overemphasize the opposition between the deontological and the teleological. It is more the secondary interpretation of the system of relationship which is quite complex. We do not have to assign it exclusively to Kant's moral philosophy. I insist that what we need is only the basic connection between norm as the objective side of imputability and commitment as the subjective side of imputability.

To my mind, the real difficulty starts with the appropriate location of the term *ethics*. We can look to Hegel's term *Sittlichkeit*, which has been translated by most English translators as "ethical life. " This covers the system of institutions related to what Hegel, the great systematic thinker, called "objective mind"—that is to say, family, economic structures, state, and so on. By the way, I should say that, like Charles Taylor, I admire very much Hegel's philosophy of right. We have got to be Hegelian too, because it is only Hegel, in a sense, who has a complete philosophy of action, which is maybe a lacking component in Kant, who has something about desire and law but not about action. We have, then, the first use of the term *ethics*: there is, on the one hand, the grounding level of the whole moral philosophy, and, on the other hand, the field of applications. It is in that way that we speak of medical ethics, bioethics, business ethics, and so on.

My problem is, why do we need two apparently opposite uses of the term *ethics*? And what is the role of morality in relation to the two usages of the term *ethics*, ethics in the sense of the grounding foundation and ethics as the field of application? I suggest that the basic structures of ethics in the first sense are so deeply rooted that they need what Hannah Arendt would call a public sphere of appearance to become readable, visible. Their deep-rootedness makes them hidden to the moral look. What I try to show is that the function of morality is to connect two levels of ethical life, the basic one and the applied one. It is not only the deductive order of my first presentation, the problem, which should be reconstructed, but the transition also. We have too much emphasized the distinction and even the opposition between the deontological and the teleological. I think that this opposition is not implied by the basic texts themselves. It is more or less a construction of the tradition. And, in that sense, I would say that if there is something to deconstruct in "moral philosophy," it is precisely this quickly stated opposition between the deontological and the teleological.

Let us proceed from the middle, as it were, and show that it is the normative that implies, on the one hand, a basic ethics, and, on the other hand, an applied ethics. First, this is true in terms of Kant himself. The first proposition of *The Foundation of the Metaphysics of Morals* is the assertion that nothing can be conceived as higher under the sky and in reality at large than a good will.[3] A teleological concept governs the whole attempt of a so-called deontological ethics. Second, and once more in Kant himself, the subjective side of imputation relies on moral feelings that constitute what he called the rational motives of action. As everyone knows, only one motive, one moral feeling, is considered by Kant: respect. But to my mind, one of the tasks of moral philosophy today would be to enlarge, to expand, the field of moral feelings concerning shame, courage, admiration, enthusiasm, veneration, indignation. These feelings have to do with dignity, a kind of immediate recognition of the dignity of a moral subject.

Furthermore, the so-called unconditional imperative, the categorical imperative, called for a series of secondary formulations that point in the direction of several fields of application, the first one about "the self," the second formulation, "the other," and the third formulation, "political commitment." We could say that Kantian ethics, Kantian moral theory, points in the direction of the grounding structure of ethics with the notion of good will, and to the fields of applied ethics thanks to the three formulations of the categorical imperative. As for our last point, we should not forget that there is a work called *The Metaphysics of Morals*. It is not only about the foundation of morality. This work has two parts, the virtues as moral obligation and the laws as legal obligation. In this way the so-called deontological version of morality points both ways, backward toward the roots of good will, and forward toward the field of application.

We should have to say the same concerning the so-called teleological approach. It is true that it provides the main structures of moral action: choice, deliberation, rational desire, preference, and, above all, the wish for the good life. These basic structures are enough to construe the general concept of virtue as rational habit. But what about the virtues? These virtues make visible and credible the general concept of virtue (i.e., rational habit) in terms of the available cultural experience of the Greeks, starting mainly from Homer and the tragic poets. Do they not delineate a variety of fields of application according to cultural traditions and the historical allegiance of belonging to, of membership in, a historical community? And is it not here that we have to find the transition from the general idea of virtue to the plurality of virtues secured by a normative or prenormative concept, that of mediation, the mean between the excess and deficiency that forecasts, in a sense, the radical categorical imperative? The so-called golden mean of Aristotle is a kind of preimperative in the teleological ethic.

My problem proceeds from this more accurate reading of both Aristotle and Kant, liberated from the prejudice of lazy interpretations, among which I could include my own, despite the work of so many commentators! If we proceed from common experience and the problem that it raises, we will be more attentive to the smooth transitions from one realm to the other. What has been said concerning the mediating role of the interpretative self is in full agreement with what I just said, and proceeds from the inquiry into the implications, the basic concept of imputability, which belongs to the philosophical anthropology of capability, of the "I can." If these general remarks are sound, then we will agree that the main emphasis has to be shifted to the field of applied ethics, which is ethics as such. In my *petite ethique*, my chapter devoted to practical wisdom still looks like an appendix, and it should become the crucial chapter. It is, in the language of Hannah Arendt, "the public sphere of appearance," and precisely the basic structure of human action, the basic structure of desire, action, preference, choice, judgment, and so on. The largely invisible structure, the basic structure of the ethical unconscious, requires the screening of norms in order to be brought to the field of application where they are put to the test at the level of what Martha Nussbaum called "tragic situations," the agonistic side of action.

As to the screening or testing stage of norms, we should not let ourselves be caught in the difficult, but not unsolvable, problem of the test of universalization. Everybody agrees that it is thanks to its dialogical structure in public discourse that the alleged universality of any norm—what I called in my work inchoate universals—should be put to the test. And in that sense we should say that the process of universalization, the testing of the universal capability of our projects, already belongs to the sphere of applied ethics, the field that I called the field of practical wisdom. Following the suggestion of Aristotle's book 6 in his *Nicomachean Ethics* about *phronesis*—which has been translated in Latin as *prudentia*, the prudential component—the prudential component is ethics itself at work. To emphasize this complexity of the moment of testing, we not only should have to say that it implies a dialogical testing, but we should confess the radical plurality of the field of testing. It is quite possible—here I feel very close to Michael Walzer's *Spheres of Justice*—that the tests of universality may be themselves scattered according to a variety of spheres of application.

It is at this point that I should have to introduce my attempts to explore some specific spheres of applied ethics. I proposed in my recent articles and published works to consider four fields of applied prudentiality: the political field (and I agree entirely with what has been said in the lecture by my colleague Fred Dallmayr), but secondly the field of historical judgment, the field of judiciary judgment, the field of medical judgment. These would be the places for testing the concept of judgment in the practical sphere, because we may have a kind of typology of the different uses of language, uses of judgment, putting them in pairs. We should have to compare, for example, judging as a judge or historian, as Carlo Ginzburg does in his work, judiciary judgment in courts of justice and medical judgment, but also political judgment for the sake of citizenship. I give only an example of this exploration of the structure of judgment in comparative fields. Let us take the problem of decision-making in the two fields of judiciary judgment and medical judgment. We have to do with two different fields, since, on the one hand, we have the problem of justice because there are conflicts, there is violence, and we have to arbitrate between conflicts at the level of discourse. On the other hand, concerning the medical act, we have not only conflict but also suffering. So two fields have the structure of the tragic, as was said this morning. We have a parallelism between them at the level of the process of decision-making, arriving at the prescription on the one hand, at the sentence on the other hand.

And then we have to consider the concatenation between the argumentative component and the interpretative component. Let us take quickly the example of judiciary judgment. On the one hand, we have to apply laws to cases, but which law and which case? We have to choose among the jurisprudential interpretations of the laws that are considered as fitting with the case, as appropriate to the case. And then it's a law under the consideration of this or that tradition of interpretation. We have to do with a case that has to be described correctly, in agreement with the qualification, the alleged qualification of the acts. And we know from the same facts we may have several narrative descriptions. So one has to combine a legal interpretation with a narrative interpretation to proceed in the direction of the sentence that comes as the last word, the word of justice.

The Duration of Human Things

I do not want to say more. But once more I repeat that we have in Hegel the appropriate model to consider not only the interpersonal relationship implied in all these procedures but also the institutions. Institutions have the basic function of providing a temporal framework for human action. We are mortal beings. We attempt to put our action under the aegis of institutions that last longer than each of us. We have a concern for the duration of human things. Again I quote Hannah Arendt, "the continuation of action" may be the ultimate concern of ethical action.

That is the conclusion of my response, since I opened a variety of things. Allow me to thank you for the wonderful opportunity that you give me to remain for a while the contemporary of my successors.

Notes

1. This essay is based on a transcription of Paul Ricoeur's talk given October 22, 1999, at the conference "Ethics and Meaning in Public Life: Paul Ricoeur and Contemporary Moral Thought," The University of Chicago Divinity School. The transcription was made by Judith Lawrence and the text was edited by John Wall and William Schweiker. The editors have attempted to retain the flavor of Ricoeur's oral presentation while also clarifying, when needed, the transcription. Section headings as well as footnotes are the addition of the editors.
2. David Tracy is a well-known theologian at the Divinity School of the University of Chicago and a longtime colleague of Ricoeur's. Tracy made introductory and concluding remarks at the conference to which Ricoeur here refers.
3. Ricoeur is calling to mind the famous opening of Kant's text: "Nothing can possibly be conceived in the world, or even out of it, which can be called good without qualification, except a good will."

Contributors

Pamela Sue Anderson is reader in philosophy at the University of Sunderland.

Don Browning is Alexander Campbell Professor of Ethics and the Social Sciences in the Divinity School of The University of Chicago.

Helen M. Buss is professor of English at the University of Calgary.

Fred Dallmayr is Dee Professor of Political Theory in the Department of Government at the University of Notre Dame.

Bernard P. Dauenhauer is professor of philosophy at the University of Georgia.

Peter Kemp is professor of theology and philosophy and executive director of the Centre for Ethics and Law at the University of Copenhagen.

David E. Klemm is professor of religion at the University of Iowa.

W. David Hall is assistant professor of religious studies at Centre College, in Danville, Kentucky.

Linda M. MacCammon is assistant professor of theology at Carroll College.

Martha C. Nussbaum is Freund Distinguished Service Professor of Law and Ethics at The University of Chicago.

Paul Ricoeur is Nuveen Professor Emeritus and professor of philosophical theology at The University of Chicago.

William Schweiker is professor of theological ethics at The University of Chicago.

John Wall is assistant professor of religion at Rutgers University, Camden.

Mark I. Wallace is associate professor of religion at Swarthmore College.

Glenn Whitehouse is assistant professor in the College of Arts and Sciences at Florida Gulf Coast University.

Index of Names

Antigone, 56, 65–70, 72
Apel, Karl-Otto, 219
Arendt, Hannah, 229, 287–288, 290
Aristotle, 15, 17–19, 33, 38–39, 41, 47, 50–51, 61, 71, 73–75, 88, 105–106, 124, 169, 214, 216–217, 219, 221–223, 225, 229, 234, 246, 255, 257, 265, 271–272, 281–282, 284–285, 288

Barth, Karl, 99, 119
Benhabib, Seyla, 26, 187
Betz, Hans Dieter, 126, 129
Bonhoeffer, Dietrich, 80, 90–92

Derrida, Jacques, 48, 121, 167, 187–201
Descartes, René, 83, 104, 124, 215, 281

Ebeling, Gerhart, 44, 161

Farley, Edward, 251–252
Foucault, Michel, 48, 83, 187
Freud, Sigmund, 198, 258

Gadamer, Hans-Georg, 48, 49, 198, 253–256

Habermas, Jürgen, 42, 48–50, 57, 60, 219–220, 222, 225, 253, 255, 258
Hegel, Georg Wilhelm Friedrich, 41–42, 61, 99, 104, 108, 124, 181, 198, 215, 218, 220–224, 229, 257, 268, 270–271, 273–274, 286, 289
Heidegger, Martin, 33, 44, 48, 161, 197–198, 204, 214, 216, 224–225, 282, 284
Hillel, 54, 257
Huber, Barbara, 67–69, 75, 77
Hume, David, 24, 123
Husserl, Edward, 33, 48–49, 51, 81, 105, 124, 214–215, 223, 226, 281

Irigaray, Luce, 66, 67, 75

Jaspers, Karl, 32, 44, 214

Kant, Immanuel, 15–27, 39, 41–42, 47, 48, 51, 54–55, 82, 89, 99, 103, 106–108, 117, 120–121, 123–124, 126–129, 133–134, 136, 144–145, 152, 154, 160, 166, 168–169, 200, 204, 214–224, 257, 265, 271–273, 283–287
Kearney, Richard, 196, 198

Index of Names

Kierkegaard, Søren, 147, 194–195
Kosellech, Reinhart, 235–236
Kristeva, Julia, 73, 74

Leibnitz, Gottfried Wilhelm, 177, 181, 282
Lévinas, Emmanuel, 23–24, 37, 42, 54, 61, 80, 83, 85–86, 88, 92, 105, 119, 121, 159–161, 187, 217, 222–223, 226, 284
Luther, Martin, 44, 50
Lyotard, Jean Francois, 52, 187

MacIntyre, Alasdair, 36, 48, 50–51, 57, 59, 213–214, 216, 221
Marcel, Gabriel, 32, 214–215
Merleau-Ponty, Maurice, 226, 280
Moltmann, Jürgen, 118, 143, 145

Nietzsche, Friedrich, 104, 125, 129–131, 167, 187
Nussbaum, Martha, 260, 287
Plato, 98, 190, 283, 285–286

Popper, Karl, 221, 224

Rawls, John, 54, 160, 167–170, 172–173, 176–177, 181, 183, 218, 220, 227, 258, 271
Rosenzweig, Franz, 43, 145, 147–148, 156, 158–160, 162, 181, 283

Schleiermacher, Friedrich, 50, 98, 99, 113, 114
Sophocles, 218, 268–269

Taylor, Charles 48, 224, 286

Van der Ven, Hans, 253, 258

Walzer, Michael, 267, 272–273, 289
Weber, Max, 237–238
Weir, Allison, 67, 72–73

Index of Subjects

Action, 20, 24, 25, 32, 35, 40, 89, 120, 124, 126, 131, 135, 152, 160, 182, 216, 235–236, 267, 270, 280–282, 287–288
Agents/ Patients: 23, 33–34, 54, 65, 68, 69, 71, 74, 124, 127, 135, 238, 282
Attestation, 18, 49, 51, 70, 86, 216

Capacity, 15, 17, 49, 51, 53–55, 84–85, 119–120, 124, 128, 200–201, 205, 234–235, 260, 279–290
Care (*Sorge*), 84, 244, 282
Conscience (*Gewissen*), 44, 83–85, 88–92, 103, 105, 112, 122, 127, 129, 132, 134, 137, 159, 161–162
Creation/ New Creation, 42, 110, 123, 126, 128–135, 137, 138, 143–148, 153–154, 157, 160–161, 171, 203, 283–284

Duty, 19, 23, 104, 120, 124, 156, 217, 266–267, 273

Evil, 16, 19, 33, 39–40, 43–44, 89, 102–108, 123–129, 131, 133–135, 143–148, 159–160, 177, 217, 266–267, 273

Fallibility/Fault, 32, 43, 49, 100, 102, 105, 111, 123–124, 126,128, 133, 135
Feminism, 15, 26, 64, 65, 70, 71, 72, 74, 76, 77
Forgiveness, 84, 242–245
Freedom, 16–19, 25–27, 48–49, 51, 61, 65, 75, 101–103, 105, 108, 118–120, 125–126, 134, 144–149, 154, 157, 200–202, 205–207, 213–215, 221

Gift, 56, 108, 119, 124, 128, 129, 153, 158, 165, 171–174, 178–180, 183, 188, 193–199, 202–207
God, 43–44, 55, 81–82, 84–87, 91, 107, 109, 110–112, 114, 117, 120, 128–130, 133, 136- 137, 145–148, 151, 154–157, 165, 170–178, 181–184, 187–189, 195–197, 199–204, 207, 252

Hope, 43, 55, 100, 104, 107, 118–126, 128–133, 135–137, 143–148, 160, 203
Human Nature, 48, 100–101, 103, 112, 117, 132–133,

Index of Subjects

Imagination, 35–37, 40, 42, 58–59, 80–81, 84, 108–111, 113, 124, 127, 129, 131, 133, 136, 166

Jesus Christ, 92, 108–112, 125, 128, 136, 150–151, 155, 170, 173, 178–184, 188, 195–196, 204, 206
Justice, 17, 19, 33, 35, 40, 43, 52, 61, 105–107, 112, 119, 123, 129, 144, 148–154, 157–160, 164–185, 188, 190–197, 200–202, 206–207, 217–222, 227–229, 264, 271–272

Language, 32–33, 40, 49–50, 72–73, 82–83, 85, 102–103, 109–110, 112, 124, 191–192, 198–202, 280–282
Law, 16, 20–23, 33, 39–42, 67, 86, 88, 104, 117, 121, 126–128, 132, 134–136, 147, 150, 156, 171–174, 177, 181–182, 196, 200, 228, 264, 271, 289
Logos, 188, 204, 207
Love, 43, 56, 61, 67–68, 71, 86, 104, 110, 112, 114, 118, 123, 125–126, 128–131, 133–135, 137, 138, 143–144, 147–149m 152–158, 162–167, 171–175, 178–185, 206–207

Moral Theory, 26, 149–155, 167–170, 176–178, 213–229, 264–275, 279–290

Narrative, 24, 32–40, 42–44, 47–48, 51–54, 56–58, 60–61, 64, 66–73, 76–77, 101, 105, 109, 111, 122, 130, 138, 161, 204, 243, 253–257, 280–282, 289

Political Theory, 25, 99, 213–229, 233–246
Practical Reason/ Practical Wisdom/ Practical Judgment (*Phronesis*), 21–22, 24–25, 27, 40–42, 56–57, 61, 74, 88, 90, 104, 106, 112, 117, 126, 128–129, 134

Regeneration (moral), 97–98, 103–104, 106–107, 109–114, 123, 125, 127–128, 134, 136
Religion/ Religious, 61, 81, 82, 84, 97–99, 102, 106–114, 117–118, 122, 125, 132, 135–137, 138, 144–146, 164–167, 170, 173–174, 185–188, 192–195, 198–199, 202, 223, 264, 268–269, 284

Self, 16–18, 21–22, 24–27, 34–37, 43–44, 47–48, 50–56, 58–61, 64, 65, 67, 69, 71–72, 74, 76, 77, 80–86, 88, 89, 92, 98, 100, 104–106, 112–114, 121, 122, 124, 149, 152, 156–158, 161, 169, 172, 182, 190, 200–201, 205, 214–218, 222–223, 226, 253, 287
Solicitude, 17, 19, 52, 80, 84–85, 132, 134, 155, 160, 216–219, 221–223

Texts/ Textuality, 32, 49–50, 53, 55, 59, 80–81, 86–88, 92, 103, 106, 108–109, 124, 132–133, 135, 175–178, 191, 196–199, 281
Theology, 55–56, 81–82, 87, 91, 97, 112, 114, 122, 130–131, 135, 137–138, 143–148, 154, 159–161, 164–165, 207, 251–261, 283
Time, 25, 33–34, 103, 118, 121, 136, 147–148
Tragedy, 56–59, 218, 257, 264–275, 289

Utopia, 37–38, 119, 131

Voluntarity/ Involuntarity, 32, 48–50, 53, 55, 124

Welt, *Umwelt*, 133, 135, 199
Will, 16–18, 32, 48, 54–55, 60, 98, 101–104, 107–108, 111, 119–120, 125, 127–129, 137, 145, 147, 160, 177, 215, 285